HERTFORDSHIRE
1731–1800

as recorded in

The *Gentleman's Magazine*

The *Gentleman's Magazine:*

Lond. Gazette
Read's Jour:
Craftsman:
Daily Adver-
tiser.
St James's E-
vening Post.
London Even-
ing Post.
Gen. Evening
Post:
Lond. Gazet-
teer
Gen. Adver-
tiser
Westminster
Journal.
Old England
Whitehall Eb
Post
Remembran-
cer
Lon. Review

St JOHN's GATE

Bark 2 News
Dublin 3:
Edinburgh 2
Bristol :: 3:
Norwich 2
Exeter 2
Worcester
Northampon
Glaucester I
Stamford :
Nottingham
Chester Jour
Derby ditto
Ipswich 1:
Reading :: 2
Leeds Merc:
Newcastle 2
Canterbury
Sherborn
Birmingham
Manchester
Bath
Cambridge
Glasgow

For FEBRUARY 1750.

CONTAINING,

[More in Quantity and greater Variety than any Book of the Kind and Price.]

Illustrated by a representation of *Nova Scotia* PLANTS, ANIMAL and INSECTS; a plan of the harbour of *Chebucto* and town of *Halifax*; the arms of *Nova Scotia*, and its baronets, neatly engraved on copper.

By *SYLVANUS URBAN,* Gent.

LONDON: Printed by E. CAVE, jun. at *St John's Gate.*

HERTFORDSHIRE
1731–1800

as recorded in

The *Gentleman's Magazine*

Edited by Arthur Jones

HERTFORDSHIRE PUBLICATIONS
1993

HERTFORDSHIRE PUBLICATIONS

(Hertfordshire Libraries, Arts & Information,
in association with
The Hertfordshire Association for Local History)

New Barnfield, Travellers Lane, Hatfield AL10 8XG

ISBN 0-901354-73-2

Printed by Stephen Austin and Sons Ltd, Hertford

CONTENTS

PREFACE

Arrangement

This volume has aimed to include all Hertfordshire material of substance in the Gentleman's Magazine, 1731–1800. It is arranged here in a single main chronological sequence, with separate lists of births, marriages, bankruptcies and deaths. Within the main sequence, stories which have been supplemented in one or more later issues have been brought together for convenience in a block, in which case they have been given an opening headline and a final horizontal line to separate them from items which follow.

The production of this volume

Production has been a complex team effort, spread over five years. The main credit for its inception must go to Reg Auckland who proposed to the Publications Committee in 1988 a more selective volume, and offered his typing and computing skills. He remained undaunted when the committee responded enthusiastically, but wanted a full transcription of Hertfordshire material with annotations wherever necessary. When our requirements out-grew his equipment he cheerfully updated it, and in spite of ill-health has remained the corner-stone of our operation.

The identification, and in some cases, transcription, of Hertfordshire items from seventy years of Gentleman's Magazine was undertaken by Alan Ruston (who has also written the Introduction), using the set of volumes in Dr. Williams's Library. Since the volumes are tightly bound, with narrow margins, photocopying was seldom possible and most of the remaining transcriptions had to be done by hand, using the sets of volumes in the Hertfordshire Record Office and at Hatfield House. In several cases the transcriptions in the Gentleman's Magazine itself needed to be checked, mostly from the standard county histories or locations within the county, but involving in one case a visit to the parish church at Woodchurch in Kent. When fully checked and edited, transcriptions were then passed to Reg Auckland, whose own part-set of the magazine enabled him to make a further quality check in some cases before typing the entries into the computer. Many of the entries clearly needed annotation, either to make their meaning clear or to add interest by the provision of background information. For this purpose we called upon the great wealth of specialized knowledge which is available among Hertfordshire historians, and met with the heartening and generous response which will be apparent, particularly to anyone who reads through the main sequence. In addition, Robin Harcourt Williams has been an ever reliable referee on many points of difficulty.

Conventions adopted when transcribing

Spelling. After much agonizing it was decided to adopt modern spelling of place-names, though a few others may have slipped through. Purists may object, but with so many people involved in the transcription process it seemed the only practical course. The original contributors, editors and printers had great difficulty in distinguishing between Hertfordshire and Herefordshire: errors have been corrected as far as possible.

Contributors to the Gentleman's Magazine. Main contributions were always anonymous. Letters to the editor were addressed to 'Mr. Urban', and this has been omitted, though the name does survive in a few places in the text. Letters were commonly published without a signature, or over a pseudonym or initials, very occasionally over a real name. Names and initials have only been retained if they apparently identify the correspondent.

Cross references. References sometimes occur in the text to other issues of the magazine, using either date or volume number. These have not been systematically converted. The magazine was first published in 1731 (volume 1). Subsequently there was a single volume number each year. (After 1783, when there were two volumes each year, they were lettered A and B). Thus, to convert volume number to year of publication, add 1730.

Arthur Jones.
January 1993.

INTRODUCTION

by

Alan Ruston

The Gentleman's Magazine (henceforth GM) first appeared in January 1731 and thereafter was published every month until September 1922. During the last fifteen years of its existence, from 1907 to 1922, the magazine became merely a four-page number produced for the sole purpose of maintaining a continuous run and preserving the title. In its heyday, well into the nineteenth century, it was the most popular and widely read of all current periodicals, but in the 1850s its character began to change and its importance declined. From being a miscellany of parliamentary reports, news both domestic and foreign, obituaries, book reviews, poetry, a theatrical register, scholarly essays and topographical notes, it became a fiction magazine and ceased to have any significant genealogical or news interest. The complete change came after 1863.[1]

The amount and quality of textual material relating to the topography of the British Counties was first brought to wider attention with the appearance of *The Gentleman's Magazine Library*[2] in several volumes late in the nineteenth century. This Library consisted of topographical extracts covering the period 1731–1868, edited by G.L. Gomme. Volume 5 of this series, which appeared in 1894, comprised four counties, and included just 32 extracts on Hertfordshire. The present volume contains more than ten times that number in the main sequence alone, many of them extensively annotated.

The very large amount of resource material in the GM has not hitherto been satisfactorily indexed and has not therefore been easily accessible to researchers. The reason why these records of relatively local interest should have been published in the first place becomes evident from a study of the early history of the magazine and the philosophy of its owners. The GM was founded and run by Edward Cave (1691–1754) until his death. Its early years were understandably occupied in establishing itself and building up a circulation amongst the all-important county gentry. They wanted to see news from their own or neighbouring county (and gossip if possible) and so an emphasis in this direction was necessary. However, by 1741 Cave could boast in his Preface: "The GM is read as far as the English language extends, and we see it reprinted from several presses in Great Britain, Ireland and the Plantations." The formula was therefore successful and did not vary under the later proprietorship of David Henry and Richard Cave. John Nichols took over the editorship in 1778 and it was the preoccupations of the Nichols family, who were partners and proprietors of the GM between 1778 and 1856, which are probably the chief reasons for the continuing emphasis placed on English county affairs. They were all deeply interested in English local history and antiquarian matters in general. They printed and published many local histories as well as the GM and participated, often from their inception, in many of the learned societies which were formed in this period.[3] Their commitment to local history and topography is very much our gain as through it we are given a fascinating glimpse of eighteenth century life, albeit reflected through its oddities and often its most unpleasant aspects. It cannot be considered as a representative or systematic account of county life, but in the circumstances it could hardly be otherwise.

The bound annual volumes were quite slim in the early years and the amount of Hertfordshire material they contained was at first quite small. However, their size increased as the century wore on, and in 1783 the material appearing increased greatly. From then on the monthly issues could only be contained in two volumes per year, each of which can consist of over a thousand pages of tiny and often ill-printed type.[4]

Readers with differing interests will find a rich source for their researches here—history, news items of every kind, reports of robberies, court hearings, executions, fires, burglaries and theft, and of course obituaries. There are also lists of bankrupts for the earlier part of the century, taken from the London Gazette; the name, place of origin and occupation is given, generally under the quaintly headed title "B—K—TS", an odd euphemism in a non-squeamish age. Until about 1750, accounts of assaults, murders and executions were often given in the most gruesome detail, making our present day supposedly sensational journalism tame by comparison. A person charged with murder, for example, was considered by the correspondent or editor as guilty from the start. Therefore entries like: "The murderer (name given) will no doubt receive his just condemnation at the next Assizes", are not infrequent occurrences.

Throughout the century there are numerous reported cases of people being bitten by rabid dogs in the obituaries and elsewhere. It seems to be the most oft-reported human disease, and shows that worries over rabies is a continuing feature of British life. In the 1790s the columns included many bizarre treatments for this terrible condition. However, up until about 1760 the readership was apparently more interested in reading about cures for sickness in farm animals than how to treat their own bodies. This feature is not unexpected as it was a major concern of the farming gentry to learn how to cure, for example, coughs in horses. Of course, these matters were not specific to Hertfordshire but the farming community no doubt avidly absorbed every word at a time when reading material was not readily available. The influence of the GM in rural life should not be underestimated as its position was unique in the eighteenth century in a way that could not be repeated in the nineteenth century.

One of the acknowledged glories of the GM is the obituaries, which provide a unique source in the period up to 1760. There is nothing else to match them in detail or coverage. The printed journal obituary, as we know it, is essentially a nineteenth century invention, and the form they took was based on the pioneering work which appeared in the GM in the previous century. The obituaries, while centred on the gentry, are not exclusively taken from this class of society; there is also the deserving poor, those who died nastily or from an odd cause, the very aged or those whose death was considered as a morally uplifting example for the readership. Unfortunately the age at, or place of death, is not given in every instance, some entries being short, imprecise or so general as to be useless, while others are detailed and of considerable length and may contain obviously tendentious and sensational material. The large number of centenarians will cause some surprise, but must often no doubt be attributed to the gullibility, or deliberate exaggeration, of friends and relations. The birth and marriage announcements are of lesser interest but can be of obvious value to the genealogist. A valuable adjunct to many marriage entries in the earlier period is the amount in pounds noted against the bride's name, showing how much she was worth in marriage settlement. A round sum is shown in thousands of pounds up until the late 1750s, and this has been included in the extraction where it appears in the original. After this date the tide of feeling turned against including this financial detail and within a few years it had entirely disappeared as a feature.

The GM throughout its life could never be considered as an unbiased journal. Its pages do not contain any support for radical views in the fields of politics, society or religion; for most of the eighteenth century anything which could show Nonconformists, Quakers and particularly Methodists or Roman Catholics in a bad light was readily included. Support for the ancient privileges and position of the Church of England was maintained however indefensible a reported anomaly might be. This consistent stand obviously affected what was printed about Hertfordshire as well as other counties. However, at times the GM could be amazingly open-minded and the coverage of religious topics late in the century was extensive. The introduction of a Bill in Parliament which might affect the standing of the Established Church was the signal for numerous articles and letters. However, the opposing view was often printed in order to foster interest and circulation.[5]

It was the Revolution in France that created the greatest alarm in the minds of editor and correspondents of the GM, a reflection no doubt of feeling amongst the gentry in the country as a whole. The proprietors fought the good fight as they saw it, the editor in his Preface to the 1791 opening number pointing out: "It is the glory of the Gentleman's Magazine to be founded on true Protestantism and true Patriotism, superior to the clamours of the day, whether extorted by mistaken humanity, misguided faith, or interested policy".

This meant that the GM adopted public figures whom it "loved to hate". Perhaps one of the leading examples was Rev. Dr. Joseph Priestley, the libertarian Unitarian scientist who preached disestablishment of the Church of England and the need for constitutional change in Britain. The GM attacked him on every score, so much so that in the index for certain volumes up to 1794 his name appears more than that of any other public figure. Unfortunately we know the identity of few of the writers and correspondents of this or later periods, most contributions being anonymous or signed with just a couple of initials. This means that while it is feasible to work out the views of the editors on a particular point, it is impossible to say whether the often venomous articles were from their pens.

It is not possible to sum up a journal of the range or length of the GM in the eighteenth century. A great deal of what was printed has not been mentioned here, like the articles on higher mathematics and natural science that were bravely included on a regular basis and which must have strained the patience of much of the readership. To obtain the full flavour of the GM in the flower of its popularity it is necessary to read the original volumes. I recommend those who are likely to make much use of this extraction to venture on the task of looking through a typical volume selected at random, and try in their reading of it to put themselves in the place of a moderately educated reader living in central Hertfordshire who had just received the latest issue hot off the press. In this way it may be possible to get some idea of the challenge and breadth of vision that the GM could provide to a farmer living a dull, hard and repetitive life in this county. C.Lennart Carlson probably gets near to a proper evaluation of the GM's importance in the intellectual and social life in the eighteenth century when he writes:

"In the final analysis the Gentleman's Magazine must be viewed as an integral and particularly revealing document of the time in which it originated. No type of publication in the eighteenth century succeeded more completely than the magazine in showing the dual character of the age, in revealing its baseness and idealism, its egotism and humanitarian aspiration, its smugness and enquiring spirit, its self-sufficiency and liberal adventuresomeness".[6]

References

1. Peter Jackson, London Illustrations in the Gentleman's Magazine 1746–1836, *London Topographical Record*, Vol. XXVI, p.177–179.

2. *Gentleman's Magazine Library: a classified collection of the chief contents from 1731 to 1868*, English topography, part V. Hampshire, Herefordshire, Hertfordshire and Huntingdonshire. Edited by G.L. Gomme, London, 1894, pp.209–302.

3. Trevor Hearl, The Gentleman's Magazine; a nineteenth century quarry, *Local Historian*, Vol. 16 No. 6, May 1985, p.346–350.

4. The extraction, which took about two and a half years to complete, was made from the run of the GM held in Dr. Williams's Library in London, and I wish to express my thanks to the Library staff for their help in this undertaking.

5. Peter Christie, The Gentleman's Magazine and the Local Historian, *The Local Historian,* Vol. 15, No.2, May 1982, p.80–84.

6. C. Lennart Carlson, *The First Magazine, a history of the Gentleman's Magazine*. Brown University, USA, 1938, p.239.

ANNOTATORS

The contributors of annotations have been identified by their initials in square brackets at the end of the annotations. We acknowledge our indebtedness to the following :

Nigel Agar	[NA]	Nicholas Maddex	[NM]
Reg Auckland	[RA]	National Rivers Authority	[NRA]
Lionel Baker	[LB]	Jack Parker	[JP]
Peter Clayton	[PC]	Ann Pegrum	[AP]
David Dean	[DD]	David Perman	[DP]
Tom Doig	[TD]	Eileen Roberts	[ER]
Jack Edwards	[JE]	Tony Rook	[TR]
Noel Farris	[NF]	Alan Ruston	[AR]
Mary Forsyth	[MF]	Brian Sawford	[BS]
Henry Gray	[HG]	Gillian Sheldrick	[GS]
Alan Greening	[AG]	Alan Thomson	[AT]
Graham Javes	[GJ]	Liz Wagstaff	[LW]
Arthur Jones	[AJ]	Peter Walne	[PW]
W.J. Killick	[WK]	Brian Warren	[BW]
Ann King	[AK]	Robin Harcourt Williams	[RHW]
Peter Kingsford	[PK]	Wally Wright	[WW]

MAIN SEQUENCE

September 1731. Account of a murder in Hertfordshire, in the 4th year of King Charles I [1628–29] taken in writing from the depositions, by Sir John Maynard Serjeant at Law. ([Daily Courant] Sept. 21.)

Jane Norcott, the wife of Arthur Norcott, being found murdered in her bed, the coroner's inquest on view of the body and depositions of Mary Norcott, her husband's mother, Agnes his sister, and her husband John Okeman, gave their evidence that she was *Felo de se*; the said persons giving information that she went to bed with her young child, her husband being abroad, and that no body had been or could come to her without their knowledge, they lying in the outer room. But divers circumstances manifesting that she could not murder her self, 30 days after the jury prayed the Coroner to have the body taken out of the grave, whereupon they changed their verdict; and the above persons being tried with the husband at Hertford Assizes, were acquitted; but so much against evidence, that Judge Harvey advised an appeal, which was accordingly brought by the young child against his father, grandmother and aunt and her husband Okeman.

On trial, the minister of the parish where the fact was committed, deposed, that the body being taken up out of the grave thirty days after the party's death and lying on the grass, and the four defendants being required each of them touched the dead body, whereupon the brow of the dead, which before was of a livid and carrion colour, began to have a dew, or sweat arise on it which increased by degrees till the sweat ran down in drops on the face, the brow turned to a lively and fresh colour and the deceased opened one of her eyes, and shut it again several times; she likewise thrust out the ring or marriage finger three times, and pulled it in again, and the finger dropped blood on the grass.

Chief Justice Hyde seeming to doubt the evidence, asked who saw it besides ? To which he replied, That he believed the whole company saw it, but was sure his brother, minister of the next parish, saw it as he did. That person being sworn, gave evidence exactly as above.

Other circumstantial proof was: 1. That she lay in a composed manner in bed, and the bedclothes not disturbed. 2. Her throat was cut from ear to ear, and her neck broke, both which she could not do her self. 3. There was no blood in the bed. 4. There were two streams of blood on the floor, but no communication betwixt them, and turning up the mat there were clots of congealed blood on the straw. 5. The bloody knife was found sticking in the floor, the point towards the bed. 6. There was the print of a thumb and four fingers of a left hand: And lastly, the prisoners had before said, no stranger could come into the room.

Okeman was acquitted, but the other three found guilty; the grandmother and husband were executed; but the aunt was not, on account of her being with child. Sir John adds, that they confessed nothing at their execution.

Sir John Maynard's record of this trial was printed in 1915 by William Gerish, who was fascinated by the element of 'trial by ordeal' implicit in the requirement that the four accused should touch the body. It was reprinted in Hertfordshire Folk Lore *by William Gerish (S.R. Publications Ltd., 1970). The place where the murder occurred has not been identified, but the marriage of Agnes Norcott (or Norkett) and John Okeman took place at Berkhamsted in 1615 and most references to the Norcott family occur in the area between Hemel Hempstead and Tring. However, the marriage of Arthur Norcott and his wife Jane has not been traced. [AJ]*

21 March 1732. William Newton and Richard Curral were executed at Hertford, the first for burglary, the other for robbing on the highway. Curral had been tried on the evidence of Newton for the murder of one Adams a farmer, 3 years ago, and acquitted. At the place of execution their behaviour was uncommonly rude, and they died denying every thing laid to their charge. Four others were condemned, but reprieved.

Richard Coral (probably baptized at Hatfield 17 February 1697/8, son of Christopher Currall) and William Newton (? baptized at Hatfield 9 August 1708, son of Thomas Newton), were buried at Hatfield 21 March 1731/32. [HG]

22 April 1732. Mr. Petit, gardener to Sir William Leman of Northal [Northaw] in Hertfordshire, Bart., presented to His Majesty a ripe melon, the first produced this year, as he has done for these ten years past.

19 July 1732. Her Majesty, with the three eldest Princesses, visited John Sambrook, Esq., at Gubbins in Hertfordshire, viewed his fine gardens, waterworks, and his collection of curiosities.

This reference should be to Jeremy not John Sambrook(e). He bought Gubbins, now known as Gobions, in 1709 with money from the East India Company in which members of his family had been directors. He inherited a baronetcy in 1740 from one of them. A bachelor, he employed Charles Bridgeman and James Gibbs to develop the mansion and estate into pleasure grounds famous throughout the eighteenth century until in 1834 R.W. Gaussen of Brookmans bought the estate, demolished the mansion and left the gardens to nature. The pleasure grounds are now being restored by the Gobions Woodland Trust. [PK and WK]

CORRUPT ELECTION IN ST. ALBANS

24 January 1733. John Merril, Esq., was elected Representative in Parliament for St. Albans, when the Corporation gave him the following instructions under their common seal, viz,
SIR,
We have chose you to be our representative in Parliament, which is the highest trust we can repose in you, and in return for so great a confidence, we expect you will have a constant regard for the interest of your country, and especially of this Borough, but as this is a very critical con-

juncture, we think it necessary to give you more particular instructions. In the first place, sir, as we are in profound peace, we are surprized to find no reduction of the land forces, which we conceive to be dangerous to our constitution, and we feel to be very burdensome and oppressive to us. In the next place, we are alarmed with an attempt to be made this session of Parliament, for extending the excise laws to commodities not yet excised. We hope, however, that these reports are false, and raised by the enemies to our constitution, and to his Majesty's government. But if any one who calls himself an Englishman should be so much an enemy to his Majesty and us, as to propose such a scheme, we expect, sir, from you, the most vigorous opposition to it for we shall look upon the continuance of so great a body of land forces, and an increase of excise officers, under our present circumstances, as a sure presage of an entire subversion of our ancient constitution, and all the valuable privileges belonging to it, which have so long distinguished us from our neighbouring nations.

A constitution, sir, that our fore-fathers have, at the expense of their lives and fortunes, delivered down safe to us, and which, we hope, we shall have the virtue and courage to deliver to latest posterity, under a succession of princes issuing from his present most sacred Majesty, whose family came in on the principles of liberty, and who can be maintained on no other. Whoever, therefore, tries to sap the foundations of liberty, is at the same time undermining his Majesty's title to the crown, which thoughts give us the utmost abhorrence, and we expect from you, sir, a constant and steady pursuit of such measures as will keep our constitution as near as may be in the same situation under which it has long flourished, and we don't doubt but in such conduct you will have the assistance of our other worthy member, and of all honest Englishmen.

17 February 1733.
A Letter from St. Albans.

The instructions pretended to be given, under the common seal of the Corporation, to their new representative (See our last p.44) were obtained in the following manner:

As soon as the election was over (which was not without opposition) Mr ——————— entertained a large number of the inhabitants at the house of Wm C ——————— Mayor of St. Albans. After dinner, the mayor (who is also post-master) and two or three of the aldermen were called out by Mr M ——————— and going into his chamber, signed a paper of instructions, which was ready ingrossed, but not by the Town-Clerk nor any person in town, and which, we have reason to believe, was brought down by the secretary of a certain gentleman, once honourable, but now not so much as a Justice of the Peace. The same paper was afterwards presented to others of the aldermen to sign, and to some at their own houses. After the signing, the mayor fixed the Corporation seal to it; for doing which he is challenged to produce the consent and approbation of his brethren, and it is expressly charged on him, that he did it without a Court being called, and without the previous knowledge of his brethren.

It is very surprizing to see so great a profession of zeal for the constitution, and liberty of the subject, made by a body of men, who, in defi-
ance of their oaths, and the rights and privileges of the inhabitants of
St. Albans, have arbitrarily made great numbers of non-resident
Freemen, not warranted by their charter or constitutions. About 200
have been made by this mayor and his brethren, of gentlemen, servants,
and near 30 clergymen, collected out of London and 5 or 6 countries,
who are all inrolled in the Company of Mercers or Inholders; and, when
summoned to serve a party, come to over-power the inhabitants and
legal Freemen; a proceeding agreeable to the model set by the late King
James, under whose arbitrary reign the first non-resident Freemen and
aldermen were made.

*Corrupt elections attracted unscrupulous parliamentary candidates to St. Albans
well before the start of the eighteenth century. Votes were secured by: (a) straight
bribery of resident voters, and (b) enfranchising non-resident supporters of the
preferred candidate. The latter was achieved by the Mayor and Aldermen granting Freedom of the Borough, usually gratis.*
*William Carr was elected Mayor in September 1721. In the first six months of
his mayoralty, prior to the 1722 parliamentary election, Freedom was granted to
163 persons. This can be compared with grants to a total of 35 over the following
two years.*
*Carr was elected Mayor for a second time in September 1732, shortly before the
parliamentary by-election at which John Merril was elected. A modest 31 new
Freemen were created in the available time.*
*The published entries dated January and February 1733 may both have come
from the same informant, evidently with a view of exposing corruption. William
Carr will no doubt have read them before he died in March of that same year.
The abuse of granting Freedom reached its climax in about 1743. From that time
onward, straight bribery became the chief means of influencing elections in St.
Albans. The Borough was disenfranchised following the findings of the Bribery
Commission of 1851. [DD]*

May 1734. List of such Cities, Boroughs, &c. whose elections have been
controverted in the House of Commons, placed under general heads
according to the last Determinations there, together with the dates
thereof.
[Includes:]

> In List of Freemen and Householders:
> St. Albans, April 12, 1714
> In List of Mayors, &c. and Freemen:
> Hertford, Dec. 6, 1705.

Note: By an old Statute 23 Henry 6 c 25 for regulating the elections of
Knights, Citizens and Burgesses to serve in Parliament, Citizens are to
be chosen by citizens of the same city, and Burgesses by burgesses of
the same borough; but, as many corporations, either by prescription or
charters, choose their Members in right of freeholds, inhabitancy, and
other different qualifications, according to the custom or law of the
place, so they could not be brought under general heads without some
exceptions; which, however, being observed with due regard to the

heads they are called under, will discover a greater exactness than perhaps would be expected in such a concise method. And if there is any room for doubt, the Journals of the House, which are referred to, will explain it. In the intricacy of these rights, Returning Officers have a guide, such votes only being deemed legal which have been so declared by the last Determination of the House of Commons . . .

5 March 1735. At Hertford Assizes. John Smith was condemned for returning from transportation, and robbing a gentleman of goods to a great value.

30 August 1735. As some labourers were lately cleaning a fish pond at Hempstead in Hertfordshire, they found a bottle of sack covered with mud a yard thick. On it were inscribed these words: 'New Canary put in to see how long keep good, April 1659, Ri. Combe.' The mouth of the bottle was waxed over, and the wine good, but the cork was almost decayed.

March 1736. A list of small livings, by Lot agreed to be augmented by the Governors of Queen Anne Bounty, 1735.
[Included among seven curacies, to be augmented 'in conjunction with other benefactors', is 'Market Street [i.e. Markyate] Hertfordshire'].

2 August 1736. A very extraordinary cause was tried at Hertford Assizes, on an action brought against the defendant for debauching the plaintiff's daughter (both persons of fortune) and having a child by her under marriage promises. A special jury gave her £150 damages, and directed her to bring an action in her own right upon a marriage contract.

31 March 1738. A horse started the 19th from Shoreditch, to go to Ware in an hour, for 100 guineas, which was performed in 57 minutes and a half; but on the person's alighting, the horse bled violently at the nose and feet, and died the next day. He carried 9 stone.

25 July 1738. About noon a dreadful storm of thunder, lightning and hail happened at Dunstable, which put the whole town in the utmost consternation . . . This storm was felt also at Watford, Bushey, St. Albans, and places adjacent in Hertfordshire. Between three and four o'clock in the afternoon they had a like storm of hail about Bungay in Suffolk, preceded by an uncommon clap of thunder. The windows of the churches were shattered, the corn laid flat, turkeys and other poultry killed in great numbers.

December 1738. A continuation of the accounts sent to Mr. Harding, bookseller in St. Martin's Lane, by those who have taken Mrs. Stephens's medicine. [One of seven letters in the December 1738 issue]:
    I, John Baker, of Buntingford, in the County of Hertford,
    was afflicted with the gravel in my kidneys some years,
    took several medicines, but found no relief till advised to

Mrs Stephen's Powders, in the year 1730; which I took and found immediate relief, having been free from the complaint ever since; unless making too free with liquors that are hurtful brings something of it, but then two or three papers of the above-said powder entirely carry it off.

Witness my Hand,
JOHN BAKER.

16 March 1739. A foot race for £100 was run by the famous Pinwire and an Irish footman, from Highgate to Barnet and back again (13 miles) and won by the latter performing it in 1 hour 19 minutes and half.

GEORGE WHITEFIELD IN HERTFORDSHIRE

20 May 1739. The Rev. Mr. Whitefield not being admitted to one pulpit in city or suburbs, continued his preachments at Moorfields and Kennington Common to vast numbers of people. On Monday the 21st he made an excursion to Hertford, and thence to Bedford, Olney, Northampton, Hitchin, St. Albans, and—being denied the pulpits—preached at Northampton from the weighing chair on the horse-course, elsewhere in the fields; and having sowed the seeds of Methodism throughout his progress, returned the following Saturday evening to Kennington Common.

George Whitefield (1714–1770) was probably the greatest preacher of his age, who led a frenetic life both in this country and in America where he died. It is said he preached some 18,000 sermons. Educated at Oxford he dated his conversion to 1735 after having met Charles Wesley. Ordained priest in the Church of England early in 1739, he was already a highly successful preacher. A Calvinistic Methodist by persuasion he was soon in trouble with church authorities, and in consequence adopted open air preaching in February 1739. This increased his popularity and even Dr. Philip Dodderidge, the famous dissenting divine, went to hear him at Kennington in May. Whitefield noted that at St. Albans he "preached to a congregation of 1500 people, in a field at 7 in the morning" (he always wore his clerical robes). In July the same year he preached to 20,000 at Stoke Newington. [AR]

31 January 1740. This month the frost, which began the 26th of last [month], grew more severe than has been known since the memorable winter of 1715–16 . . . In Hertfordshire, numbers of oaks were riven by the frost, and split into the solid timber as far as a case-knife could be thrust; and at Buntingford in that county a new spring forced its way out of the ground and filled the road with ice so as to make it unpassable . . .

22 April 1741. Came on before the Court of Common Pleas the cause relating to the Right of Presentation to the rectory of Northchurch, near Berkhamsted, Hertfordshire, worth £300 per annum, between the Prince of Wales and the Dean and Canons of Windsor; and the jury brought in a verdict for his Royal Highness, so that Dr. Ayscough (who is his chaplain) is confirmed therein.

11 December 1741. At 45 minutes after 12 (the sun shining) appeared at Bushy [Bushey?] a ball of fire 45 deg. high in the clouds, which ran about the seeming distance of 4 yards and then disappeared. It grew larger as it ran, and ended in appearance as big as a man's hand. The same phenomenon was seen at Reading and several other places. Its course was nearly from West to East.

May 1743.

THE LASS OF BALDOCK-MILL. A B A L L A D.

To the tune of The abbot of Canterbury.

Who has e'er been at *Baldock*, must needs know the *mill*,
With the sign of the *horse* at the foot of the hill;
Where the *grave* and the *gay*, the *clowns* and the *beau*,
And the *old* and the young all promiscuously go.
Derry down, &c.

To this *mill* tho' a multitude daily repair,
It is not for the sake of the *drink* or the *air*;
For the far greater part, let them say what they will,
Go to see and admire the sweet lass of the *mill*.
Derry down, &c.

For, the *man* of this *mill* has a daughter so fair
With so easy a shape and so graceful an air;
That *once* on the river's green bank as she stood,
I believ'd it was Venus just sprung from the flood.
Derry down, &c.

But in looking again I perceiv'd my mistake,
For *Venus*, tho' fair, has the look of a *rake*;
While nothing but *virtue* and *modesty* fill
The more beautiful looks of the *lass* of the *mill*.
Derry down, &c.

Sweet *Molly* (for that is the name of the fair)
Is the joy of each neighbouring swain, and the care;
Her glances can warmth to the aged impart,
And the young are all wounded quite *thorough* the heart!
Derry down, &c.

Prometheus stole fire (as the poets all say)
To enliven the *man* which he model'd of *clay*;
But had *Molly* been with him, the *beams* of her *eyes*
Had sav'd him the trouble of robbing the skies.
Derry down, &c.

Were the *goddesses three* for the *apple* to vye,

And chuse me their *Paris*, and *Molly* stand by!
The prize should be hers, without studying about it,
And the *goddesses* e'en go to *Heaven* without it.
Derry down, &c.

Hold, hold (cry'd my friend) prithee stop your career
A truce with your muse, and pray help off the beer;
The bottle stands next you,—a bumper then fill,
It's the health of the *lass*, who's the *pride* of the *mill*.
Derry down, &c.

Baldock Mill lay on the outskirts of the town on the south side, and the miller ran the adjoining public house, the Black Horse. Both still existed in 1857 but seem to have been pulled down soon afterwards. The story of the 'The Maid of the Mill' was published by W.B. Gerish in 1912, and included in the collection of his writings re-issued by S.R. Publishers Ltd. in 1970 as Hertfordshire Folk Lore. *His source was the* Autobiography *(1809) of the Rev. Percival Stockdale—'a very curious cleric'—who stated that the poem, written by the curate of Baldock, had caused great annoyance to the girl's parents through the number of curious sight-seers it attracted. Stockdale claims to have been one of these, and—in spite of her father's general veto—to have obtained a brief interview with the girl in 1756, when she was about thirty—and he himself only twenty. The girl, Mary, shortly afterwards married Henry Leonard, but died aged 43 on 26 April 1769. Gerish quotes a note written in 1862 by the then rector of Baldock beside the entry in the burial register: "This was the celebrated lass of Baldock Mill".*
Stockdale quoted only four verses from the ballad—the first, third, fourth and sixth in the version above. Neither he nor Gerish seems to have been aware of the longer text. [AJ]

May 1743. A List of Corporations in England, includes in Hertfordshire:

St Albans.   A Mayor, Recorder, 12 Aldermen, 24 Assistants.
Hertford.   A Mayor, Recorder, 9 Aldermen, 16 Assistants.

8 September 1743. A fire consumed Archdeacon Cole's house in St. Albans. His son saved his life by jumping out of a window.

January 1744. Ecclesiastical preferments. Mr. Johnson, second master of Westminster School, to the vicarage of Watford, Hertfordshire. James Johnson, D.D., has a dispensation to hold the vicarage of Watford, Hertfordshire, with the rectory of Mixbury, Oxfordshire.

March 1744. Promotions from the London Gazette.
   Richard Chase of Hadham, Esq., High Sheriff of Hertfordshire, and Jeffrey Ellways [Elwes] of Hoddesdon, Esq., were knighted upon presenting the Hertford Address.

This address, presented by the High Sheriff on behalf of the County of Hertford, was an address of loyalty to the King at a time of a threat of invasion by the French and of abhorrence at French plans and the possibility of their placing a Catholic king on the British throne. [PW]

3 May 1744. At Watford, Hertfordshire, a Dutch soldier, in a quarrel with a farmer's man, stabbed him in the belly and cut him in the face. Upon which, being carried before his Captain, he ordered him to be immediately hanged on the sign-post, and accordingly had a ladder brought out and a rope put about his neck. But a Justice of the Peace coming, prevented the execution by acquainting the Captain that if the man died the civil power would demand the murderer; and in the meantime, desired a guard might be kept on him, with which the officer at length complied.

March 1745. Mr. Edm. Castle, rector of Barley, Hertfordshire, chosen master of Bennit College, Cambs., the Bishop of Chichester having resigned.

10 December 1745. The guards and other regiments which were sent on the 7th to Highgate, Enfield and Barnet in order to form a camp at Finchley Common, were countermanded.

MAIL ROBBERY NEAR ST. ALBANS

22 April 1747. The Chester mail for London was robbed between St. Albans and Barnet by three highwaymen, who carried off all the letters out of 41 bags. For each of these robbers there is a reward promised of £200 upon conviction, besides the reward by Act of Parliament.

Friday 1 May 1747. Ended the session at the Old Bailey, when . . . Robert King Parkinson, who was committed to Newgate the 25th ultimo, on information of a Jew (to whom he offered, by a broker, the negotiation of two £50 banknotes) on suspicion of robbing the Chester mail was ordered to remain till next session. Two young fellows, brothers, of the name of Bibbie, concerned with him, being impeached by him, are in custody at Bristol, being taken on board a privateer.

Friday 10 July 1747. The two Bibbies, charged with robbing the Chester mail; Curtis, alias Pollard, the smuggler; and William Cox, charged with forgery and marrying several wives; broke out of Newgate.

Friday 17 July 1747. William Bibbie, apprehending he was pursued, and endeavouring to escape over some pales in Church Lane, Whitechapel, was killed by a fall.

Friday 11 September 1747. Ended the sessions at the Old Bailey, when . . . Bibbie [was ordered] to be sent to Hertford.

Friday 11 March 1748. At Hertford Assizes, Thomas Bibby was convicted of robbing the Chester mail, in company with King Parkinson, who died in Newgate, and William Bibby his brother. He was afterwards hung in chains near St. Albans.

23 August 1747. A fire at Royston consumed 36 houses, several stacks of corn, and a great quantity of meal and grain.

January 1748. George Pembroke of St. Albans, and Lord Earl Cowper, appointed Land Tax Receivers.

8 January 1750. Between 12 and 1 o'clock afternoon, an earthquake was felt throughout London and Westminster . . . On enquiring we find that the shock was felt at Deptford, and Greenwich to Gravesend, . . . at Woodford, Walthamstow, Hertford, Highgate, Finchley — not at Barnet.

8 March 1750. This morning, at half an hour after five o'clock, the town was again alarmed with another shock of an earthquake, which is generally allowed to be more violent, and of longer continuance than that felt this day month; great numbers of people were awakened from their sleep merely by its violence, which however has done no other mischief than throwing down several chimneys, and damaging some houses. The shock was so great in some parts, that people ran from their houses and beds almost naked.
[Here is recorded what happened in different parts of London and finishes up with]:-
The shock was felt at Cheshunt, Hertford, Ware, Copthall near (not at) Epping, Beckenham in Kent.

3 June 1750. At Mile End in the parish of Rickmansworth, Hertford, in a great storm of thunder and lightening, which began at 9 and lasted till noon, ten sheep were struck dead, others wounded, the bark of an elm was shivered, and much other mischief done in other places.

August 1750. [Letter from L.W. of Royston, concerning treatment for the bite of a mad dog, and other medical matters].

5 February 1751. Was interred the coffin and remains of a farmer at Stevenage in Hertfordshire, who died, February 1, 1720, and ordered by will that his estate, which was £400 a year, should be enjoyed by his two brothers who are clergymen and, if they should die, by his nephew, till the expiration of 30 years, when he supposed he should return to life, and then it was to revert to him. He also ordered his coffin to be affixed on a beam in the barn, locked, and the key to be inclosed, that he might let himself out. They stayed four days more than the time limited and then interred him.

This seems to be a variant of the story of Henry Trigg, grocer of Stevenage, (died September 1724), who had become apprehensive lest his body after death should fall into the hands of body-snatchers. He therefore provided in his will that his property should be inherited by his brother, a clergyman, on condition that he did not allow the body to be buried: instead, it was to be laid upon the roof beam in the old barn behind his house to await the 'General Resurrection'. The house subsequently became the Old Castle Inn, and is now the National Westminster Bank. In 1906 the coffin was opened by the East Hertfordshire Archaeological Society and found to contain "about two-thirds of a male skeleton". Stevenage Museum has summarized the facts in a four-page leaflet. [AJ]

30 March 1751. At Hertford 9 persons were condemned: one of them was for murder, another for firing a barn, in which a person was burnt to death, and 7 for highway robberies. Four are executed.

MOB VIOLENCE AT TRING

23 April 1751. At Tring in Hertfordshire, one B——d——d, a publican giving out that he was bewitched by one Osborne and his wife, harmless people above 70, had it cried at several market towns that they were to be tried by ducking this day, which occasioned a vast concourse. The parish officers having removed the old couple from the workhouse into the church for security, the mob missing them broke the workhouse windows, pulled down the pales, and demolished part of the house; and seizing the governor, threatened to drown him and fire the town, having straw in their hands for that purpose. The poor wretches were at length for public safety delivered up, stripped stark naked by the mob, their thumbs tied to their toes, then dragged two miles, and thrown into a muddy stream; after much ducking and ill usage, the old woman was thrown quite naked on the bank, almost choked with mud, and expired in a few minutes, being kicked and beat with sticks, even after she was dead; and the man lies dangerously ill of his bruises. To add to the barbarity, they put the dead witch (as they called her) in bed with her husband, and tied them together. The coroner's inquest have since brought in their verdict of wilful murder against Thomas Mason, William Myatt, Richard Grice, Richard Wadley, James Proudham, John Sprouting, John May, Adam Curling, Francis Meadows, and 20 others, names unknown. The poor man is likewise dead of the cruel treatment he received.

2 May, 1751. Tring. Though your account of the riot and murder that lately happened in this place is in general true, yet several names were mistaken, and some circumstances omitted. These I have corrected, and supplied; and added some account of the incidents which for several years past have gradually been tending to produce this unhappy event.

A little before the defeat of the Scotch in the late rebellion, the old woman Osborne came to one Butterfield, who then kept a dairy at Gubblecote, and begged for some buttermilk, but Butterfield told her with great brutality that he had not enough for his hogs. This provoked the old woman, who went away, telling him, that the Pretender would have him and his hogs too. Soon afterwards several of Butterfield's calves became distempered; upon which some ignorant people, who had been told the story of the buttermilk, gave out that they were bewitched by old mother Osborne, and Butterfield himself, who had now left his dairy, and taken the public-house by the brook of Gubblecote, having been lately, as he had been many years before at times, troubled with fits, mother Osborne was said to be the cause. He was persuaded that the doctors could do him no good, and was advised to send for an old woman out of Northamptonshire, who was famous for curing diseases that were produced by witchcraft. This sagacious person was accordingly sent for and came. She confirmed the ridiculous opinion that had been propagated of Butterfield's disorder, and ordered 6 men to watch his house day and night with staves, pitchforks, and other weapons, at the same time hanging something about their necks, which, she said, was a charm that would secure them from being bewitched themselves. However these extraordinary proceedings produced no considerable effects, nor drew the attention of the place upon them, till some persons, in order to bring a large company together, with a lucrative view, ordered by anonymous letters that public notice should be given at Winslow, Leighton and Hempstead, by the cryer, that witches were to be tried by ducking at Long Marston on the 22nd of April. The consequences were as you have related them, except that no person has yet been committed on the coroner's inquest except one Thomas Colley, chimney-sweeper, but several of the ringleaders in the riot are known, some of whom live very remote, and no expense or diligence will be spared to bring them to justice.

30 July 1751. At Hertford assizes was condemned Thomas Colley for the murder of Ruth Osborne near Tring. The facts proved at this trial were as related [above], with the addition of the following particulars. Such was the folly and superstition of the crowd, that when they searched the work-house for the supposed witch, they looked even into the salt-box, supposing she might have concealed herself within less space than would contain a cat. Having wrapped the deceased and her husband in two different sheets, first tying their great toes and thumbs together, the most active of the mob dragged the deceased into the water by a cord which they had put round her body, and she not sinking, the prisoner Colley went into the pond and turned her over several times with a stick. After a considerable time she was hauled to shore, and the old man was dragged into the pond in the same manner and this they repeated to each three times. The deceased, after she was dragged in the third time, being pushed about by the prisoner, slipped out of the sheet and her body was exposed naked. Notwithstanding which, the prisoner continued to push her on the breast with his stick, which she with her left hand endeavoured to catch hold of, but was prevented by his snatching it away. After using her in this manner till she was motionless, they dragged her to shore and laid her on the ground where she expired; and then the prisoner went among the spectators, and collected money for the pains he had taken in shewing them sport. The old man afterwards recovered, but did not appear as an evidence.

24 August 1751. Thomas Colley for the murder of Ruth Osborne was executed at Gubblecote Cross, and afterwards hanged in chains on the same gallows, near 30 miles from the place of his confinement; the people about Marston Meere having petitioned against hanging him near their houses. The day before his execution he received the sacrament, and signed a solemn declaration† of his faith relating to witchcraft, which was read at his request by the minister of Tring, who attended him, just before he was turned off. He was escorted from Hertford gaol by the sheriff and his officers and a guard of 108 men, 7 officers, and 2 trumpets belonging to the regiment of horse blue. The procession was slow, solemn, and moving. Friday night he was lodged at St. Albans gaol, and at 5 the next morning was put into a one-horse chaise with the executioner, and came to the place of execution about eleven. The infatuation of the greatest part of the country people was so great that they would not be spectators of his death (perhaps from a conscious-ness of being present at the murder as well as he); yet many thousands stood at a distance to see him go, grumbling and muttering that it was a hard case to hang a man for destroying an old wicked woman that had done so much mischief by her witchcraft. As he passed through Tring, just as the prisoner's wife and daughter were permitted to speak to him, a pistol went off by the carelessness of one of the troopers, which put the whole corps in some consternation, taking it at first to be fired from a window; but no other accident happened. He behaved very penitent.

The Declaration of Thomas Colley

GOOD PEOPLE!

I beseech you all to take warning by an unhappy man's suffering; that you be not deluded into so absurd and wicked a conceit, as to believe that there are any such beings upon earth as witches.

It was that foolish and vain imagination, heightened and inflamed by the strength of liquor, which prompted me to be instrumental (with others as mad-brained as myself) in the horrid and barbarous murder of Ruth Osborne, the supposed witch, for which I am now so deservedly to suffer death.

I am fully convinced of my former error, and with the sincerity of a dying man, declare that I do not believe there is such a thing in being as a witch; and pray God that none of you, through a contrary persuasion, may hereafter be induced to think that you have a right in any shape to persecute, much less endanger the life of a fellow creature.

I beg of you all to pray to God to forgive me, and to wash clean my polluted soul in the blood of Jesus Christ, my saviour and redeemer.

So exhorteth you all, the dying
Thomas Colley.

8 June 1751. The jury sat on the body of Thomas Nash, blacksmith of South Mimms, Hertfordshire, murdered the 31st ultimo by Daniel Derbyshire, servant to a major in the army. This fellow and another livery servant, passing through South Mimms, saw the deceased at play with some girls at stool ball; at which he said *"What does such a black dog do playing with such pretty girls?"* to which the deceased replied *"I am not so much a dog as you, for I wear my own coat and you wear your master's."* On this, Derbyshire fell to lashing him with his whip, which Nash getting hold of, pulled off the thong, but returned it, and ran into a house for shelter. Derbyshire pursued him with a pistol in his hand, and knocking at the door in vain, broke the window with the butt end of his pistol, and spying the deceased in a corner of the room, fired, and shot him through the body, of which he died the next morning. The villain then drew another pistol and intimidating those who would have stopped him, rode after his master, who was gone before, and changing horses with him, on what pretence is uncertain, escaped.

August 1751. Hugh Bell, Esq., [appointed] collector of excise for Hertfordshire.

23 September 1751. A man ran driving a coach wheel from the Bishop's Head in the Old Bailey, to the 11 mile stone at Barnet, and back again, in 3 hours 51 minutes, having 4 hours to do it in, for a wager of £50.

2 October 1751. A man, for a wager of 20 guineas, walked from Shoreditch church, to the 26 mile stone near Ware, and back again in 7 hours.

16 October 1751. £100 was paid by Paggen Hale, Esq., of King's Walden, Hertfordshire, towards St. Luke's hospital for lunatics.

16 January 1752. Transactions in Parliament. [Were read and referred] petitions from St. Albans, Birmingham and Liverpool, praying bills for the more easy recovery of small debts.

29 February 1752. The whole town of Southwold, with a considerable part of Lowestoft in Suffolk, the children of the foundling hospital, the poor of the workhouses at Ware, Hertford[shire], and Richmond, Surrey, and the charity boys of West Ham, Essex, are employed in spinning twine and making nets for the herring fishery; by this seasonable labour the poor rates are already fallen from 4s. to 2s. in Southwold.

March 1752. At the last Hertford assizes, Charles Smith was condemned for the murder of his own son, a youth of about 17 years of age, whom he stabbed in his bed in many places of his body, swearing at the time he'd have his heart's blood.

At the same assizes were condemned Thomas Hurry and Alice Andrews (who lived as wife to Hurry) for the murder of his own daughter by repeated acts of torture.

13 March 1753. The Rev. Dr. Young of Welwyn in Hertfordshire, author of *The Tragedy of the Brothers* lately acted, has given to the Society for Propagating the Gospel 1000 guineas.

17 April 1753. [Royal assent given to an Act] for repairing the roads from Enfield in Middlesex to Hertford, &c.

8 March 1753. Accounts of the shock felt early in the morning on 8 March, 1749–50. XV. By Dr. Cowper, Dean of Durham.

The earthquake was felt very much at Northaw and Gubbins in Hertfordshire, and by a farmer and family three quarters of a mile northeast of Hatfield but not by the inhabitants of Hatfield, also at Hertingfordbury, a mile west of Hertford, but not at Hertford. At his own house in Panshanger, two miles west of Hertford, the noise was heard twice, with an interval of about half a minute, resembling the rumbling of a cart, but no shock felt; whence he concludes the force of the vapour was spent, and there was the northern limit of the earthquake.

15 October 1753. His Majesty has been pleased to promise his most gracious pardon to any accomplice, for the apprehending and bringing to justice the person or persons who sent two incendiary letters to Hale Wortham junior of Royston in Cambridgeshire, Esq., requiring him to lay £100 at his gate and, in case of failure, threatening to murder him and fire his house; and Mr. Wortham promises £50.

JOHN SCOTT OF AMWELL

December 1753. Mr. URBAN, Accidentally looking over your magazines for July and August 1752, I was agreeably entertained with a critical dissertation on that beautiful description in the 12th. chapter of Ecclesiastes. I thought your correspondent's explication was just, and having a mind to see how the passage would look in a modern poetical dress, I attempted the following version of it, on his plan; to which, if you please to allow a place in your next magazine, you will extremely oblige

Your friend and constant reader,

Hertfordshire, Dec. 18, 1753.   R.S.

Epidemick Mortality, from Eccl. xii

To move unthinking youth to just regard,
On Judah's plain thus sung the royal bard;
Thy maker God in early time revere!
'Ere evil days, those dreadful days, draw near,
When health shall fly and pleasure leave the plain,
And woe and languor and distress remain . . .

Because the time of desolation's come,
And man swift passes to his final home;
And pensive mourners range about the street,
And rend their garments and their bosoms beat.

John Scott (1730–1783) of Amwell House, Amwell End, the poet, Quaker and grotto-builder, was an assiduous reader of the Gentleman's Magazine and an occasional correspondent. This poem (not transcribed in full) was the first of his work to be published here, over the initials 'R.S.' A description of the workings of the Aeolian Harp in the magazine of February 1754 occasioned Scott's poem under the same title in the November issue, again signed with the initials R.S. and dated Hertfordshire, Nov. 15, 1754. In July 1758 Scott contributed a poem 'On Fear' without any signature or initials. The attribution of these poems to John Scott was made by James Hoole in his life of Scott, printed with the 'Critical Essays' in 1785. In August 1777 Scott contributed a long letter in which he unmasked the Rowley forgery, showing on stylistic grounds that the poems were not medieval but contemporary, and probably written by Thomas Chatterton. This letter, written anonymously, was subscribed 'A Detester of Literary Imposition, but a Lover of good Poetry'. London, June 19. In the following year he wrote two letters defending his friend, Dr. James Beattie of Aberdeen, against a correspondent writing under the name of Crito, signing each 'John Scott, Amwell'. [DP]

21 August 1754. A girl of three years old was struck dead by lightning at Sage Hill in the neighbourhood of St. Albans. Her father, who stood close by her, was unhurt but on taking up the child, whose clothes were on fire, the flame communicated to his own but was soon extinguished without doing him any injury.

9 December 1754. The malefactors under sentence of death were executed at Tyburn, amongst whom was Henry Mansell, condemned on Saturday, for the murder of Isaac Overton at Barnet.

Mansell, one of a party of soldiers hunting for deserters, was billeted at the Waggon & Horses public house, Barnet, where he murdered Isaac Emmerton (not Overton as G.M.) with a bayonet, on 6 November, 1754, following a dispute, apparently over who should pay for drinks. He was convicted at the Old Bailey on 6 December and sentenced to death: his body to be delivered to the surgeons to be dissected and anatomized. [GJ]
Sources: Guildhall Lib. Old Bailey Proceedings pt. 1 1714–1793. GLRO Old Bailey Sessions Book OB/SB/11.

8 March 1755. The assizes ended at Hertford, when Isaac Shuffle and Thomas Wood, bargemen, were capitally convicted for the murder of Francis Prior, three years ago. It appeared that these villains had waylaid the deceased, knocked him down with a bludgeon and then threw him into the river Ware, because he had threatened to prosecute them for frequently dragging his waters.

April 1755. List of capital convictions in 1755. Hertford. Isaac Shuffle and Thomas Wood, for murder; Robert Freeman and Henry Freeman, for the highway; Thomas Hanscombe and Richard Gurry, for housebreaking.

30 January 1756. Richard Hitch, aged upwards of 60, formerly a hog butcher at Islington, was committed to the New Gaol in Southwark by William Hammond, Esq., for the murder of his wife eleven years ago. The night this murder was committed, the prisoner, by his own confession, fled to Hitchin in Hertfordshire, and has been strolling up and down the country ever since in a wretched condition. Last Thursday being accidentally met at Ditton upon Thames by two butchers who knew him, they treated him till they came to Wandsworth, and there seized him. Since his commitment he hath confessed that he was in the room when his wife's throat was cut, but says she snatched the knife from him, and did it herself.

THIEF APPREHENDED AT POTTERS BAR

4 August 1756. At 1 o'clock this morning, the Hon. Captain Brudenel was stopped in his chair, just as it entered Berkeley Square, from the Hay Hill, by two fellows with pistols, who demanded his money; he gave them five six-pences, telling them he had no more, which having taken, they immediately made off; the captain then put his purse and watch under the cushion, got out, drew his sword, and being followed by one of the chairmen with his pole, and the watchman, pursued them up the hill, where the Hon. Captain West, who was walking, having joined them, one of the fellows having got off, they followed the other into Albemarle meuse [mews], where finding himself closely beset, he drew a pistol, and presented it, upon which the captain made a lunge at him, and run him through the body. The fellow at the same instant fired his pistol, which the captain being still stooping, went over his head, and shot the watchman through the lungs. At the instant the pistol was discharged, while the fellow's arms was extended, the chairman struck it with his pole and broke it. He was then seized, and carried with the watchman to the round-house in Dover Street, where Mr. Bromfield and Mr. Gataker, two eminent surgeons, came, but the captain would not suffer the villain to be dressed, till he discovered who he and his confederates were, when he acknowledged they were both grenadiers in Lord Howe's company. The poor watchman died in half an hour after he was shot; and the soldier was so disabled by his wound that he was carried in a chair to justice Fielding, who sent him to New Prison, where he died. It is but a year since Mr. Boudeler was robbed in that square, in whose defence a chairman was shot.

6 August 1756. Jonathan Hurst, the accomplice of Browning, who robbed Captain Brudenel, as already related, was after a most diligent search, traced to a cottage near Potter's Bar, beyond Barnet, and there apprehended. Most of the robberies that have been committed in Berkeley Square within these 2 last years are supposed to have been committed by these two fellows.

23 August 1756. The sessions at the Old Bailey, which began the 19th. ended, when five criminals were capitally convicted, viz. William Higgins and James Raythorne, for stealing wearing apparel; John Hughes, for forgery; Jonathan Hirst, for robbing Captain Brudenell; and Francis Mugford, for returning from transportation.

September 1756.
The ODDITY
Being a journal for the greatest part of a month, which may be of great service to poor travellers, and poor housekeepers. [Two verses from a very long poem.]

> Veal cutlets for supper, punch, breakfast, horse, maid,   4s 10d
> At Buntingford stopt, where for dinner I paid.   2s 3d
> A town famous for nothing that I can tell,
> Except that John Frisby keeps the sign of the Bell.
>
> At Hodsdon I lay, and found great relief,
> By a pretty large slice from a buttock of beef.   3s 8d
> Next morning arriv'd safe in London by nine,
> The roads were all good, and the weather was fine.

12 December 1756. The postboy carrying the Worcester mail was robbed by a footpad near Shepherd's Bush, who opened a great number of the letters, stripped them of their bills, and then made off. He afterwards, by travelling post in post-chaises with four horses through Barnet, Hatfield, Stevenage, Bugden, Caxton, Royston, Ware and Enfield, put off several of the bills and notes, which he endorsed by the name of James Wilson.

15 April 1757. John Wright, a dragoon belonging to Lord Ancram's regiment, was shot on Colney Heath, near Barnet, for desertion. It was the third offence for which he suffered.

July 1757. An abridgement of the new Act for better ordering the Militia Forces in the several Counties of England . . .
> The number of private men serving in the militia shall be, for
>   Hertford[shire]   560 . . .
> The Lord Lieutenant of the County on whom the execution of
> the Act wholly depends [is]
>   Hertford[shire]   Lord Cowper

6 April 1758. Field Officers of embodied militia battalions in 1759: Lord Lieutenant Earl Cowper, Colonel John Sabine, Lieutenant-Colonel Jacob Houblon.

MARTYRDOM OF ST. AMPHIBALUS

12 April 1759. The antique figures that were discovered in the roof of a small chapel at Wakefield in Yorkshire in May 1756 (see Vol xxvi p.559) and the year following publicly shown in London, excited my curiosity to take a view of them, particularly that of St. William, the 30th archbishop of York, most accurately explained by the learned and ingenious Mr. Paul Gemsege. Amongst those of alabaster, I took notice of a piece of sculpture representing a bishop under the act of martyrdom, with his bowels winding out with a spit turned by two lictors . . .

I take the subject to be a piece of pagan persecution, and to represent the martyrdom of St Amphibalus, who converted our British proto-martyr, St. Alban, to the Christian faith, and both suffered in the time of the tenth persecution, under the emperor Diocletian. Our historians much vary concerning the precise time of their martyrdom; some of them placing it about the latter end of Diocletian but Cressy (on better authority) fixeth it in the third year of that emperor's reign, AD 286. They agree no better in their accounts of this Amphibalus; for Boethius, with other Scottish historians, make him to be bishop of the Isle of Man; whilst Giraldus Cambrensis, with many of the writers of our church history, say, he was by birth a Welshman, and bishop of the Isle of Anglesey; that after converting Alban to the faith of Christ, he fled from Verulam into Wales, to escape the execution of the severe edict made by that emperor against the Christians, and was there seized, and brought back to Redbourn in Hertfordshire, where he was put to death in the cruel manner above represented. Bishop Usher exposes this story as a piece of monkish fiction, and says his name nowhere occurs till Geoffrey of Monmouth's time, who is the first author that mentions it. And Fuller, with his usual drollery, wonders how this compounded Greek word came to wander into Wales; and thinks it might take its rise from the cloak wherewith he was wrapped; or it might be, from changing vestments with his disciple Alban, the better to disguise his escape. It is certain, that Venerable Bede, who was a Saxon, and to whom most of our monkish historians are beholden for the history of St. Alban, makes no mention of his name, only calling him Presbyter, a priest, or clerk. Though Copgrave, Harpsfield, and others, pretend the lives of these saints were written by an anonymous author, prior to Bede, found in the monastery of St. Albans. This work, Bishop Nicholson, in his *Histor. Library*, p.95, says, was translated into Latin by William Albanensis, a monk of that house. Matthew Paris, in his history of the abbots of St. Albans, tells us, that Aedmer, the 9th abbot, in searching among the ruins of Verulam, found a small chest filled with books in the ancient British language; that he sent for Unwon, an old priest, well versed therein, who translated one which treated on the life of Alban; but the others, containing the rites and ceremonies of the old inhabitants of Verulam, he destroyed: Leland laments the loss in these words.—*Cætera pro dolor! fatuus et idem poene impius Abbas, non sine ingenti antiquarum rerum jactura, vulcano commisit.* See his work, intitled *Commentarii de Scriptoribus Britannicis*, published by Anthony Hall, A.M. Vol I. p.166.

Notwithstanding the obscure accounts of Amphibalus in those early days, ample amends were made to his memory in succeeding times; for when Offa, king of Mercia, founded the stately abbey of St. Albans for Benedictine monks, he bestowed on it large possessions; which were much increased by other kings his successors, who obtained for it great privileges from divers popes; and Adrian IV granted to the abbot thereof precedency of all others in England. As it had the pre-eminence in wealth and grandeur, so it likewise abounded most of any with learned monks, who were particulary lavish in their histories and legends of these saints; nor were several abbots less backward in bestowing honours to their memory and remains. I shall only mention a few instances, as I find them recorded in M. Paris, and other writers.

Garine, 20th abbot, caused a coffin and shrine to be new made, wherein he deposited the reliques of St. Amphibalus.

Roger, 24th abbot, caused to be made three tuneable bells for the steeple, two to the honour of St. Alban, and the third to St. Amphibalus.

And the convent of St. Albans had such a care that the reliques of Amphibalus should be devoutly preserved, that Thomas de la Mare, the 30th abbot, made a decree, that a prior and three monks should be appointed for so sacred an office; for which they were to receive £20 yearly allowance. vide Weaver, p.585.

In an ancient and fair copy of the *Sanctilogium Britanniæ* of Johannes Tinmuthensis, a monk of St. Albans, and preserved in the Cotton library, is the following note of Thomas, the above abbot. *Hunc Librum dedit Dominus Thomas de la Mere, Abbas Monasterii Sancti Albani Anglorum Proto Martyris Deo et Ecclesiae B. Amphibali de Redburn, ut Fratres ibidem in cursu existentes per ejus Lecturam poterint caelestibus instrui, et per Sanctorum Exempla virtutibus insigniri.* Nicolson's Hist. Lib. p.98.

Besides this church of Redbourn, Camden says, the collegiate church at Winchester was dedicated to this saint, though now to the Holy Trinity. See Brit. Bishop Gibson's 1st Edit, p.120.

To conclude, whether he was the real or pretended instructor of St. Alban, and when and where the name had its first rise; whether in that monastery, which I think is not unlikely; this much is certain: it was in after times held in high veneration, and made no inconsiderable figure in the Roman calendar.

The above passage brings together some of the facts, misunderstandings and legends relating to Amphibalus, an unjustly derided saint. He is the earliest described Christian evangelist to Britain, as authentic as Alban, his famous convert. (See Hertfordshire Countryside, *vol. 36, no. 262, (1981) 14–15). The author refers to the date of the martyrdom, and to the complex problems involved in establishing it. St. Amphibalus' passion he dismisses as a "piece of monkish fiction" and the "pretended" life, but internal evidence suggests it may have been rooted in an oral epic of the Anglo-Saxon period.* Alia Acta . . . *or Other Doings . . . is translated in* Hertfordshire Archaeology, *vol. 8 (1983) 67–77. The proper name "Amphibalus" and the supposed church in Winchester dedicated to him, go back to the corrupt copy of Gildas'* Ruin of Britain *which Geoffrey of Monmouth strove to make sense of in writing his* History of the Kings of Britain. *Amphibalus' Welsh origins and his status as a bishop are nothing more than later legendary accretions. A twin cult of SS. Alban and Amphibalus was practised at St. Albans with the utmost solemnity for almost four hundred years and the building was modified to accommodate it; these are unimpeachable facts. A serious study of the confused cult of St. Amphibalus is in preparation at the present time. [ER]*

---

16 June 1759. [An account of the effects of thunder and lightning at Rickmansworth in Hertfordshire, 16 June 1759. The correct date was 16 July 1759].

This account, though written by a lady, Mrs. Anne Whitfield, is one of the most regular, consistent and particular narratives of the kind that was ever published. As there is nothing superfluous in it, nothing can be omitted without rendering it imperfect; there is not, however, anything peculiar in the effects of this storm, except that one of the rooms which suffered was so filled with sulphur, smoke and dust that nothing in it could be seen, and the person that went in to open the window was obliged to feel about for it; and a young lady that was in the room when the accident happened was preserved from having her arm broken by accidentally having her comb tray under it, which was shattered to pieces, and if it had not happened to have been there her arm would probably have been in its place.

16 July 1759. The chimneys of the house of Mr Whitfield, lord of the manor of Rickmansworth, were beaten down by the thunder and lightning, and the windows on one side broken. As a lady was combing her hair at the window, the comb in her hand was shivered to pieces, and the bed in her room split and rent in a surprising manner, yet she did not receive the least hurt. Some of the bricks of the chimneys were carried 100 yards from the house.

8 June 1761. The Hertfordshire regiment of militia, commanded by Colonel Sabine, began their march for Bristol, as did the Norfolk for Chatham camp.

DISTURBANCE BY REAPERS AT KINGS LANGLEY

8 August 1761. A dispute having happened between the farmers of Kings Langley and the Irish reapers, about wages, the latter, in order to oblige the farmers to comply with their demands, assembled to the number of 200, armed with pistols, swords, guns and clubs, and threatened to fire the town. Upon which the Royal Foresters, quartered at Watford, being sent for, a great skirmish happened this day, in which several were wounded. Six were taken and committed to St. Albans jail and the rest were dispersed. Some of these after made a riot in the Isle of Ely.

Records of the Hertfordshire Quarter Sessions report an indictment of six men in August 1761 for riotous assembly in Kings Langley and causing assault, shooting and wounding Gilbert Campbell, gentleman, Thomas Bean, husbandman, William Durrant, cordwainer and John Coleman, labourer, on the information laid by John Gee, collarmaker, and John Sutton, baker, both of Kings Langley. The defendants were named as Patrick Marrow, Edward Kinant, Richard King, and Richard, Thomas and Matthew Plunkett. Their trades were not specified and there was no report that they were Irishmen although the surnames suggest that was perhaps what they were.

The six were found guilty and, with the exception of Patrick Marrow, who undertook to enlist as a soldier, all the defendants were sentenced to one shilling fines and either one or two months in gaol. Their names appear in the Calendar of Hertford gaol for September 1761.

This entry in the G.M. is an example of journalism putting flesh on the bones of an incident illustrated in the court record. Without the magazine entry we would have no reason to associate this minor fracas with either migrant farm workers or Irishmen.

The testimony of the article seems dubious in some respects. Early August sounds a bit early in the year to have a dispute about harvest wages. Harvest workers might well cause trouble if expected wages were not paid but surely not at the very start of the harvest season. Workers who were recalcitrant at the bargaining stage would not be taken on at all.

I think we can take the threat to burn down the town with a pinch of salt. In the same session another man who 'appeared to be a madman' was similarly indicted for threatening to burn down Puckeridge. Easier said than done.

'Pistols, swords and guns' sound a little expensive for roaming Irish labourers although likely enough, if, say, they were discharged soldiery. Even serving soldiers stationed in country districts took on casual farm work on occasion and militiamen were sometimes in the habit of taking their sickles with them when serving away from home.

Mention of the army raises the question of the mysterious 'Royal Foresters' quartered at Watford. The use of capital letters suggests a regiment of that name although they could equally well be keepers or verderers of a Royal forest, although there is not one nearer than Windsor. There is no mention of the foresters in the court records. Indeed, the recognizance entered into by the two initial witnesses, John Gee and John Sutton, both ordinary residents of Kings Langley, suggests that the case was brought before the county magistrates in the ordinary way without any aid from the military. There is more than a trace of sensationalism about this report. [NA]

1762. New Militia Act. The number of private men to be raised in each county shall be:

Bedfordshire	400
Buckinghamshire	560
Cambridgeshire	480
Essex	960
Hertfordshire	560

[Transcribed for Hertfordshire and neighbouring counties only]

January 1762. A list of the Field Officers of the Fifty One Battalions of Militia embodied in 1759:

Hertfordshire:
Embodied 8 October
Lord Lieutenant Earl Cowper
Colonel John Sabine
Lieut. Colonel Jacob Houblon
Major William Cowper

6 January 1762. A lady in Bond Street, said to be nearly related to the young officer who was wounded in Hyde Park, shot herself through the head with a pistol, and died in great agonies. She was the daughter of a family of fortune at Northaw in Hertfordshire, and had married against her friend's [sic] consent.

August 1762. Rev. Mr. Dixon of Ware, appointed master of the grammar-school of that place.

August 1762. It is remarkable, that in the five counties of Hertford, Essex, Kent, Sussex and Surrey, on the home circuit, only three men were condemned, who were afterwards reprieved; and, according to the gaolers' calendars throughout England, only 18 persons have received sentence of death, four of whom, for murder, have been executed.

FARMER GLASSCOCK ROBBED BY HIGHWAYMEN AT HATFIELD

13 October 1762. One Miller was apprehended at Luton in Bedfordshire, on suspicion of robbing on the highway. On his examination, he owned, that he, with five others, had robbed the house of Farmer Glasscock of Hatfield, of £300 and that they were all to meet that very evening, to consult what other rich farmer to rob. Two of the five accomplices have been apprehended; one a rat-catcher, well known in that country; the other a poacher, who having been detected by Mr Hutchinson's park-keeper, had practised with three Irishmen to murder the poor man, and to throw his body into a hole. The detecting of this desperate gang is looked upon as a benefit to the country; the farmers, for many miles round, being under the most terrible apprehensions on their account. [See also 7 September 1764].

Miller was Ganselius or Ganzelous Miller, son of Cornelius Miller and nephew of Ganzelous Miller, innkeeper of the Salisbury Arms in Hatfield. Farmer Glasscock was Thomas Glasscock, tenant of Lord Salisbury's Coldharbour Farm, and Mr. Hutchinson was lord of the manor of Hatfield Woodhall. [HG]

11 December 1762. Fudge Harrow, a notorious thief and house-breaker, and one of the gang who robbed Farmer Glasscock of Hitchin, in Hertfordshire, of £300 was apprehended at Worlibank in Staffordshire, and safely lodged in Gloucester gaol. He had for some time resided at Wotton, near Gloucester, under the character of a deserter from one of his Majesty's ships of war, but being suspected of worse practices, and a description of him sent to Sir John Fielding, he thought fit hastily to retire, with a woman who came to Wotton along with him. On the arrival of Fielding's men at Wotton, they soon discovered which road he had taken, and being active in the pursuit, the thief takers surprized both him and his woman in bed; and, though Harrow had three brace of pistols charged by his bed-side, yet they broke in upon him so suddenly, that he had not presence of mind to make use of one, but surrendered himself quietly, and was carried to gaol in a post-chaise.

Here 'Hitchin' is an error for Hatfield. Sir John Fielding was the blind police magistrate at Bow Street, half-brother of Sir Henry Fielding, the magistrate and novelist. The Fieldings' "thief-takers" were the originals of the body later known as the Bow Street Runners. [HG]

14 March 1763. William Harrow (the supposed flying highwayman), Thomas Jones, the noted travelling rat-catcher and William Bossford, for robbing the dwelling house of Thomas Glasscock of £300, and John Wright for a robbery on the Buntingford Road, were all executed at Hertford.

William Harrow (a member of a long established Hatfield family of bricklayers) and Thomas Jones, "hanged at Hertford for Housebreaking", were buried at Hatfield 16 March 1763. William Botsford, also "Hang'd for Housebreaking", was buried at Essendon the next day. A copy of a contemporary "Narrative of the Lives, surprizing Robberies, Behaviour, Confession, and Dying Words of the Four Malefactors", is in St. Albans Library. [HG]

27 October 1762. By the rains that fell for some days past, a high tide in the river Thames, and a strong gale of wind at North, the rivers within twenty miles of London were so raised, that the like has never been known in the memory of man; and the damage that has been sustained, more especially on the river Lee, is almost incredible. In less than five hours the water is said to have risen 12 feet in perpendicular height . . .

Buntingford bridge in Hertfordshire is [likewise] broken down, and the post-boys were carried away by the stream; but the mail, after continuing ten hours under water, has been recovered, the boys were saved, but the horses drowned. The letters received at the general post office were obliged to be dried by fires, and several of the mails did not come in.

The waters at Mimms rose so high that the stage-waggons durst not attempt to pass.

1 November 1762. John Batt of Potter's Bar, blacksmith, was committed to Bridewell, to hard labour, for cutting and destroying several young beech trees upon his Majesty's chace of Enfield, where he was detected with a cart and horse, in carrying away such trees unlawfully cut and destroyed. He is to be publicly whipped in the market town of Enfield, once every month during his confinement, pursuant to statute.

Sunday 23 June 1763. During the time of divine service a fire-ball fell upon the church of Hertford, penetrated the same, and greatly terrified the congregation. It burst in the blue coat boys gallery, with a terrible explosion that was heard in every house in the town, but did no other damage than singeing a boy's hair. The like accident has happened to several other churches, particularly that at Mangotsfield in Gloucestershire, and Wilbraham church near Cambridge.

THIEF APPREHENDED AT SAWBRIDGEWORTH

8 July 1763. Thomas Usher, clerk to the Bristol waggon, who lately carried off £1800 delivered to him by the captain of a ship to be forwarded to London; and also £200 of his master's cash, and two watches belonging to his servants, was secured in Newgate, having been traced by his master to the Oxford Arms in Oxford Road, where he learnt that he had been taken out of a post-chaise and four the preceding day by an hackney coach. This intelligence being communicated to Sir John Fielding, it had the desired effect; and it was soon discovered that Usher had paid the coachman extraordinary to carry him by Islington to the Black Bull in Whitechapel, from whence he was pursued and apprehended at Sawbridgeworth in Hertfordshire. Most of the Portugal money of which the £1800 consisted, was found on searching his wife's lodgings, and on a more particular search, near £100 more was found, and also one of the watches. A letter was also found, wrote to his wife, wherein he desired her to meet him at Fairfaxe's on Epping Forest, and to invite her brother and sister to come along with her, having got joyful news to tell them; no less, says he, than £1000 in the lottery, which I have got about me.

4 May 1764. Thomas Usher for defrauding William James, the Bristol carrier of £2200, was executed at Bristol. During the execution, a highwayman committed a robbery in sight of many thousand spectators, but was afterwards taken.

February 1764. In a description of the County of Bedfordshire—"At Millbrook near Ampthill was a small cell of Benedictines, belonging to the abbey of St. Albans, a market-town of Hertfordshire, dedicated to St. Mary Magdalene . . . In a wood near Market-street [Markyate], about three miles from Dunstable, was a nunnery of the Benedictine order, dedicated to the Holy Trinity. The site and some adjacent lands were given by the Dean and Chapter of St. Paul's, London, in 1145; and it was soon after built and endowed by Geoffrey, abbot of St. Albans. Dugdale values this nunnery at £144.16.1d per annum, and Speed at £143.18.3d."

June 1764. Some account of the life of the late Stephen Hales, D.D., F.R.S . . . : His mother was Mary, the daughter and heiress of Richard Wood of Abbots Langley, in Hertfordshire. They had many children and Stephen was their sixth son. He married about 1711 Mary the daughter and heiress of Dr Newce, Rector of Hailsham, Sussex, but resided at Much Hadham, Hertfordshire.

23 June 1764. A most violent tempest of thunder, lightning, and rain, did incredible damage from Beaconsfield to Hatfield; it shivered trees, cut off and laid flat whole fields of corn, destroyed the fruits of the earth, broke the windows that were exposed to its fury, and ruined many farmers, and others totally.

8 August 1764. At Hertford assizes, a cause was tried, in which a citizen of London was plaintiff, and a farmer of Stanstead defendant, for a horse bought of the latter, warranted sound, which soon after proved defective in his eyes. The jury without going out of court, gave a verdict for the plaintiff, and the judge, L.C.J. Mansfield, took occasion to declare, that if at any time, any horse-dealer should take a sound horse-price for an unsound horse, the warranting, or not warranting, should make no difference in the decision.

7 September 1764. Farmer Glasscock of Hatfield was again robbed by a daring fellow [see 14 March 1763] who attacked him in his own fields, made him go home to furnish him with money, and when he entered the house knocked him down, and carried off whatever he thought most valuable. The villain has been since taken.

18 December 1764. A young lady of fortune who had eloped from her guardian the night before was overtaken a little beyond Barnet concealed in a mourning hearse; her lover, who is said to be a military gentleman, acted as coachman on the occasion, and both were bound for Scotland; but luckily their journey was stopped.

May 1765. A chimney-sweeper at a village in Hertfordshire has sixteen children, sons, who all follow the occupation of their father.

September 1765.

TRING—PARK Tragedy

By the late Dr. Redman, of Berkhamsted.

Par Nobile fratrum.

A Brace of bucks in friendship bound
(such as with man is rarely found)
Together walk'd, together lay,
And fed together every day:
Whatever pasture one approv'd,
The other for that reason lov'd:
Contented with their gay retreat,
They envy'd neither rich nor great.
All their ambition, all their strife,
(Mark this, and blush, O man and wife!)
Was, which shou'd love his brother most,
To all, but one another, lost,
 One fault they had; and, what was that?
A fatal fault! they were too fat;
For this alone condemn'd to die:
So wills the keeper, and lets fly.
One falling cries, 'Farewell, dear mate!
Fly, swiftly fly, and shun my fate.'
 Speaking he died. Confus'd, amaz'd,
On the dead corpse his brother gaz'd;
He sighed and sobb'd : Adown his cheeks
Fast flow the tears while thus he speaks:
'Thy dying words I nought will heed,
Nor quit thy side, but by thee bleed:
One half is gone; 'twill be unkind,

Should t'other linger here behind;
Come, Libitina, quickly come,
And lead me to my faithful chum!'
    While thus he mourn'd with grief unfeign'd
Achilles like, his murder'd friend,
Out steps the minister of death;
Shoots him his wish, and stops his breath.
    If life's the price for fatness paid,
Tremble for thy devoted head,
O* Trig! lest thou, in sin as deep,
Shouldst not, so plump, in whole skin sleep.
But hold! for thy dear† lady's sake,
Still keep thy broad expanse of back,
To screen her, when she mounts thy beast,
From the rude blasts of North or East.
    Goddess of health! attend the fair,
Wait on her steed, and bless the air!
Through the mild air they balm convey
Smile on her cheek, and bloom without decay!

                              August 7, 1750.
*The keeper.
†Mrs Gore being then in a bad state of health, used to take the air behind the keeper.

The above verses are founded on a true fact. The keeper was ordered to shoot two bucks in the two parks. But after he had shot the first he had mark'd, his comrade came and stood by him in the manner here described; whereupon the keeper shot him also.
            Quis talia fando temperet a lachrymis ?
                [These notes by the Editor, G.M.]

This curious and apparently allegorical poem was dated 1750, but not published in the Gentleman's Magazine until 1765. The author seems to have been Jones Redman, a Fellow of King's College, Cambridge, who became Master of King's College School. He subsequently studied physic and practised at Berkhamsted, where he died 6 May 1763. (Alumni Cantabrigienses). He can possibly be identified with John Redman, Esq., whose monumental inscription in St. Mary's Northchurch (transcribed by Clutterbuck) recorded his death 5 May 1763, his wife Susannah having died 14 March 1756. The possibility that the poem might contain allusions, offensive to some local people, might itself have caused publication to be deferred till after the author's death. The head of the Gore family in 1750 when it was written was Charles, who had inherited the estate in 1739, but he did not die until 1768. [AJ]

September 1765.

Q U I N's Soliloquy on seeing Duke Humphrey at St. Albans.

A Plague on Egypt's arts, I say!
Embalm the dead ! on senseless clay
    Rich wines and spices waste !
Like Sturgeon, or like brawn, shall I
Bound in a precious pickle, lie,
    Which I can never taste ?
Let me embalm this flesh of mine
With turtle fat, and Bourdeaux wine,

And spoil th' Egyptian trade !
Than Humphry's duke more happy I —
Embalm'd alive, old Quin shall die
A mummy ready made.

D.G.

3 September 1765. A most desperate attack was made upon the Rev. Dr. Yarborough, of Tween [Tewin], near Hertford, by a young fellow, who having left his horse at the gate, entered the parlour where the doctor was, and clapping a pistol to his breast, demanded his money. The doctor offered him some silver, and protested what other money he had was at Hertford, on which the young villain withdrew, saying it was not silver he wanted, took his horse, and rode off without further mischief.

August 1766. [A long poem, with no apparent Hertfordshire relevance, is 'Inscribed to Miss B.B. of C——— in Hertfordshire.']

18 August 1766. At an entertainment on account of the opening of a new organ at Watford, the Indian chiefs were present, and sang several of their warlike songs.
    [The G.M. had recorded the arrival of the Indian chiefs on 2 August, as follows: "Arrived in London, the Indian chiefs, with their ladies and an Indian attendant. According to their own account, they are chiefs of two of the five tribes of Iroquois Indians, inhabiting the country between New York and Lake Ontario, and are come with letters of recommendation from General Sir William Johnston in order to settle the limits of their hunting grounds, which they complain are encroached upon by the settlers from New York . . . "]
The new organ installed at Watford in the summer of 1766 was in St. Mary's Parish Church. Vestry minutes of 1 May 1766 record the decision that "an organ for which several of the inhabitants of Watford and others have subscribed shall be erected in the gallery at the west end of the church." On 6 August 1766 Joseph Hodsdon, sexton, was appointed blower to the organ at 40s. a year. A note inserted at the back of the minute book records that the organ was put up by Thos. Parker, organ builder, at a cost of £190. No reference has been found to an inauguration ceremony, or to the presence of 'the Indian Chiefs' in Watford. [MF]

1 December 1766. It is remarkable that No. 20,99 in the present lottery, was purchased in the alley for Pagan Hale, Esq., of Hertfordshire; and the same number was also divided into shares, at a lottery-office near Charing Cross, and some of the shares actually sold. The number purchased in the alley was the real number, but that divided was done by mistake, for which the office-keeper paid a proportionable sum for what he had sold.
The Gentleman's Magazine had reported in April 1766 (page 144) the origin of this lottery, as follows: "The House of Commons came to a resolution of raising £1,500,000, two-fifths of which by annuities of 3 per cent, two-fifths by way of lottery, the tickets £10 each, the blanks £6; and the remaining fifth by way of tontine, or annuities upon lives, at 3 per cent with benefit of survivorship . . . . The new tickets have already been done in Change Alley, at £12.3s. . . ." (Change Alley, near the Royal Exchange, is presumably the 'alley' referred to again on 1 December 1766). [PW]

7 January 1767. Peter the wild man, who was taken in the Hartz Forest in Hanover when a youth, and sent as a present to his late Majesty on his accession to the throne, was brought from Cheshunt in Hertfordshire, (where he has been kept for many years at the expence of £30) to be seen by the Royal Family. He, like Shakespeare's Caliban, can fetch wood and water, but can speak no language articulately. The tale in the papers of his being a poor Hanoverian idiot, sent here in a drunken frolic to be maintained, deserves contempt. [See also February 1785, November 1785].

17 September 1767. Was held a court at Christ's hospital, when the president declared that a benefaction of £200 had been received from Sir James Cockburn, Bart., upon which the thanks of the court and staff were voted to that gentleman. Dr. Pitcairne received his charge as a governor, as did John Small, Esq., who gave £100. The report from the committee of almoners was also read, in relation to the residue of the estate of Mr John Butteris, late of Hertford, amounting to £546 which he bequeathed to the hospital, on condition, that the corporation might have always one child there, and it was unanimously agreed to accept the same.

17 March 1768. Some malicious persons set fire to a plantation of young oaks belonging to Timothy Earle, Esq., near Rickmansworth, which in three hours time consumed several acres.

May 1768. List of members of Parliament [includes]:
ST. ALBANS   Richard Sutton, under-secretary of state
         John Radcliffe of Hitchin, Hertfordshire.
HERTFORDSHIRE   Thomas Halsey of Great Gaddesden, Hertfordshire.
         William Plumer, son-in-law to Viscount Falkland.
HERTFORD TOWN   John Calvert of Albury, Hertfordshire.
         W. Cowper, nephew to Mr. Cowper, clerk of the House of Lords.
BOROUGHBRIDGE, YORKSHIRE James West of Alscot, Warwickshire, recorder of St. Albans and Poole, FRS.
OAKHAMPTON, DEVON Thomas Brand of Hoo, Hertfordshire.
TEWKESBURY, GLOUCESTERSHIRE Nicholson Calvert of Hunsdon, Hertfordshire.

16 October 1768. A farm house belonging to John Lemon, Esq., of Northaw, in Hertfordshire, was maliciously set on fire, and entirely consumed, together with the barns, and a great quantity of grain.

3 December 1768. A horse belonging to Mr. Delimore of Hanstead [Hempstead?] in Hertfordshire, was cut for the stone, and a calculus extracted which weighed 17 lb. The horse died immediately after the operation.

THE DATCHWORTH TRAGEDY

23 January 1769. A man, his wife and two children were found perished to death in one of the poor-houses belonging to the parish of D—— [Datchworth] in Hertfordshire. They were found lying upon a little straw, without clothes and without covering, and a third child, a boy about eleven years old, alive but unable to stand, lying by them, who could give no account how long they had been dead. Upon enquiry, it was found that they had been taken ill about three weeks before, and that only one half-crown had been given them during the whole time by one the overseers of the poor.

This discovery in Datchworth was given wide publicity by a pamphlet entitled An Account of the Four Persons found Starved to Death at Datchworth, *written by Philip Thicknesse. Thicknesse was instrumental in securing an inquest, in spite of attempts to hush-up the affair. An account appears in* Five Hide Village: a History of Datchworth in Hertfordshire, *by T.O. Beachcroft and W.B. Emms, (Datchworth Parish Council, 1984). [AJ]*
See also the next two entries.

4 May 1769. The court of King's Bench was moved against the parish officers of Datchworth in Hertfordshire, to shew cause touching their conduct relative to the poor of the said parish, in consequence of nine affidavits being read in court on that subject.

29 June 1769. Cause was shown in the court of King's Bench by the parish officers of Datchworth in Hertfordshire, why an information should not go against them. When, upon a full hearing, the court was unanimously of opinion that there was not the least ground for such an information, and ordered the rule to be discharged.

———————————

22 March 1769. A pretended clergyman, for attempting to commit a rape upon a child under ten years of age, was tried at Hertford assizes, convicted, and sentenced to be imprisoned six months, to stand twice in the pillory during that time, and to find security for his good behaviour for one year.

9 May 1769. A baronet was convicted by a bench of justices at Barnet, in the penalty of £300 for making his own candles; but the penalty was mitigated to £110 before the justices left the court.

A search through the Chronological List of Statutes from 1558 (1st year of Queen Elizabeth I) to 1769 reveals no Act of Parliament relating to candles or chandlers. The conviction could be for breach of a monopoly for chandlers only to make candles. Or it could have been for breach of the excise laws by non-payment of duties due from making candles. [PW]

January 1770. Writs issued for electing Members [of Parliament] in the room of those dead or promoted.

Hertford, in room of William Cowper, Esq., deceased.
Candidate   Paul Field 244 {Returned}
                         Mr. Lyde 122

November 1770.

Average prices of corn
From Nov. 5 to Nov. 10 1770.
Published by Authority of Parliament
[per Winchester bushel]

	Wheat s d	Rye s d	Barley s d	Oats s d	Beans s d
Bedfordshire	4.8	2.1	2.3(?)	2.1	3.0
Buckinghamshire	5.1	?	?	2.1	2.10
Cambridgeshire	4.10	2.11	2.10	2.2	3.1
Essex	4.5	3.4	2.8	2.1	2.9
Hertfordshire	4.10	—	2.7	2.1	3.7

[Transcribed for Hertfordshire and neighbouring counties only]

1771. Sheriff. Hertfordshire. George Prescott of Theobalds.

27 March 1771. Executed at Tyburn [with four others]: Richard Mortis, for firing a loaded pistol at Thomas Parkinson, in Hertfordshire . . . Birch, Sidey, Mortis and Peak behaved in the press-yard in a most audacious manner, and struck the executioner when put into the cart.

7 August 1771. There was a great storm of thunder at Caddicot [Codicote?] in Hertfordshire, succeeded by a violent rain which lasted several hours and overflowed all the adjacent marshes.

24 September 1771. [Capitally convicted at the Old Bailey]. Robert Walker, for stealing a mare out of a field at Hatfield in Hertfordshire.

30 September 1771. One of the lunatics confined in Bethlem hospital made his escape from thence, and took his course towards St. Albans. He was immediately pursued by two of the keepers, who overtook him at Barnet, and having seized and handcuffed him, left him by himself while they got fresh horses. In the meantime he ran off and went through a field into Dock's Wood. The keepers made diligent search after him, but he has not been heard of since.

30 November 1771. Report from the Public Office in Bow Street relative to the commitment of offenders: Levi Weil, Solomon Porter, Mark Asheburg, Hyam Lazarus, Lazarus Harry Asheburg, and Asher Weil, being charged on the oath of an accomplice with breaking open the house of Mrs. Deighton at Wormley in Hertfordshire, in February last, and stealing a quantity of plate, etc.; and on suspicion of robbing the house of Mrs. Hutchins at Chelsea, and murdering her servant; and of being guilty of other felonies and burglaries: Esther Moses and Elias Jacobs, otherwise Polock, charged with receiving part of the goods stolen from Mrs. Deighton's at Wormley as above-mentioned, knowing the same to be stolen. Three of the last-named principal offenders were apprehended at Birmingham; a fourth was stopped on the road as he was riding post to Birmingham to give his companions notice to escape; the others were taken about Duke's Place and that neighbourhood. The three following persons belonging to this horrid gang are not yet taken: Abraham, otherwise Aaron, Linevil; one Coshay, a little man, born in England of German parents; and Solomon Lazarus, otherwise Blind Zelie, about 60 years of age.

1772. Sheriff. Hertfordshire. Samuel Moody of Watford.

June 1772. "What remained of Theobalds in Hertfordshire, King James's sumptuous palace, was pulled down, 1765, by the present proprietor George Prescott, Esq. Among the rest, was the room in which James I died, and a portico with a genealogical tree of the house of Cecil painted on the walls".
From *Anecdotes of British topography; or an historical account of what has been done for illustrating the topographical antiquities of Great Britain and Ireland* [by William Gough, Esq.] London, 1768.

1773. Sheriff. Hertfordshire. John Dorien of Berkhamsted, St. Peter.

19 April 1773. A gentleman of St. Albans attended at the Weavers Arms, in Spitalfields, and assembled a company of poor weavers, to the number of 485, whom he took with him to St. Albans, on pretence of setting them to work to dig a canal; but when they arrived, it appeared that the gentleman was out of his senses, and that the whole was a crazy man's trick. The mayor of St. Albans, however, by his prudent conduct, prevented any tumult that might have been expected from such a disappointment. He ordered lodgings and victuals to be provided for them the night of their coming, and next day gave every man sixpence to return; which they did, without the least disturbance.

11 August 1773. Dispensation. Rev. Caleb Hill, to hold Clothall rectory with Baldock rectory in Hertfordshire.

August 1773. [Booklet]. *The Happiness of the Saints in a separate state.* A Sermon, preached at Hitchin, in Hertfordshire, August 27, 1771, at the funeral of the Rev. Mr. Samuel James, A.M. By Benjamin Wallin, M.A. 8vo. 6d. Buckland.

12 December 1773. In the dead of night, the house of Mr. Cooper, attorney in St. Albans, was robbed of money to the amount of £700.

1774. Sheriff. Hertfordshire. Sir Abraham Hume, Bart.

TWO ANCIENT BRITISH COINS

January 1774. I have here inclosed a drawing of a coin, which I have reason to think is a Unic. The piece, by the appearance of it, seems to be

Saxon. It is of copper; and, having never seen nor heard of a Saxon copper regal coin, should be obliged to any of your curious readers for an explanation. M.

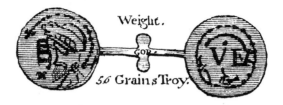

February 1774. I have seen a coin with a head like that in your last magazine, the reverse with VER upon it. I think this may the same coin, as the last letter seems to have been an R. The above coin is supposed to be one of Cassibelin, who was governor of Verulam; so that it is not Saxon. This is all the information I can give upon the subject. F.D.

July 1774. Your correspondent in your February magazine has endeavoured to explain the coin mentioned in your magazine for January last; for which we are much obliged to him. He there says, that he has seen such an one with VER on the reverse, and ascribes it to Cassibelin, Governor of Verulam, upon which he says, that it is not Saxon. Speed, in his *History of England*, gives us a coin with VER on the reverse (which coin is what that gentleman saw), and he likewise ascribes it to Cassibelin. The ingenious Mr. Pegge, in his *Essay on the Coins of Cunobelin*, has likewise given us a draft of the same coin mentioned by Speed, and ascribes it to Cunobelin: but this is foreign to the purpose; the coin in the magazine is quite different from Cunobelin's, which I here give you a draft, and I hope it will deserve a place in your magazine. M.

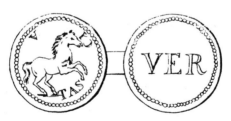

August 1774. . . . The plate in your last magazine . . . Nothing needs to be said [on the figure] as it is only engraved to illustrate the gentleman's observations on the old copper-coin given us in your magazine for January last. I shall add a word, however, on that coin. It is undoubtedly British, and coined at Verulam, or St. Albans, though it is impossible to tell by what king. The letters are apparently Roman, and not Saxon; and, indeed, I am of opinion, that the Saxons had not the use of letters so early as this coin implies. Your correspondent remarks there he had never seen nor heard of a Saxon copper regal coin; forgetting that we have many Sticas of the Northumbrian kingdom, and that few cabinets are without some of them. T. Row.

August 1774. Pray communicate the following question to M. As the coins with the word or letters TASCIA have different representations on the other side, and are all ascribed to the same person (Cunobelin), why may not those with VER, and different representations of the other side, be likewise ascribed to the same person, whether Cunobelin or Cassibelin ? I should be also glad to know his reasons for thinking the coin in the magazine for January to be Saxon. F.D.

October 1774. I must once more trouble you with a few words on M.'s coin, and endeavour to exculpate myself. The coin which I compared to his, was not that set down by Speed (as he might have perceived where I speak of a head being upon it, whereas there is none on Speed's), but a coin which I have actually seen and heard the opinions of many learned antiquaries upon, who have all attributed it to Cassibelin; but I did not absolutely affirm it to be the same as his; however, be that as it may, I am very certain his coin is British, and am very glad to find the ingenious Mr. Row of the same opinion. In your last magazine M. says, I may find several obverses like his in the Saxon, but none in the Old British Kings, whereas that of Cassibelin in Speed is British, and has VER on it like his own; nor is there one coin like his among the Saxon ones in Speed. I hope this will be satisfactory, and put an end to your dispute, as the subject is hardly worthy of such a long one. F.D.

G.M. EDITOR'S NOTE. The coin illustrated in the January magazine has 'TAS A' on the reverse. Is this, then, a coin of Tasciovanus ? Had not this ruler been discovered by the year 1774 ?

The coin illustrated in GM January 1774 appears to be a mule or hybrid since there is an attempt to show the laureate head (of Apollo) facing left, with the VER reverse. Amongst the relevant issues from Verulamium there are only two with head facing left, and both have the usual Celtic horse reverse, not the legend VER. The head left is unusual (it is normally in this series to right) and there are only two such varieties recorded for Verulamium under Tasciovanus (van Arsdell 1715 and 1745; Mack 158 and 182, respectively).

The GM July 1774 coin is a well-known type, the VER legend is actually the obverse ("heads") side whilst the horse is the reverse. It is a small silver unit, weighing around 1.4gms. According to van Arsdell it belongs to Tasciovanus's first coinage of c.25–20 BC (VA 1699; Mack 161). Tasciovanus, otherwise unknown except from his coinage, appears to have been the father of Cunobelin and reigned c.25–10 BC as king of the Trinovantes. He made the important innovation of adding mint names to the coinage, first VER(ulamium, followed by CAM(ulodunum).

A specimen of this particular coin was recently found in Great Gaddesden and has since passed into the possession of the Dacorum Museum Advisory Committee.

William Camden, Britannia (revised by Gibson),1695, p.298, illustrated this coin and says: "And I have seen several pieces of ancient money which in all probability were coined at this place [Verulamium] with this inscription TAS-CIA; and on the reverse VER, which that most inquisitive and learned Antiquary David Powel S.T.D. interpreteth to be the tribute of Verulam. For the Tasc (he tells me) in the British tongue signifies Tribute, Tascia a Tribute-penny, and Tascyd the Chief Collector of Tribute . . . Some will have it, that these pieces were coined before the coming in of the Romans. But I am not of that mind . . . For before the Romans coming, I can scarce think that the British ever coined money."

Sir John Evans (of Apsley) was amongst the pioneer scholars working on ancient British coinage and he published his seminal book, The Coins of The Ancient Britons, *in 1864.*
References:
R.P. Mack. The Coinage of Ancient Britain. *London, 1975.*
R.D. van Arsdell. Celtic Coinage of Britain. *London, 1989. [PC]*

---

13 January 1774. A few days ago, the house of Mr. Cater, at Bell Bar, in Hertfordshire, was burnt to the ground, together with all the outhouses. Mr. Cater, his wife, two children, and a maid-servant, perished in the flames. It is supposed to have happened by the floods reaching some lime, a great quantity of which happened to be in the house where the fire broke out.

The site of this house has been tentatively located at Russells Bottom, on the south-east corner of the Westfield crossroads. [BW]

20 March 1774. A number of ruffians have infested the neighbourhood of Barnet, and committed the most daring robberies, which has thrown the inhabitants into the utmost consternation.

July 1774. Dispensation. The Rev. Edmund Gibson, M.A., Chaplain to Lord St. John, of Bletso, to hold Bishop's Stortford vicarage in Hertfordshire, with the united rectories of St. Bennet's and St. Peter's, Paul's-Wharf, London.

13 August 1774. Great quantities of new wheat were brought to market at St. Albans, in Hertfordshire, which sold at 33s. 6d. the bag of five bushels. At the same time the best old wheat sold for 32s. the bag.

29 October 1774. Some villains broke into the house of Mrs. Cooley, near Cheshunt, in Hertfordshire, and after tying her, her niece, and maid-servant, in their beds, they stripped the house of money and effects to the value of £100.

1775. Sheriff. Hertfordshire. Rd. Emmott of Goldings.

29 August 1775. General Harvey went to General Cornwallis's seat near Hatfield, and returned to town to dinner, after which he waited on his Majesty at Kew.

Lt.-General the Hon. Edward Cornwallis (1713–1776), 6th son of the 4th Baron Cornwallis, and twin brother of Frederick Cornwallis, Archbishop of Canterbury. He was Lieutenant-Governor of Nova Scotia 1749–52, and Governor of Gibraltar 1762–76. Married Mary (died 1776) daughter of 3rd Viscount Townshend by his wife Audrey Harrison of Balls Park, Hertford. His seat was Bird's Place, Essendon (pulled down in 1833). [HG]

December 1775. Dispensation. Rev. Ed. Bouchier, M.A., to hold All Saints vicarage, in Hertfordshire, together with Bramfield rectory, in the same county.

This was the second of three rectors named Edward Bourchier who served the parish of Bramfield during the period 1740 to 1840.

Edward Bourchier I was instituted 30 September 1740, and served until his death on 17 November 1775, aged 68. He had also held, from 1741 to 1771, the vicarage of the united parishes of All Saints and St. John's, Hertford, but resigned that post in favour of his eldest son.

Edward Bourchier II succeeded his father as rector of Bramfield in 1775, and served for eleven years until his death in 1786. At that time his own son, Edward Bourchier III, was a child of only nine years. Edward II was therefore succeeded as rector by William Lloyd, who resigned in favour of Edward Bourchier III fourteen years later, in 1800. Edward III served as rector for forty years, until his death in 1840. [AJ]

December 1775. The original letter, of which the following is a faithful copy, was lately dusted out of a folio, where it had lurked near 20 years in my library. The book had been borrowed, and returned in the year 1753, by Dr. Cornewall Tathwell, a young physician, since eminent, and who died, I am told, at Stamford, in Lincolnshire, but then newly settled in my neighbourhood at Hitchin, Hertfordshire.

[Here follows an account, headed 'Hertfordshire, Oct. 31' dealing with "An entertaining Tour through several Parts of Burgundy, Switzerland, Savoy, and Dauphiny." The communication is unsigned].

February 1776. Dispensation. Rev. Anthony Hamilton, to hold Great and Little Hadham rectories, in Hertfordshire, together with the vicarage of St. Martin in the Fields, in Middlesex.

March 1776. Dispensation. Rev. Robert Dolling, LL.B., to hold the vicarage of Aldenham, Hertfordshire, together with the rectory of Titsey, in Surrey.

June 1776. Dispensation. Rev. John Law, M.A., to hold the rectory of Westmill, Hertfordshire, together with the rectory of Much Easton, Essex.

October 1776. John Stratford, Esq., of Ireland, was created in 1769 Baron Baltinglass, of that kingdom, a title to which (I have been told) an English gentleman [Godolphin Roper, Esq., of Hertfordshire] if he claimed it, has an hereditary right.

1777. Sheriff. Hertfordshire. John Serancke of Hatfield.

THE STORY OF MARY LOFTY OF REDBOURN

January 1777. A extraordinary Instance of the Vicissitude of Fortune, exemplified in a genuine Story of Real Life.

In the village of Redbourn, in Hertfordshire, is the little tenement of Mary Lofty, who is about eighty-four years of age, and obtains a livelihood in a manner so very extraordinary, as to make her the general conversation of the neighbouring people. She was the daughter of a country schoolmaster who had received an academical education and was intended for a clergyman, but his parents dying, and his patron deserting him, an honest country farmer, who was a freeholder in the parish, took him under his protection, and had interest enough with one of the knights of the shire to get him appointed a supernumerary officer in the excise, where his good behaviour soon promoted him to the station of an established officer in a country district. He continued in several removes as an exciseman till he was near sixty years of age, and was highly respected by the publicans and tradesmen whom his office obliged him to visit; for though he was punctual in his duty, he was never impertinent in the execution of it. He was caressed by the lord of the manor, and much esteemed by the vicar as a man of learning, and an agreeable companion, which gave so much jealousy to a young imperious supervisor, that he took every opportunity of mortifying him, by watching his conduct, and officiously reported him to the board. Being ill of the rheumatism, and unable to set out upon his round so early as usual, his supervisor took occasion to charge him with wilful neglect. This offence lost him his employment, nor could he tell how to make any provision for his daughter, till the honest vicar advised him to open a little school for the education of the neighbouring children. He took this advice, formed a school, and procured a tolerable livelihood, with great credit and esteem, till he was turned of seventy, and then died, leaving his daughter in the twenty-second year of her age.

The daughter had been tenderly bred up by her father, who took care to cultivate her mind according to those principles which he thought necessary to render her virtuous and amiable. She was for some time inconsolable for the loss of so good a parent; but her agreeable person, well-known economy, and irreproachable character, had for some time made an impression on a neighbouring farmer, whose name was Lofty, and who held a considerable farm in his hands, whereby he obtained a very decent competency; and as he had paid his addresses to this young woman before the death of her father, she consented to marry him a few months afterwards.

His industry and her frugality were conspicuous to all in the parish; the plough and the dairy were constantly employed; plenty was seen at their table, content always surrounded their hearth, and inviolate love crowned their nuptial bed with two fine daughters, who were carefully educated by the mother, and tenderly cherished by the father. Their matrimonial felicity had subsisted near twenty years, when farmer Lofty was unhappily thrown from his horse as he was returning home from Hempstead market, whereby he got a contusion, of which he languished for some time, under the care of an unskilful apothecary, and then died, to the inexpressible grief of his family.

The loss of so good a husband renewed the grief of Mrs. Lofty for her father. She was now without parent or husband, yet she was herself a parent, and she found some relief from the affection of her children, the eldest of whom was now about nineteen, and the youngest sixteen years of age. She bred her daughters up with as much reputation as she had herself been bred by her father, whose memory, with that of her husband, still made her greatly regarded by all her neighbours; but though her economy at home was very extraordinary, she was incapable of inspecting the conduct of her servants abroad, and lost so much money by carrying on the farm, that she found herself obliged to quit it in less than four years after her husband's decease.

With the mortification of having diminished the little portion that had been left her children by their father, Mrs. Lofty was thrown into the utmost anxiety to know how to make them a decent provision. She might have been married again to a farmer who had been the friend of her husband, and well knew the value of her as a wife, but she retained so great a regard for the memory of Mr. Lofty, and preserved so much affection for his children, that she could not be prevailed upon to trust them and herself to the control and management of another husband. However, the farmer continued her very worthy friend, and married his nephew to her eldest daughter, with whom she lived very happily for several years, and then died without issue. The younger daughter was also well married to a substantial mealman, who took Mrs. Lofty to his home, and decently provided for her till he died. His death was soon followed by that of his wife, and they likewise left no children behind them; but their effects came into the hands of one of his relations, who took out administration to him, and nothing was left for Mrs. Lofty but a prospect of misery.

In this calamity she relied on providence, and soon became contented with her humble situation. She took a little cottage, had a matted bed, a small table, and two old chairs. The lark was her clock to summon her to rise; and the nightingale was the sweet monitor of her repose. She employed herself in weeding a nobleman's garden in spring; she went to hay-making in summer; in autumn she gleaned up the refuse of the harvest; and in winter she was constantly turning her spinning-wheel. Her labour blest her with health, and temperance gave her content: she had the highest reverence for religion, and the remembrance of her Redeemer's sufferings made her never repine at her own. Her poverty, honesty, and industry, caused her to be much regarded by the parishioners, who gave her the place of what is called a searcher of dead bodies, to see that the deceased are buried in woollen, pursuant to act of parliament; and in this office she got fourpence upon every death; though, as the parish is far from being numerous, such accidents seldom happened; and when she was turned of seventy the parish allowed a charity of sixpence a week.

A long fit of sickness confined her to her bed; but she was not suffered to perish for want of assistance by her neighbours. She recovered, but was much enfeebled: yet her honest and generous temper put her upon a strange kind of industry, rather than make herself entirely dependent on the beneficence of her neighbours, or throwing herself wholly on the bounty of the parish. The village of Redbourn is a great thoroughfare to London; it forms one street, and has four or five inns, where the waggons generally set up. Manure is very scarce in this county, which abounds chiefly in arable lands, and the farmers are always ready to purchase any that is offered them. Mrs. Lofty, in her infirm state and advanced age, conceived the thought that she might gather up the horse-dung that fell in the street, and sell it to the farmers. Accordingly she began this uncommon employment; but for some time she had only an old wrapper to put the dung in which she gathered; and she was so assiduous, that she watched every horse or carriage that passed through the town, being always up at three o'clock in the morning, nor would she ever go to bed till the last waggon came in. By these means she collected some little quantities of dung, and then got a few spare pence, with which she purchased an old box, and flung it with a strap round her body, whereby she had an opportunity of getting more manure together, with more conveniency than in her wrapper. Her indefatigable diligence in watching the carriages, and the peculiarity of such an employment, made her be taken notice of by her neighbours, who readily entered into a subscription to purchase the well-respected old woman a wheelbarrow.

Here is an uncommon scene of industry, and a melancholy idea of adversity. She, who was once the happy mistress of a plentiful farm, at eighty-four years of age, when nature requires the cherishing hand of time, was reduced to the pitiful condition of what has been related. Blush affluence! that such merit should have been suffered to languish under such adversity; for where can the cherub Charity so properly extend her hand as in the relief of so much undeserved and such deplorable distress?

EPITAPHIUM LUDIMAGISTRI J.B.

Scripsit J.C.

February 1777. [An epitaph in Latin, to which the editor of G.M. had added: 'An English translation is requested'. The following are the opening lines of a translation (69 lines in all) by an anonymous contributor to the next issue].

Epitaph for a Schoolmaster, J.B.

Written by J.C.

At length, the Pedagogue resigns to Fate
Ordain'd by Heav'n to bear a tenfold weight
Of troubles, as with tears he oft confess'd,
When wine unlock'd the secrets of his breast.
O'er num'rous captives absolute he reign'd,
But, tho' a monarch, was himself enchain'd.
A perfect galley slave, so mean, so poor,
He from the wolf cou'd scarcely guard his door.
No language can describe the stunning sound,
The cares revolving in the ceaseless round,
The foul aspersions, and vindictive rage,
From day to day experienc'd by our Sage . . .

The original author was John Carr (1732–1807), the Master of the Hertford Grammar School, and his subject James Bennet, Master of the Free Grammar School at Hoddesdon. As the mocking tone and complete abandoning of pious sentiments show, the two schoolmasters were close friends as well as distinguished scholars. The jokes are perhaps more subtle in the Latin original which quotes Virgil's Aeneid, Homer *in Greek and John Clark's* Introduction to the Making of Latin. *But the translator—possibly John Hoole (1727–1803), a friend of Carr and a former pupil of Bennet—was also a literary stylist of note, clearly privy to the identity of the subject. Hoole was also a friend of Dr. Johnson and the Quaker poet, John Scott of Amwell. James Bennet edited the works of the Elizabethan scholar, Roger Ascham, as well as propounding advanced ideas on education at Hoddesdon. John Carr, who was awarded an honorary doctorate by Aberdeen University in 1781, was made an Alderman of Hertford in 1791 and was Mayor of the borough in 1792 and again in 1807. More information on this circle of friends can be found in* Illustrations of John Carr, LL.D. *by Chris Marris, who published it privately in Canada but has deposited a copy in the Hertford Record Office. [DP]*

CHESHUNT CONNECTIONS OF THE CROMWELL FAMILY

June 1777. Your magazine has at sundry times preserved some anecdotes of the Cromwell family, and in the 116th page of that for March last a correspondent has corrected a mistake in the daily papers, which represented an Oliver Cromwell, who died lately at Hampton, to be a descendant of the Protector Oliver; but, as he founds his correction upon a presumption only, from his not being mentioned by Dr. Gibbons in his account of that family, I must beg leave to add a more positive testimony. From an intimate acquaintance in that family for near 40 years, I can assert that within that space there have been no descendants in the male line living but William Cromwell, Esq., whose decease gave occasion to Dr. Gibbons's account of the family, and his four younger brothers, Richard, Henry, Thomas and an Oliver who died in 1748, and the children of Richard and Thomas, of whom also only one male descendant remains, viz., Mr. Oliver Cromwell of the Million-Bank . . .

In page 202 of the 3rd volume [of Hughes's letters] Mr. Luson begins his account of Richard Cromwell, eldest son of Oliver, who in May 1649 married Dorothy, daughter of Richard Major, Esq., of Hursley (not Hunsley as he calls it) in the county of Southampton. He says Richard Cromwell, the Protector, had only two daughters and one son, and mistakes the rank and age of Elizabeth. By the inscription in Hursley church, of which I have a copy, it appears he had two sons and seven daughters, of whom one son and three daughters only lived to maturity. Elizabeth, instead of being the youngest daughter, was the eldest child; she died unmarried, in Bedford-row, April 8 1731, in her 82nd year. Anne, the 6th daughter, married Dr. Gibson, a member of the College of Physicians, and died without issue December 7, 1727, in her 69th year, and was buried with her husband in the yard belonging to St. George's Chapel in London. Dorothy, the 7th daughter, married John Mortimer, Esq., of Somersetshire, and died without issue May 14, 1681, in her 21st year . . .

As to the sons of Richard, the eldest died an infant, the youngest, Oliver, reached the 49th year of his age and died unmarried, May 11, 1705.

This may complete the account of Richard the Protector's family, which is now extinct; as to whose character, while travelling abroad, I cannot speak; but, during the latter years of his life, which he finished at Cheshunt, in Hertfordshire, under the name of Mr. Clarke, it was respectable and unblemished. He was buried at Hursley, in Hampshire.

Richard Cromwell, who briefly succeeded his father as Lord Protector in 1659–60, fled the country at the Restoration but returned in 1689 to lodge at the house of his friend Thomas Pengelly in Finchley. When Pengelly died in 1700, Richard Cromwell continued to lodge with his widow who moved to a house in Churchgate, Cheshunt. During this period Richard Cromwell used the pseudonym 'John Clarke'. He died in 1712 and was buried in the family vault at Hursley, Hampshire.

Richard Cromwell's twelve years residence in Cheshunt was unrelated to a later Cromwell connection with Cheshunt, through the inheritance of a moiety of Cheshunt Park by Robert, a great-great-grandson of Protector Oliver. When Robert died unmarried in 1762 the moiety went to his sisters, and eventually passed to his cousin Oliver, the last surviving descendant of the Lord Protector in the male line. This Oliver, a London solicitor, died in 1821 and is buried in a table tomb in St. Mary's churchyard. In 1860 the Cheshunt Park estate was leased by his descendants to Frank Gissing Debenham, whose daughters purchased it in 1912. It remained in the Debenham family until 1970. [JĒ]

1778. Sheriff. Hertfordshire. Thomas Blackmore of Hunsdon, Esq.

July 1778. Dispensation: Rev. Stephen Eaton, M.A., to hold the rectory of St. George the Martyr, Middlesex, with the rectory of Chorley, Hertfordshire.

July 1778. Dispensation: Rev. Robert Richardson, D.D., to hold the rectory of Wallington, Hertfordshire, with the rectory of St. Anne, Westminster.

December 1778. Dispensation: Rev. W. Bingham to hold Great Gaddesden vicarage with Hemel Hempstead, Lincoln diocese.

1779. Sheriff. Hertfordshire. Rd. Baker of Hertingfordbury.

CONSECRATION OF THE NEW CHURCH AT AYOT ST. LAWRENCE

28 July 1779. A new church, on the Grecian model, lately built at Ayot St. Lawrence in Hertfordshire, at the sole expense of Sir Lionel Lyde, Bart, was this day consecrated by the bishop of Lincoln. On this occasion the neighbouring nobility and gentry, with their ladies, attended, together with many hundred persons of all denominations from different parts of the county. The procession was preceded by a band of music; upwards of twenty men and women, dressed in neat uniforms at the expense of Sir Lionel, followed the music, and after them the bishop, clergy, and the rest of the company in regular procession. When they arrived at the church the doors were thrown open (each of the populace eager to enter first) when the usual service was performed, after which the company were regaled (under tents fixed for the purpose) with wine, cakes, etc. They then returned to the mansion house where an elegant dinner was provided, after which the company dispersed in the adjoining fields, where they diverted themselves in innocent rural games till the close of day, and at last parted highly delighted with the pleasure they had received. A wedding was the only thing wanted to complete the festivity, which was intended but the consecration of the church was not over till past twelve. [See also November 1789].

August 1779. In the churchyard of Ware, Hertfordshire, is the following inscription:

In memory of
William Mead, M.D.
who departed this life
the 28th of October, 1652
aged 148 years
and 9 months

If any of your numerous readers is in possession of any particulars relating to this same Dr. Mead, it is presumed a communication of them would be very acceptable to the public. [See May 1781]

2 August 1779. At a meeting of the nobility, gentry, clergy, and freeholders of the county of Hertford, held at the Shirehouse, a general debate took place on the propriety of offering to the crown the extraordinary assistance of the county, in the present state of national affairs; when the sense of the meeting appeared against concurring in the measures proposed, and the motion was withdrawn.
[Similar meetings were also reported in other counties]

The nature of the assistance to be offered to the crown is not specified but similar meetings held in other counties, such as Devon and Sussex, agreed to raise extra volunteer companies for the militia. Spain had declared war on Great Britain on 17 June 1779, following the example of France which had done so the year before. Taking advantage of British preoccupation with the war in America (independence had been declared in 1776) both countries were hoping to win back possessions, particularly in the West Indies, which they had lost in the Seven Years' War. The combined enemy fleets were at sea and fear of invasion prevailed in Britain throughout the summer. The meeting in Hertford was called by Lord Cranborne, as Lord Lieutenant of the county and as a supporter of Lord North's ministry. He found himself outnumbered by the government's opponents, such as the Whig MP for Hertfordshire, William Plumer, who rejoiced at this "defeat of ministerial attempts" (letter to Duke of Portland, 2 August 1779, printed in R.W. Goulding, ed., Letters ... from the originals at Welbeck Abbey. 1909). [RHW]

6 September 1779. This day a dispute arose at Barnet between two recruiting parties of the 52nd regiment and the Duke of Rutland's regiment, about a recruit whom each claimed from the other. The man alleging that the former had only dropped the guinea into his shoe, and the mob beginning to take his part, he was carried into the Red Lion at the foot of the hill. The mob pressing in after him, the officers imprudently opposed them with their drawn swords, and wounding several so provoked the rest that they broke all the windows of the house, together with all the china and glass in the bar and larder, to the amount of upwards of fifty pounds; and had not the officers, at the request of the landlord, dismissed the man, it is believed the house would have been pulled down. Fortunately no lives were lost in the riot, though one or two of the country people were cut, and the mistress of the Red Lion, who is near her time, was very much frightened. Two of the rioters were taken into custody.

30 October 1779. A man discharged from Hertford gaol brought the gaol fever into Ware workhouse, which has been very fatal to the inhabitants in general.

1780. Sheriff. Hertfordshire. J. Hunter of North Mimms.

A PETITION TO PARLIAMENT

17 January 1780. A very respectable number of freeholders of the County of Hertford met at the Shirehouse, in consequence of an advertisement from the sheriff, in order "to endeavour, in the present state of the British empire, and the distressful situation of individuals, to concert measures, in a constitutional way, for the public safety, and for their own relief." Lord Cranbourn opposed the purpose of the meeting, declaring that this was not a proper time to concert measures distressive to government. This occasioned some disturbance, which, however, was handsomely apologized for by the sheriff; and the result was, to follow Yorkshire in petitioning parliament.

High taxes caused by the war with France, Spain and independent America made Lord North's government unpopular. The Yorkshire Association, led by Dr. Christopher Wyvill, petitioned for "economical reform": for the reduction of government expenditure and for the abolition of sinecures and pensions which, it was contended, were corruptly distributed by the King's ministers to procure majorities in parliament. Hertfordshire was among twenty-five counties and eight cities and towns that sent similar petitions, which were debated in parliament in February 1780. For a time the movement achieved some success, culminating in the passing of Dunning's motion "that the influence of the Crown has increased, is increasing and ought to be diminished", which was carried on 6 April 1780 by a majority of eighteen votes.
The letter requisitioning the Sheriff to hold the Hertford meeting was signed by regular critics of the government, like William Plumer and William Baker, but they also managed to secure the support of many independent county gentlemen for their petition. Lord Cranborne's speech against it is the only one which he is

recorded as having made during six years in the Commons. In September 1780 he was appointed Lord Treasurer of the King's Household, succeeding to the Earldom of Salisbury a fortnight later. He was Lord Chamberlain of the Household from 1783 until 1804. [RHW]

August 1780. (11 February 1780). Summary of Proceedings in the present Parliament.

Mr. P———m———r [Plumer, M.P. for Hertfordshire] presented a petition from Hertfordshire, similar to that from Yorkshire.

Lord C———nb———ne [Viscount Cranborne, M.P. for Great Bedwyn] had opposed this petition, and had procured a counter protest, that by no parliamentary mode however would be introduced to the house, which Mr. B———g [George Byng, M.P. for Wigan] lamented, as the means of procuring the protest would then have appeared. He asserted, that at the general meeting, though there were more than 400 gentlemen present, Lord C———bn———e, on a division, had only five hands.

Lord N———g———t [Earl Nugent, M.P. for St. Mawes] warmly approved the petition, which, he said, would have become more popular, had some points been suppressed.

Mr. T. T———nsh———d [Thomas Townshend, M.P. for Whitchurch] congratulated his lordship on his candour, but added, that it would still have been more noble in his lordship to have attended the meetings in those counties where he had property, and avowed his opinion, approving what he thought right, and opposing what he judged wrong. He was very severe upon the protestors, whom he deemed libellers of the people; among whom he pointed at Lord H———sb———gh [Earl of Hillsborough, Secretary of State for Southern Department] as foremost in that train.

Lord N———th [Lord North, M.P. for Banbury and Prime Minister] objected to the Hertfordshire petition on the ground of its title. It was certainly not the Petition of the Noblemen, Gentlemen, Clergy, and Freeholders, of Hertfordshire, he said, therefore should have been intituled, The Petition of the Noblemen, &c. whose Names were thereunto subscribed.

Mr. B———g observed, that if a few protestors were to disannul the business of a county, then no county business could ever be done. The worst administration that ever existed never wanted emissaries to oppose the remonstrances of the people. And if his lordship rested his cause upon that ground, he would find it in the end a rotten foundation.

The petition was ordered to lie upon the table.

August 1780. From a review of the book *British Topography; or, an historical Account of what has been done for illustrating the Topographic Antiquities of Great Britain and Ireland.*
2 vols. 4to. £2.12s.6d. in Boards, Payne.

p.420. "Paul Wright, B.D., formerly curate and lecturer of All Saints, Hertford, now vicar of Oakley, in Essex, having received some MS.

papers relating to Sir Henry Chauncy's *History of Hertfordshire*, proposed to publish an accurate edition of that elaborate work, with continuations to the present time, from his own actual view of every parish, as well as from the communications of others." [See also October 1784; obit. 8 May 1785].

p.429,434. "I am well informed, that the late Dr. Stebbing, when a young man, wrote a pamphlet or two in favour of Jane Wenham [condemned for a witch at Hertford, 1712]. This poor woman, against the opinion of the judge who tried her, was found guilty by the jury. She however received a pardon from the Queen; and a gentleman in the country provided her an apartment over his stables, sent her victuals from his table, and suffered her to attend on his children. She was ever after looked upon by the family as an honest, good-natured woman. Mr. Bragge, in his evidence on her trial, declared, on the faith of a clergyman, he believed her to be a witch; whereupon the judge told him, that therefore, on the truth of a judge, he took him to be no conjuror." He also told the jury that they should not look for witches among the old women, but among the young".

An account of the trial of Jane Wenham was published in 'Hertfordshire Folklore,' edited by W.B. Gerish (reprinted 1970). He recorded that after the trial judge, Mr. Justice Powell, had obtained for her a free pardon from Queen Anne, she found a home first on the estate of Colonel Plumer at Gilston and, after his death, in a cottage on the Cowper estate at Hertingfordbury where she remained until her own death, said to be on 11 January 1730. The diary of Lady Sarah Cowper (HRO D/EP F234) makes it clear that Colonel Plumer and her father the first Earl Cowper had joined with Mr. Justice Powell in making representations to Queen Anne. She wrote further: "Jane herself always said that the principal evidence against her [presumably the Rev. Francis Bragge] was a person to whom she had denied favours in her youth, and who always bore a spite to her for that reason . . . . My father and mother always protected this poor woman, and since their death our family has continued that protection; my brother [the second Earl Cowper] paid 40s. per annum for her house rent . . . ." When Jane was near to death she expressed "her earnest desire that her character might be justified if possible from the aspersions thrown upon it. I engaged if it could be done without riot, that a sermon should be preached something applicable to her misfortunes. With these promises this poor creature was more pleased than with anything I could do to make her remains of life comfortable . . . ." The sermon was duly preached by Mr. Squire, the curate of Hertingfordbury, who reported that the parish church was "prodigiously crowded, the fullest that ever I saw it on any occasion, and there was the utmost decency during the whole service, no whispers, no noise or disturbance, no tendency in the least to mirth and laughter." (With acknowledgement to the executors of Lady Ravensdale). [AP]

August 1780. Some few weeks ago the post-boy bringing the mail from Stevenage to Welwyn in Hertfordshire, was robbed by a man on foot, who at first was thought to be a farmer in that neighbourhood, whose case was somewhat singular. Soon after the robbery was committed, not being conversant in bank-notes, he had joined the half of one note of £10 to the half of another of £20 and had paid the same to a tradesman in Hertford. This being brought to the bank for payment caused a suspicion, and, on enquiry, the fact was easily traced to the farmer, who, being under no fear of danger, was taken out of his bed without resistance, and carried to Hertford gaol for trial.

The cutting in half of banknotes and their despatch by separate mails was a common security measure in the risky conditions of those days, with no registered post, no postal orders, and very limited use of cheques. Indeed, the Post Office Directory for 1802 gave details of the best way to do it. Bank of England and most country banknotes had their numbers in the top left and bottom right hand areas, and so, however divided, could be matched and joined for presentation for payment. The practice in fact continued to a limited extent right to the early years of this century. Banker's records contain indemnities for payment of half notes where the other half had gone astray. Until around the 1820s cheques were sometimes treated in the same way. [JP]

1 August 1780. At Hertford assizes Mardell Lawrence was tried for robbing the mail, and acquitted.

October 1780. A very old customer of yours will be very thankful to you for a list of the Royston Club in Cambridgeshire [sic], which was so famous in the time of George the First. There are the portraits of Lords North and Grey, Judge Pemberton, and Dr. Savage their chaplain, in pretty good preservation; but the names of the rest of the club are unknown even to the master of the inn (the Red Lion), who, being asked lately for a catalogue, could not produce one, and said it had been lost a great while ago. If, Sir, by the means of your numerous and learned correspondents, you could procure an accurate list of the members of this club, you would rescue their names from oblivion, and would extremely oblige, CANTAB. [See October 1783]

7 October 1780. James, Earl of Salisbury, [was appointed] high steward of the borough of Hertford.

16 November 1780. Some rogues broke into Cheshunt church, and carried off several books, and an old curtain before the organ.

1781. Sheriff. Hertfordshire, Theo. Clutterbuck the Younger of Watford.

16 January 1781. A new mode of burglary has been of late adopted. The houses of Messrs. Barwick and Jessop, at Waltham Abbey, and of Mr. Hughes, at Hoddesdon, Hertfordshire, were last week broke open and robbed of their plate, &c. by two persons in a one-horse chair.

THE MEAD FAMILY OF WARE

May 1781. [See also August 1779]. The assistance you are always ready to give to British biographers, induces me to send you the following particulars of a person hitherto little noticed. I shall think myself amply rewarded if any further light can be produced from these imperfect hints. In the churchyard at Ware, Hertfordshire, on the s. side of the church, is an altar-tomb of brick, with a blue marble slab, inscribed to

"William Mead, M.D., who died Oct. 28, 1652, aged 148 years and 9 months." [Transcribed in full, August 1779].

Upon further enquiry after this remarkable instance of longevity, I found that this inscription had been renewed by the trustees of his benefactions to this parish, and that the original slab lay at the steps of the N. door within the church, so much worn by the weather before its removal, or treading on since, that the following words could scarce be read.

. . . .
which William departed
this Life the E . . H . . . . .
1652, being of the Age of 148
Yeares and 9 Moneths;
. . . . this Parish . . . . to the
how . . . . Overseers Pew
on Sund . . . .

The register expresses his benefaction in the following terms:
"Mr. George Meade, Dr. of Phisick, who dyed the 28th of October att Tunbridge Wells, was buryed at Ware the 4th day of November 1652, and in his last will and testament (among several other legacies) hee gave to the poore of Ware £5 a yeare for ever, to be paid by the overseers of the said parish out of the George inn in Ware, upon the feast day of St. Thomas the Apostle. Mr. Humphrey Parker, sen., and Mr. Stephen Lamas were trustees to see this legasie performed and paid."

The George inn is now a private house, inhabited by Mr. Lister.

The following anecdote about it is entered in the register:
"June 8, 1691, Mr. Wootten of London was killed at the George by 5 Dutch troopers, and another gentleman wounded; 3 of them sent to goale; buried in the chancel, Dec. 19, 1694. Suf. Flint, a widow, was blown up with gunpowder at the George tavern."

'Old Parr' exceeded Dr. Mead but four years, dying at the age of 152. Even the celebrated Countess of Desmond only reached some years, it is not said how many, above 140 (Granger, Suppl. 164. Sir Wm. Temple on *Health and Long Life*). Mr. Robert Shrimpton, mayor St. Albans, was but a shrimp in age, dying at 103 (*Brit. Top.* II. 462). Henry Read, minister of Hardwicke, co. Northampton, reached but to 132 (Bridges, *Northamptonshire*, II, 101). The 'Cricket of the Hedge', a Lancashire woman, but to 140 (Brokesby's Letter to Hearne, *Leland's Itinerary*, VI. p.84). Henry Jenkins, whom Mr. Granger (II. 462) calls "the oldest man of the Post-diluvians, of whom we have any credible account," reached to 169.

The parish registers of Ware, which begin in 1558, 1 Eliz. and are remarkably well kept, furnish the following persons of the same name and family:

Geo. Mead, M.D., buried 4 Nov. 1652.

Susan, wife of Thomas; May 15, 1652

Nicholas and Widow Powell, married Jun. 1, 1641.

Alex. and Eliz. Weld, mar. Jan. 1, 1651.

Mary, wife of Sam. died Dec. 13, 1664.

Mary, daug. of Alex, Esq: died Jul. 14, 1662.
Mr. George Mead of the Parsonage, Sept. 21, 1662.
Anne Mead penconer, Dec. 27, 1661.
Mr. Thomas Mead of the Parsonage, buried Nov. 7, 1658.

The memorial to 'William' Mead continues to excite as much debate as it did in the eighteenth century. Although most of the memorials and gravestones have been removed to the edge of the old churchyard, this one remains, lying flush with the grass to the south of the church. It appears to have been added to since these extracts, for it now reads:

In Memory of
WILLIAM MEAD M.D.
who departed this Life
28th October 1652
aged 148 years
and 9 months
3 weekes and 4 days

As the 1781 correspondent stated, the church register records the burial of George Meade, Dr. of Physick, on 28th October 1652. He was undoubtedly a member of the wealthy Mead or Meade family who lived in the Crib Street area during the sixteenth and seventeenth centuries, occupying at one time or another the Rectory (now the Manor House), Copt Hall (now Collett Hall) and the Parsonage (which was situated on the north side of Church Street and later became an extension of the graveyard). But no mention is made of the age of Dr. George Meade. It is interesting to note that during the nineteenth century one of the chemists in the High Street sold "Dr. Mead's patent medicines". It could well be that, when the trustees of Dr. (George) Meade's bequests renewed the inscription during the 1770s, the evidence of longevity was added by an earlier chemist with an eye to the sales of his medicines. [DP]

The inscription in its earlier form, as recorded in the entry dated August 1779 (without the last line noted above) was recut in January 1797 by David Cock, stonemason of Hertford. His account book (sold to private buyer at auction at Hertford, March 1993) records charge to churchwardens of Ware "to cutting 84 letters on a Portland ledger in memory of Doctor Mead, aged 148 and 9 months. Letter at 1d. : 0 . 7. 0 ." [RHW]

July 1781. Dr. Mark Hildesley was first presented to the vicarage of Hitchin, Hertfordshire, where he resided many years, and distinguished himself by a diligent attendance on the parochial duties, especially in catechising and instructing the youth in the principles of the Christian religion two evenings in a week, at an hour when the business of the day was over, and they could be best spared. After this he was presented by ——— Ratcliffe, Esq., of Hitchin, to the rectory of Holwell, Bedfordshire, about three miles from thence, whither he used to go over alternately with his curate to preach, &c. When Mr. Ratcliffe gave him the living of Holwell, he said to him, "Mark, there is something to keep you a journeyman." It was, I am told, his being so good a parish minister, that was the occasion of his having the bishopric of Man conferred upon him. For when bishop Wilson died, and the Duke of Athol, patron, was inquiring for one of like pious zeal to succeed him, Dr. Hildesley was recommended to him as such a person as he wanted. When he took the bishopric of Man, he resigned Hitchin, but retained Holwell. [He held also with his bishopric the mastership of an hospital at Durham, given him by that bishop]. I.M.

c. September 1781. Mr. Heath, master of Harrow, is presented to the valuable rectory of Walkern in Hertfordshire worth £400 a year, with a good house and beautiful ground; not, as well observed in a daily paper "through any of his connexions with the school but from King's College, Cambridge".

January 1782. Dispensation. Rev. John Ramsay, B.D., Abbots Langley vicarage and Bushey rectory, Hertfordshire.

January 1782. Sheriff. Hertfordshire. J. Michie of North Mimms.

January 1782. Epitaphs in Welwyn Church, Hertfordshire.

Mary Harper 1771, 58.
To thee my great Redeemer do I fly,
It is thy death alone can change my dye.
Tears mingled with thy blood can scour so
That scarlet sins will turn as white as snow.
Sarah Harper died 1776, aged 41.

Richard East 1776, 16.
Drop not the tear, suppress the needless sigh,
Tho' early called, I did not fear to die:
This jarring life I willingly resign'd
For one more suited to a tuneful mind.
Where my enraptur'd soul I hope shall sing
Unceasing praise to heaven's all-gracious King.

ANOTHER
True as the Scripture says, man's life a span,
The present moment is the life of man.
Of life, the present moment's all we are sure,
We can't call back one part, nor one to come insure.

"I would by no means be understood to abet the vulgar error, that the Rector of Welwyn's son was a Lorenzo, or an Altamont; but when I assert, on undoubted authority, that his father refused the most powerful solicitations of his friends to see him on his death with this severe reply, "It cannot be, consistently with the happiness of either of us"; it would suggest no unfair suspicion, that he treated him with a severity to which the worst excesses are hardly entitled on such an occasion, though all the world lays to his charge were only the errors, or the follies of youth." R.H.

These epitaphs cannot now be located. They may have been on wall slabs; every wall was rebuilt and memorials relocated in 19th and 20th century improvements. The names do not appear in a list of graves made by W. Andrews in 1906 and a survey of the churchyard recently completed by the Welwyn Archaeological Society does not include them.

The rector referred to in the closing paragraph is Dr. Edward Young. In his

Night Thoughts *Lorenzo is "an atheist, whose remorse ends in despair." (Brewer,* Dictionary of Phrase and Fable*). He was identified with Young's son, Frederick, to whom the Prince of Wales was godfather. This idea was, however, debunked by Herbert Croft in Samuel Johnson's* Lives of the Poets*. Altamont, friend of Lorenzo, is a hero with feet of clay: ". . . the brave, the gallant Altamont / So called, and then he fled the field. / Less base the fear of Death, than fear of Life."* [TR]

March 1782. "If you think the inclosed worthy of a place in your valuable repository, you are welcome to insert it. You will probably wonder at the baldness of the language of the biographical part; but it is in general extracted from an old MS book preserved in the family, and I thought it would be more agreeable to some of your readers to see it in its plain, unadorned garb, though an hundred years old, than to mar its naiveté and originality, by attempting to dress it in new and finer clothes."

Memoirs of the Family of Sir John King.

John Le Roy, alias King, of London, merchant, came out of France at the time of the massacre there in August 1572, for refuge into England, and married Mary, daughter of James Blit, elder of the French church in London; by whom he had issue:

John b.1604 m. 1. Elizabeth Hale.   Issue John, Richard, Mary and
Elizabeth.
2. Elizabeth Roberts. Issue John, Ann, Samuel, 2nd daughter, Ann,
James, Asahel and Bethiah.

John King, the eldest son by the second venter, was born at St. Albans, February 5, 1638/39, and took the rudiments of learning in the free school there very strenuously, so that in a short time he was of the highest form of the school. . . On December 10, 1674, John received the honour of knighthood from King James II. [As amended April 1782].

SIR RALPH SADLEIR OF STANDON

May 1782. "Having formed an idea, grounded on the similarity of the name, and on one of those traditions which so frequently pass current in families, unexamined, from generation to generation, that the subject of the following narrative was the ancestor of a family from which I am descended, I took what pains I could to ascertain the truth; and though upon enquiry I found a well-authenticated pedigree of my own family, which begins probably several years before the existence of Sir Ralph Sadleir, and therefore his history is of no immediate consequence to me, yet I thought some memoirs of him might be acceptable to some of your readers; if you are of the same opinion, you are welcome to publish them."

Memoirs of the Right Honourable Sir *RALPH SADLEIR,* Knight Banneret, and his Descendants.

Ralph Sadleir was descended of an ancient family, seated at Hackney, in Middlesex, where he was born about the year 1507, to a fair inheritance; he was educated under Thomas Cromwell, Earl of Essex, vicegerent to the King in all ecclesiastical matters, &c. &c. and married Margaret Michell, a laundress to the earl's family, in the life-time, though absence, of her husband Matthew Barré, a tradesman in London, presumed to be dead at that time, and he procured an act of parliament 37 H. VIII for the legitimation of the children by her. Being secretary to the Earl of Essex, he wrote many things treating of state affairs, and by that means became known to King Henry VIII who took him from his master in the 26th year of his reign, and appointed him Master of the Great Wardrobe; this was a happy circumstance for him, as it removed him from the danger of falling with his noble patron.

In the 30th year of his reign, Mr. Sadleir was sworn of his Majesty's privy council, and appointed one of his principal secretaries of state. The King sent him divers times into Scotland both in war and peace, appointed him by his will one of the privy council, who were to assist the sixteen persons that he appointed regents of the kingdom during the minority of his son and successor Edward VI (at which time it appears he was a knight), and bequeathed to him £200 as a legacy. Ann. I Edward VI, Sir Ralph was appointed treasurer for the army (a more proper name for the office than that of paymaster general, especially as it has been managed in modern times).

He was present at the battle of Musselburgh in Scotland, September 10, 1547, under Edward, Duke of Somerset, lord protector, and gained such honour in that victory, that he was there, with two more, Sir Frances Bryan and Sir Ralph Vane, made a knight banneret. The King of Scots' standard, which he took in that battle, stood within these 50 or 60 years (and, for aught I know, still stands) by his monument in the church of Standon in Hertfordshire, one of the principal manors that was given him by King Henry VIII; the pole only is left, about 20 feet high, of fir, encircled with a thin plate of iron from the bottom, above the reach of a horseman's sword.

In the time of Queen Mary he resigned, and lived privately at Standon, where he built a new manor-house upon the site of the old one. He was privy counsellor to Queen Elizabeth the first year of her reign, and chancellor of the Duchy of Lancaster the tenth, which place he held till his death.

Buchanan speaks of him as "Eques notæ virtutis, qui (1559) Bervici publicis muniis præfectus erat," *Re. Scot. Hist. Lib.* 16. 46. The following coat of arms was granted to him by Christopher Barker, Garter, by his letters patent dated May 14, 34 Henry VIII. Party per fess azure and or, gutty, and a lion rampant, countercharged, in a canton of the last a buck's head caboshed of the first; crest, on a wreath, a demi lion rampant azure, gutty d'or. But this (to use the language of the last century) "being deemed too much confused and intricate in the confused mixture of too many things in one shield, another was ratified and assigned to him February 4, 1757, by Robert Cook, Clarencieux, and

William Flower, Norroy, viz., Or, a lion rampant party per fess azure and gules, armed and langued argent; crest, on a wreath. a dei, lion rampant azure, crowned with a ducal coronet or; motto, 'Servire Deo sapere.' He was of the privy council above forty years, and during the greatest part of that time one of the knights of the shire for Hertfordshire, particularly in the parliaments 6 Edward VI, 1, 5, 13, 14, 27, 28 Elizabeth and probably in several temp. Henry VIII as all the writs and returns throughout England from 17 Edward IV to 1 Edward VI are lost, except one imperfect bundle, 33 Henry VIII, in which his name appears as Sir Ralph Sadleir, Kt. He was always faithful to his prince and country, and a great promoter of the reformation of the church of England. He died at his lordship of Standon, March 30, 1587, in the 80th year of his age, leaving behind him 22 manors, several parsonages, and other great pieces of land, in the several counties of Hertford, Gloucester, Warwick, Buckingham, and Worcester. He left issue 3 sons and 4 daughters; the daughters were Anne, married to Sir George Horsey of Digswell, Kt., Mary to Thomas Bollys, aliter Bowles, of Wallington, Esq., Jane to Edward Baesh, of Stanstead, Esq., (which three gentlemen appear to have been sheriffs of Hertfordshire, 14, 18, and 13 Elizabeth); and Dorothy to Edward Elryngton of Berstall, Buckinghamshire, Esq. The sons were Thomas, Edward and Henry.

Thomas Sadleir, Esq., succeeded at Standon, was sheriff of the county 29 and 37 Elizabeth and knighted, and entertained King James there two nights in his way from Scotland. He married, 1st, a daughter of Sir Henry Sherrington; 2ndly, Gertrude, daughter of Robert Markham of Cotham, Nottinghamshire, Esq., by whom he had issue Ralph, and Gertrude, married to Walter, the first Lord Aston of the Kingdom of Scotland. He died January 5, 1606, and was succeeded at Standon by his son Ralph Sadleir, Esq., sheriff of the county 7 Jac. I. He married Anne, eldest daughter of the famous Sir Edward Coke, chief justice (successively) of the courts of common pleas and king's bench, with whom (says my author) "he lived in good correspondence 59 years in the same house, yet, according to the tradition of the neighbourhood, never bedded her;" and, dying without issue, was succeeded in his lordship of Standon, and other estates in Hertfordshire, by Walter, the 2nd Lord Aston, eldest surviving son of his sister Gertrude Lady Aston beforementioned.

In his descendants the estates, and the representation of this eldest branch of Sir Ralph Sadleir's family, continued for three successive generations, till the death of James, the 5th lord, in August 1751, who left two daughters coheiresses, married into two very ancient and respectable families, professing the religion of their ancestors; Mary, to Sir Walter Blount of Sodington in Worcestershire, Bart.; and Barbara, to the Hon. Thomas Clifford, posthumous son of Hugh, the 3rd Lord Clifford of Chudleigh, whose issue will now divide the representation.

In the chancel of Standon is the burying-place of the family; against the south wall is a monument for Sir Ralph Sadleir, with the effigies of himself in armour, of his three sons and four daughters, and three inscriptions, in Latin verse, in English verse, and in English prose. Against the north wall is another for Sir Thomas, with the effigies of himself in armour, his lady, son, and daughter, and an epitaph in English prose. There are several inscriptions for various persons of the Aston family, but no notice is taken of Ralph Sadleir, Esq.; and from thence, and from some very observable peculiarities in the following epitaph, which is inscribed on the marble stone in the vestry fixed against the wall, one might be led to infer that his wife acknowledged and felt the truth of the tradition before-mentioned:

"Here lyeth the body of Ann Coke, eldest daughter of Sir Edward Coke, Kt., lord chief justice of the common pleas, by his first and best wife, Bridget Paston, daughter and heir of John Paston, of Norfolk, Esq. At the age of fifteen she was married, in 1601, to Ralph Sadleir of Standon in Hertfordshire. She survived him, and here lies in assured hope of a joyful resurrection."

Upon Edward Sadleir, Esq., 2nd son of Sir Ralph Sadleir, he settled his manor of Deneslai, hod. Temple Dinsley, in the parish of Hitchin, and county of Hertford. This Edward married Ann, daughter, and at length sole heiress, of Sir Richard Lee, or A'Leigh, of Sopwell, in the parish of St. Peter at St. Albans, Kt., which Sir Richard, on account of the good services performed by him at the siege of Boulogne, had the following coat of arms granted to him by patent, bearing date October 4, 1544, those which he had before borne being erased: "Party per chevron golde and gouls, in the chefe ii lyons fallyant encountrant sables, armed and langued gouls."

His eldest son, Leigh Sadleir, was grandfather of Sir Edwine Sadleir of Temple Dinsley, Bart., so created by patent bearing date December 3, 1661, who was succeeded in title and estate by his son Sir Edwine Sadleir, Bart., who was living and married, but does not appear to have had any issue, in 1692. With him I apprehend the title and eldest male branch of the family to have ceased.

Richard Sadleir, next brother to Leigh Sadleir above-mentioned, had the estate at Sopwell settled upon him, and was succeeded by his eldest son Robert, whose daughter and heiress was married to Thomas Saunders, of Beechwood, in the parish of Flamstead, and county of Hertford, Esq., who left an only daughter, married to Sir Edward Sebright, of Besford, Worcestershire, bart., whose grandson, the present Sir John Sebright, Bart., as representative of those families, quarters the arms of Saunders, Sadleir, Lee or A'Leigh, Chute, and Newbury.

Henry Sadleir, Esq., third son of Sir Ralph Sadleir, was twice married; 1st, to Dorothy, daughter of ... Gilbert, of Everley, near Hungerford, Wiltshire, by whom he had 5 children, viz., Gertrude, Grace, married to Robert Sadleir of Salthorp, Wiltshire; Helen, or Ellen, Thomas, and a 5th whom Sir Henry Chauncy calls in one place Henry, and in another place Dorothy, but I have no farther account of his descendants. He married, 2ndly, Ursula, daughter of John Gill, of Wyddial, Hertfordshire, Esq., by whom he had no issue. As to the family of Sadleir of Salthorp, I have a pedigree of it for five generations (of which the above Robert is the fourth), taken in 1623, but its origin and farther continuation I am totally ignorant of.

REV. DR. EDWARD YOUNG OF WELWYN

June 1782. "In return for the entertainment I have long received from your agreeable Miscellany, I send my quota in addition to the common stock, consisting of several anecdotes relative to the excellent author of the *Night Thoughts* [Dr. Young]. You may depend on their authenticity, as they are copied from the letters of Mr. Jones (who was some years his curate at Welwyn) to a confidential friend in the metropolis. If they discover the foibles of a great mind, they illustrate a material part of his history, and Mr. Croft has well remarked, that we should say, De vivis nil nisi bonum, de mortuis nil nisi verum." M. Green.

The letters dated 2 April and 13 April 1765 are printed in The Correspondence of Edward Young, 1683–1765, *edited by Henry Pettit (Oxford, 1971). They are there addressed by John Jones to the Rev. Dr. Thomas Birch (the historian and biographer) in Norfolk Street in the Strand. Dr. Birch, therefore, was the "confidential friend in the metropolis" who communicated them to M. Green.*
In the letter dated 2 April 1765, 'Dr. Cotton of St. Albans' was Dr. Nathaniel Cotton, who ran a college for the insane in Spicer Street, where the poet William Cowper was one of his patients. Dr. Yate of Hertford may have been Thomas Yate, M.D. In 1767 John Jones, the author of these letters, became vicar of Shephall, Hertfordshire. [AJ]

I
Welwyn, July 25, 1762.

The old gentleman here (I may venture to tell you freely) seems to me to be in a pretty odd way of late, moping, dejected, self-willed, and as if surrounded with some perplexing circumstances. Though I visit him pretty frequently for short intervals, I say very little to his affairs, not choosing to be a party concerned, especially in cases of so critical and tender a nature. There is much mystery in almost all his temporal affairs, as well as in many other of his speculative opinions. Whoever lives in this neighbourhood to see his exit, will probably see and hear of some very strange things (time will show), I am afraid not greatly to his credit. There is thought to be an irremovable obstruction to his happiness within his walls, as well as another without them, but the former is the more powerful, and likely to continue so. He has this day been trying anew to engage me to stay with him. No lucrative views can tempt me to sacrifice my liberty or my health to such measures as are proposed here. Nor do I like to have to do with persons whose word and honour cannot be depended upon. So much for this very odd and unhappy topic.

II
St. Neots, August 18, 1762.

How are matters altered since my letter to you above-mentioned of the 25th past! You remember what I suggested to you about my resolution of leaving Welwyn, of which I had given very early notice to the worthy Doctor, that he might have sufficient time to provide. After repeated trials, and repeated disappointments, though seven or eight offered, he thought proper to apply to me anew, and though lucrative motives could not, earnest importunities did, prevail with me at last to cheer up his dejected heart, by promising to continue with him for some time longer at least, although my necessary measures in respect of other affairs are hereby disconcerted. But compassion and humanity will, I hope, ever dwell in my breast. By the way, I privately intimated to you the Doctor is in various respects a very unhappy man. Few know so much of him as I do in these respects, and have often observed with concern. If he would be advised by some who wish him well, he might be happy, though his state of health is lately much altered for the worse. These things you see, Sir, are between ourselves.

[Another letter mentions,"that he will not be like to get a curate but by dint of money and force upon himself. Then his great age; and if he has any foibles in temper and conduct, they will be sure not to be forgotten on this occasion."]

III
Welwyn, January 1, 1763.

The mismanagement too well known unhappily continues, and, still more unhappily, seems to be increasing, to the grief of friends, and, I need not say, to the ridicule of others; who are not a few. What a pity! what a loss! but no advice will be taken, nor can it well be offered. Penuriousness and obstinacy are two bad things; and a disregard to the general judgement and friendly wishes of the wiser part of mankind, another, there seems to be no hope so long as the ascendancy is so great. Enough to a friend, and to a friend only.

IV
Welwyn, September 4, 1764.

My ancient gentleman here is still full of trouble, which moves my concern, though it moves only the secret laughter of many, and some untoward surmises in disfavour of him and his household. The loss of a very large sum of money (above £200) is talked of, whereof this vill and neighbourhood are full. Some disbelieve, others say it is no wonder, where about 18 or more servants are sometimes taken and dismissed in the course of a year. The gentleman himself is allowed by all to be far more harmless and easy in his family than some one else, who hath too much the lead in it. This, among many others, was one reason for my late motion to quit.

V
Welwyn, April 2, 1765.

As soon as I got home I enquired after Dr. Young, and found that he had gone through very great pains since I left him, and the pains return pretty frequently. Dr. Cotton of St. Albans, and Dr. Yate of Hertford, meet at his house every day on consultation. But whatever they may think of his disorder, and the probable consequence, little or nothing as yet transpires, only all that attend him constantly imagine there is little or no hope of his doing well again. For my own part, I judged so from the beginning. I find that opiates are frequently administered to him, I suppose to render him less sensible of his pain. His intellects, I am told, are still clear; though what effect the frequent use of opiates may by degrees have upon him I know not. I am pretty much of his son's sentiments as to this, viz. that those ingredients, if for some time longer continued, may have an ill effect upon the brain. Having mentioned this young gentleman, I would acquaint you next that he came hither this morning, having been sent for, as I am told, by the direction of Mrs. Hallows. Indeed she intimated to me as much herself. And if this be so, I must say it is one of the most prudent acts she ever did or could have done in such a case as this, as it may prove a means of preventing much confusion. I have had some little discourse with the son. He seems much affected, and, I believe, really is so. He earnestly wishes his father may be pleased to ask after him, for, you must know, he has not yet done this, nor is, in my opinion, likely to do it. And it has been said farther, upon a late application made to him on the behalf of his son, he desired that no more might be said to him about it. How true this may be, I cannot as yet be certain. All I shall say is, it seems not improbable. Mrs. Hallows has fitted up a suitable apartment in the house for Mr. Young, where I suppose he will continue till some farther event. I heartily wish the ancient man's heart may grow tender towards his son; though, knowing him so well, I can scarce hope to hear such desirable news. He took to his bed yesterday about eleven in the forenoon, and has not been up since. I called soon after my coming home, but did not see him; he was then in a doze. I imagine his farther stay upon earth can be of no long duration.

VI

Welwyn, April 13, 1765.

I have now the pleasure to acquaint you, that the late Dr. Young, though he had for many years kept his son at a distance, yet has now at last left him all his possessions, after the payment of certain legacies. So that the young gentleman, who bears a fair character, and behaves well as far as I can hear or see, will, I hope, soon enjoy and make a prudent use of a very handsome fortune. The father on his death-bed, and since my return from London, was applied to in the tenderest manner by one of his physicians, and by another person, to admit the son into his presence, to make submission, intreat forgiveness, and obtain his blessing. As to an interview with his son, he intimated, he chose to decline it, as his spirits were then low, and his nerves weak: with regard to the next particular, he said, I heartily forgive him; and upon mention of the last, he gently lifted up his hand, and gently letting it fall, pronounced these words, God bless him! After about a fortnight's illness, and bearing excessive pains, he expired a little before eleven of the clock, in the night of Good Friday last the fifth instant, and was decently buried yesterday about six in the afternoon, in the chancel of this church, close by the remains of his lady, under the communion table. The clergy, who are the trustees for his charity school, and one or two more, attending the funeral, the last office at interment being performed by me.

I know it will give you pleasure to be farther informed, that he was pleased to make respectful mention of me in his will, expressing his satisfaction in my care of his parish, bequeathing to me a handsome legacy, and appointing me one of his executors next after his sister's son (a clergyman of Hampshire), who this morning set out for London in order to prove the will in Doctors Commons. So that, much according to my wishes, I shall have little or nothing to do in respect of executorship.

November 1783.   MR. SAMUEL RICHARDSON, Printer
                              (A GREAT GENIUS)

(Extract from an anonymous account of Samuel Richardson)

Mr. Shotbolt tells me that when Mr. Richardson came down to Welwyn, with the late Speaker Onslow and other friends, to visit Dr. Young, he took up his quarters with Mr. Shotbolt, there being no room enough at the Doctor's; and that, getting up early, about five of the clock, he wrote two of the best letters in *Sir Charles Grandison* in one or two mornings before breakfast. Mr. Onslow had a high esteem for him, and not only might, but actually would have promoted him to some honourable and profitable station at court, but the good man neither desired nor would accept of such posts, etc., being much better pleased with his own private way of living.

'Mr Shotbolt' was John Shotbolt, tanner, of Ivy Cottage, Welwyn, Dr. Young's next door neighbour. In letters to Edward Young, Samuel Richardson (1689–1761) sent his compliments to 'your bachelor friend next door' (9 September 1749) and 'to your next door neighbour—not married yet, I doubt! Poor man!' (October 1749?). Shotbolt, however, was married by 1758. He made frequent visits to London, and very often acted as go-between for Young and Richardson. George Harrison of Balls Park, Hertford, referred to Shotbolt in his will as 'kinsman.' [AJ]

MIGRATING WHIMBREL

July 1782. "Some months ago, I and all my neighbours, were alarmed with a whistling, which, on going out of doors, seemed to be in the air, and at such a height, that every one thought it just over his head. This made me recollect having heard of a bird called The Seven Whistlers, and reminded me of a passage in Spenser, where, among "the nation of unfortunate and fatal birds" that flocked about Sir Guyon and the Palmer, it is thus introduced,
            "The Whistler shrill that whoso hears doth 'die'"
                    Fairy Queen, B.II, cant. 12. st.36.
Can any of your correspondents inform me where else it is mentioned, or whether it is described in any book of Ornithology?" [Hertfordshire].

October 1782. "In your magazine for July I find an enquiry from Hertfordshire concerning a bird called a Whistler. I immediately recollected, that about seven years ago, I and many of my neighbours heard in the evening (I think the month August, and nine o'clock the time) exactly such a whistling in the air as your correspondent describes. It was very like a bird's note uncommonly shrill, very rapid in its flight, and frequently changing its place. The noise was heard three or four nights successively, and then it ceased.

At length after it had been canvassed amongst us for some little time, an adept in such matters satisfied us by affirming, that the noise we heard was the Smuggler's Whistle, established amongst that respectable society, as an evening signal well known to themselves. From that time to this I thought no more of the matter.

The fact, however, I am very sure of: whether the noise proceeded from a bird or was a smuggling signal, I pretend not to determine . . . "
A.D. Freemantle.

Once fairly widely in vernacular use, 'The Seven Whistlers' related to Whimbrel Numenius phaeopus. *Looking rather like small curlew, these wading birds nest upon open moors and tundra from Iceland across northern Europe to Siberia, including a small population in northwest Scotland. After the breeding season, they migrate southwards to eventual wintering grounds in West Africa. Migrations, often in small flocks, mainly take place at night with daylight hours being used for rest and feeding. From late July into September, some Whimbrel will be passing across southern Britain. To retain contact with one another, particularly at night, they utter far-carrying flight calls which sound as a series of whistle-like 'pu' notes, usually repeated about seven times in quick succession. Night migrating Whimbrel may still be heard high over Hertfordshire in late summer, also during April and May as they head north to breed. Now however, with so much extraneous noise from road, rail and air traffic, the poignancy of their calls is severely muted. [BS]*

September 1782. In the old chapel of Lord Bute's house is preserved a fine Gothic wainscot in oak richly sculptured, which was put up by Sir THOMAS POPE, the founder of Trinity College, Oxford, in the chapel of his house at Tyttenhanger in Hertfordshire, about the year 1548. It was removed from Tyttenhanger to Luton, in entire preservation, by the family of Napier, tenants to Trinity College, in the beginning of the reign of James the First.

November 1782.   EPITAPHS

In the Church-Yard, Wheathampstead

HANNAH LUKE, 1773. Aged 79.

The Spirit wrought my faith and love,
And hope and every grace;
But Jesus spent his life to work
The robe of Righteousness.

On a Board against a south buttress of the Chancel,
Wheathampstead Church.

SARAH MOULIN, DIED FEBRUARY 5, 1775.

While Health and Pride and Folly laugh and sleep,
Affliction slumbers but to wake and weep:

Thus did the virgin eyes beneath the sod
In pious anguish pour their tears to God.
Toss'd on the thorny bed of pain she lay
Five times five years, nor saw the cheerful day.
That storm is past; in brightest heavens above
Secure and happy sits the trembling dove.
Dust with her dust, and free among the dead
Reclines her honest father's hoary head.
The worm feeds sweetly while the body lies;
Faithful in thee, O Lord, supreme to save,
I saw their end, and honour thus their grave.

In All Saints Church-Yard, Hertford

Transform'd from what I was, how am I grown
A frightful spectre to myself unknown!
With trembling steps and soggy puffs of breath
My very limbs crawl to the edge of death.
The mouldring clay seeks out its first abode,
With a stiff plant supports the tottering load.
Open thy bosom, Earth, and in the womb
Of Nature let me find a quiet tomb.
To thy cold breast my colder limbs receive,
They are the very clod thou once didst give.

January 1783. Sheriff. Hertfordshire. Robert Macky of Tewin.

February 1783. Dispensation. Rev. Peter Thomas Burford, LL.B., to hold Magdalen Laver rectory, Essex, with Braughing vicarage, Hertfordshire.

March 1783 Table of monumental inscriptions at Bath Abbey includes:
ASTEY, Elizabeth Herts 1736
COWPER, Rebecca Herts 1762

March 1783. At Hertford assizes, one Hemmings, a noted footpad, whose father was shot when he was taken, and his elder brother made his escape, received sentence of death. This family had long been the terror of that part of the country.

June 1783. APPARITIONS, &c.   November 30, 1759.
"Dr. Yarborough, rector of Tewin, Hertfordshire, who had a long and intimate acquaintance with the late General Sabine, governor of Gibraltar, whose country seat was at Tewin, told me this story, which he had from the General's own mouth, who was a person of great honour and veracity, and much good sense.
That when he once lay dangerously ill of his wounds after a battle abroad, and began to recover, as he lay awake one night in his bed, having a candle in his chamber, he saw on the sudden the curtains drawn back at his bed's feet, and his wife then in England (a lady whom he greatly loved) presenting herself to his full view, at the opening of the curtains, and then disappearing. He was amazed at the sight, and fell into deep reflections upon this extraordinary apparition. In a short time after he received the melancholy news from England that his beloved

consort was dead, and she died at such a time; which, as near as he could possibly recollect, was the very time on which he had seen that strange phenomenon.

This he immediately entered down in his note-book, continuing ever afterwards fully persuaded of the certainty of some apparitions, notwithstanding the general prejudice to the contrary; "which," said he often, "I can, from my own knowledge in this instance, confidently oppose upon the strongest grounds."

This is the story, and I here set it down as I heard it from the above-mentioned worthy Doctor, without making any remarks . . . ".

July 1783. "We have many orchards about Derby [and] of course plenty of hedge-pigs; but Hertfordshire is a county where they abound so much as to gain the natives of it the ludicrous appellation of "Hertfordshire Hedge-Hogs." It will eat any thing that another pig will eat."

July 1783. On Sunday evening, July 20, between seven and eight o'clock, the lightning burnt a cottage near the Rev. Mr. Browne's at Wildhill near Hatfield, and between 10 and 11 the stables of Sir Richard Chase, at Hadham, Hertfordshire. The servants were just gone to bed, in order to set out early next morning, and were awakened by the hay blazing from one end of the loft to the other. The horses were with difficulty saved.

THE ROYSTON CLUB

October 1783. [See also October 1780]. The ROYSTON CLUB is so totally unnoticed by our tourists, and so little known out of its own neighbourhood, that the following account of it may not be unacceptable to your inquisitive readers, and it is to be hoped may draw forth fuller and more correct information on the subject.

The precise year of its institution does not appear. It certainly was prior to the year 1698, and perhaps began at the Revolution. The only book of entries now known to exist by the present landlord and his waiter opens with a list of members from the institution to 1698. Among these members the following have been extracted, not in regular succession, nor as a complete list, but as persons most likely to be known beyond their own counties, though after exhausting his talent in naming their respective places of abode, your correspondent finds himself obliged to leave several of them to the sagacity of others. Their meetings were held on a Thursday.

Their mode of election was by a majority on ballot on the club-day succeeding that of nomination. The candidate was admitted on his first appearance within a year after his election, otherwise a second ballot was allowed. The steward for the day entered the nomination and election. Each member who was steward furnished the wine, or five guineas in lieu of it. No wine was to be drunk out of the club-room, and what was left after each meeting was to be put into a chest, and the key delivered, sealed up by the steward or his deputy, to the master of the house, for the next steward. In 1760 there was so much wine in the cellar that it was resolved that no member should be chosen steward for 3 months to come. In September 1783 there remained, of Claret, Madeira, Port, and Lisbon, about 3 pipes. The bill of extraordinaries was to be delivered in on the first Thursday in July. No cyder, wine, or beer, or tobacco, to be allowed as extraordinaries; only fire and venison fees.

The place of meeting was the Red Lion Inn, which is the Post-house. Two handsome rooms, a smaller and a larger, were built, at the expense of the members, at the back of the house, for this purpose, and furnished with portraits, still preserved there, though the rooms, having lost their original destination, and the larger serving occasionally for an assembly and having an orchestra, and the smaller for an ordinary on market-days, or other public occasions, are going fast out of repair.

In the first, or ante-chamber, are two very good half-lengths of James I and Charles I; whole lengths of Charles and James II, William, Mary, and Anne, in an inferior style: a good head of Dr. Savage,* in a gown and band: and over the chimney the Judgement of Paris.

Round the top of the larger room, above the wainscot, are the following heads:
At the upper end of the room an old man in his hair and a gown, and over his head a crown carved on the gilt frame.
A head in robes, with the George.
A man in a wig, cravat, and blue coat.
One in judge's robes. [Qu. Pemberton ?]
One in a flowing wig and armour.
One in a gown and wig,
Portrait of a chancellor, with the great seal. [Qu. Harcourt ?]
A man in a flowing wig, cravat, and starched sleeves.
Another in a like wig and gown.
Another in a like wig and open sleeves.
A nobleman in robes, holding a white staff. [Qu. Earl of Oxford ?]
A gentleman in a yellowish coat, blue belt, short hair.
Another in a pink coat and cravat.
Another in a gown and short cravat.
Over the chimney the Angel appearing to the Shepherds.†

The chaplain to the club was Hugh Parnel, on whose decease Francis Gulston, rector of Wyddial, was elected, 1763, and occurs in that character in 1777. He is still living, and resident at Wydial, though the estate has been sold out of the Gulston family, first to Stephen Comyn, barrister at law and bencher of the Inner Temple, and by him to Brabazon Ellis, Esq., whose son, John Thomas, now enjoys it, and has improved the hall by the addition of two bow windows, and by a new road to it from Buntingford.

I am credibly informed that the divisions in the county on the general election 1754, when Hale, Gore, and Gardiner, were candidates (and the latter lost it) occasioned an almost total desertion of this club.

Another Cantab.

*Rector of Bygrave, then of Clothall, Hertfordshire; and lecturer of St. George, Hanover Square, London. In his younger days he had travelled with James 5th

Earl of Salisbury, who gave him the great living of Clothall, where Dr. Savage rebuilt the rectory house. In his more advanced years he was so lively, pleasant, and facetious, that he was called the Aristipus of the age. . . . One day, at the levee, George I asked him, "How long he had stayed at Rome with Lord Salisbury?" Upon his answering how long, "Why," said the King, "you stayed long enough, why did you not convert the Pope?" "Because, Sir," replied he, "I had nothing better to offer him". Having been bred at Westminster, he had always a great fondness for the school, attended at all their plays and elections, assisted in all their public exercises, grew young again, and, among boys, was a great boy himself. He used to attend the schools to furnish the lads with extempore epigrams at the elections. The King's scholars had so great a regard for him that, after his decease, they made a collection among themselves and, at their own charge, erected a small tablet of white marble in the cloisters to his memory. (See it in the 'Anecdotes of Bowyer', p.644). He printed two Sermons; 1. On the "Election of the Lord Mayor, 1707;" 2. "Before the Sons of the Clergy, 1715." He died March 24, 1747. Editor, G.M. [See also October 1786, and obituary 24 March 1787].

†Arthur Chauncey was paid eight guineas for cleaning and mending these pictures in 1745.

James Willymot	of Therfield and Kelshall.
Edward Chester	of Cokenhatch in Barkway.
Sir Peter Soame, Bart.	of Berkesdon, now living.
Francis Floyer	of Brent Pelham.
Giles Dent	of Newport, Essex.
John Mead	of Wendon Lofts, Essex.
Richard Freeman	Qu. of the Aspeden family?
James Goulston	of Wyddial.
Sir Thomas Brograve, Bart.,	of Shephall and Braughing.
Henry Guy	of Tring.

Qu. mayor of St. Albans in 1685 (Chauncy 457,458) and alderman by the charter 1 James II; recorder of Berkhamsted 1638 (ibid. 581); groom of the bed-chamber, clerk of the treasury, temp. Charles II, James II and William III; member for a borough in Yorkshire in all their parliaments (ibid. 592). He built an elegant house [at Tring] and laid out large and beautiful gardens there, and a park, and then sold it to Sir William Gore, Knt, lord mayor. (Salmon, Herts, 130).

This house, one of the best works of Sir Christopher Wren, being entirely his own plan, was built for Mr. Guy with the treasury money. It is the property of the present Charles Gore, Esq., great grandson of Sir William. Editor, G.M.

Robert Elwes	of Amwell and Throcking.
Sir Thomas Middleton, Knt.	Qu. serjeant at mace to Charles II who held Bedwell Park in Essendon. (Chauncy 277).
John Turner	Qu. of Great Hormead?
William Calvert	of Pelham Furneux.
Robert Chester	of Bygrave, and Cokenhatch in Barkway.
Thomas Newland	Qu. of Newsells, or of Queenbury in Reed?
John Pargiter	
William Dyer	Some of this family were burgesses of Hertford from 1630 to 1651.

Sir Henry Puckering, Bart.	Qu. who sold Weston, 1654 ? (Chauncy 374).
Felix Calvert	of Pelham Furneux and Hadham.
Sir Charles Barrington, Bart.	who died 1714–15.
Sir Edward Turnor, Knt.	member for Hertford 1661.

Speaker of the House of Commons, knighted, and solicitor to the Duke of York; 1663, treasurer to the Middle Temple; 1670, solicitor general; 1671, serjeant at law and chief baron of the Exchequer. (Chauncy 250).

Sir Alexander Rigby, Knt.	
Henry Earl of Suffolk and Bindon	created Earl of Bindon and Baron Chesterford in his father's life, became Earl of Suffolk in 1709, and died in 1718.
Ralph Freman	of Westmill and Standon.
Richard Gulston	of Wyddial; died 1686.
William Levinz	of Mold Hall, Depden, Essex.
Sir Richard Hutchinson	
William Gore [son of Sir William]	of Tring.
John Essington	of Ashlim [Ashlyns] in Great Berkhamsted.
William Robinson	of Lytton Strode.
Sir Charles Buck, Bart.	of the Grove, Watford.
Robert Gilsthorpe, Esq.	of Welwyn, died 1731.
Henry Coghill	of Pen's Place, Aldenham.
Francis Pemberton	Qu. afterwards knighted, serjeant, chief justice of the King's Bench and Common Pleas; died 1627. (Chauncy 469).
Edward Nightingale	Qu. of the family at Newport in Essex?
John Coghill	
William Hanley	
William Webb	Qu. of Barkway?
Robert Hare	
Edward Fitzgerald viscount Villiers	
William Freman	
Jeffrey Elwes	impropriator of Amwell.
William Harvey	of Braughing.
Jacob Houblon	of Braughing and Hormead Magna, died October 16, 1783.
Robert Trefusis	left the club in 1737.
John Savage, D.D. 1733	Fellow of Emmanuel College, Cambridge.
Thomas Rolt	of Bengeo and Sacombe.
Edward Bayntun	
Adolphus Meetkirk	of Bradfield and Rushden.
Catesby Freeman	
William Plummer	of Eastwick, member for Hertfordshire, father to the present.
Edward Chester	of Cokenhatch, admitted 1734, quitted 1745.
Lucius Charles, Viscount Falkland 1735	died May 27, 1776.
Alexander Cottle	

Thomas Carleton
John Thomlinson
Thomas Milner   of Langley Lawn, in Clavering, in the county of Essex, died 1733 or 1742.
William Benn   alderman of London; of Tillers End, Westmill.
Edward Gardiner, 1746   of Thundridge.
John Cheshire
William Hale   of King's Walden.
William Pym   of Radwell Hall in Norton.
William Wright   of Barkway.
Ralph Freman, D.D.   of Hamels, in Braughing. Uncle to the first lady of the Right Hon. Charles Yorke, whose son now possesses the estate.
Sir Thomas Salisbury [Salusbury], Knt.   of Offley, judge of the Admiralty.
Thomas Whetham   of Bradford.
Christopher Anstey, D.D.   of Trumpington, co. Cambridge, father to the author of the New Bath Guide.
Richard Hale   of Codicote.
Francis Bowyer   of North Mimms.
Thomas Clarges
Robert Philipps
Richard Chase   now Sir Richard Chase, Knt. of Hadham, sheriff of Herts 1745, when he was knighted. He is or was Lieut. Col. of the Herts Militia.
John Robinson Lytton   of Knebworth.
Gilbert Thornton Heysham   probably the younger son of Jane, daughter of the next member.
Robert Thornton   of Little Munden.
Nicholson Calvert   of Hunsdon.
Paggen Hale, 1747   died 1754, member for Herts County.
Edward Webster   of Littlecourt. [Buntingford]
James Coltee Ducarel 1741,   quitted 1757.
Samuel Smith   Qu. of King's Langley?
John Gardiner, 1742   quitted 1748. Of Thundridge, or Pishobury?
Honourable James Aston   of the family of Lord Aston of Standon.
William Woolball   [of Walthamstow. (Cussans, Odsey H., 89)].
Edward Gould
George Jennings   of Newsells in Barkway, son to the admiral.
James Gordon   of Moor Place.
Sir John Hynde Cotton, Bart. 1732,   of Maddingley, co. Cambridge: living.
Thomas Plumer Byde, 1754   of Ware Park, late a banker in London.
Edward Otto Bayer, 1754
Henry Pennant, quitted 1757   of Little Ayot.
George Wright   of Beeches.
Frederick Halsey, 1758   of Great Gaddesden, deceased. Eldest brother to the present member for the county.
William Plummer, jun., 1758   the other member for the county.

John Radcliffe   of Hitchin, member for St. Albans.
Earl of Essex, 1765   William Anne, of Cashiobury, now living.
R. Cox, 1766   of Aspeden.

November 1783. Letters from Hitchin, in Hertfordshire, speak of houses and barns being set on fire, in that neighbourhood, for the villainous purpose of robbing the inhabitants. No less than five fires have happened in the course of last month, though none of the incendiaries have yet been detected, except a girl, who at Bedford assizes, was sentenced to be hanged for setting her master's house on fire.

December 1783. Dispensation. Rev. John Hewit, M.A., Royston vicarage, Hertfordshire, with Feltham vicarage, Middlesex.

1784. Sheriff. Hertfordshire. J. Thomas Ellis, Wyddial Hall.

May 1784. List of the new House of Commons [includes]:
HERTFORDSHIRE. * W. Plumer, and Viscount Grimston, vice T. Halsey.
HERTFORD. * Baron Dimsdale, and J. Calvert, vice W. Baker.
ST. ALBANS. * Colonel Sloper and Hon. T. Grimston, vice Lord Grimston.
*Chosen for their former Seats.

PAUL WRIGHT AND HIS HISTORICAL COLLECTIONS

October 1784. The following specimen of my Collections towards the History of Hertfordshire may afford some amusement to your readers, and shew, that if a generous public will support me, the whole work shall be published. Other specimens shall be occasionally communicated.
Paul Wright [obit. 8 May 1785].

HINXWORTH PLACE. Arms in the parlour window. Argent, on a bend Vert between two cottises dauncette Gules, a crescent for a difference Or.
Second shield. The same coat, impaling quarterly, first and fourth Sable, three dexter hands couped Argent. Hanchett second Gules, three chevrons Or. Montfitchet. An ancient baron. Third Gules, three lozenges in bend Argent, a martlet Or for a difference. Underneath Grey and . . . , it was formerly Hanchett.
Third shield. Quarterly, first and fourth, Or, a lion rampant queüe furché Gules within a border of the same. Second and third Azure, a

bend Argent between seven billets, Or. Underneath Malory and . . . 1570.

In the chamber window. First shield. Quarterly first and fourth. Quarterly, per fesse indented Gules and Or. Bromley. Second Argent, on a chevron within a border ingrailed Gules, five Bezants. Third Argent, on a Fesse Sable, three cross crosslets Or, between six fleurs de lis. Impaling, Quarterly, first and fourth Azure, a bend ingrailed Argent, cottised Or. Fortescue. Second and third, Argent frettee Azure, on a chief of the second, three roses of the first, barbed and seeded gold. These were the arms of Sir Thomas Bromley, knight, who was solicitor general in 1569; and in 1579 was made lord chancellor. Dugdale's Chronica Series, pp. 93 and 94. He married Elizabeth, daughter of Sir Adrian Fortescue. This shield, by the blunder of some glazier repairing the window, has been turned outwards; so that, as it now stands, the second quartering in the Fortescue arms is the first coat.

Second shield in the chamber window. Quarterly, first Argent, a lion passant in fesse Gules, between two bars Sable, charged with three bezants, in chief, three stags heads caboshed of the third. Parker Lord Morley and Monteagle. Second Argent, a lion rampant Sable, crowned Gules. Sir Robert Morley temp. Edward the First. Third Quarterly. First and Fourth Barry Nebulee or six Or and Gules. William Lovell, who, by his marriage with Eleanor, daughter and heiress to Robert Lord Morley, had the title of Lord Morley. Second and third azure, a lion rampant Argent.

Fourth coat. Gules, a bend fusilee Or. Crest. Out of a ducal coronet Or, a bear's head Sable, bridled gold.

Alice, sister to Henry, only son of the said William, was married to Sir Henry Parkes, knight, whose son Henry was, at Henry VIII summoned to parliament by the title of Lord Morley.

Third shield in the chamber window. Twelve coats formerly quartered. First Argent, three bars Azure, in chief three torteauxes. Grey. Second Argent, a chief indented Azure, Glanville. Third Or, a maunch Gules. Hastings Earl of Pembroke. Fourth Argent, a double tressure floree counterfloree, in the honorary point an inescutcheon Gules. Scott Earl of Huntingdon. Fifth is almost demolished; but part of the field, and the top of a garb appearing, shews that it was Azure, three garbs, Or. Blundeville Earl of Chester. Sixth Gules, three leopards heads jessant fleurs de lis, Or. Cantelupe. Seventh Azure, a lion rampant, Or. Eighth, Barry of ten Argent and Azure, nine martlets, Gules. Audomare de Valentia Earl of Pembroke, Ninth, Newburgh, or Berkley, demolished. Tenth, demolished, except part of the field Or; and it was probably, Or, three inescutcheons Barry of six Vaire and Gules; being the arms of Joan Montchensy, mother of Audomare de Valentia Earl of Pembroke. Eleventh, almost demolished, but part of the field Argent, and the chief Azure, charged with three crosses pattee fitchee of the field. Strongbow. Twelfth, Sable, three garbs Argent. Mackmurrough. Dermot MacMurrough, knight, of Leicester, married Eva, the only daughter and heir to Richard Strongbow Earl of Pembroke. The second, third, eighth, tenth, and eleventh coats are in Dugdale's Origines Juridiciales, p. 300, quartered by the Lord Grey of Wilton; and many of them are likewise quartered by the present Earl of Stamford.

There is no account of these several shields in Sir Henry Chauncy. And Salmon's description of them is very short and imperfect.   *Paul Wright.*

October 1784. From Dr. Plot's Analecta in Bibliothecâ Bodleianâ, October 5, 64, inter MSS. Browne Willis, Armig.

Near St. Albans, not many years since, quicksilver sprang out of the earth.

Hertford. The Danes made a strong intrenchment on the River Lea, where Hertford now is. *Life of King Alfred,* p. 72.

Verulam. Ophiomorphites found there. Mr. Ray, p. 115.

Between Puckeridge and Ware, on the banks of an hollow lane, the great whitish ash-coloured shell-snail*, eaten much in Italy, found there by Mr. Martin Lister, p. 404.

**I myself saw, a few years since, near Braughing, some of the snails mentioned by Mr. Martin Lister, p. 404. He was afterward M.D.* Paul Wright.

October 1784. An account of the first Aerial Voyage in England, in a Series of Letters to his Guardian, Chevalier Gherardo Compagni, written under the Impressions of the various Events that affected the Undertaking, by Vincent Lunardi, Esq., Secretary to the Neapolitan Ambassador. 8vo.

. . . "At twenty minutes past four I descended in a spacious meadow in the parish of Standon, near Ware, in Hertfordshire. Some labourers were at work in it. I requested their assistance. They exclaimed, they would have nothing to do with one who came in the Devil's house; and no intreaties could prevail on them to approach me. I at last owed my deliverance to the spirit and generosity of a female. A young woman took hold of a cord which I had thrown out, and calling to the men, they yielded that assistance to her request which they had refused to mine. A crowd of people from the neighbourhood soon assembled, who very obligingly assisted me to disembark. Gen. Smith was the first gentleman who overtook me. I am much indebted to his politeness. He kindly assisted in securing the balloon, having followed me on horseback from London; as did several other gentlemen, amongst whom were Mr. Crane, Captain Connor, and Mr. Wright. The inflammable air was let out by an incision, and produced a most offensive stench, which is said to have affected the atmosphere of the neighbourhood. The apparatus was committed to the care of Mr. Hollingsworth, who obligingly offered his service. I then proceeded, with Gen. Smith, and several other gentlemen, to the Bull Inn at Ware. On my arrival, I had the honour to be introduced to William Baker, Esq., member for Hertford in the last parliament. This gentleman conducted me to his seat at Bayford Bury, and entertained me with a kind of hospitality and politeness which I shall ever remember with gratitude, and which has impressed on my mind a

proper idea of that frank liberality and sincere beneficence which are
the characteristics of English gentlemen.

The general course of the second part of my voyage, by which I was
led into Hertfordshire, was three points to the eastward of the north
from the Artillery Ground, and about four points to the eastward of the
north from the place where I first descended.

This is the general account of my excursion.

VINCENT LUNARDI."

The young woman who first assisted Lunardi is identified in the fuller text of his
narrative quoted by Cussans as Elizabeth Brett, servant to Mr. Thomas Read,
farmer of Standon. Mr. Hollingsworth, to whose care the 'apparatus' was com-
mitted, was probably John Hollingsworth, a surveyor or land agent of
Puckeridge, who had acted as intermediary in the sale of Old Hall (now St.
Edmund's College) to the Roman Catholic Bishop Talbot in 1772. [AJ]

November 1784.
ON A GRAVESTONE FOR JOSEPH
CHAPMAN, A TALLOW-CHANDLER, IN
THE CHURCH-YARD AT
BISHOP STORTFORD,
HERTS.

> Like leaves of trees the race of man is found,
> Now green in youth, now withering on the ground;
> Another race the following spring supplies,
> They fall successive, and successive rise.
> So generations in their course decay;
> So flourish these when those are pas'd away.

1785. Sheriff. Hertfordshire. William Phillimore of Aldenham.

PETER, THE WILD BOY

February 1785. Lord Monboddo's Account of PETER THE WILD BOY,
formerly brought from the woods of Germany. [See also 7 January 1767,
November 1785].

"It was in the beginning of June, 1782, that I saw him in a farm-
house, called Broadway, within about a mile of Berkhamsted, kept there
upon a pension which the King pays. He is but low of stature, not
exceeding five feet three inches; and, although he must now be about
seventy years of age, has a fresh healthy look. He wears his beard. His
face is not at all ugly or disagreeable; and he has a look that may be
called sensible and sagacious for a savage. About twenty years ago he
was in use to elope, and to be missing for several days; and once, I was
told, he wandered as far as Norfolk; but of late he has been quite tame,
and either keeps in the house, or saunters about the farm. He has been
the thirteen last years where he lives at present; and before that, he
was twelve years with another farmer, whom I saw and conversed with.
This farmer told me, that he had been put to school somewhere in
Hertfordshire, but had only learned to articulate his own name Peter,

and the name of King George, both of which I heard him pronounce very distinctly. But the woman of the house where he now is (for the man happened not to be at home) told me, that he understood every thing that was said to him concerning the common affairs of life; and I saw that he readily understood several things that she said to him while I was present. Among other things, she desired him to sing Nancy Dawson; which he did, and another tune which she named. He never was mischievous, but had always that gentleness of nature which I hold to be characteristical of our nature, at least till we became carnivorous, and hunters or warriors. He feeds at present as the farmer and his wife do; but, as I was told by an old woman (one Mrs. Collop, living at a village in the neighbourhood, called Hempstead [Hemel Hempstead], who remembered to have seen him when he first came to Hertfordshire, which she computed to be fifty-five years before the time I saw her) he then fed very much upon leaves, and particularly upon the leaves of cabbage, which he eat raw. He was then, as she thought, about fifteen years of age, walked upright, but could climb trees like a squirrel. At present he not only eats flesh, but has also got the taste of beer, and even of spirits, of which he inclines to drink more than he can get. The old farmer above-mentioned, with whom he lived twelve years before he came to this last farmer, told me, that he had acquired that taste before he came to him, which is about twenty-five years ago. He has also become very fond of fire, but has not yet acquired a liking for money, for though he takes it, he does not keep it, but gives it to his landlord or landlady, which, I suppose, is a lesson that they have taught him. He retains so much of his natural instinct, that he has a fore-feeling of bad weather, growling and howling, and shewing great disorder, before it comes . . . .

November 1785. Peter the Wild Boy, of which you inserted Lord Monboddo's account, and related his death, having been buried in the church-yard of the parish where he resided, he was buried at the expense of Government, a brass plate, with a short inscription to his memory, was erected in the church, which has also been paid, on application, by the Treasury, and a more particular account has been inserted in the parish register. As both these inscriptions are worthy of a place in your magazine, I wish you to insert them, that the particulars of this extraordinary person may be transmitted to posterity. [See also 7 January 1767].

Extract from the Parish Register of North-Church, in the County of Hertford.

"Peter, commonly known by the name of Peter The Wild Boy, lies buried in this church-yard, opposite to the porch. In the year 1725 he was found in the woods near Hamelen, a fortified town in the electorate of Hanover, when his Majesty George I with his attendants, was hunting in the forest of Hertswold. He was supposed to be then about 12 years of age, and had subsisted in those woods upon the bark of trees, leaves, berries, &c. for some considerable length of time. How long he had continued in that wild state is altogether uncertain; but that he had formerly been under the care of some person was evident from the remains of a shirt-collar about his neck at the time when he was found.

. . . In [1726] he was brought over to England, by the order of Queen Caroline, then Princess of Wales, and put under the care of Dr. Arbuthnot, with proper masters to attend him. . . . He was afterwards intrusted to the care of Mrs. Titchbourn, one of the Queen's bed-chamber women, with a handsome pension annexed to the charge. Mrs. Titchbourn usually spending a few weeks every summer at the house of Mr. James Fenn, a yeoman farmer, at Axter's End, in this parish, Peter was left to the care of the said Mr. Fenn, who was allowed £35 a year for his support and maintenance. After the death of James Fenn he was transferred to the care of his brother, Thomas Fenn, at another farmhouse in this parish, called Broadway, where he lived with the several successive tenants of that farm, and with the same provision allowed by Government, to the time of his death, February 22, 1785, when he was supposed to be about 72 years of age. . ."

A brass plate is fixed up in the parish church of North-Church, on the top of which is a sketch of the head of Peter, drawn from a very good engraving of Bartolozzi, and underneath it is the following inscription:

"To the memory of PETER, known by the name of the Wild Boy, having been found wild in the forest of Hertswold, near Hanover, in the year 1725. He then appeared to be about 12 years old. In the following year he was brought to England by the order of the late Queen Caroline, and the ablest masters were provided for him. But, proving incapable of speaking, or of receiving any instruction, a comfortable provision was made for him at a farmhouse in this parish, where he continued to the end of his inoffensive life. He died on the 22nd day of February, 1785, supposed to be aged 72."

February 1785. [See also July 1790]. The following epitaph is in the east part of the church-yard at Cheshunt.

In memory of
MR. EDMUND SOUTH*,
who departed this life
Jan. 11, 1784, aged 66.

When thoughts of guilt invade the troubled breast,
The spirit's wounded, and farewell to rest;
But he his life of innocence so led,
That peace in sickness made an easy bed.
Art thou a husband ?—to thy partner yield,
As he Love's tribute, by Affection seal'd.
Art thou a parent ?—to thy children show
A love like his, a debt which parents owe.
Art thou a Christian ?—learn of him to blend,
Sound faith, good deeds, and manners to the end.

Also MR. EDMUND SOUTH,
son of the above
who departed this life
Jan. 21, 1779, aged 27 years.

*A celebrated dancing master, as well as his father. [Editor, G.M.].

April 1785. EPITAPH in Amwell† Church-yard, Hertfordshire, on the Stone of Thomas Monger, who died in August 1773, ætat 64.

> That which a Being was, what is it ? shew;
> That Being which it was, it is not now:-
> To be what 'tis is not to be, you see;
> That which now is not, shall a being be!

†Celebrated by the late ingenious John Scott, Esq., in his descriptive poem. See his poetical works just published. [Editor, G.M.].

May 1785. To follow the good example of a correspondent in volume LIII, I transmit to your universal Repository of Curiosities, the few remarks that have occurred to me in the course of an attentive perusal of Mr. Nichols's *Memoirs of Hogarth.* P. Pindar.

Hogarth said himself, that Lord Lovat's portrait was taken (at the White Hart at St. Albans) in the attitude of relating on his fingers the numbers of the rebel forces —"Such a general had so many men, &c." and remarked, that the muscles of Lovat's neck appeared of unusual strength, more so than he had ever seen. When the painter entered the room, his lordship, being under the barber's hands, received his old friend with a salute, which left much of the lather on his face.

May 1785. Memoirs of the Life and Writings of Arthur Ashley Sykes, D.D. By John Disney, D.D., F.S.A. 8vo.

Mr Sykes, we learn from these Memoirs, was born in London, about the year 1684. The profession or business of his father, Arthur, cannot be ascertained; but his great-grand-father and grandfather were successively vicars of Ardeley, or Yardley, in Hertfordshire, and the former was also rector of Cottered, in the same county, which was held in trust, after his death, for our author's elder brother, John, who died in 1723. . . .

16 May 1785. A fire broke out in the stables of the Green Man at Barnet, occasioned by a stone-horse kicking down the candle, which burnt eight horses belonging to a waggon.

June 1785. List of all the Parishes in Middlesex, with Incumbents, &c., includes :

> *South Mimms*, vicarage. Patron Mr. Marsh. Incumbent Mr. John Heathfield, vicar of Northaw, Herts.
>
> St. Martins in the Fields, vicarage. Patron Bishop of London. Incumbent Anthony Hamilton, D.D., chaplain to the King, Archdeacon of Colchester, Precentor of St. Paul's, Rector of Great and Little Hadham, Hertfordshire, FRS.
>
> Mr. Heald, Lecturer of Watford, Hertfordshire.

29 September 1785. A wheelwright at Hatfield, in Hertfordshire, completed his 100th. year; on which occasion Lord Salisbury, by whose family the old man has been employed from his youth, ordered the neighbouring inhabitants to be invited into his park, where a very numerous company were sumptuously entertained with roast beef and

London porter. The family of this industrious old man consists of himself, a daughter 79, another of 76, and a son of 75 years of age. The common earning of the father is 3s.6d. per day.

This was John Palmer, whose age indeed can be verified. He was baptized at Digswell 27 September 1685, married a Hatfield girl (Mary Lamb), and settled there. Held various parish offices, and was churchwarden for some 20 years. The details of his children are somewhat inaccurate—he in fact had two sons living at this time, aged 68 and 62, and two daughters, aged 55 and 53. Direct descendants of the centenarian continue to live in the town. [HG]
[See obituary, 26 January 1786].

December 1785. In a severe storm of thunder and lightning, at Baldock in Hertfordshire, on the 19th. of July, a ball of fire entered a barn, and in an instant set fire to that and the adjoining buildings. The men who were threshing had scarce time to save their lives.

1786. Sheriff. Hertfordshire. Jeremiah Mills, of Pishobury.

REV. HENRY ETOUGH, RECTOR OF THERFIELD 1734–57

January 1786. Mr Etough, such was his name, was in truth an ecclesiastical phenomenon, and a most eccentric, dangerous character. He began his career by setting out from Glasgow with a pack on his back, being a Scotch Presbyterian, afterwards halloo in election mobs at Lynn, and, in consequence, being worshipped, like the Indians, by the Devil through fear, he was converted, ordained, and preferred, by the means of Sir Robert Walpole; the valuable rectory of Therfield, Hertfordshire, and another, being his reward. The degree of M.A. he obtained at Cambridge, by mandamus. On Sir Robert's marrying Miss Skerret, Etough performed the ceremony, none of his dignitaries probably accepting that dirty business; and after dinner he requested a favour, which Sir Robert previously promised to grant, not doubting that it was some preferment; but in truth it was only a certain political secret, which, as far as he knew, the minister disclosed.

I remember him often in company at Cambridge, where he attended at the commencements; odd was his figure, and mean and nasty was his apparel; his stockings were blue, darned, and coarse, and without feet; and so hot and reeking was his head, that when he entered a room he often hung up his wig on a peg, and sat bare-headed. So have I seen him, in particular, at the lodge of the worthy primitive master of Bene't, Mr. Castle, where Dr. Ben Ellis, of Norwich, (the elephant and rhinoceros) attacked him generally with wit, keenness, and asperity. He had compiled a "History of his own Times" (a political Atalantis), somewhat in the manner of Burnet, which, I am told, he had carried down as far as the characters of Frederick Prince of Wales and Lord Bolingbroke. But his sarcasms were too free and too libellous ever to be printed. Many more anecdotes are well remembered at Cambridge. He left his good fortune (for he lived penuriously) and his papers to Archdeacon Plumptree, though he had poor relations, one of whom, Rebecca Hopley, of Pipemakers Alley, Houndsditch, was put into an hospital at Canterbury by Archbishop Secker, at that archdeacon's desire (his chaplain) in 1762.   Yours, &c. J.D.

April 1786. The . . . peculiarities of [Mr. Etough's] body and mind, which form the principal matter of your [former] correspondent's communications, were such as, without injury or loss to any one, might and ought to have been buried with him. Not having been so, or, in the prevailing rage of collecting anecdotes, having been dug up and brought into public view, the following traits of his character and conduct should in justice accompany them.

That he counteracted his bodily infirmities by a strict attention to cleanliness, going into a cold bath, or using other means of a very general washing twice in a day, and observing a strict temperance in his diet. That this consisting principally in milk and vegetables, his own mode of living was, of necessity penurious; but his friends were received at his house with the degree of hospitality suited to his situation and circumstances. That, at his coming to his living of Therfield, he borrowed £800 and laid it out in putting his house and appurtenances into good repair, and a decorous state; and, afterwards, was very attentive to keep them so; was diligent in the discharge of his parochial duties, watchful over the conduct of his parishioners, and humane in his conduct to them. That he gave away considerable sums to hopeful young men of moderate circumstances, in the University of Cambridge, to enable them the better to prosecute their studies; and, in assistance to other meritorious objects of benevolence. That, whatever the fortune left by him to Archdeacon Plumptre amounted to, he reaped no other personal benefit from it, than the satisfaction of causing Mr. Etough's bounty to flow in its usual channels during his life, and of planning measures since carried into execution by his elder brother, the executor of his will, for its continuance and perpetuity.
                              Yours, &c. D.M.

Rev. Henry Etough (1687–1757) attracted criticism and admiration from opposing viewpoints. Fellow Anglican clergy despised his north country non-conformist background: others questioned his friendship with Sir Robert Walpole, his vegetarian teetotal discipline, and his amazing good fortune at securing the well-rewarded living of Therfield.
Etough was also Rector of Colmworth in Bedfordshire.
It was necessary for Etough to repair and extend the neglected Rectory because he planned to live there; unlike many of his predecessors, who found London more attractive. [AK]

MEMOIRS OF THE LATE REV. JOHN DUNCOMBE, M.A.

March 1786. . . . John Duncombe was born 1730. He was the only child of William Duncombe, Esq., younger brother of John Duncombe, Esq., of Stocks near Berkhamsted, Hertfordshire. His mother was sister to Mr.

Hughes, author of the *Siege of Damascus*. When a child, he was of an amiable disposition, had an uncommon capacity for learning, and discovered, very early, a genius for poetry; after some years passed at a school at Romford, in Essex, under the care of his relation, the Rev. Ph. Fletcher, afterwards Dean of Kildare, and young brother to the Bishop of that see, he was removed to a more eminent one at Felsted, in the same county. . . .

July 1786. I have wondered at not seeing in any of the papers an account of a remarkable wind in this neighbourhood on the last day of July about 6 o'clock in the evening. Its effects were mostconspicuous in Sacombe Park, the seat of Timothy Caswall, Esq., where many very large trees were almost instantaneously torn up by the roots, many others snapped in two, and carried to a considerable distance from where they had been standing in perfect security for some centuries. The blast came in a northwest direction, and defied all opposition. The wall of Mr. Caswall's kitchen garden, though stout enough in appearance to withstand a storm of cannon balls, fell before it; a man at work in it concluded the end of the world was come, and for once (it is hoped) was wise enough to apply to him, who "rides in the whirlwind and directs the storm."

10 August 1786. About one o'clock in the afternoon a fire broke out in a stack of hay belonging to one Brand, dealer in hogs, in Sun Street, Waltham Holy Cross, which in two hours time consumed several barns full of hay besides other stacks and sheds belonging to Harvey the town-carrier, and a sow in pig; and had not the wind providentially turned to the southeast and driven it off from a barn, wherein were 500 faggots, and other contiguous thatched buildings; the whole street, if not the greater part of that ancient town, being principally old wooden houses, must have been destroyed. By the exertion of two engines from Cheshunt, and two belonging to the town, under the direction and assistance of Mr. Justice Berwick, the fire was got under by five o'clock, with the loss of 300 load of hay, and the next day large quantities of the damaged hay was spread on the adjoining fields, and a large rick, which had been some time cut open to prevent its firing and should have been removed sooner, was cut up almost in a state of calcination. On Sunday evening some fire being discovered in the ruins of a barn, the engines played on the adjoining buildings to prevent ill consequences, and in removing some hay which had been bound for sale, several of the trusses were found burnt to a coal.

September 1786. At Hertford assizes, in open court, a very genteel well-dressed man was observed, by a by-stander, to press hard against an honest farmer, and presently to pick his pocket of his purse, and then to make off. The by-stander (an officer belonging to the court) whispered to the farmer, and followed the thief, seized him in the street, brought him into court, had him committed, and a bill found against him by the grand jury. He was put on his trial, found guilty, and sentence of death passed upon him. Thus in less than three hours he was at perfect liberty, in custody of the gaoler, on his trial in court, and under sentence of death in the condemned hole. The judge, in passing sentence, enlarged on the nature of his crime, committed in the face of the court, where the lives of others were, at the very moment, depending for the like offence.

TURNER, FORDHAM AND ETOUGH MEMORIALS AT THERFIELD

October 1786. Having lately visited the church of Therfield in Hertfordshire, about three miles southwest from Royston, I send you the following notices of two persons who have lately made some figure in your useful Miscellany.

On the south side of Therfield church, in the yard, on a raised base is a square stone ending in a point. On the east side is this inscription, on a tablet of black marble:

I.
To the memory
of Sir BARNARD TURNER, Knight,
Alderman and Sheriff of London
and Middlesex,
Major of the Honourable Artillery Company,
and Member of Parliament for the
Borough of Southwark,
who
signalized his early years
in the naval service of his country,
and became eminently distinguished
in social and civil life,
by unremitted activity and undaunted
courage,
unshaken integrity and firmness as a
Magistrate,
spirited support of order and decency
in the execution of justice,
humane attention to the distresses of the
wretched,
and
disinterested ardour for the public good,
merited and adorned
that dignity and those important stations
to which
his Sovereign and Fellow-Citizens had
raised him.
The Artillery Company[1]
having attended their much-lamented Officer
and Friend
here to his grave,
dedicate this Inscription.
He died by a Fall from his Horse the 15th
of June, 1784, ætat 42[2].

[1] The officers of which make an annual visit to this tomb on the anniversary of its erection.

[2] Sir Barnard was proposed for election into the Society of Antiquaries three days before this unfortunate accident happened. [For a further reference to the circumstances of his death, see Leson obituary notice, 25 December 1787.]

This memorial stone was removed to a site opposite the south porch when Therfield church was partially rebuilt 1874–78. The Honourable Artillery Company continues an active interest in the well-being of the memorial. On 18 September 1991 a portrait of Sir Barnard commissioned by the Company and showing him attired in H.A.C. uniform was returned to the Company by Barnard's Australian descendants. [AK]

On the south side:

> Under this tomb are interred
> the remains
> of Mrs. SARAH PERRY TURNER[1]
> who died 7th March, 1782, aged 39 years,
> leaving to her affectionate and afflicted
> husband the following Children:
> Anne Tillet Turner, born 23 April, 1769,
> William Sackville Turner, born 4 October, 1770,
> Sarah Perry Turner, born 28 March, 1772,
> Edward George Turner, born 25 August, 1774,
> Sophia Perry Turner, born 31 December, 1775,
> and
> William Swiney Turner, born 7 March, 1782,
> who died 13th following,
> six days old.

[1] Her maiden name was Tillet, of Latton, Essex.

Sarah Perry Turner (née Tillet) was daughter of William Tillet of Watton, Norfolk. His second wife was Lucy Swiney, daughter of George Swiney of Pontefract, Yorkshire. [AK]

On the west side:

> 1782.
> As a memorial of love and attachment
> to a most deserving and beloved Wife
> this tomb was erected
> by BARNARD TURNER, Commanding Officer
> of the London
> Military Foot Association
> during the memorable Riots in June 1780,
> Major
> of the Honourable Artillery Company,
> and Alderman of the City of
> London.

North side blank.

II.

On an altar tomb by the south side :

> Under this stone lies the body of
> EDWARD TURNER, Gentleman,
> who was born the 6th of September,
> 1590, and attained the age of 86 years.

He left William Turner, his son,
Richard Gammon and Elizabeth
Swaine, his grandson and grand
daughter, his Executors,
who erected this stone,
which being greatly defaced was
recut at the expence of
Sackville and Barnard Turner,
his great great grandsons,
in 1772.

III.

On a blue slab on a tomb at the feet of this :
Here lies the body of Mrs. ANNE TURNER,
Wife of Edward Turner, Gentleman,
whose soul it pleased God to call to
him March 3rd, 1737–38,
aged 72 years.
By love unfeigned and all other good qualities
desirable as a Wife, which lasted near 50
years, and (that too in trying times) highly
intitled to her Husband's affections, and by an
exemplary performance of her duty to
GOD and Man, highly deserving the esteem of
everybody; and it may not be forgotten that
(to complete her character) her precious
soul was lodged in a body suitable for its reception.
Not a covering of gold, with a flood of tears
and groans, can sufficiently express the bounden
duty of love and respect that is due to her memory from her most affectionate and therefore
most affected husband Edward Turner.
Of the abundance of the heart his mouth speaketh. Luke vi. 45.

Very near adjoining lies the body of
EDWARD TURNER, A.M.
who ventures his character of being a
Nonjuror from 1688 with posterity.
He died 6 December, 1755, aged 92 years,
looking for the resurrection of the dead, and
the life of the world to come. Amen.

Another, by the side of the last:
Under this stone lies the body of
WILLIAM second son of
EDWARD and ANNE TURNER,
died 27 March, 1754,
aged 62 years.
Could Death have spared the man
beloved by all who knew him,
he had not died.
Also the body of ANNE his wife,
who died September the 9th, 1763,
aged 62 years.
Who, with a thorough resignation
to the will of her Creator,
patiently bore the loss of her dear Husband,
and fulfilled the character

of a good Christian
and a true Widow.

IV.

Ground-slab:

To protect the Remains of
a much-respected Grandfather,
Edward Turner, A.M. this
stone was placed by
Sir Barnard Turner,
in the year 1784.

V.

Here lies the body of
WILLIAM FORDHAM,
who left this world January 1st, 1765,
aged 57, to receive a reward
suitable to his merit in a better.
Also Mrs. MARTHA FORDHAM,
Wife of the above William Fordham,
and youngest daughter of Edward
and Anne Turner, of Tuthill, in this
parish. She died universally lamented
January the 12th, 1777, aged 72.

VI.

On a stone against the wall of the church:
In memory of
EDWARD eldest son of
WILLIAM and ANNE TURNER,
who died of the small pox at
Bapaume in French Flanders,
June 19, 1756,
aged 21 years.
Wisdom to him was grey hairs,
and an unspotted life old age.

*All other external memorials and tombs for Turners and Fordhams (here num-
bered II—VI) have vanished. Many were decaying, others were damaged during
church rebuildings, 1874–78. [AK]*

VII.

On a white marble tablet, with a pediment and urn, against the south
pillar of the nave entering into the chancel:
To the memory of
SACKVILLE TURNER, Esq.
A Captain in his Majesty's 33rd Regiment,
and of
SARAH his wife,
(the only child of Edward Crockley,
of Watton in Norfolk, Gentleman,)
who were cast away and drowned in their
passage
to Ireland, on the night of the 5th of
September, 1774,
this stone is dedicated

by their most affection and afflicted brother
BARNARD TURNER.
To enumerate their virtues were an endless
task,
And to number his sighs were vain.
Patience here
Her meek hands folded on her modest breast,
In mute submission lifts to the adoring eye,
E'en to the power that wounds her.

Arms: A. a chevron between 3 fer de molines S. quartering Az, on a fess O. between 3 martlets O. 3 fleurs de lis S. On a shield of pretence G. a lion rampant. A. debruised by a bend Az. Motto, Optimum quod evenit ('Whatever is best').

Sackville Turner's memorial is now located on the south side aisle wall. The arms were repainted in 1976. [AK]

The first of the family of Turner settled here was Dr. Francis, son of Dr. Francis Turner, dean of Canterbury, and canon-residentiary of St. Paul's. He is supposed to have been born at Canterbury, and was successively bishop of Rochester and Ely, and one of the seven bishops committed to the Tower for refusing to read James II's Declaration for liberty of conscience. Being deprived of his bishopric after the Revolution, 1690, he ended his days in retirement, 1700. He probably retired to this rectory, to which he had been presented December 20, 1664. He was educated at Winchester School, and thence elected fellow of New College, Oxford, where he proceeded B.A. 1659, M.A. 1663, B.D. and D.D. 1669, being a compounder, and in December following was collated to the prebend of Sneating in St. Paul's. He succeeded Dr. Guming, bishop of Chichester, in the mastership of St. John's College, Cambridge, 1669, Dr. Durell in the deanery of Windsor, 1683, and Dr. Dolben in the see of Rochester the same year, and the year following, Dr. Guming in the see of Ely. Against the south wall of Therfield chancel, which he rebuilt in a handsome manner, 1676, is a singular monument of wainscot, erected by him to the memory of his wife, who died . . . , and was buried in a vault made by him for her. This monument is adorned with the images of Time and Death on each side of the inscription; on the pediment are two female figures reclining on skulls, with their hands and eyes uplifted, and by them two flaming urns. In the middle of the pediment is a blank shield. In the centre of the monument is an oval tablet, with an inscription on a gold ground, and below it a square tablet, with an inscription, both of which may be seen at large in Chauncy (p.88) and Salmon (p.348). On the covering stone of the vault is, in capitals,
E X P E R G I S C A R,
the only memorial of the bishop, who was buried in it. . . .

Chauncey, and after him Salmon, say, the manor of Merdlay, in this parish, of which they give no intermediate lords from the time of Edward III, was for a great while in the possession of the Turners, till sold, 1630, by one of them, of the name of William. They say nothing of that of Tuthill, which seems to have been their residence, and whose site, with remains of moats and banks, is still to be seen in a field northwest from the church, in the way to a house inhabited by the present curate, Mr.

Ferriby. To this manor belongs a pew in the upper end of the nave on the door of which is cut TVTHILL, as on two others, MANERIUM DE GLEDSEYS & DE GLEDSEYS and MA^{R}DE LIMBVRY.

From the epitaph N^{O}II, here given, it appears probable that Edward Turner, who was born in 1590, was lord here, and that from him the property descended to the late Sir Barnard, or his grandfather; though these epitaphs do not allow us to fill up the succession with that accuracy which a close examination of the parish registers would enable us to do (they begin in 1538, 30 Henry VIII).

The property of this family here was sold by the late Sir Barnard's father, who was a dealer in foreign spirits, and lived and died at Turnford, in Cheshunt parish, in an old house on the north side of the London road, not far from the 14th mile-stone, where were born Sir Barnard and two brothers and a sister (she married ———— Lilly, an apothecary at Hodsdon, against her friends' consent). He or his father sold the family estate here to Mr. Fordham, who married a daughter of Sir Barnard's grandfather, Edward, whose epitaph is given N^{O}III. Edward Turner, M.A. is recorded as glorying in the bishop's anti-revolution principles.

The bishop's munificence to the chancel is celebrated in a Latin poem, signed Thos. Wright, printed in Chauncy, p.89, dated 1678, two years after the work was done, which the register places in 1676. The bishop hung one of the bells, 1689; Dr. Stillingfleet, dean of St. Paul's, and Dr. Tillotson, another; Dr. Holder, a successor of the bishop, gave another of the five old bells, and added a treble bell (Salmon (p.349) adds a saint's bell), built the loft or gallery in the belfry, 1689, and gave a communion cloth and two prayer books for the desk and table.

William Turner settled in Therfield from Shropshire towards the end of the fifteenth century. He farmed land, Mardlebury, as tenant of the Priors of Royston. William, a husbandman, according to his will, died in 1544. Another branch of the Shropshire family settled in Berkshire. Francis Turner (1637–1700) descended from them through his father Thomas Turner, dean of Canterbury.

Thomas Turner, (c.1512–1608) yeoman, bought the Manor of West Reed (Mardlebury) from William Hyde in 1562. William Turner, grandson of Thomas, sold the Manor to the Willymotts in 1630. The Therfield branch of the Turner family descends thus :-

William	from Shropshire husbandman died 1544	married Joane — 5 children
Thomas	c.1512–1608 yeoman	married Margaret Priest 7 children
Thomas	1542–1627 yeoman	married Agnes Game 8 children
Edward	1590–1677 yeoman	married Mary Fordham 6 children
William	1615–1684 yeoman	married — 3 children
Edward 1	661–1755 gent.	married Ann Sackville 6 children
William	1693–1754 gent.	married Ann — 5 children
Sir Francis Barnard, Kt.	1741–1784	m. 1. Sarah Perry Tillet 2. Lucy Swiney 8 children in all

After being deprived of his Bishopric, Francis Turner retired to Wyddial (not to Therfield, as suggested by the author of this article) to reside with his daughter Margaret and son-in-law Richard Goulston. In 1700 his body was brought to Therfield for burial beside his wife Ann.
In 1731 William Turner (1693–1754) commenced trading in Valenciennes in cambric, lace and linen. Barnard Turner was baptized at St. Nicolas church, Valenciennes, on 14 December 1741. William's factory was at Bapaume, where his eldest son died in 1754 aged 21. Turner and his wife, with their other surviving children returned to England in the year of his death and lived in Cheshunt. William was buried in the family vault at Therfield. [AK]

The church, situate on high ground, nearly in the centre of the village, consists of a nave, separated by three pointed arches supported by clusters of large and small pillars, and clerestory windows over them, from an aisle on each side. In the south wall of the south aisle at the end is a holy water-hole under two pointed arches resting on three round pillars. The chancel, fitted up by Bishop Turner, has a stuccoed roof, with a large oval wreath; the floor paved with stone, and within the rails with marble. On a coffin-fashioned stone on entering the chancel is cut RESURGAM. In a north pillar of the nave is an opening, leading to the rood loft, which, on the rebuilding of the chancel, was succeeded by the King's arms, on which, and their supporters, Mr. T. Wright descants so sweetly in his poem before referred to. Under the opening is a locker, with a door, now locked up. The font is octagon, on an octagon shaft. At the west end of the nave is a good brass figure of a priest (now headless), habited in his pontificals, his robe faced with thistles and small buds alternately, and under him was a very small plate. A blue stone contiguous preserves the cavity of another priestly figure. These may have represented rectors, and been removed from the chancel on rebuilding. Nothing remains in the windows; but the register preserves this inscription, formerly in the east window of the north aisle: "Orate pro a'i'b's D'ni Wi Paston & Agnetis ux'is ejus benefactorum hujus ecclesiæ A.D. 1418," with this remark: "The parish church of Therfield was founded by Sir William Paston and Agnes his wife, in the year of our Lord and Saviour Jesus Christ 1418, as appears by an inscription," &c. Salmon makes the register say he founded the north aisle.

Therfield church was in a bad state of repair in 1874 and was partially rebuilt. Some memorials were relocated. Turner's "beautification of the chancel in 1677" was removed. His stucco ceiling had disintegrated and fallen in 1873. The Royal Arms of Charles II were placed over the south door after the rebuilding. In 1977 they were stolen but later retrieved and replaced. During their absence from the church the authentic colouring was removed and bright non-heraldic colours substituted. Regrettably it has not been possible to restore the accurate colours. The north side aisle chapel built by William and Agnes Paston was demolished in 1874–8 during rebuilding. Agnes Paston (née Berry) had received Horwellbury, a small Kelshall estate, from her father as part of her dowry. She refers to it several times in correspondence. (See The Paston Letters). [AK]

The succession of rectors, as made out in Chauncy, and continued, is as follows:
John Overall, D.D., dean of St. Paul's, died 1619.
William Alabaster, D.D., prebendary of ditto, died 1640.
John Mountford, D.D., another prebendary, who rebuilt great part of

the parsonage house. (Rector of Ansty and Ware, and ejected, 1643, by the parliament, from these and other spiritualities).

John Barwick, LL.D., prebendary of St. Paul's, died 1664.

Francis Turner, D.D., December 20, 1664.

John Standish, D.D.

William Holder, D.D., residentiary of St. Paul's 1672, prebendary of Ely, and subdean of the King's chapel, 1691; died January 24, 1697–98, aged 82, and was buried in the undercroft at St. Paul's.

Thomas Sherlock, D.D., dean of St. Paul's; died 1707, having resigned this rectory in favour of Thomas Sherlock, D.D., his son, master of the Temple, dean of Chichester, bishop of Bangor 1727. He held this rectory in commendam till translated to Sarum 1734, and London 1748; and died 1761.

Henry Etough, M.A., rector almost 23 years, died August 10, 1757, aged 70.

Philip Yonge, D.D., bishop of Norwich 1761, when he resigned this rectory, and was succeeded by Charles Weston, M.A., March 23, 1762, prebendary of Durham, and present rector, 1786.

The Dean and Chapter of St. Paul's are patrons of the rectory, whence it has been usually held by one of their body, except that on the promotion of two of its rectors to bishoprics, the King has presented.

The rectory house, to the southeast of the church, a handsome, uniform, and commodious structure, had been in great part rebuilt by Dr. Mountford; and we are told, in your present volume, p.281 [April 1786], that Mr. Etough laid out £800 on it and its appurtenances; but the present rector rebuilt it a second time, 1777, leaving only a part at the east end, which is of ancient style; and in the kitchen windows are these arms:

In a garter, St. George's cross.

R.S. R.S. joined by a bow-knot.

S. a chevron between 3 towers, A.

On another field the chevron is charged with 3 escallops A.

A. a bend nebulè Az. between 3 crescents, out of which issue as many fleurs de lis S.

Over the parlour chimney-piece is the engraved portrait of Sir Barnard Turner, in a gilt frame, with an inscription, setting forth that it was the gift of the London Military Foot Association.

The Rectory, now the Old Rectory, contains none of the glass. There is no trace of the engraved print of Barnard Turner. [AK]

Over the south door of the chancel is the following epitaph, on a white marble table, the letters vanishing apace:

In memory of
HENRY ETOUGH, M.A.
being 23 years Rector
and faithful Pastor of this parish.
A firm integrity
placed him above fear,
and the strict love of truth
above all dissimulation.

His eager beneficence
was tempered only
by his own abilities
and the indigent merit of others.
He was the warmest friend in private life,
but his ruling passion was
a disinterested love of the public.
With a robust constitution,
thro' a singular habit of body,
he lived many years
without the use of animal food,
or of any fermented liquid,
and died suddenly August 10, 1757,
in the 70th year of his age.

In the register is this entry:- "1757. The Rev. Henry Etough, M.A., Rector of this parish almost 23 years, died August 10, aged 70 years, and was buried August 15, in the chancel of the church, near the door." [See also January and April 1786].

Much of the register during his time is kept in his own hand; the rest by his different curates.

His death is not noticed in your Obituary. We are enabled to add to his other benefactions recited p.281, that he left an annuity of £5 to St. Luke's Hospital, which, being sold to Dr. Plumptree, his executor, at 25 years purchase, produced £125 to that excellent charity. (A Rev. Henry Etough of Catherine Hall, Cambridge, was married to Miss Anderson, February, 1779).

Here is a school. Bishop Turner rebuilt the house, and vested £50 in trust for the master; the indenture was, in 1723, in the hands of Ra. Fordham. The present master is Mr. Thomas Wing.

Edward Shouldham, of Norfolk, LL.D., master of Trinity Hall, Cambridge, rebuilt a fine casting roof of the church, and was buried there 1503. He was of the ancient family of this name, of Shouldham, co. Norfolk, ordained priest by Bishop Barnet, of Ely, April 17, 1473; master of Trinity Hall 1502, where he had been fellow and educated; canon of Exeter 14.., and of Lincoln 1488; rector of Kelshall 14 . . . , and of this place 14. . . . His sister Elizabeth was abbess of Barking.

Bishop Tanner mentions a free chapel or hospital of St. John and St. James, for a master and seven brethren, at Royston, as early as the reign of Henry III. This, in the new edition of Ecton (p.514), is placed in Therfield parish. G.K.

A National School was built beside Therfield village green in 1855–56, and children were transferred to it from the old schoolhouse referred to above. For a time the old building continued as the home of teachers at the National School, but eventually it was sold by the Schoolhouse Trust, and the income was invested to provide educational assistance for village children. [AK]

December 1786. Your correspondent G.K. in your magazine for October, p.832, has my thanks for the epitaphs in Therfield church. That on the late Sir Barnard Turner is pompous enough, and will serve, like most inscriptions of the kind, to deceive posterity. That by Sir Barnard on his first wife is a complete piece of bombastic egotism, and made me laugh very heartily, for I knew the man. G.K. informs us that Sir Barnard's father "was a dealer in foreign spirits at Turnford, in the parish of Cheshunt." This is true, for he kept a public house there; though Sir Barnard always spoke of his father (to strangers) as a merchant in London.

It is generally supposed, that the account of Sir Barnard and his family, published some few years ago in the *Westminster Magazine*, with his head prefixed, was drawn up by himself, or from materials furnished by him; and I think it probable. I have not the book by me, but well remember the vanity of narrative; and that his first wife's father (Tillet) is there called a hair merchant, who was literally a shaver.

The motto of every biographical writer ought to be, TRUTH ABOVE ALL THINGS.

G.K. says, Sir Barnard was born at Turnford, and he may be right; but I heard it asserted, that he was born abroad, and that TURNER was only a translation.

Other familes of Turners lived in the south and east of the county bearing similar Christian names to these Therfield Turners. There are several references in H.R.O. to Barnards—(one a goldsmith, another a spirit dealer), but Hertford Mayor William Turner was a grandson of Thomas, of Therfield (1542–1571). Barnard Turner, M.P. for Southwark, sheriff and alderman of the City of London, has a well-documented career. It is unlikely Barnard Turner wrote the account in Westminster Magazine. His untimely death followed two days after a riding accident. [AK]

October 1786. In addition to the account of Dr. Savage, [October 1783] I send you his epitaph in Clothall church, transcribed from the papers of Dr. Paul Wright.

H.S.E
JOHANNES SAVAGE, S.T.P.
Hujusce parochiæ per 39 annos
Rector non indignissimus,
Qui
Domi male habitus
Ad exteras regiones annis plus octo
Sponte exulavit,
Unde
Totâ fere Europâ perlustratâ
Reversus
Ædes rectorias in formam augustiorem extruxit,
Aream, hortos, horrea, ampliavit, decoravit.
Templum etiam hoc Deo sacrum
Si vires illi sufficerint
Aliquando exornaturus.
Obiit 24to die Martii Anno Salutis Christianæ MDCCXLVII.
Ætatis suæ LXXV.
Et hanc sibi epigraphen
vivens designavit.

From the same papers take the epitaph of another member of the same club, in Westmill church:

Near this Monument
in a family vault are interred the remains of
WILLIAM BENN, Esq.
Alderman of the City of London,
President of Bridewell and Bethlem Hospitals,
Sheriff of the County in the year 1739,
elected Sheriff for the City of London 1742,
and with Dignity and Applause filled the station
of Lord Mayor 1747.
A true Christian, a sincere Friend, an untainted Patriot.
Sensible of his approaching end
He calmly resigned his breath,
In hopes of a joyful resurrection
through the merits of his blessed Saviour,
August the 10th, 1755, aged 53 years.
In regard to whose memory, and as a lasting testimony
Of affection, this monument was erected
by his surviving Brother.

1787. Sheriff. Hertfordshire. J. Roper, Berkhamsted St. Peter.

25 March 1787. A fire broke out in the stables of the Bell Inn at
Hertford, which destroyed them, with four horses; and the house was
with difficulty saved.

17 April 1787. This day a great boxing-match was fought on Barnet-
course between Mendoza, a Jew, and one Martin, a Bath butcher, on
which bets to a great amount depended; and was, after about half an
hour's fair boxing, decided in favour of the Jew. There were many thousand spectators, and among them some of the first personages of the
kingdom.

*Mendoza the Jew and Martin the Bath Butcher were well-known prize fighters.
'Barnet-course' would be the race course on Barnet Common. [GJ]*

June 1787. I send you some corrections of Mr. Kearsley's Supplement to
the *Tour through Great Britain,* just published; in which I do but fulfil
the wishes of that public-spirited editor, who exerts his utmost to give
us as much information in as little compass as possible, whether in Tax-
tables, or the Beauties of England. . .
Hertfordshire. *Pishobury,* pulled down, and rebuilt by Mr. Milles,
who married the heiress of Gardener. *Gorhambury,* pulled down, and
rebuilt by the present lord, though Mr. Walpole praised his father's
taste for letting it stand. *More Park,* if not pulled down, neglected.
Pendley Lodge, let to any tenant that will take it. *Wotton, Wotton Park,*
one and the same. The venerable mansion and estate of the Botelers for
centuries, sold to a Nabob, who pulled down what the fire spared, and
built a costly modern house in a new and more exalted situation.
Hunsdon House, not at all remarkable, and but a small part of the original mansion. *Hatfield,* restored to its primitive splendour. *Hertford
Castle,* rebuilt at great expense with little taste. *Balls,* improved in
some respects, in others not. . . . . . P.B.

GENERAL AUGUSTIN PREVOST, EAST BARNET

July 1787. As no account of the late General Prevost has appeared in your valuable Repository, you are requested to insert the following inscription on a neat monument erected to his memory in the churchyard at East Barnet, Hertfordshire.

"SACRED to the memory of Augustin Prevost, Esquire, major-general in his Majesty's army, colonel of the 2nd battalion of the 60th regiment of foot, &c &c. by birth a native and citizen of Geneva. He entered the service of Great Britain in 1756, in the rank of major, and uniformly distinguishing himself with the zeal and honour of a true soldier, he merited, and on repeated occasions received, the thanks, both public and private, of the generals under whom he served. He finished his more active military career with the memorable defence of Savannah in Georgia in 1779, where he commanded, and, in a post intrenched merely on the spur of the occasion, sustained a formal siege against the combined armies, French and American, commanded by the Count D'Estaing, of above three times his own number, supported by a powerful fleet, and furnished with a numerous and well-served artillery: he repulsed them in a general and well-maintained assault; and finally compelled them to raise the siege, thirty-three days from his being closely invested, twenty-six of open trenches, and fifteen of open batteries. As a man, he was mild, unassuming, and modest, perhaps approaching to a fault; as a soldier, manly, firm, determined, possessing himself equally in the hour of danger as in that of calmest retirement. His solicitude on every occasion of public import was solely directed to the honourable discharge of his duty to the King and country he had chosen for his. A kind husband, a tender father, a sincere friend. He was also eminent in all the virtues and in all the duties of private life. He died May 4, 1786, aged 63.

This monument is erected by the companion of some of his most trying scenes, now his afflicted widow, in pious and affectionate testimony of her gratitude to him, who was the best of husbands, and the best of men."

September 1787. To your account of General Prevost's monument, add: At the West end are his arms ——— A. a hand holding a dagger, hilted, Or, issuing out of a cloud proper; in chief, 2 mullets, Or; impaling, G. 2 chevrons A. on a pale A. the sun Or; crest, on a helmet the hand and sword; over the shield, A.P.; under it, "Ob. May 4, 1786, aged 83. [This age at death was wrongly copied by G.M. It should be 63.]". The slab of the tomb rests on four clustered columns, and covers the inscription on a table on the North side, the South side being plain. The whole was executed by Mr. Bacon.

---

9 August 1787. The most alarming and general display of lightning, though not rendered awful alike in all places with thunder, spread a terror over the whole metropolis ... At St. Albans [this] storm was attended with such a shower of hail and rain as no man alive ever remembered in that part of the country. The hail stones were as big as moderate-sized peas. . . .

September 1787.
In East Barnet church-yard:

M.S.
of John Berry,
a faithful servant
to Mr. Richardson's family
at Mount Pleasant.
He died Dec. 6, 1773,
aged 73 years.

Here lies old John, who in licentious days
Dar'd to be faithfull and to merit praise;
Cheerfull in duty, obstinately just;
Stop, reader, then, and mark this servant's dust.

Mount Pleasant, a former East Barnet estate earlier known as Belmont, was once the seat of Elias Ashmole, founder of the Ashmolean Museum. [GJ]

5 January 1788. In the evening, as the St. Ives waggon was passing over Ware bridge, just as the horses were over, some of the planks gave way, and let in the waggon. Fortunately the pole-pin breaking in the instant disengaged the horses, and the waggon with contents was received into an empty barge under the bridge, all recovered, except the hind wheels, which flew off and sunk in the river, whence they were not got out till some time after. The bridge was new-built of timber not above 25 years ago.

16 January 1788. Hertford. One Judd, a substantial farmer of Stocking Pelham, in this neighbourhood, has lately been apprehended, on the oath of his plowman, for hiring, inciting, and encouraging him and others, to set the barns, out-houses, and premises of Mr. Sworder, of Stocking Pelham, on fire, by which his whole year's crop was consumed, and much other damages sustained. The incendiary, during the late snow, was providentially discovered by the impression of two rows of nails on one shoe, and only one row on the other. He resolutely persisted in his innocence till the discovery of this singular circumstance, when he confessed the fact, and charged the farmer above-mentioned as his abettor. The public opinion of the county is much divided respecting his guilt or innocence. Judd, till lately, held a farm of Mr. Calvert, the lease of which expiring some time ago, that gentleman refused to renew it at the old rent, and it was let to Mr. Sworder, who agreed to give more. This person, ever since he took possession, has been harrassed every possible way. His house has been beset in the dead of night; his barns and stacks set on fire thrice; and lesser mischiefs daily. Judd was carried before William Plomer, Esq., who committed him to the custody of a constable in his own house, till the quarter sessions, three weeks after, when he was fully committed to Hertford gaol, and £10,000 bail refused.

THE SPRING AT AKERLEY HOLE,
HERTINGFORDBURY

March 1788. In the parish of Hertingfordbury, about two miles from Essendon in Hertfordshire, is a spring of water, known by the name of Aquatile-hole, vulgo, Akerley Hole, now in the tenure or occupation of Samuel Whitbread, Esq., of the most copious or singular nature in the island, supposed to deliver a quantity of water at the mouth or opening sufficient for the discharge of a pipe of the bore of three feet and a half in diameter. This spring arises within 100 yards of the river Lea, into which it disembogues; and, in that short space, actually furnishes a greater quantity of water than what is contained in the river itself, which is well known to take the aggregate springs from Leagrove Marsh, near Dunstable, in Bedfordshire, to that place. What most astonishes me is, that none of your historians, geographers, or noters of antiquity, have noticed this extraordinary natural curiosity, or that none of the mechanical geniuses of the present day, considering its contiguity to the metropolis, and considering its unbounded ability, should not have thought it, long ere this, an object of serious attention and experiment.

For the contemplation of the curious, however, and of the Antiquary in particular, this communication is meant; and, if noticed by the mechanic, so much the better; not but that I could wish that some of your valuable and intelligent readers, whose time may be more their own than mine, and whose inclination is constantly tending towards the information and benefit of mankind, would favour the public with the exact quantity of water issuing therefrom; and, at a future period, with a comparative table of the productions of other large springs throughout the kingdom; and, if it were not too arduous an undertaking, with the quality as well as quantity of each. J.B.

The spring which is referred to above as Akerley Hole is marked as Arkley Hole on the 6″ Ordnance Survey map. It is situated at Grid Reference TL 28981004, about half-a-mile southeast of Letty Green. The present status of the spring is not known, but no current or recent use is recorded. The area is underlain by Upper Chalk with recent drift cover consisting mainly of Glacial Gravel. Alluvium covers the gravel along the path of the River Lee and Boulder Clay overlies them on the valley sides. It is from the gravels that the springs emerge. [NRA]

CROMWELL LETTERS TO COLONEL COX OF ST.
ALBANS

April 1788. Observing in your valuable magazine for March a copy of an original letter of the Protector Cromwell; it has induced me to submit one from the original in my possession. T.C.

Note that the two letters which follow were published in consecutive issues of G.M., but because of the incorrect date on the second letter they appeared in reverse chronological order.

For Colonell Cox*, Captain of the Militia troop in our county of Hertford. These. For our special service.

To be left with the Post M'r of St. Albans—to be speedily sent.

Sir,

By our last letters to you, we acquainted you what danger the commonwealth was then in from the old cavalier party, who were designing new insurrections within us, while their head and master was contriving to invade us from abroad, and thereupon desired your care and vigilancy for preserving the peace and apprehending all dangerous persons. Our intelligence of that kind still continues, and we are more assured of their resolutions to put in execution their designs aforesaid within a very short time, being much encouraged from some late actings of some turbulent and unquiet spirits, as well in this town as elsewhere. . . .

Judging these things to have in them very dangerous consequences to the peace of this nation . . . we thought it of absolute necessity to dissolve the present Parliament, which I have done this day, and to give you notice thereof that you, with your troop, may be most vigilant for the suppressing of any disturbance which may arise from any party whatsoever. . . . And we do further let you know that we are sensible of your want of pay for yourself and troop, and do assure you that effectual care shall be taken therein, and that without delay; and I rest, your loving friend,

Oliver P.

Whitehall, February 4th, 1657.

*Colonel Cox then lived at Beaumont's, a farm little more than a mile from St. Albans. [Editor, G.M.]

May 1788. ORIGINAL Letter from O. CROMWELL.

Whitehall, 24 April, 1665. [sic; should probably be 1655 or 1656]
For Colonel Alban Cox in Hertfordshire.

Sir,

Haveing occasion to speak with you upon some affairs relating to the publique, I would have you, as soone as this comes to your hands, to repair up hither; and upon your comeing you shall be acquainted with the particular reasons of my sending for you. I rest your loveinge friend, OLIVER P.

Colonel Alban Cox(e) was living at Beamonds in 1634. Given custody of the King's Stables at St. Albans in 1636. Ordered to train the St. Albans Volunteer troop of horse in July 1642. Member of a variety of local committees during and after the Civil War. Became commander of the county volunteer horse which was used to defend the county against incursions by the royalists. Helped round up Royalists in south Bedfordshire after Naseby. Sided with the army under Fairfax & Cromwell against the more conservative Parliamentarians in 1647. Appeared to gain more influence after Pride's Purge as became a local JP in 1649. Though Cox was appointed Governor of Guernsey he returned after a few months and in May 1650 was sent with troops raised in Hertfordshire to help Cromwell defeat the Scots. By January 1652 he was back in St. Albans appointing a Treasurer for the Assessment Committee and quarrelling with the local Chairman Dr. John King. He served the Republic as JP for the Liberty of St.

Albans. After the dissolution of the Rump he was used by Cromwell to regulate local religious affairs and was returned as MP for St. Albans in the first Protectorate Parliament. He served on the Parliamentary Committees for Scotland and Ireland and was a militia commissioner and then Colonel of the new Militia under the Deputy Major General William Packer in 1655–56.

Assuming that the second extract should be dated 24 April 1655 and not 1665, the following would be the immediate background.
1. Cromwell had dismissed the first Protectorate Parliament on 22 January 1655.
2. March 1655 was the height of Penruddock's royalist rising.
3. August 1655. Major Generals appointed and sent instructions.
This would probably mean that Cox was being summoned to Whitehall to discuss the immediate military problems following Penruddock's rising, but before the appointment of the Major Generals. Given that the Major General experiment was ended in January 1657, it was probably again, either interim military arrangements that were being discussed in February in the other letter to Cox, or problems in the second Protectorate Parliament, but given the letter was sent to him specifically as captain of militia, I would assume the former.

Cox was elected for St. Albans to the second Protectorate Parliament in September 1656 but the election was contested by his defeated opponent Richard Jennings, who petitioned the committee for elections, accusing Cox of using force to prevent his supporters from voting. The petition failed and Cox sat on a number of Parliamentary Committees supporting Cromwell's position when he refused the Crown and opposing the idea of creating a House of Lords. Cox continued to sit as a JP locally and was returned to Richard Cromwell's Parliament. However with the restoration of the Rump, Cox was replaced as commander of the militia and bound over on two sureties of £1000. He petitioned General Monck for a full and free Parliament, and though defeated in the elections to the Convention, produced his own poll in an unsuccessful attempt to overturn the result. After 1660 he faded from the political scene and no longer held any political or military office. [AT]

19 May 1788. Was held at Enfield church, by the Lord Bishop of London, a confirmation for that and the adjoining parishes of Edmonton, Hadley and South Mimms, when upwards of 300 persons of both sexes were confirmed. This commences the general confirmation throughout London.

July 1788. Civil Promotion. William Hart, gentleman of Hemel Hempstead, Hertfordshire, and Marmaduke Prickett, jun., Esq., of Bridlington, Yorkshire, appointed masters extraordinary in the Court of Chancery.

July 1788. Dispensation. Rev. Thelwall Salusbury, LL.B., rector of Gravely with Chivesfield, Hertfordshire, to hold Weston vicarage in the same county.

September 1788. The enclosed impression is taken from a brass seal ploughed up, about a year ago, in a field about two miles from Puckeridge in Hertfordshire. I should be glad if you could favour me with an explanation of it. S.R.

The position of this small engraving, close to the spine of the tightly bound volume of the Gentleman's Magazine, makes reproduction here impossible. It shows, however, a small oval medallion bearing (obv.) a crudely drawn profile of King Charles I, with the words: 'Gloria Angl. Emigravit: — Ja. the 30 1648: Gloria

Vanitas'; and (rev.) a skull between two crowns, between the words (left and right) 'Gloria Vanitas'. The medallion, with its message 'The Glory of England has departed: Fickle Glory', commemorates the execution of Charles I on 30 January 1648/9. [AJ]

PROPOSAL FOR A BISHOP'S STORTFORD— CAMBRIDGE CANAL

11 September 1788. At a meeting of the committee for improving the navigation of the river Thames, Mr. Alderman Clarke reported the resolution of a meeting of the noblemen, gentlemen and other freeholders of the counties of Hertfordshire, Essex, Cambridge, and Huntingdon, and the Isle of Ely, at Great Chesterford, on the 5th instant, when it was resolved, That an extension of the navigation to Bishop Stortford into the Cambridge river will be of great public utility, that such extension will be beneficial in a still greater degree, by empowering commissioners to cleanse the Old Ouze from Hermitage sluice to the junction of the Granta or Cambridge river; that it is the opinion of this committee, that it will tend more to the public utility, if, in the execution, the navigation is carried to the town of Saffron Walden, than if carried west of Audley End House, as proposed by the plan taken by order of the commissioners of the city of London for the Thames navigation and canal; and that they be requested to order a fresh survey of that part of Essex, necessary to explain the line of carrying it without injury to the proprietors of the land through which it is to pass, &c.

A survey of the line of the proposed canal was carried out by John Rennie in 1789, but this route was opposed by Lord Howard of Audley End as detrimental to his property, and many other local landowners voiced their opposition and the scheme was dropped. In 1811, another line was surveyed by John Rennie, which would have involved the building of reservoirs and two tunnels in the Saffron Walden area at the cost of £870,000. In 1812, an Act of Parliament was passed authorising the work, but the amount to be raised before work started, £425,000, was not found and once again the scheme did not materialize, and it was never revived.
Observations on the Prospectus of the London to Cambridge Canal *(Printed B. Flower, Harlow) asks* "Would not an Iron Railway suffice?" *[WW]*

16 December 1788. By the violence of the frost, the New River was so frozen over, without snow, that the water obstructed by the ice in the common fields on the west of Broxbourne overflowed the high road, to the great obstruction and danger of travellers, and some horses were thrown down and killed; but a number of men being employed in the removal of the ice, the river was restored to its bed, which it had overflowed in several other places.

January 1789. Sheriff. Hertfordshire. Drummond Smith of Tring Park, Esq.

January 1789. The Traveller's Companion, or New Itinerary of England

and Wales, with Part of Scotland, arranged in the Manner of Copper Plates; being an accurate and complete View of the principal Roads in Great Britain, taken from Actual Surveys, wherein every Object worthy of Notice is pointed out; illustrated by Two Maps. To which are annexed, the Circuits of the Judges, the Ports from whence the Packets sail, and a copious Index, where the Market Days of each Town are particularised. By Thomas Pride and Philip Luckombe.

It passes our comprehension how authors or booksellers, after such professions, can obtrude such incorrect and erroneous works on the public;- for such we are authorised, from our own knowledge, to call this Traveller's Companion. We have owners of houses whom we know to have been dead above twenty years, and living ones mis-named, just as they were set down in surveys by foreigners. Thus, in p.112, . . . At Bayfordbury we find Sir. W. Baker. At Cheshunt, Mr. Ashforby . . . , Mr. Tottenham for Tatnall. At Cheshunt Priory, Mr. Jenson, for Jansen . . . , Amwellbury never was Mr. Lake's . . . , Thunbridge is Thundridge. . . . Ayot St. Lawrence are not two distinct places. If such errors abound near London, what must we apprehend at a distance?

EPITAPHS IN WARE CHURCH

July 1789.

To the valued memory of
CATHERINE wife of RICHARD CHANDLER,
bookseller of London and York,
whose remains are deposited under the white
pavement in this aile, opposite the overseers' pew,
next two of her children, who died in their
infancy, and are buried near her husband's
father and several of his family.
She departed this life, with the greatest
resignation to the divine providence, agreeable
to her life and conversation, 22 January 1742,
in the 25th year of her age,
and 7th of her marriage-state, leaving
one daughter, Judith, aged 4 years.
She left this transitory life with the lasting
character of a most valuable woman, and
was a pattern truly worthy of the imitation of her sex.
In memory of the many virtues she possessed,
which are very rarely centered in one person,
this tablet was erected by her husband.

The memorial to Catherine Chandler still exists above the north door of the church, leading now to the extension. The transcript omits "after three days of illness" after the date of her death, which probably indicates that Mrs. Chandler died in one of the numerous outbreaks of the smallpox which occurred in the 1740s and 1750s. [DP]

In the Church-yard.

William Lester, 34 years pastor of a church
of Baptist Dissenters in this town,
March 16, 1778, aged 62.

William Mead*, M.D., October 28, 1652.
aged 148 years and 9 months.

Ralph Grindal, M.D., January 6, 1740, aged 67.

George Harris, of Winchmore Hill, in the
parish of Edmonton, October 30, 1771, aged 61.

*see August 1779 and May 1781.

October 1789. Your epitaphs from Ware churchyard, I should suspect,
are incorrectly copied. Mr. Lister, not Lester, was certainly pastor of a
congregation of Dissenters, but not of the Baptist denomination. It is
scarcely likely his relations or friends would record a fact untruly on his
tomb. He was father to Dr. William Lister, a young physician of some
eminence, now practising in the metropolis.

Ralph Grindall, M.D., I presume to be the father of a gentleman long
known and distinguished for his abilities in this city, Richard Grindal,
Esq., of Austin Friars . . . .

*LISTER. The Ware register records the burial of William Lister on March 23rd
1778. The gravestone has now been removed to the edge of the churchyard. There
is no evidence that the Rev. William Lister or his son, Dr. William Lister, were
related to the family of Lord Lister (1827–1912) who introduced antisepsis into
surgery. [DP]*

October 1789. I send you the following epitaph just put upon an altar-
tomb over the late Dr. King, of Wormley.

Here lie the remains
of the reverend
JOHN GLEN KING, D.D.
late rector of this parish.
He died the 2d of November, 1787,
in the 56th year of his age.
He married, first, Anne Magdalene,
daughter of Michael Combrune, Esq.,
by whom he had
one daughter, Anne Henrietta.
He married, secondly,
Jane, daughter of John Hyde, Esq.

November 1789. In a late excursion into Bedfordshire, a little way from
Welling [Welwyn], I was struck with a beautiful appearance of a new-
built church. It is situated at Ayot St. Lawrence, in Hertfordshire: the
church I found to be a new erection, a model of ancient architecture, at
the sole expense of Sir Lyonel Lyde, Bart., by that eminent architect,

and great antiquary, Mr. Nichol Revett, who, forty years ago, travelled into Greece, and Asia Minor, with Messrs. Wood, Stuart, and Dawkins, and afterwards with Dr. Chandler, at the expense of the Dilettanti Society. The effects of his labours and researches will for ever remain monuments of his memory and talents as an artist, whilst those noble publications of Palmyra, Balbeck and the Ionian antiquities, are admitted into the cabinets of the curious. I am happy to acquaint the world, that Mr. Revett is still living, and constantly enlivens a small select circle of friends with his lively conversation. I.R.

NICOLAVS REVETT, Suffolciensis,
Qui plurimos annos
Romæ, Athenis, et Smyrnæ commoratus,
Hanc ecclesiam,
Ad antiquæ architecturæ exemplaria
Quæ in Græcia, atque Asia Minori,
Adhuc visuntur,
Designavit, extruxit, decoravit;
Hoc monumentum posuit
Sumptibus
LYONELLI LYDE, Baronetti.
MDCCLXXXVIII.

January 1790. Sheriff. Hertfordshire. S. R. Gaussen, of North Mimms, Esq.

9 January 1790. The wind blowing extremely hard, a fire broke out at six in the morning at Waterford Mill, near Hertford, which in a short time consumed the whole, with the dwelling house adjoining, in which only two workmen slept. It is supposed to have been occasioned by some neglect of greasing the mill wheels, which were left early the preceding evening. The whole was insured by Mr. Hickman the owner, but not to the full value, a large sum having been expended in repairs not long before.

14 January 1790. Mr. Bentley, grocer of Hertford, riding to London about five in the morning, with a considerable sum of money, which, the night before, he had been overheard to boast he would defend against any man, was attacked, on the edge of Hertford Heath next Hoddesdon, by a single footpad, whom he knocked down. A second fired a pistol, which frightened his horse so that he reared up and threw him, and ran home. Mr. Bentley being now left at the mercy of three villains, was robbed of eighty pounds in banknotes and fifty in cash; and, after beating him with some violence, they made off across the heath. Three men were afterwards apprehended at a public-house on Cheshunt Common; but Mr. Bentley not being able to swear to them, they were detained for other offences, and have impeached a large gang.

April 1790. The following circumstance may be depended on as a fact. A gentleman, who had missed his road a few days ago near Hoddesdon, in

Hertfordshire, made up to a cottage to get directions. Here, with an old ballad stuck against a broken pane in the window was a banknote for £20 which, as the aged couple belonging to the place could neither read nor write, was only looked upon as an ornament, &c. It appeared that this, with another which had been lost, was found in the lining of a pair of breeches, which belonged to a stranger who died about two years since at an inn in that neighbourhood, and which had been given to the cottager by the landlord, on account of his acting as a bearer to the corpse.

June 1790. Civil Promotion. Rt. Hon. James Bucknell Grimston, Viscount Grimston, created Baron Verulam of Gorhambury, Hertfordshire.

June 1790. In your obituary, [May, 1790] is recorded the death of "Mrs. Hallows, aged upwards of 80, many years housekeeper to the late celebrated Dr. Young, author of the Night Thoughts, &c." Now, if Mrs. Hallows really was the housekeeper of Dr.Young many years, how erroneous was the information which Mr. Herbert Croft so morally laments he received in his life of that poet! His words are these: "Of the domestic manners and petty habits of the author of the Night Thoughts, I hoped to have given you [Dr. Johnson] an account from the best authority; but who shall dare to say, tomorrow I will be wise or virtuous, or tomorrow I will do a particular thing? Upon enquiring for his housekeeper [1780], I learned that she was buried two days before I reached the town of her abode." I congratulate Mr. Croft upon the veracity of his intelligence; but equally condole with him that he could not obtain what he so ardently desired. This will probably teach him, if the experience has not taught him already, the vanity of depending too minutely on transitory report; and that, in literary cases in particular, that information may for the most be doubted which is not local or evident.

THE HALLOWES FAMILY OF HERTFORD

July 1790. The mention of the death of Mrs. Hallowes, Dr. Young's housekeeper, in your obituary for May last, p.476, and the rap of Mr. H. Croft's knuckles, in the following month, p.520, induce me to trouble you with an epitaph on the frame of a north window in the choir of the church of All Saints, Hertford, commemorating that lady's father:

"DANIEL HALLOWES,
Rector 40 years,
October 6, 1741, æt. 71."

"Prope in cœmiterio,
Spe lætæ resurrectionis in Christus,
dormit
DANIEL HALLOWES,
hujus ecclesiæ per 40 annos

rector indignus.
Obiit 6 die Octobris, anno æt. 71,
A.D. 1741.
Dawn, glorious day, when Christ shall say,
Awake, and be new-drest.
Resume thy spirit, and for my merit,
Be thou entirely blest.
This inscription was by his own appointment."

Over Mr. Hallowes' grave, in the churchyard, at the northeast corner of the chancel, is a slab thus inscribed:

The remains of
DANIEL HALLOWES,
40 years vicar of this parish,
were here buried the 10th day of
October, 1741.
Anna Hallowes, relict
of the above Daniel
Hallowes, was buried
. the 16th day of February, 1777.
Their hope was in Christ.
"I will ransom them from the power of
the grave: I will redeem them from death."
Hosea [xiii.14.]
"Believe, and look with triumph on the
grave." YOUNG.

This stone is fenced with a cradle of iron rails; and close to it, on the north, is the turf grave of their daughter, the late housekeeper to Dr. Young, who ended her life on a small sufficiency, which barely paid for her board, at a house in Castle Street, Hertford.

Mrs. Hallowes was dead to all Mr. Croft's poses of enquiry, for her mental faculties were deranged some time before her decease.

Against the east wall of the church, without, is a head-stone for (it is presumed her brother) Mr. John Hallowes, who died May 2, 1787; and Letitia, his wife, who died December 15, 1781, aged 66. D.H.

The burial of Mary 'Hollows' Spinster on 25 April 1790 is recorded in the burial register of All Saints' Hertford (Hertfordshire Record Office D/P48/1/25) and her gravestone (as transcribed by L.Turnor in his History of the Ancient Town and Borough of Hertford (1830), p.226) read: 'In memory of Mary Hallowes, daughter of the Rev. Daniel Hallowes, who died 20th April 1790 aged 80 years'. Mary Hallowes' father, Daniel, was vicar of All Saints' church from 1701 (he was instituted on 16 July 1701) until his death in 1741. Turnor (pp.197 and 215) records both the window frame and monumental inscriptions, with slightly different (and almost certainly more accurately copied) wording from that in the G.M. He also records (p.226), again more accurately, the monumental inscriptions for John and Letitia Hallowes: John Hallowes actually died on 3 May 1757, and was buried on 7 May; in the All Saints' burial register (D/P48/1/25) he is described as 'Upholsterer from London'. His wife Letitia died on 13 December 1781. Turnor also records (pp.226–227) the monumental inscriptions for two other daughters of Daniel Hallowes, Frances Heath, died 1753, and Susanna Russell, died 1777. [GS]

CHESHUNT EPITAPHS

July 1790. If the enclosed epitaphs, collected from Cheshunt church-yard, by a traveller, while his dinner was dressing, will entertain your readers, or correct your obituary, they are at your service. [For first epitaph, see also February 1785].

In memory of
Mr. EDMUND SOUTH*
who departed this life
January 11, 1784, aged 66 years.
Where thoughts of guilt invade the troubled breast,
The spirit's wounded, and farewell to rest.
But he—his life of innocence so led,
That peace in sickness made an easy bed.
Art thou an husband—to thy partner yield,
As he—Love's tribute by Affection seal'd.
Art thou a parent—to thy children show
A love like his—a debt which parents owe.
Art thou a Christian—learn of him to blend
Sound faith, good deeds, and manners to the end.
Also Mr. EDMUND SOUTH,
son of the above,
who departed this life
January 21, 1779, aged 27 years.

*An eminent dancing master. [Editor, G.M.]

On an altar tomb:

In memory of
GEORGE BARNE, Esq.,
who departed this life March 14, 1780,
aged 67.
Here humble Barne, rejoin'd to kindred clay,
Sleeps but to wake in Heaven's eternal day.
Manners so simple, morals so refin'd
Such warm affections, with so meek a mind,
Faith so well founded, Hope by Joy confest,
And Charity by Bounty so exprest,
Through life attendant to his latest breath,
Forc'd Truth with tears to tell it at his death.

In memory of
JAMES CRAIG, Esq.,
who departed this life the 20th
of April, 1789, aged 64 years.

In memory of
Mrs. MARY STOW, widow,
who died 12th March, 1788,
aged 82 years.

On a head-stone:

Sacred
to the memory of
the Rev. THOMAS GRIFFIN, B.D.
who died March 24, 1788, aged 32.

ELEANOR LANG, died June 13, 1785, aged
13 years. WILLIAM, her brother, died 13th
January, 1786, aged 2 years. MARY, their
sister, died 31 January, 1788, aged 13.
Weep not for us, parents dear,
We are not dead, but sleeping here.
Our debts are paid; our graves you see;
Therefore prepare to follow we.

On an altar tomb, supporting a pyramid, with urns at the four corners,
and on it a chevron between three owls, impaling paly of six on a bend
three etoiles: Here lyeth the body of MARY PRESCOTT, daughter of
GEORGE PRESCOTT. Esq., and MARY his wife, of Theobalds Park, in
this parish, who departed this life the 2nd of November, 1775, in the
20th year of her age.

On an altar tomb:
Beneath
are deposited the remains
of
ELIZABETH, daughter of JOHN FIELD,
citizen and apothecary of London,
who died December 9, 1781,
aged 23 years.

Arms, a chevron engrailed between three gerbes, impaling a lion rampant.

Here lieth the body of
SARAH ETHERINGHAM, widow,
who died March 3, 1786,
in the 75th year of her age.
Upwards of 50 years of her life
were spent with the friends
who erect this stone in memory of,
and in gratitude for,
her faithful
and affectionate service.
He that is faithful in that which is least, is
faithful also in much.

To the memory of
PHEBE WALLIS,
who departed this life
December 18, 1778, aged 2 years and 2 months.
Why should we mourn thy quick remove,
And overlook thy gain,
Stranger to all the ills we prove,
As conflicts, trials, pain ?
While terror reigns, and wild dismay,
When Judgment shall descend,
What crowds will wish their mortal day
Had found as quick an end!

In memory of
Mr. JOHN MORRICE,
who died February 13, 1788,
aged 49 years.

In memory of
Mr. JOHN COOKE,
cooper and citizen of London.
He died 3 March, 1785,
aged 75 years.

Here are to lie the remains of
THOMAS and REBECCA PALMER,
who endeavoured so to live as to obtain
a happy resurrection.
He died the 31st day of August, 1789,
aged 83 years.
She died the 18th day of May, 1782,
aged 76 years.

Within this church lies the body of
Mrs. SARAH PALMER,
their only daughter,
who lived beloved, and died lamented.
Sincere in her piety to God and charity to the
poor, dutiful to her parents, and most
affectionate to her brothers. She died in
April 1766, in the 34th year of her age.
Be ready, the present time is only yours.

Here lieth the remains of
Mr. JOHN BUSH,
of Oxford, who died
27 November, 1783, aged 42.
Now troubles cease, now earthly joys are fled,
Now cease to mourn, ye sorrowers for the dead.
To heavenly joys behold his soul aspires,
And mingles with the blest immortal choirs.

On the base of a pyramid, on which is a saltire engrailed, charged
with a shield of pretence, in an orle of cinquefoils; crest, a muzzled bear:
and by the lower side of this coat the escutcheon of pretence single, and
the saltire engrailed, impaling a pelican vulning herself.

On the east side:

In a vault under this monument
is deposited all that is mortal
of JOHN ASHFORDBY, Esq.,
late of this parish,
who died February 25, 1747,
aged 70 years.
As an instance of the regard and esteem
he bears to the memory of
the best of fathers,
JOHN ASHFORDBY his son
erected this monument.

On the north side:

Also here lies deposited
all that is mortal of
Mrs. FRANCES ASHFORDBY,

relict of JOHN ASHFORDBY, Esq.,
who died 16 April 1774,
aged 86 years.

On the west side:

Also near this place is interred
MARY ASHFORDBY, first wife
of the said JOHN ASHFORDBY,
who died 17 April 1717, aged 39 years.
Also two children by his last
wife, FRANCES ASHFORDBY,
who both died in their infancy.

On the south side:

In memory of the late
JOHN ASHFORDBY, Esq., whose
exemplary, wise, and amiable qualities
did honour to his posterity. He was
a dutiful son, an affectionate husband,
a tender parent, and a sincere friend
he departed this life September 30, 1778,
aged 52 years.

JOHN CARTIER, Esq., died January 25, 1774,
aged 89 years.
MARY his wife, died June 21, 1782,
aged 86 years.

In this vault are interred
the body of Mrs. MARY CHOLMLEY†
who died 30 July, 1764,
aged 76 years.
Also her daughter MARY, the wife of
WILLIAM TATNALL,
of Theobalds, who died 17 March, 1771,
aged 68 years.
Likewise WILLIAM TATNALL,
the husband of the said MARY,
who died November 21, 1785, aged 75 years.

†She was aunt to the late John Howard, Esq.

Here rests all that was mortal
of the late reverend, learned, and pious
JOHN MASON, M.A.*
who was minister of the congregation of
Protestant Dissenters in this parish 17 years.
He ceased from his labours, and was called to
receive his reward, February the 10th, 1763,
aged 58 years.
"Be followers of them who through faith
and patience inherit the promises."
And MARY his wife died the 8th of May,
1771; aged 72.

*Author of *Self Knowledge, the Lord's Day Evening Entertainment*, a set of practical sermons, in six or eight volumes, and other excellent works.

John Mason was pastor of Crossbrook Street Chapel. [JE]

On wood:

WILLIAM WILLIAMS, died September 24, 1782,
aged 21 years.
In silence here beneath a youth is laid,
By whom the sports of Nature were survey'd;
With ravish'd breast o'er mead he did pursue
The startled hare which o'er the landskip flew;
Plung'd in the stream which Nature thought so sweet.
But soon the stream a change to Nature gave,
And plung'd this youth deep in the silent grave.
URSULA, daughter of RICHARD and URSULA
BRETT, died June 30, 1777, aged 12 years.
The life of youth may well compared be
Unto the blossoms of a fruitful tree,
That one day seems both pleasant, fine, and gay,
And on the morrow fades and dies away.
So did this youth drop in the midst of bloom,
Her day was short, her sun was set at noon.
ANN, her sister, died June 3, 1780,
aged 3 years and 7 weeks.
Sweet babe, adieu! short was thy stay,
Just look'd about, and call'd away.
RICHARD (their father) died July 5, 1783,
aged 49 years.

SARAH JONES. wife of THOMAS JONES,
of Enfield, Middlesex, gent. and daughter of
Mr. PHINEAS PATISHULL,
who died 21 June, 1785, aged 34.
She lived beloved, and died lamented.

JOSEPH PATISHUL, of Leominster,
Herefordshire, died May 3, 1764, aged 76.

PHINEHAS (sic) PATISHUL, his son, of Fenchurch
Street, London, died 31 December, 1771,
aged 56 years.

Mrs. SARAH LINDOE,
wife of Mr. DAVID LINDOE,
died January 31, 1789, aged 23 years.

Against the north wall of the church:

In memory of
Mrs. KATHARINE YOUNG,
who departed this life January 13,
1743, aged 54 years.
She lived by faith, and died in hope.
Also, the body of JOSHUA YOUNG, M.D.
who departed this life the 30th of September, 1755,
aged 55 years.

July 1790. On a robin red-breast being found in the gaol chapel at Hertford, June 27.

> Ah, gentle stranger! take thy flight
> From these dreary mansions, where the light
> But dimly penetrates the gloom,
> Faint image of our future tomb!
> Say, why so musical thy throat ?
> Why lengthen thus thy cheerful note,
> Mid horrors wild, the prison's light,
> Where wretches, doom'd t'eternal night,
> Rattle their adamantine chains,
> Corroding links, corroding pains!

[Nineteen more lines]   J. Moore, Ordinary.

September 1790. I send you a drawing of an ancient gold ring, lately in the possession of Mr. Wilson, one of the clerks of the New River Company, who died at Cheshunt this summer, at the house of a friend who had the ring in his possession as executor, together with the included illustration of it, in a letter from the late Mr. J. White of Newgate Street. D.H.

KNEBWORTH HOUSE

November 1790. Having lately had an opportunity of seeing the ancient mansion of the Lytton family at Knebworth, near Stevenage, in Hertfordshire, your topographical readers may not be displeased with some account of it.

It stands about a mile out of the road from Stevenage to London, two miles from Stevenage, and four from Welwyn, and about thirty from London, on a lofty hill at the southwestern extremity of an extensive and woody park, commanding from its east front a beautiful view of richly timbered and cultivated hills.

It is a large structure, built of brick, round a quadrangle, of which the east front may be seen in Sir H. Chauncy's *History of Hertfordshire*, p.352. The approach to it is by iron gates in a court walled round, corresponding with an arched gateway in the centre of a part of the front, sided by imitations of embattled towers, from which extend two unequal wings. The north side is partly formed by a colonnade of seven light round arches on pillars, opening to a garden, and supporting a gallery 76 feet long by 14 wide, floored with oak, and as many windows over the arches. The south side of this colonnade is lighted by windows corresponding with the rest of the quadrangle. At the west end of this colonnade is a suite of rooms with modern sashes, as is the greater part of the west side to the park. In this side is a spacious hall, fitted up in a later style, with a gallery at the upper end, and communicating with the kitchens and offices at the southwest end. In the west side is another gateway corresponding with the former, sided by a tower in the stair-case, in the spandril of whose door is the Lytton rebus, a tun in an L. Under a long window on this side is a tun richly flowered, and over this window the Lytton arms. Over the inside of the first or eastern gateway are the arms of Lytton, quartering Booth, Oke, and Wayland, and the date 1563, which fixes it to Rowland Lytton, great-grandson to the first purchaser of this family, sheriff of Hertfordshire 1568, 10 Elizabeth, and afterwards knighted. He died 1582, and was buried in the church. On the grand staircase are the portraits, three-quarters, of Sir Rowland, lieutenant of the county, and commander of their troops at Tilbury, 1588, and his lady. Anne, daughter of Oliver lord St. John, baron of Bletsoe. He is represented in dark hair, whiskers, and peaked beard, armed completely in plate armour, almost to the knees, on which appear flowered silk or linen drawers, with red garters, reaching to his black boots, which just appear, red sash and tassels to his sword. In his right hand he holds a heavy tilt-lance; his left hand is akimbo; his hel-met stands on a table behind him. Above behind his head, are his arms quarterly:

Ermine, on a chief indented G. 3 crowns O. Lytton

S. on a fess A. between 6 trefoils, 3 oak leaves G. Oke.

A. 3 boars' heads S. Booth.

Erm. a cross G. charged with 4 bezants. Weyland.

Motto, HOC VIRTVTIS OPVS.

Crest, A bittern in rushes, and over it 1588, with another motto. Before his face a tree, with an inscription, which, as well as the second motto, the height of the stairs prevented from being seen.

His lady is represented in her hair, ruff, black gown, double gold chain, supported by her left hand, and in her right a silver ball.

On another staircase is a portrait of a man in red hair and enormous ruff, his left hand on his belly. By him is written A^o ætatis 23, 1586.

Below these is a three-quarters portrait of Sir Watkin Williams Wynne, in a tye-wig, brown coat, laced waistcoat; in his left hand, "An act for the more effectually preventing bribery and corruption of Members to serve in Parliament."

On the landing place a whole-length portrait of a man in his hair, whiskers, and falling beard, black coat and mantle, trunk hose, roses to shoes, standing, on a red and white lozenge pavement, his right hand on a table, his left on his sword. Behind him, in the left corner, is a view, as seems, of St. Mark's Square at Venice.

In one of the rooms are high-backed wooden chairs, painted with R.L. in cypher, and this coat: 1, 4, gules over a fret Or a fess Azure. 2. 3. Azure.

In the gallery a whole-length portrait of the last Mr. Lytton, leaning on his gun, in a gold laced green coat, ribbed stockings, square-toed high-quartered shoes, and tye-wig; a pointer running, looking back to him. At the right corner below: "Ferrers; surdus & mutus pinxit, 1710."

A whole-length of a young gentleman, in a similar style of composi-tion, seems of the same master.

A small head on board, in armour, with ruff and red hair, super-scribed: "Le Duc Mateas Davstriche."

Another small head on board of a lady, in small cap and coronet, ruff and standing cape, with a double-headed spread eagle pendant from her necklace.

A man with flowing hair, in armour, in a red gown with white sleeves under it.

A coat of arms, of quarterly: 1, 4, Lytton. Q: 2. Erm. in a canton S. a crescent A.; 3. Erm. on a chief indented Az. 3 crowns. Lytton. On a shield of pretence G. an anchor O.; on a chief O. 3 torteaux.

Crest, a bird with wings extended S.

Another small woman's head on board, in a ruff, small cap, black and ermine gown, and rich stomacher, superscribed: "Chaterina d Holande."

A pedigree of the Lytton family, by Peter Le Neve.

Two portraits of ladies, in the style of Lely.

In a room contiguous to the gallery over the chimney, are rude bas-reliefs of Venus and Adonis, with churches in the distant landscape. This and another adjoining room are hung with old tapestry.

In another room, a head of Lord Strafford, in armour,

>A lady in a black veil.

>Le Prince d'Orange, small.

>La Princesse d'Orange, small.

On another staircase:

A fine three-quarters portrait of a handsome young man, in light curled hair, long laced neckcloth, coat with buttons to the bottom, open, and showing loose drawers with bunches of tapes or straps at the knees, such as also hang from the shoulders and from the waistband, the line of the sleeve falling from under a cuff with three buttons; the sword, with a plain hilt, hangs from a rich broad belt embroidered or quilted.

A head, in a ruff, beard, and whiskers, superscribed: "Bussy d'Amboyse, homme de sang &c de feu."

Another head, superscribed: "Boulainville de Montmorency."

An emblematical painting, of a landscape with the figure of a woman reclining over a skull on a sarcophagus adorned with reliefs of a sacrifice. At her head a pillar, on whose base is this inscription, pointed to by a man in a moresque dress or blanket, barefooted:

>*In illo tempore memorabo & sepulchrum qui*
>*illustrissimo addorato percitò*
>*mento more qu*. . . Triumph.*

Under a statue of Diana, or a woman with a dart:
>Nemo magis felix.
>Anno D. 1685.

"In Romæ Onnobibus", under a Cæsar's laureate bust.

A man like a porter carrying water or milk in pails slung over his shoulders up a large stone staircase.

Other inscriptions illegible.

A head of James I holding a blue garter from his neck in his left hand, as at Hatfield. On one side of him SERIO.

---

*This space has letters hid by the figure pointing to it.

At the upper end of the hall, in a gallery, hangs a large group of whole-length portraits of the last Mr. Lytton, his lady, and three young ladies, (two with fishing-rods and fish, a third in a riding-dress) and a young gentleman standing by Mrs. Lytton who holds a music book with some notes and these words, "Blow winds, blow winds, and bear me to some grove!"

In 1811, some twenty years after this visit, the red-brick house built around a courtyard, as described in these notes, was substantially remodelled by Mrs. Elizabeth Bulwer-Lytton, who found it "old fashioned and too large". Three sides of the courtyard were demolished, and the surviving bricks covered with stucco. Of the original building only the west wing—the present entrance for visitors— remains. The rest of the present building is of the early nineteenth century. Within the west wing are preserved the picture gallery and the banquetting hall, with its minstrels' gallery remaining at the upper end. The former dining parlour is now the White Drawing Room. In the entrance to the dining parlour a section of wall painting dated 1630 was uncovered during the last major phase of restoration. [LW]

The church stands in the park, at a small distance southeast from the house: a neat structure, fitted-up in a modern manner; the nave and chancel of one pace, with a west tower and small spire, and a south porch. A north chapel to the chancel is the burial place of the family, and contains the following monuments.

Rowland Lytton, 1582; and his two wives, Margaret Tate and Anne Carleton, with their figures in brass, and an inscription in black letter.

Anne St. John, 1601, wife of his son Rowland.

Judith their daughter, wife of Sir Thomas Barrington, 1657.

Jane another daughter, wife of Sir Charles Crofts, 1672.

Judith their great-grand-daughter, wife of Maurice Abbot.

George Strode, her second husband, 1707.

Sir William Lytton, 1794; and his two wives.

Mary Harrison and Phillipa Keyling.

Lytton Lytton, his sister's son by George Strode, 1710.

These three heavy marble monuments, the two first with recumbent figures, the last with a standing figure in a long wig and neckcloth, and a coat buttoned down to his toes, are the work of Edward Stanton of London.

(Mr. Walpole, vol. III, p.150, mentions Thomas Stanton, a statuary, who made a tomb in the church of Stratford upon Avon, which, Vertue says, is in good taste).

As the inscriptions on these, and several others of lesser note, may be found in Chauncy, p.356–7, and Salmon, p.201, I forbear to repeat them. But I shall describe a monument of white marble erected since their time to the last heir of the family, the son of Lytton Lytton, 1732. It represents a man in a stiff coat, and a woman in a gown, kneeling at the end of a sarcophagus, on which are carved in relief three boys holding a snake biting its tail (the emblem of eternity), an hour-glass, and a skull. In a panel above a man stands holding a skull, his wife sits by him, their youngest daughter stands, and at her right another daughter leans on an urn of flowers. The arms are Lytton quartering the fret, and on a shield of pretence the anchor, and in chief 3 .. . . .

Inscription:

In spem beatæ resurrectionis,
sub hoc marmore conduntur
reliquiæ
Gulielmi Robinson Lytton Strode, arm.
uxorem duxit filiam
cohæredemque Gulielmi Heysham, arm.
Ex eá genuit liberos
tres filios quatuorque filias:
tres è vitâ excessêre; relictis
Elizabetha, Anna, Barbara,
cum Johanne natu minimo,
Ab hâc vitâ ad meliorem emigravit
decimo nono Novembris,

anno $\begin{cases} \text{æt. 44,} \\ \\ \text{sal. 1732.} \end{cases}$

His relict died March 13, 1790, aged 67,* and was buried in a brick grave in the churchyard, just by the chancel door. The estate on her death has devolved to Warburton Lytton, Esq.

*[In the next issue of G.M. the Editor pointed out that there must be an error in these figures: for the husband to have died in 1732, aged 44, and the wife in 1790, aged 67, is scarcely possible!]

Against the north wall of the chancel is a black marble monument, with a female bust in white marble in a niche, subscribed IVDITHA, and under it an inscription for Judith daughter of Sir Rowland Lytton, wife of Sir Nicholas Strode, who died 1662, aged 24.

At the entrance of the Lytton chapel lies a slab inlaid with the following inscription in five brass lines, in the black character:

Hic procerum de stirpe satum cum conjuge clari

Joh'is Hotoft iterum tellusis co. . . urnis,

Hospicii regis qui thesaurarius olim

Henrici Sexti merito pollebat honore.

Sit lux p'petua sibi post haec horrida lustra!

A sixth line, of which Chauncy gives only 'Corpora spiritibus. . . .' is now torn away, and the ends of the others are hid by the iron railing. On the slab are the arms of Hotoft, 3 pikes' heads, twice single, and once quartering A. 2 bars G. in chief 3 ogresses. In Chauncy's time this made part of an altar tomb on the north side of the chancel. Sir John Hotoft, sheriff of Hertfordshire 7 Henry IV, treasurer of Henry VI's household, knight of the shire 1, 2, 3, 5 Henry V and 1 Henry VI, was lord of this manor from 13 Henry IV to his death; and his daughter Idonea conveyed it to Sir John Barre, by whose daughter Isabel it passed to Sir Thomas Bourchier; and on his death, 6 Henry VII, was purchased by the Lyttons.

In the chancel, on a slab:

John Ham, clerk,
3rd son of John Ham, of Widhayes, Devon, Esq.
died May 20, 1684.

On the floor of the chancel lies a fine brass figure of a priest in his cope, adorned with Saints; and under him this inscription, in black:

> Hic incet d'nus Simon Bache, cl'icus quonda'
> thesaurar' hospicii illustrissimi
> principis d'ni henrici quinti, regi Angl', &
> chanonic' eccl'ie cathedralis s'ci Pauli London',
> q'i obiit XIX° die Maii, A° D'ni MCCCCXIIII.

At the east end of the church, in the yard, is an altar tomb, inscribed:

> The rev.
> Mr Peter Ellice,
> rector of this parish,
> died January 24, 1788,
> aged 76.

He was of Jesus college, Oxford, M.A., 1736, B.D. 1743; and is succeeded here, and at Letchworth in the same patronage, by ———— Price, brother of Mr. Price, steward for the estate.

The rectory house is pleasantly situated at the northeast end of the village. Just above it is a good brick house built by Mr. Price, the steward. R.K.W.G.

---

15 November 1790. A violent storm blew from the southwest.. . A barn belonging to Mr. Hutchinson of Hatfield Woodside, in Hertfordshire, was blown down, and killed a poor man just got to work in it.

23 November 1790. Between four and five o'clock in the morning, a second but more violent storm blew from the southwest, attended with successive flashes of lightning and continued rolls of loud thunder, succeeded by heavy showers of hail and rain.

At Harrow on the Hill and St. Albans, both elevated situations, the electrical shock was very sensibly felt, but no mischief done; though at the latter the fire was seen to play through and about the Abbey steeple in a singular manner.

1791. Sheriff. Hertfordshire. Matthew Raper, of Ashlyns Hall, Esq.

14 May 1791. Ended the sale of the valuable library of the late Dr. Lort, which had continued 25 days, with the interruption of Easter holidays, the produce of which amounted to £1269. Among a variety of curious articles which the proprietor had amassed from his first entering on a collegiate life, and which his extensive acquaintances with men of letters enabled him to pursue to the last, those books on our National History and Antiquities, enriched with the MS. notes of his friend, that well-known antiquary, the Rev. George North, rector of Codicote, in Hertfordshire, were not the least interesting. The Doctor's notes in his books were chiefly references to authors who had treated the same subjects, or keys to particular publications. His prints were sold May 26, and the six following days, and produced £40.1s.6d.

June 1791. In a letter to the editor from E.J. of Uppingham, and dated May 31, is the following: "Having traced him [Bishop Taylor] as accurately as I could in the register of this parish, of which he was rector, I have been also gratified by a present lately made me, a small octavo book, intituled, *The Life of Bishop Taylor, and the purest Spirit of his Writings*, extracted and exhibited by John Wheeldon, A.M., rector of Wheathampstead, Hertfordshire, and Prebendary of Lincoln. London. 1789."

1792. Sheriff. Hertfordshire. James Bourchier of Little Berkhamsted.

30 March 1792. A very melancholy accident happened lately near Rickmansworth, Hertfordshire. Mr. Dundas, a gentleman of that neighbourhood, was driving his wife and sister in a small country cart. The carriage got entangled with a wagon on the road and in consequence overset. Mrs. Dundas fell under the wheel of the wagon on the road, and was crushed to death. Mr. Dundas had both his legs broken, and the other lady was thrown into a ditch but luckily escaped with only a few slight contusions. The unfortunate lady has left 3 children thus dreadfully deprived of maternal care.

May 1792. In the parish church at Bushey, in Hertfordshire, is a small blue altar-stone, about four feet long, and two broad, with an inscription thereon. It seems more inclined to puzzle than inform a reader. I enclose you an exact copy, and shall be much obliged by any of your correspondents who can explain the two centre lines; no doubt the writer thought them very ingenious, but he appears to have a much better hand at conundrums, than at epitaphs: A.B.

In the centre: Here's two in one, and yet not two, but one,
                    Two sons, one tomb, two heires, one name alone.
Right border: HERE LYETH YE BODY
Top border: OF ROBERT BLAKWELL, SONNE OF RICHARD
Left border: BLAKWELL, GENT.
Bottom border: WHO DYED YE 11TH OF DECEMBER, 1643.

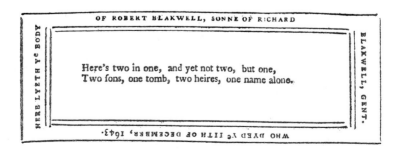

September 1792. [A long discourse by Ferd. Stanley includes the following:] ... Edward Waterhouse, Esq., who was, I believe, of an Hertfordshire family, and collaterally related to Sir Edward Waterhouse, one of the Privy Council in Ireland, and Chancellor of the Exchequer there (in the reign of Queen Elizabeth), [referred to as] 'the learned, industrious, and ingenious, Edward Waterhouse, Esq., of Sion College.' ... Sir Edward is said to have been of an ancient and worshipful family, deriving their descent lineally from Sir Gilbert Waterhouse, of Kirton, in Low Lindsay, Lincolnshire, temp. Hen. III, and to have been son of John Waterhouse, Esq., of Helmstedbury, [Hempstedbury, i.e. Hemel Hempstead] Hertfordshire, by Margaret Turner, of Blunt's Hall, Suffolk, and to have died S.P. at Woodchurch, in Kent, October 13, 1591. ... [See also June 1796].

September 1792. A college was opened at Cheshunt for the educating of young men to preach at the chapels belonging to the Countess of Huntingdon. A great concourse of people were assembled on the occasion; exhortations were given by four gentlemen who received their education at the college in Wales. The committee, who assisted her ladyship in the management of the affairs of the chapels, have had it in contemplation for several years to remove the college from Wales, but her ladyship would not consent. Since her death, the committee have purchased a spacious house at the above place for £950, and the college in Wales is to be given up.

1793. Sheriff. Hertfordshire. George William Prescott, of Theobalds.

WYDDIAL HALL

January 1793. I enclose you a drawing of Wyddial-hall, Herts. In 1789 I published a "Descriptive Sketch" of the place, and will now add a few farther particulars to accompany the drawing.
H.G. Oldfield.

Wyddial is about 15 miles from the county town; the manor house is on the south side of the park. The entrance, in the centre of the front, is through a porch, with a rustic doorway over which used to be a stone carved with the Gulston arms. A Doric cornice and frieze run through the whole length of the building, and in the parapet, over each window, is an open ballustrade. Going through the porch, you enter the hall, fitted up with pillars of the Doric order. On the right hand are the drawing room and library, which contains a very good collection of books; on the left are the drawing room and staircase. The offices are at the back part of the house, and the stables, etc. in a detached building, north of the mansion.

The manor of Wiggele, in the Saxon times, was held by Edgiva, a noble woman, who in the days of Edward the Confessor bestowed it upon the church of St. Paul, London, as Dugdale in his history of that place mentions.

The arms of John Thomas Ellis, Esq., the present lord of the manor, are Ermine, a lion passant guardant; crest, a lion's head, ducally crowned, issuant from a coronet of the same. He married Miss Heaton, daughter of John Heaton, Esq., of Bedfords, near Havering, Essex.

July 1793. The pictures of the Kit-cat Club were at Barne Elmes [Surrey], in the house of Jacob Tonson, eldest son of old Jacob Tonson, secretary, or rather printer and publisher, to the Club; on whose death, 1767, they descended to Richard Tonson, his brother, at Water Oakley, where he built a room for them; and, after his death, the house was sold. Sir W. Baker married the elder of the two daughters of old J. Tonson; the younger married Mr. Lempriere, and died S.P. Mr. Baker's house at Hertingfordbury is called the Park, and not Hertingfordbury Park.

August 1793. Richard Waring, who married a daughter (not a sister) of Dr. Wall, had 17 children (besides his wife having once mis-carried); namely, Sampson, Catharine, Richard, William, Ann, Edward, Thomas, Sarah, Elizabeth, Cecil, Walter (who died within the month), Mary, Walter, Rebecca, John, Jane, and Dorothy; all of whom are deceased except Walter (now residing at Barnet), Jane (now of Maidstone, widow of the late Rev. Mr. Waterhouse, of that place), and Dorothy (also of Barnet, who remains unmarried). My having married a great grand-daughter of the said Richard Waring enables me to give you this information.

August 1793.

INSCRIPTION ON A HERMITAGE
in the centre of a Copse, intersected by irregular
Walks, at MICKLEFIELD GREEN [Rickmansworth], HERTS,
the Residence of LORD EDWARD BENTINCK.
By the author of CALVARY.

Here sleep, Ambition! be this cell thy tomb;
Vanish, and give the calmer passions room.
Avaunt, vain world! this solitary grove
Nor fears thy malice, nor invites thy love.
And, though like thine its dark and winding maze

'Tangles our path, and for a while betrays,
Let patience guide, and, one short trial past,
Content shall greet us in the spot at last.

WALTHAM CROSS

7 August 1793. The workmen made preparations for taking down the cross erected to the memory of Queen Eleanor 1293, in the parish of Cheshunt, in order to remove it into the grounds of George Prescott, Esq., lord of the manor, for its better preservation; but, after removing the upper tier of stone, finding it too hazardous an undertaking, on account of the decayed state of the ornamental parts, the scaffold was removed on the 20th; and we hear the proper measures will be taken to repair this ancient memorial of conjugal affection. The like attention has been paid to that near Northampton, by replacing the steps round its base.

Forty years were to pass before a proper restoration was undertaken. [JE]

September 1793. . . . Sir William Humfreys, Kt., and Bart., so created November 30, 1714, [Humfreys of Jenkins, in the parish of Barking, Essex, Bart.] died in October, 1735. He was succeeded by his son and heir, Sir Orlando, who died at Jenkins, June 14, 1737, aged 59, and was buried in the parish church, having had three sons, who died before him, and two daughters, Mary, wife of William Ball Waring, Esq., and Ellen Wintour Humfreys, married December 3, 1741, to Thomas Gore, Esq., a younger brother of the family of Tring, Hertfordshire, and afterwards member for the borough of Cricklade, from whom the estate came by marriage to Smart Lethieullier, Esq., lord of the neighbouring manor of Alderbroke, an attentive and respectable F.S.A. who died, leaving only a daughter, now the wife of Edward Hulse, Esq., (eldest son of Sir Edward Hulse, Bart.), the present representative of these families, who has two sons, and perhaps other children.

November 1793. James Penrose, Esq., of Hatfield, Hertfordshire, appointed surgeon extraordinary to His Majesty.

James Penrose baptized at Bicester, 8 May 1750, son of Francis Penrose, surgeon and medical writer (see D.N.B.). Settled at Hatfield as a young man and in practise there as physician and surgeon throughout his life. Died 23 November 1818, and buried in Hatfield churchyard. [HG]

DINING WITH DUKE HUMPHREY

November 1793. Will you be so obliging to an old correspondent as to insert the following queries in your next magazine. Why dining with Duke Humphrey signifies to go without a dinner.

December 1793. In Ray's *Collection of English Proverbs*: it is said, that "To dine with Duke Humphrey, is to fast, to go without one's dinner. This Humphrey, Duke of Gloucester, was uncle to King Henry VI and his protector during his minority, renowned for hospitality and good house-keeping, and commonly called the good duke of Gloucester. Those were said to dine with duke Humphrey who walked out dinner-time in the body of St. Paul's, because it was believed the duke was buried there. But, saith Dr. Fuller, that saying is as far from truth as they from dinner, even twenty miles off; seeing this duke was buried in the church of St. Albans, to which he was a great benefactor."   H.D.B.

February 1794. "To dine with Duke Humphry" is to go without one's dinner. Duke Humphry was ordered to be executed before he had his dinner; therefore, if you dined with the duke, you were likely to have none.   S.N.

March 1794. One word, one more word, on the subject of a very melancholy text, "Dining with Duke Humphry" ———— a text, like many others, obscured rather than illustrated by comments. Your humorous correspondent has, I fear, puzzled the cause more completely than ever. Duke Humphry, he says, was ordered to be EXECUTED before he had his dinner. "Homo sum," Mr. Urban; "humani a me nihil alienum puto." I can enter into the fine feelings of a Bristol gentleman on this melancholy subject, and give him credit for all his sensibilities. To execute a fellow-creature in any way is bad enough; but to execute him fasting ———— fie upon it, Mr. Urban! Bristol men, who oftener feel the pangs of repletion that those of inanition, must account the doom of poor Duke Humphry a severe one indeed! IGNOTUM OMNE PRO MIRIFICO EST!

  We may perhaps, however, contrive to afford your tender-hearted friend a little comfort, by reminding him, that poor Duke Humphry came to his untimely end without halter or guillotine, and without suffering the pangs of starvation. On the contrary, he was, if fame says true, poisoned, in the act of eating a hearty dinner (MORE BRISTOLIENSI), by the ambitious and malignant Beaufort, Cardinal of Winchester. Shakespeare's Henry the Sixth, if not historical, is at least poetical, evidence on this subject. Let S.N. then sit down to his municipal feasts in peace, as far as Duke Humphry is concerned.

  Seriously, the proverb originated from the accidental circumstance of a wit in the last century being shut up in the abbey at St. Albans, where the remains of Humphry (the good duke regent) are yet to be seen, while a party of his friends, who came down to that ancient and loyal borough with him on an excursion from London, were enjoying the hospitalities of the worthy Mrs. Langford's unknown predecessor at the White Hart.

Yours, IMPRANSUS, G.

Humphrey, Duke of Gloucester, ca.1390–1447, was the youngest brother of King Henry V, under whom he served as commander during the whole of the French campaign, including Agincourt. He was a lifelong supporter of retaining English rule in France, unlike his more statesmanlike elder brother, John of Bedford, who realised it was beyond the resources of England to maintain. Humphrey was dissolute in his private life, convivial and of great personal charm, hence a popu-

lar figure amongst Londoners. His ambitions for the regency after the death of his brother were opposed by Parliament, which granted him only the protectorship. Humphrey was an early and dedicated student of the Renaissance and a collector of books. His gifts of volumes to Oxford, to house which 'Duke Humphrey's Library' was added to the Divinity School, ensured that the study of classical humanism would modify the curriculum at Oxford. He was an intimate friend of Abbot John of Wheathampstead, also a Renaissance scholar and he often visited St. Albans, his favourite monastery. Humphrey died while under arrest on a charge of treason. It was probably not foul play, but the failure of a dissipated constitution under stress which caused his death. Although he was buried at St. Albans in a favoured spot just south of the shrine, it was popularly believed that the tomb of Sir John Beauchamp in St. Paul's cathedral, London, was his, and the promenade which it overlooked was called 'Duke Humphrey's Walk'. The proverb 'to dine with Duke Humphrey' meant to 'go dinner-less' and was used by the poor who had no meal to go to and by debtors who feared arrest if they left the sanctuary of the cathedral. There is a reference to it in Shakespeare's play, Richard III, Act IV, scene iv, line 176. [ER]

---

10 December 1793. Between one and two o'clock this morning, a terrible fire broke out in the brewhouse of Mr. Langford, brazier, in Sun Street, Hitchin. It was occasioned by the ends of the joists (that were laid in the chimney) taking fire, which in a rapid manner communicated to the dwelling house, which was nearly consumed, with the whole of the brewhouse, wash-house, and all the out buildings. The progress of the flames was so rapid, that Mrs. Berwick, aunt to Mr. Langford, narrowly escaped being burnt in her bed, being taken out of the bedroom with only her shift and under petticoat on, just as the bed caught fire. The assistance of the neighbourhood, with the engines, and the wind being quite still, kept the fire from spreading farther, so that about six o'clock it was got under. The principal inhabitants of the town have begun a subscription for Mr. Langford, as only a small part of the property was insured.

A FUND TO AID THE CLERGY

December 1793.   Cheshunt, November 9.

In p.805 the corporation for the relief of the widows and orphans of the poorer clergy in Suffolk is duly commended. One, on the same plan, has been very long instituted in Essex, including too the deanery of Braughing, and arch-deaconry of St. Albans, Hertfordshire: the contributions last year amounted to £635 5s 4d. This, with the interest of some money in the funds, and the application, unfortunately, from increasing claimants, of the principal of some late legacies amounting in the whole, to £759 was distributed in 54 pensions, the largest, and that one only, being £24. In this corporation are 458 rectories, vicarages, and perpetual curacies. Yet allowing for those clergymen, who (though contrary to the rules) pay their contributions for two parishes that they hold under the one where they reside; and for those that, occasionally, pay for two years under one; yet not more than 250 rectors, vicars or perpetual curates, communibus annis, ever appear on a contribution, which, though an act of charity in the laity, is, in the clergy, little more than one of insurance.

Yours, &c. [Not signed]

January 1794. Your anonymous correspondent from Cheshunt considers the contributions of the clergy to charities, similar to the one of which I lately sent you an account, as acts of insurance, not of charity. We disdain the imputation; it is an illiberal observation; it is, if applied to the Suffolk clergy, I can take upon me to say, an unjust one; and I believe it to be equally unjust if applied to the Essex clergy or the clergy of any other county in England. We owe much to the contributions of the laity, we own ourselves on this account much their debtors; even your Cheshunt correspondent allows them to be influenced by no other motives than those of the purest charity; and the same ought surely in justice to them to be said of the more opulent clergy, who cannot entertain the most distant idea of other recompense for what they thus bestow, than that treasure which they lay up for themselves in heaven. As to the clergy in less affluent circumstances, neither can it be fairly supposed that even they, in contributing their mite, act on self-interested motives, since, whether they contribute or not, their families, when in distress, receive the same assistance from the fund. J. Ord.

1794. Sheriff. Hertfordshire. Samuel Leightonhouse, of Orford House, Esq.

April 1794. . . . I apprehend the stone in Mr. Martin's garden at Naseby was the shaft of an old cross in the churchyard at Dallington, where I do not recollect a monastery. Mr. Martin will have the goodness to explain why the "niche, or small bit taken out as with a file, in the inside, just under the crown or head" made the seal-ring appear to him to have "belonged to an ecclesiastic, a member of some monastery." Dallington rectory belonged, from before 1220 to the Dissolution, to the nunnery of Woodchurch, or St. Giles in the Wood, near Flamsted, Hertfordshire. Bridge, I, 494. H.D.

August 1794. Lately there has been placed a white marble slab on the inside of the south wall of Broxbourne church, in Hertfordshire, with the following inscription on it:

Near this place lies interred
the body of THOMAS JONES, Esquire,
late one of his Majesty's judges
of the supreme court of the province of New York,
in North America.
Who, having suffered severe hardships, and great
personal injuries, during the troubles in America,
for his firm attachment to the British Constitution,

and unshaken loyalty to his present Majesty,
(under whom he had held different civil
commissions,)
came to England for the recovery of his health;
and being, by an act of attainder passed in the
State of New York, deprived of his large
property,
and prevented from returning to his native
country,
settled at Hoddesdon, in this parish;
and having, by the polite and friendly atten-
tions of
the inhabitants, found it a most desirable residence,
he died there July 25, 1791, aged 61 years.
His widow, from tender respect to his memory,
erected this monument
to an affectionate and most indulgent husband,
a sincere friend,
a kind master,
a benevolent member of society,
and a loyal subject.
By strangers honoured!
By strangers mourned!

In the burying ground belonging to St. Margaret's chapel, near
Hoddesdon, is the following on a grave-stone:

Here lye interred the body of Capt.
HENRY GRAVES,
who departed this life the 17th day of
August 1702, in the 52nd year of his age.
Here in one grave more than one Grave lies;
Envious Death at last hath gain'd his prize.
No pills or potions here could make Death tarry,
Resolv'd he was to fetch away old Harry;
Ye foolish doctors! could you all miscarry?
Great were his actions on the boist'rous waves;
Ah! Colchester, lament his overthrow!
Unhappily you lost him at a blow.
Each marine hero for him shed a tear;
St. Margaret's too in this must have a share.

28 November 1794. About 10 o'clock at night a fire broke out in the
stables of Mrs. Vincent, in Cooper's Lane, Northaw, which in two hours
destroyed them, with two saddle horses, a third was saved, but terribly
singed. It is supposed to have been occasioned by a candle, left while the
servant went into the house to fetch some gruel for a sick horse.

December 1794. Gazette. George William Prescott of Theobald's Park
created baronet.

1795. Sheriff. Hertfordshire. James Harding, of Tring, Esq.

January 1795. I have been, during the last spring, over a considerable
part of Hertfordshire, and made many sketches; one of which, from
Hunsdon church, as it is mentioned by Salmon, p.254, as uncommon, I

think may perhaps merit your attention. Under it, in capitals is inscribed:

"Beloved of all whilst he had lyfe,
Unmoan'd of none when he did die,
JAMES GRAY, interred of his wife,
Near to this Death's signe brass doth lye;
Years thirty-five in good renown
Park and housekeeper of this town.
Obiit 12 die Decembris, a⁰ d'ni 1591,
æt. 60."

Curious as it is, it however shews the engraver was no anatomist.

Gomme also gives James Gray's age as 60, but on the brass it is 69. [AJ]

January 1795. I wish through the medium of your intelligent and curious magazine to ascertain the relationship, if any, between that eminent schoolmaster of Westminster, Dr. Richard Busby, and the family of Busby, of Addington, in Buckinghamshire. . . .

His son and heir Sir John Busby, was knighted June 25, 1661, out of gratitude to the memory of his father-in-law, Sir William Mainwaring, Kt., who was slain during the civil wars, in defence of Chester.

The name of his first wife, daughter of the above Sir William Mainwaring, was Judith, who died in 1667, as appears by the following epitaph from the church of Ridge, in Hertfordshire (in which parish her mother, who remarried Sir Henry Pope Blount, of Tittenhanger, resided).

"Here lies the lady Busby, wife of Sir John Busby, of Addington, Buckinghamshire, daughter to the Lady Blount, by her first husband Sir William Mainwaring, who was slain in defence of Chester for the King; she died the 28th of December, 1667*, in the nineteenth year of her age, in childbed of her second child, a daughter, which survives to succeed her in those admirable perfections which made her memory dear to all that knew her"†.

[More information about descendants]

*This date ought beyond doubt to have been 1661, for Sir John Busby married his second wife November 3, 1662; and the Lady, from the time of her father's death, must have been much more than 19, had she lived till 1667. [Ed. G.M.]
†Chauncy's Hertfordshire, p.503.

February 1795. The manor and advowson of Hunsdon, Hertfordshire, was purchased, about 1671, by Matthew B.[Bluck], Esq., secondary of one of the counters in London, usher of the Rolls, and one of the six clerks in Chancery, who married a daughter of Sir William Martin, of Essex, Knt., alderman of London (Chauncy, p.199); and he was succeeded by a son, also of the same Christian name (Salmon p.253), who mortgaged it to Mr. Nicholson, who left it to the late Nicholson Calvert, Esq., his nephew. The second of these Matthews is probably the subject of a poem by Elkanah Settle, mentioned in *Brit. Top.* I 428, celebrating "Young Daphnis, wonder of the plain," without a word of his history.   D.H.

March 1795. The frost this year, being severe, and perhaps so great a degree of cold not having been felt since the years 1784, and 1785, I send you the following observations, the accuracy of which may be depended on. T.C.

Fahrenheit's thermometer in the open air, N, at S. Albans.

Jan. 1795	Morn. 8 o'clock	Noon	Even. 11 o'clock	Wind at Noon	Weather
1	24	30	24	N	fine clear day
2	18	25	18	NNE	thick rime, fine
3	16	23	20	NbE	ditto
4	17	25	22	WSW	fine clear day
5	24	31	28	WSW	fine clear day
6	32	37	33	NWbN	cloudy and fog
7	34	35	33	NE	cloudy, fog, thick
8	31	33	31	ESE	cloudy the day
9	31	35	31	N	cloudy and misling rain
10	27	32	28	N	fine clear day
11	24	30	25	NWbN	ditto
12	21	30	26	NbW	fog in the morning, fine clear day
13	32	33	22	E	cloudy, misling
14	23	27	25	E	cloudy, some snow
15	27	26	19	NEbE	cloudy, cold wind and snow
16	21	27	24	ENE	ditto
17	23	25	25	NEbN	cloudy with snow
18	25	28	20	NNE	fine clear day
19	21	29	18	NNE	ditto
20	16	24	17	N	fine morning, snow in the afternoon
21	18	21	20	N	cloudy and snow, day fine
22	19	26	20	N	cloudy and snow
23	16	20	13	N	fine clear day
24	20	29	14	NW	cloudy and snow
25	25	22	20	NwbN	exceedingly fine and clear the whole day
26	16	21	30	SEbE	cloudy and snow
27	40	42	40	SW	cloudy, and thaw, rains hard at night
28	35	33	25	NbE	fog and rain, much snow fell
29	22	27	20	N	fine clear day
30	18	25		NbE	fine and clear, rime in the evening
31	18	29	30	SW	cloudy the whole day

March 1795. From every part of the kingdom, accounts have been received of the dreadful ravages occasioned by the sudden thaw. Scarcely a river but what has lost some of its bridges, overflowed the adjacent country, and impeded for a time all communication between different places. Houses have been thrown down, canal banks destroyed; stacks and provender of all sorts swept away, great quantities of cattle have been drowned, and the sheep that are lost are innumerable. . . .

From Ware to Limehouse was one continual sheet of water. . . .

13 May 1795. Between six and seven in the evening a fire broke out in the malting-house of farmer Young, at Horrels, or Hollywell, in the parish of Hatfield, near Esingdon [Holwell, Essendon Corner], Hertfordshire, occasioned by overheating the kiln to dry the malt brown, which communicated itself to the hood or cow [cowl] of the malt-house lately pitched, and presently set the whole in a flame. In so extensive a range of buildings and ricks, the most fatal consequences were to be apprehended; but by the ready help afforded, and the double-piped engine from Hatfield House, the conflagration was prevented from spreading.

About the same time, the following night, a fire broke out on the premises of Mr. Carrol, farmer, at Turner's Hill, Cheshunt, in the same county, which destroyed not only the barns and ricks on the premises where it began, but others adjoining, and put the whole neighbourhood in imminent danger.

A correspondent, who has been on both spots since the catastrophe, authorizes us to declare, that whatever were the cause of the latter, the former was occasioned exactly as above stated. Suspicion of monopoly of any of the necessaries of life is too frequently productive of the worst of consequences to society, by destroying property of the wealthy, without relieving the wants of the poor.

12 June 1795. This afternoon, between three and four o'clock, the most tremendous storm was felt near Hatfield Broad Oak and Sawbridgeworth, ever known in those parts. The storm commenced at Hatfield town, and took a direction of more than three miles over the heath, extending about three quarters of a mile wide, and hurled destruction in its course. Whole fields of wheat, &c. &c. are totally cut to pieces, and the damage to many individual farmers is very considerable. The hail-stones, or pieces of ice, measured four inches over, and drove in such torments as to be in many places upwards of five feet deep, and were several days in melting away.

July 1795. William Paley, now D.D. subdean of Lincoln, and prebendary of Carlisle, was collated by the bishop of London to the prebend of Pancras in that cathedral, vice John Harris, LL.B. who died last year in a very advanced age, having held that prebend, together with the rectory of Greensted juxta Ongar, in Essex (the latter ever since 1738).

Mr. Harris married a daughter of Adolphus Meetkerke, formerly of Julians [Rushden], Hertfordshire, Esq., by whom he was father of the present Lieutenant-Colonel John Adolphus Harris.

SOUTH MIMMS CHURCH

July 1795. I am surprised at never having yet met with a view of the parish church of South Mimms; which, from the picturesque appearance of its tower, almost covered with ivy, well deserves a place in your instructive and entertaining miscellany.

I beg leave to send you a drawing of the south side of it and should be much obliged to any of your ingenious correspondents who would give some farther account of it. P.B.

8 July 1795. The colours which had been worked by Lady Prescott and her daughter, were delivered, in Theobalds Park, to the Corps of Hertfordshire Volunteers, commanded by Sir George Prescott, Bart., when an excellent address (accompanied by a prayer suited to the occasion) was delivered to the Volunteers, by the Rev. M. MacCulloch, vicar of Bradfield, Suffolk, and curate of Cheshunt. The corps went through their several evolutions and firings with great applause, and, after partaking of a dinner, at the house of their captain, paraded through the town of Enfield, and in the evening retired to their respective homes in good order.

The Theobald Park Estates abutted the Parish of Enfield. [JE]

29 August 1795. This evening, between the hours of eight and nine o'clock, Samuel Green, drover and salesman, from Haloughton, in Leicestershire, was robbed of banknotes and cash, amounting to £408 between Kitt's End and Dancer's Hill, as he was going from London to

North Mimms, by two footpads in smock frocks, and crape over their faces; they cut his leg and horse's shoulder dreadfully with a sharp instrument.

September 1795. "A Sermon for the Fast, &c." By the Rev. Mr. John Johnson M.A., rector of Great Parndon, Essex, and vicar of North Mimms, Hertfordshire. To which is annexed, An Address to the Dissenters". [A short editorial review follows].

September 1795. Thomas Shalcrosse, of Digswell in the county of Hertford, Esq., being (as I take it) about the age of 49, in the year 1712, obtained a pass, signed by Queen Anne, to travel into France, and other places abroad. . . . Mr. Shalcrosse was out of England about two years, returning hither about the time of the Queen's decease.   J.J.

BISHOP'S STORTFORD GRAMMAR SCHOOL

November 1795. It is really a melancholy thing to reflect on the number of institutions in various parts of the kingdom, founded by our worthy ancestors in the most pious intentions, and flourishing for a length of time to the great benefit of the community, that have either been suffered to fall into decay by the negligence of those to whose care they have devolved, or been resignedly brought to ruin from self-interested motives. In addition to the instances that have been occasionally given in your useful and elegant compilation, permit me to mention that of the famous grammar school at Bishop Stortford.
    The seminary, which for many years produced a succession of learned and virtuous men, some of whom adorned elevated stations in church and state, was about the middle of the present century suffered to fall into such a state of decay as to furnish a pretext for pulling down the building in order to save the trust the charge of repairing it. It was the custom of this school for every scholar at quitting it to present the library with some book; by which means that collection was become extremely valuable on account of the number and elegance of its volumes. This library is at present taken care of by my worthy and learned friend Dr. Dimsdale, of Bishop Stortford, who gratuitously gives it room in his house, and, but for whose pious concern for this venerable repository, it would soon, in all probability, have become a prey to avarice, and been sold by the pound to the grocers and chandlers of the town. It was founded by Mr. Thomas Leigh, as I find by the MS. records of the school; where his donation is entered in the following words:
    "Tho. Leigh, A.M. è coll. Christi Cant. anno 1621. et scholæ Stortfordiensis ab eo anno ad presentem 1664. archididascalus, non solum propriis impensis biblothecam construi et ornari curavit, et libris (qui in hoc catalogo recensentur) locupletandam tum ab alumnis tum et amicis impetravit eorum etiam libros proximè sequentes, pro suo in literas amore et ut aliis exemplo esset, largitus est."
    Then follows a list of the books he gave; to the amount of several hun-

dred volumes, many of which are extremely rare and of early dates.

"Guil. Leigh, fil. natu max. prædicti magistri Tho. Leigh, et scholæ Stortf. alumnus, coll. Christi Cant. socius, & academiæ procurator electus, donavit, Demosthenis, [&c. &c. to the number likewise of some hundreds].

Tho. Leigh, fil. natu proximis prædicti magistri Tho. Leigh. Jacobus Leigh, fil. tertius, scholæ hujus alumnus, &c. Johan. Leigh, fil. quartus prædicti M. Tho. Leigh."

The successive benefactors, with their respective donations, then regularly follow, down to the year 1745.

In the same book too are entered the names of the reverend clergy who preached the anniversary sermon during a period of near a century.

In Knight's *Life of Dean Colet*, 8vo, 1724 p.428, I find the following paragraph:

"Thomas Tooke, D.D., born at Dover in Kent, was bred under Dr. Thomas Gale, master of St. Paul's school; from under whose care he was removed to Corpus Christi, or Ben'et College, in Cambridge; where he became fellow of the society, and continued so many years. He afterwards became master of Bishop Stortford School, in Hertfordshire; which, by his great industry, and happy way of teaching and governing, he raised to very great fame; so that for many years it flourished among the very best in the kingdom, and sent out many excellent scholars. It still continues to keep up an anniversary or school-feast for the gentlemen educated therein. The present Archbishop of York (Sir William Dawes), the Rev. Dr. Robert Moffe, Dean of Ely, Dr. Nicholas Clagett, now Archdeacon of Buckinghamshire, &c. have honoured these meetings by preaching on that occasion. After refusing the public schools of Norwich and Bury, he died at Bishop Stortford in the year 1720. Having by his will given to Ben'et College aforementioned, after a certain number of years, the perpetuity of the rectory of Lambourn in Essex, where he had an estate, as also the living of Braxiel Magna, in Essex."

In the archives of the school he thus appears:

"D. Thomas Tooke, S.T.P. Collegii Corporis Christi quondam socius, postea ecclesiæ parochialis de Lambourn in agro Essex rector, scholæ de Stortford ep'i per XXX & amplius ann. archididascalus dignissimus simul ac felicissimus; qui cum literis & moribus bonis juventutæ erudiendæ & formandæ ætatem contriverit, ut post mortem etiam rei literariæ consuleret & studiosis prodesset, decem libras ad augendum armarium scholæ suæ, & viginti solidos quotannis pro concione ad annuum festum scholarium habendâ extremis testamentis legavit, quam quidem summam si quo anno nullum festum agerent scholaris libris coëmendis in usum bibliothecæ scholæ suæ impendi jussit.

Quà donatione coëmpta sunt 1738. Phavorini Lexicon Graæc. fol. Cyrilli, Philoxeni, aliorumque glossaria."

Over the chimney in the apartment allotted to the books by the favour of Dr. Dimsdale are two portraits in oil, which formerly hung up in the school; one of the aforementioned Thomas Leigh ———— black coif, straight hair, and broad band; under which are the following verses:

"En qualem formam, dum vixit Leighus habebat;

Pingere virtutes quæ penicilla valent ?
Plenius has narrent, hoc qui didicere magistro
Artes, egregium queis meruere decus.
Concilio cœpto, & curis & munere adaucta
Testatur laudes bibliotheca suas."

The other portrait is that of the above-named Dr. Thomas Tooke, in a large flowing wig, band, and modern clerical habit, without any inscription.

Now, good Mr. Urban, be so obliging as to chronicle these few memorials of public-minded men in your eventful tablets, not indeed as an encouragement to others to go and do likewise, (for alas, their ungrateful posterity have defeated that part of their good intention) but to prevent their noble efforts from being entirely effaced from the notice of mankind; which otherwise must shortly be the case, as in another generation the place where this seminary stood will no longer be known. VICINUS.

1795 (Supplement). The account given of Stortford school by your correspondent Vicinus, p. 892, led me to enquire a little into its history. It appears to have been founded about the 20th of Elizabeth, in whose reign most of these substitutes to that advantage arising from the religious houses for the education of youth were founded and endowed. Mr. Deane, of London, left the first £5 towards erecting it: but the building was not erected till the commencement of the present century, by contributions of the gentlemen of Herts and Essex, at the request of that late master, Dr. Tooke; though, as your correspondent informs us, a library was founded and finished above 50 years before by another master. This school-house stood in the high-street with the West front to the church-yard, consisting of three rooms, which, with the stair-case, made a square building for a grammar-school, and took up one-quarter of it, all the front to the street; the other two were a library and a writing-school. These stood upon arches, under which were the market and shops, the property of the parish; and the library was well furnished by the diligence of the masters. (Salmon, Herts, p.175). Your correspondent can, perhaps, tell you how this useful institution fell into disuse since the decease of Dr. Tooke in 1720 or 1721, who, by his diligence and skill in teaching, had raised the school to great repute, and acquired a considerable fortune; or of Mr. Hazeland in 175., who gained one of the prizes at Cambridge;- and where the duties of the school are now performed. But so it came to pass, that Mr. Adderley, late master of the Crown at Hokeril, got the building removed as a nuisance for the making of the river Stort navigable.

How much is it to be lamented that there is so little remaining of the public virtue of our forefathers for the maintenance of free-schools! One would think that, when such a foundation was once provided with a revenue adequate to its support, it must be perpetual; yet could I tell you, Mr. Urban, of such a foundation, coeval with this, and not less distinguished by one of its masters, and for having produced eminent scholars, its revenues considerably increasing, and its building in excellent repair, not 100 miles from London, yet sinking into disuse and disrepute notwithstanding the exertions of its trustees to keep it up, when they have been instigated by the interest of the minister of the parish to support the master for his ease at the expense of the trust, without regard to doctrine or discipline. Let them blush when they recollect how the master breaks the head of English Priscian in his teaching, and pulls the ears of the poor lads in his discipline; and let them know, Mr. Urban, that he who writes this is not afraid nor ashamed of what he asserts; for, they know that he asserts nothing but truth.

Trustees of charities to great towns, at a short distance from the metropolis, are rarely sufficiently permanent to be respectable, or sufficiently attentive to the interests of the town. Thus the emolument of its endowment falls into the hands of persons ill adapted to support them with credit to themselves or their employers; the benefits intended to arise from them to the inhabitants are so unequal, that the great charge of education falls on any man who possesses the smallest ability or inclination to take it; and the poor prefer paying the man of their choice to receiving the rudiments of learning free from him whom their betters force upon them.

VICINUS ALTER

---

6 November 1795. This morning, about two o'clock, a most tremendous gale of wind arose, preceded by torrents of rain with thunder and lightning. It appears to have been very generally extensive and it is supposed that there has not been so high a wind since the year 1703. . . .

At Hertford, near half the avenues of trees which crowded up All Saints churchyard was blown down.

At St. Albans, Mr. and Mrs. Thomas, also Mr. and Mrs. Ellis, at the Bell inn, near the market place, were in a dreadful situation for some time; the chimneys giving way, the roof of the house and ceilings fell in upon the beds wherein they slept: they were extricated from their dreadful situation with their lives, though they are much bruised. Mr. and Mrs. Ellis were buried in the ruins for several hours before they could be got out.

The damage done to the Marquis of Salisbury in Hatfield Park is computed at £500.

In Lord Essex's Park, of Cashiobury, no less than 250 of the finest venerable oaks were either torn up, or shivered to pieces.

At Bennington Place, a stack of chimneys, of the additional rooms erected by Mr. Bullock, was beat down through them.

More damage was done in Sacombe Park than in the memorable whirlwind of 1789.

December 1795. A lover of our national antiquities wishes some of our Heraldic Correspondents would tell how to connect Sir John Say, of Broxbourne, who died 1478, and his son Sir William, with the ancient family of that name, which just appears in the reign of Henry or

Richard II and seems to have ended in a female about the end of the 14th century.

1796. Sheriff. Hertfordshire. John Sowerby, of Lilley, Esq.

6 March 1796. At eleven in the morning, a fire broke out in a hay-rick adjoining to the ox shed, at farmer Mason's, at Hawkshead, a farm belonging to the Rev. Dr. Gould, in the parish of North Mimms. The family being all at church except Mrs. Mason and one boy, the flames spread with such fury that the produce of 25 acres of wheat in the straw, and 80 loads of hay, were consumed, together with 15 out of 18 fat oxen, computed at £12.12s apiece at least, and one and two more so dangerously burnt, that they were obliged to be killed; the boy in his fright having neglected to turn them out of the stalls before he got on horse-back to alarm the neighbourhood; and, mistaking his way to the church, he rode over a woman, who was taken up for dead, but is likely to recover. Two engines arrived from the Sun-fire-office, just in time to save the dwelling house and the rest of the premises, which stood parallel with the range of buildings, &c. destroyed. It having been misrepresented in some of the newspapers, that this mischief was the effect of popular resentment, we are happy in having it in our power to say that no man is more respected than Mr. Mason who has long borne an unimpeachable character in his neighbourhood and will sustain the greater loss by not being insured to the full amount. There cannot be at this time too much caution used, or too strict enquiry made, on inserting these calamitous accidents.

The same day a fire broke out at a farm-house, near Hemel Hempstead, which did more extensive mischief, consuming, besides a great quantity of hay and corn, seven hundred pounds worth of wool, &c.

8 March 1796. Two farmers living near Potters Bar, near Barnet, had wheat ricks burnt down, on account of their not having thrashed any wheat since the last harvest. In the conflagration, the fire reached the adjoining stables; and one farmer lost 12 oxen, the other 12 horses.

June 1796. In the second battle of St. Albans the Duke of York's troops broke through the king's, and "at the north end of the town, called Barnard heath, toward a little town called Syndridge [Sandridge], in a place called Nomansland, they had far greater conflict with 4 or 5000 of the king's armie." Stowe's *Annals*, p.413.

13 June 1796. Between 11 and 12 o'clock in the forenoon a fire broke out in the hay-loft over the oil-mill of Messrs. Watts and Parsons in Turners Hill, Marsh Lane, Cheshunt; which in a short time consumed the whole premises, with fifty loads of oil ready to remove, not without suspicion of wilful mischief, the mill having been on fire a week before.

THE WATERHOUSE FAMILY

June 1796. I have enclosed for you some account of the Waterhouse family. [See also September 1792]. Morgan, Lib. II. p.67, speaking of the pile as a charge in arms, says, "so that family, which had its denomination ab aquæ domo, its first ancestor of note probably living in a seat upon the water; one family of them bearing the pile between two fountains; those of Buckingham, Harford (sic), Wiltshire, and Shropshire, bearing the pile engrailed, are strengthened by the pile of honourable families, from whom is descended Edward Waterhouse, Esq., and engrailed into the memory of after-ages, that the teeth of time cannot but leave the marks of his ancient family, who is descended lineally from Sir Gilbert ab Aquædomo, of Kirton, in Low Linsey, Lincolnshire; but because, in this book, I only mention the pedigree from the great grandfather; therefore, I shall only begin with John Waterhouse, Esq., who was of Hemelhempstead-bury, Hertfordshire, and by Margaret, daughter of Turner of Bluntshall, in Essex (who bore, Ermines, on a cross quatrevoided Ar. 4 milroins Sa.) had issue two sons, 1. Sir Edward Waterhouse, of Woodchurch, in Kent, chancellor of the Exchequer, and one of the privy council of Ireland to the famous Queen Elizabeth."

This man lies buried at Woodchurch under an altar tomb, on the ledge of which is the following inscription in Roman capitals:

"Edwardus Waterhous, miles, reginæ a consiliis regni sui Hiberniæ, obiit 13 die Octobris, 1591."

[The foregoing inscription, newly and more accurately copied in 1992, reads as follows: EDWARDUS WATERHOUS MILES REGINE ACONSILIIS REGNI SUI HIBERNIE OBIIT 13 DIE OCTOBRIS 1591]

Arms. 1. Or, a pile engrailed Sa.Waterhous.
      2. G. 3 bendlets vairé. Longavalle.
      3. Per pale indented, Ar. and G.
      4. Az. on a chevron between 3 crosslets fitche Sa. a trefoil Ar. Davenport.
      5. Ar. 3 towers G. Castell.
      6. Or and Az. a bend Erm. Sparke. A crescent for difference.
      Impaling,
      1. A bend Erm.
      2. Checky, A. and Sa.
      3. Ar. 9 annulets G. 3, 2, 1.
      4. Quarterly, 1 and 4, G. a bend Ar. 2 and 3, Sa. a fleur-de-lis, Ar.
      5. Sa. a chevron engrailed between 3 owls, Ar.
      6. A fess indented between 6 crosslets.
      7. G. a chevron between 10 crosses pattée, within a bordure Arg.
      8. O. on a saltire G. 6 etoiles of the field.
      9. Ar. 3 fleurs-de-lis 2, 1.*

*Copied from the church, September 1792. In this church is a curious brass plate with the following inscription on a circle, which has puzzled many:

Mestre Nichol de Gore
Gist en ceste place
Jhesu Crist prioms ore
Qe merci lui face.

"Sir Edward's brother, Thomas Waterhouse, was of Berkhamsted, Hertfordshire, and lies buried with his father in a chapel in the church of Berkhamsted. By Mary, his wife, daughter of John Kirby, of Nottinghamshire (who bore, Ar. 2 bars, and a canton Gu.) he had issue Edward Waterhouse, Esq., of Berkhamsted, who married the daughter of Sir William Lane, of Horton, Northamptonshire; and Francis Waterhous, of London, afterwards of Greenford, Middlesex, Esq., who, by Bridget, daughter of Morgan Powell, descended from Parkhall, in Shropshire (her arms, a Chief O. and lion ramp. jessant G.), had issue Edward Waterhous, of Greenford, Middlesex, Esq., now living, 1660, and lodging in Sion college, London, who married two wives, viz. Mary, daughter and heir of Robert Smith, alias Carrington, descended from the Leicestershire family by Magdalen, his wife, daughter to Robert Harvey, Esq., controller to the custom house to King James. His other wife was Elizabeth, daughter and co-heiress of Richard Bateman, Esq., by Christian, his first wife, daughter of William Stone, of London, Esq., by whom he had issue Edward, her only son, since her deceased, and two daughters, Elizabeth and Bridget, both living this August, 1660."

[Here follows much more but with no further mention of Hertfordshire]

September 1796. The inscription at Northchurch, p.460 [see June 1796], which is said to have puzzled many, may be thus translated:
Master Nichol de Gore
Lies in this place.
Jesus Christ pray we now
That Mercy (he will) him shew.

The reference here to Northchurch is a mistake by the contributor. The monument and inscription described above are both in the parish church of All Saints at Woodchurch, Kent. [AJ]

August 1796. Correct List of the present House of Commons, [includes]:

HERTFORDSHIRE.	William Plumer, Esq., 7.
	William Baker, Esq., 4.
Hertford.	John Calvert, Esq. Baron Nathaniel Dimsdale 1.
St. Albans.	Lord Bingham 1. *Thomas Skip Dyot Bucknall, Esq.

*New member at the late General Election.

November 1796. . . . .Thomas Salmon was the younger son of Thomas Salmon, 33 years rector of Mepsal [Meppershall], Bedfordshire, who died 1706, and younger brother to Nathaniel Salmon, LL.D., who was educated at Benet college, Cambridge, 1690–95; but, declining the oaths to Queen Anne, though he had taken them to King William, practised physick at Bishops Stortford, and printed the Antiquities of Essex, Hertfordshire, and Surrey, and other antiquarian tracts, and died April 2, 1742. Thomas died suddenly in London, 1743, and was buried at St. Dunstan's church, leaving three daughters. Thus much may be learned from Master's *History of Benet College*, p.365. B.B.

1797. Sheriff. Hertfordshire. Sir John Saunders Sebright of Beechwood, Hertfordshire.

TYTTENHANGER

January 1797. In the year 1547, Sir Thomas Pope, founder of Trinity college, Oxford, bought of King Henry the Eighth the ancient stately mansion house of Tyttenhanger, in the parish of Ridge, Hertfordshire, being the country seat of the abbots of St. Albans; and which, but for this purchase, would have been destroyed as an appendage to the abbey. This house was so large, that, in 1528, King Henry the Eighth, with his queen Catharine, and their retinue, removed hither during the continuance of the sweating sickness in London.

In this house Sir Thomas Pope made great improvements. It became his favourite place of residence, and the statutes of his college are dated thence. He erected over the vestibule of the great hall a noble gallery for wind music. This chapel was a spacious edifice, and beautifully decorated. The windows were enriched with painted glass, which Sir Thomas Pope brought hither from the choir of St. Albans abbey, when that church, by his interposition with the king, was preserved from total destruction. The wainscot behind or over the stalls was finely painted with a series of the figures of all the saints who bore the name of John, in memory of John Moot, one of the abbots. But Sir Thomas Pope put up a new piece of wainscot, of Spanish oak, on a very large scale, at the east end, most exquisitely sculptured, beginning at the end of the stalls, and continued towards the altar. This was to adorn that part of the chapel which was usually called the presbytery, or the space about and near the altar.

After Sir Thomas Pope's death, in 1559, Tyttenhanger House continued to be inhabited by the relations of his second wife, bearing the name of Pope-Blount. In the year 1620 it began to be lessened, or pulled down in part; about which time the family of Napier, then tenants to Trinity college (Oxford) at Luton, by the mediation of the college, removed the wainscot (abovementioned), put up by Sir Thomas Pope in the chapel of Tyttenhanger House, in entire preservation, to the chapel of the mansion house at Luton. John, Earl of Bute, about the year 1768, pulled down this old mansion house at Luton, to build a new house in its place; but, with great taste and judgement, retained the old chapel, with Sir Thomas Pope's wainscot, where it still remains. (*Bibl. Top. Brit*. VIII.69).

No traces of the old house at Tyttenhanger now remain. It was totally

demolished about the year 1652, and was soon afterwards most elegantly rebuilt as it appears at present.   T. Warton.

---

9 August 1797. This being the day on which Earl Cowper attained the
age of 21, it was celebrated by roasting an ox whole on Cole Green, near
his seat at Hertingfordbury. The beast was put down in a pit, fastened
by an iron chain to a wooden axle-tree between 2 cart wheels, before a
large wood fire, at 2 in the morning, and after being turned by 2 men
suitable habited, and decorated with ribbons, who were the same that
assisted at this ceremony on that day 21 years, being his lordship's
birth-day, was cut up and distributed, with a proportionable quantity of
strong beer, to an innumerable crowd of spectators, at 2 in the afternoon; at which time his lordship, who had previously received the compliments of the neighbouring nobility and gentry at his steward's house
on the edge of the green, was mounted on one of the beer buts, and
received the homage of the multitude in 9 successive cheers. One of the
men towards the conclusion of the business was unfortunately thrown
down into the fire and much hurt. The whole festivity concluded with a
display of fireworks from the front of the steward's house. The same ceremony was performed at Wingham, his lordship's seat in Kent.

ROYSTON CHURCH: THE SCALES EFFIGY

September 1797. It having been suggested that the curious stone effigies
of Lord Scales in Royston Church may tend to elucidate the ancient
baronial habit, etc., I send you a drawing of it hoping that your ingenious correspondents in the costume may take the trouble of comment-
ing thereon in your widely-extended and useful Miscellany.
    The figure from which the drawing is made is now loose in the
church, and may perchance soon be entirely defaced.

*The misadventures of this monument have been extremely well documented. The
earliest reference occurs in Weever's* Funeral Monuments *(1631): "In a ruinous
wall of this decayed Priory lies the proportion of a man cut in stone, which (say
the inhabitants) was made to the memorie of one of the Founders, who lieth
thereby interred." This was clearly the main source for Chauncy (1700) who went
on mistakenly to describe the figure as a monk. "In a wall of this decayed Priory
stood formerly the effigy of a man cut in stone, with a hood covering his face
reaching to the pitch of his shoulders, which was removed into the church and
the inhabitants report to have been one of the founders, but the habit (I rather
think) declares him a monk."*

William Cole the antiquary, 1714–1783 (B.M. Add. MS. 5820, f.19) attributed the subsequent disfigurement of the monument in part to the belief that scrapings of alabaster were beneficial in some disorders. He described the figure as a knight in armour, with his head on two cushions, supported by 'angels'. Salmon referred to "a lion on one side of the cushion his head rests on; there was another lion on the other side, but broken off". The lions (or angels) do not appear in the 1797 drawing, but Clutterbuck (1827) described "a lion on each side of the cushions under his head". The lions have not been noted since.

Salmon did not mention the location of the effigy, but Clutterbuck found it "in the south-west corner of the church . . . , much battered". Cussans, whose chapter on Royston was published in 1873, reported that for many years, down to the past few weeks, the effigy has been lying under a pew at the western end of the aisle, where, being of such soft material, "it has suffered much from the iron-shod heels of restless school-children." At the time of his visit however it had recently been moved, and lay "on the ground at the east end of the north aisle."

When a chancel was added to the church in 1891 a resting-place for the effigy was found in a recess beneath a window on the south side. Alfred Kingston (A History of Royston) recorded it there in 1906, and it remains there to this day. The figure is not accompanied by a sword, as in the drawing, and none of the observers quoted above has referred to such a thing. One doubts whether it ever existed. [AJ]

FLOOD DAMAGE IN ST. ALBANS ABBEY CHURCH

25 September and October 1797. St. Albans suffered much this morning from the floods. In the Abbey church, owing to the stoppage of a drain at the north door, the water rose so high as almost to bear down the person who opened the door to let it through the church, where it so thoroughly penetrated and loosened the ground, as to remove many of the grave-stones from their places, and by undermining some of the flat stones, were at one end then at the other, changed from their horizontal to nearly an upright position. . .

The drains near the north door having been stopped, the rain had made its way into the church, and caused the above disaster. Though the pavement still continued it gave away wherever I turned, I could not resist the impulse to examine if any part of the main building had sustained the least injury. Upon strict observation, I found that the force of all the destruction wrought upon the pavement had centred round the pier of the arch next to the north-west pier of the great tower.

From my representing to the churchwardens my apprehensions for the safety of the building, and that it was absolutely necessary to clear round the invaded pier of the arch, they the next day complied with my request, but it was found that the projecting foundation of the pier had sunk several inches in the centre out of its horizontal level.

I am sorry to say not any attention was paid to this dangerous appearance, as, from its relative connexion to the great tower it was incumbent to have given it permanent security. It is not at all unlikely that on this circumstance depends the future preservation of the whole building — a building which claims universal admiration and should claim universal protection. . . .

It appears, from the conversation which I had with the churchwardens and other people of the place, that they would receive more satisfaction in beholding a new gallery thrown across the eastern part of the choir, than displeased at the altar screen, one of the finest performances of the kind in the Kingdom, being either destroyed, or hid by any introduction of parochial accommodation.

Should the new innovative levelling architectural system spread its baleful influence to this hallowed spot, what intemperate zeal has left of ancient art undestroyed must, by the ruthless iron hands of these modern beautifiers, be annihilated ! . . .

AN ARCHITECT.

The scandalous neglect of the St. Albans Abbey fabric in the three centuries prior to 1835 is portrayed in this excerpt with startling vividness. A violent storm revealed how a simple maintenance matter, blocked drains, could threaten the equilibrium of the tower. Negligence persisted and only in 1870 did Sir George Gilbert Scott, after a titanic struggle, secure the tower from imminent collapse. The anonymous architect writing here is almost certainly John Buckler, 1770–1851, who devoted his life to drawing ancient buildings. Thirteen thousand of his drawings are preserved in the British Library, while seven hundred and fifty finished drawings of Hertfordshire subjects are found in the County Record Office. The classic book, A History of the Architecture of the Abbey Church of St. Alban, *published by his sons, J.C. and C.A. Buckler in 1847, helped to turn the tide in favour of serious repair. The galleries inserted near the crossing of the abbey and referred to so disparagingly by the writer, can be seen in contemporary water-colours by Thomas Girtin, 1775–1802. The abbey interior was a veritable burial ground: since churchwardens were responsible for repairs to the pavement, a fee could be charged for interments. After 1832, the Ecclesiastical Courts Commission discouraged the practice, to safeguard the stability of church fabrics as well as the public health. [ER]*
[See also Obituary of John Kent, 12 September 1798]

1798. Sheriff. Hertfordshire. Felix Calvert of Hunsdon House.

January 1798. The following fragments, from the MSS. of Mr. Jones of Welwyn, will doubtless be acceptable to your biographical readers:

"Sir William Keate, Bart., a worthy and good man, of whom all people, as far as I can find, speak well: the last baronet, I think, of the family of the Keates of Kimpton Hoo. His remains lie buried within the communion rails in the chancel of Digswell, Hertfordshire, with this inscription (as nearly as I can remember) on a prostrate stone over them:

'Here lieth the body of Sir William Keate, Bart., LL.D., rector of Digswell, who died March 6, 1757, aged 57'.

Dr. Young and others give him a great character. He was very inoffensive; and very charitable. He expended (as his successor told me) above £1000 upon his rectory house at Digswell. In his will he bequeathed the sum of £10,000 to Worcester college, in Oxford, where he had had his academical education: to devolve to that college after the death of a legatee mentioned in the said will".

June 1798.

MEMORIAL IN BISHOPS STORTFORD CHURCH

"To the memory of
THOMAS ADDERLEY. esq.
who died April 1, 1774,
in the 67th year of his age,
and his wife, in a vault in middle aile
opposite this monument.
He was equally zealous to serve his friends and
promote the public utility: upon that
principle he first suggested the idea of making
the river Stort navigable up to this town, in which
he had resided more than 45 years; and was
principally concerned in obtaining the laws necessary
for that purpose. He lived to see the good effect of
these services in respect to the publick; and the
proprietors of the navigation were so sensible of
the benefit of his advice throughout the course of
that arduous undertaking,
that they were never
wanting, as well before as since the completion of it,
to pay him the respect due to his zeal, and to
express their thankful acknowledgements.
Absent or dead still let a friend be dear;
A sigh the absent claim, the dead a tear."

Arms. A. on a bend G. 3 crosses parrée A. between 3 talbots heads S. Crest, a crane.

Thus is commemorated in the parish church of Bishops Stortford a man who, while he shewed himself a public benefactor in one instance, bears the whole reproach of having defeated the benevolent intentions of others, by destroying "the famous grammar school" of the same town, so that not a trace or drawing of it remains to gratify any of its grateful alumni.   Q.P.

[*See November 1795 and Supplement*].

MONUMENTAL INSCRIPTIONS: ST. PAUL'S WALDEN CHURCH

September 1798. Passing the other day through the village of Paul's Walden, in Hertfordshire, I happened to walk into the church, and there copied the following inscriptions on flat stones. . ..

Arms of Gilbert: [Gules], an armed leg couped at the thigh in pale between two broken spears [Argent, headed Or]. Crest, an arm embowed in armour [proper], holding a broken spear [Or], point downwards.

"Here lyeth the remains of EDWARD GILBERT, late of the Bury, in this parish, who died the 27th of May, 1762, in the 82nd year of his age, leaving behind him one daughter, Mary, now living, the widow of George Bowes, late of Gibside and Streatlam castle, in co. Durham, Esq., deceased, and one grand-daughter, Mary Eleanor Bowes, their daughter, now living".

Another: the arms of Gilbert impaling ———— a chevron between three eagles heads erased ————.

"Here lieth the body of MARY, late wife of Edward Gilbert, of the Bury, in this parish, who died the 2nd of September, MDCCLII in the XLVIth year of her age".

Another:
"Here lieth the body of JOHN GILBERT, Esq., who departed this life the 10th of May, 1768, in the 87th year of his age".

Another: Arms, an anchor, and on a chief three roundels, impaling a chevron between three sprigs of ————.

"Here lieth interred the body of JANE HEYSHAM, wife of Robert Heysham, Esq., of Stagenhoe, who departed this life the 16th day of February, 1721. Here also lyeth the body of ROBERT HEYSHAM, of Stagenhoe, Esq., who was born in Lancaster, and served that corporation in parliament fifteen years, and the city of London seven years, who died an alderman of the said city the 25th day of February, anno Domini 1722, in the 60th year of his age. He left issue only one son, Robert Heysham, in the 10th year of his age".

On another, an anchor, and in chief three roundels, impaling on a bend ———— between two cottises Erm. three lions passant ————.

"Here lieth interred the body of WILLIAM HEYSHAM, of Greenwich, Kent, Esq., who was member of parliament ten years last past for the corporation of Lancaster. He married Sarah, daughter of Richard Perry, of London, Esq., and died the 14th day of April, anno Domini 1727, in the 36th year of his age".

Another:
"M.S. Here lieth the body of JANE HEYSHAM, daughter of Robert Heysham, of Stagenhoe, Esq., who died the 14th of November, 1711, aged three years two months. Here also lieth the body of ELIZABETH HEYSHAM, daughter of William Heysham, Esq., of Greenwich, and member of parliament for Lancaster. She departed this life the 20th of February, 1720, in the 26th year of her age".

The William Heysham last mentioned was probably father of the other William.   B.L.

The following notes relate to persons recorded above :

EDWARD GILBERT. The career and genealogy of this ancestor of the Queen have so far baffled researchers. No evidence has yet been found to support the theory that he was a successful London merchant, who purchased St. Paul's Walden Bury for his country house. The only readily available clue to his ancestry is his coat-of-arms, which, according to Burke's General Armorial (1884), was first borne by William Gilbert, Esq., of Gilbert's Place, Lullington, Derbyshire, in Queen Elizabeth I's reign. Otherwise it only records a branch of the family in Selby, Leicestershire (Yorkshire?), as bearing the arms, from whom, since the senior branch subsequently assumed the name and arms of the Cooper family on inheriting their property, Edward Gilbert may have been descended. He was in his forties when he purchased St. Paul's Walden Bury. His social status may be gauged by the marriage of his daughter, Mary, to the sole male heir to the considerable estates in Durham, Middlesex and London of the wealthy Bowes family, and his pre-eminence in the locality by his undertaking, though not the patron of the living, to rebuild the chancel of the parish church; while the uncompromising addition of a decorative, baroque east end to a strictly medieval nave reveals something of his character.

MARY-ELEANOR BOWES. As Mary Bowes' daughter, she was heiress to both the Bowes and the Gilbert estates. In 1767, at the age of 18, she married John Lyon, 9th Earl of Strathmore, who, in consequence of her great inheritance, assumed by Act of Parliament the surname of Bowes. In 1777, widowed and a mother of five, Mary-Eleanor married an Irishman, Andrew Robinson Stoney, variously described as MP for Newcastle and High Sheriff of Durham (Burke's Peerage), "lieutenant in a marching regiment" (Cussans), and "a villain to the backbone" (William Howitt), who seriously ill-treated her, squandered her fortune, was divorced after twelve years, and died in the Marshalsea. The countess was, nevertheless, something of a blue stocking, and a protégée of Linnaeus' distinguished pupil, Dr. Daniel Solander. Of her children, John Bowes succeeded as 10th Earl of Strathmore and Kinghorne in 1776, and died without offspring; George, who resided at St. Paul's Walden Bury, pre-deceased his brother, also without offspring; Thomas succeeded as 11th Earl in 1820.

ROBERT HEYSHAM. Robert Heysham bought the manor of Stagenhoe in 1703. He was succeeded in 1722 by his 10-year old only son, Robert, who died unmarried at the age of 22, leaving Stagenhoe to a relation, Giles Thornton, of Aldgate, London, on the condition that he assumed the surname of Heysham. Three years later (1737), the manor house, which had been built during the Commonwealth, was burned down. Giles built the present house in 1740.

WILLIAM HEYSHAM. Nothing more is known of him than is written on the tombstone. Unlike the burials of the Robert Heyshams, his and his daughter's are not recorded in the parish register. It seems likely that he was a cousin who perhaps died at his house at Greenwich and was interred here with his daughter, Jane, to be in the family vault. [LB]

17 December 1798. This night, between 7 and 8 o'clock, a fire broke out at the spacious mansion of the Earl of Essex, in Curzon Street, Mayfair, which consumed the whole of the premises, the flames raging with such incredible fury, that scarcely any of the valuable furniture could be saved. . . .

The same day the above fire happened, a similar accident occurred at Brocket Hall, the seat of Lord Melbourne. The Duke of Richmond and a large party were at dinner, when the alarm was given that the hall was on fire; but by the timely assistance of the servants it was got under without much injury to the house. It was occasioned, it is said, by a "buzaglo" stove getting red-hot.

The same day the chimney of Lord Melbourne's house at Whitehall caught fire; but was extinguished without doing any mischief.

December 1798. Dispensation. Rev. Thomas Bargus, M.A. to hold Reed rectory with Barkway rectory, Hertfordshire.

1799. Sheriff. Hertfordshire. Archibald Paxton, of Watford, Esq.

DISCOVERY OF A VAULT, AND SKELETONS, AT ST. MICHAEL'S

May 1799. The following circumstance having lately occurred in this neighbourhood, and created some speculation among a few persons who pay some regard to what passes around them, I mentioned it to a common and much-esteemed friend; in consequence of whose request I transmit an account of it, for insertion, if you think it worthy, in your useful Repository.

On Friday the 3rd instant, as some labourers were digging for gravel in a field of wheat at the back of the house of Kingsbury, in St. Michael's parish, in the occupation of Mr. Ralph Smith, an ancient and respectable gentleman-farmer of that place; they struck against a flint-stone; and, upon turning it up, and examining farther, they found an arched vault of large flints, reaching some way; and within it a thick and heavy leaden coffin, 5 feet 6 inches long, the upper end of which seems to have been semicircular, but the lower end quite straight; it is broken in half across the middle, and seems to have had two or three holes bored through the bottom; nothing like a lid appears; the edges of the top are broke and uneven; and it is brown, from having lain so long in the earth, and vastly cankered and corroded.

In the coffin were the remains of a skeleton, consisting principally of a small skull, grown exceedingly brown, but in perfect condition, and not having lost, when first discovered, perhaps, one tooth. From all which circumstances, and the shortness of the coffin, I should incline to think it must have been a young lad. The face appears to have been rather compressed in the sides, and projecting towards the mouth. There were also, I understand, two thigh bones. Near to this coffin were several large and long iron nails, or cramps, prodigiously encrusted and corroded with rust. Two of these, with the skull, and a scrap of the coffin, are deposited in a closet in the Archdeacon's court, behind the high altar in the abbey church, where some other reliques of a similar kind are to be seen. The coffin is, at present, at a plumber's in the neighbourhood, and contains, probably, lead enough for two or three modern ones.

I visited the spot ten days after this discovery, and found it, in a direct line, nearly north of St. Michael's church at the distance, of, perhaps, a quarter of a mile, a little, as seems to me, to the west of what is called Oster Hill in Dr. Stukeley's *Vestigia Cinerum Verolami*, in vol. 1 of the *Vetusta Monumenta*, at some distance from the hedge, and without any indication upon the surface of what was to be expected below. But I found that this must have been, at some time, and upon some occasion, a common cæmeterium, for, while I was there, the labourers dug out bones. They had found no other coffin, but many bones, the remains of more skeletons; some of which, they said, were laying about in such a way, that it seemed as if bodies had been thrown in at random, and left to lie as they fell. They dug up, and shewed me another skull, which they had found, and buried again, which was much hurt by the pick-axe, but contained several very good teeth. There seemed to be black patches in the ground, and lowest parts of which were, in general, but about $2\frac{1}{2}$ feet below the surface, whereof each had probably contained a body, or bodies, with patches of the natural coloured earth between them; and the men picked up little handfuls of earth, with small black particles, spangles, among it, which they took to be the remains of decayed coffins, or might be of the bodies themselves.

They assured me they had found no coin, but one very small trifling piece. I observed thick broken tiles, probably taken out of the walls of Verulam; and a small broken piece of black earthenware, which, when washed, might be written on like a slate, and appeared to have been something of the shape of those Soucoupes, or stands, which we frequently meet with under the better sort of garden pots. I wish not to encroach too much upon your closely-printed pages; and therefore conclude.

June 1799. A list of Bampton lecturers from their first establishment, [including] Charles Wheatley, M.A. vicar of Furneux Pelham, Hertfordshire, 1738.

'THE BEGGAR'S PETITION'

December 1799. I do myself a pleasure in sending you some account of a well-known and much-admired poem, intituled, "The Beggar's Petition."

This very pleasing and pathetic poem is the production of Dr. Joshua Webster M.D. and was written at St. Albans in the year 1764. It refers to an aged mendicant, named Kinderley, or Kinder, who had once lived on his little paternal estate near Potter's Cross [Potters-Crouch, St. Michael's parish], between St. Albans and Berkhamsted, in Hertfordshire, and was for many years a farmer in decent circumstances. His ruin was occasioned by the artifices of what Pope calls a "vile attorney": yet, at the time of the above elegant composition, he had dragged on a sorrowful existence to the great age of 83; and he continued to live some years after. The ingenious author of the stanzas is now (in 1799) resident in Chelsea, and, like his subject, is far advanced in years: Animi autem maturus Alethes, cruda viridisque senectûs.

Dr. Webster has a drawing of Kinderley in water colours, representing him as begging at the door of a cottage or farmhouse, designed by the Doctor himself, and to which he has affixed the beautiful lines in MS. That justly celebrated picture of "The Woodman," painted by Gainsborough, from which an admirable print has been engraved by Simon, was done from a hale woodcutter, who worked for Dr. Webster at Chigwell Row, in the parish of Chigwell, Essex.

In early life, Dr. Webster was very intimately and professionally connected with Dr. Nathaniel Cotton, of St. Albans, author of "Visions in Verse for younger Minds"; and of a variety of other pieces, which are highly esteemed.

[The editor of G.M. has added the following note: We have already paid our respects to this excellent piece in vol. LX [1790] p.972, where however it is ascribed to the Rev. Thomas Moss, minister of Brierly Hill chapel in the parish of King's Swinford, in the county of Stafford.

The full text of the Beggar's Petition, given here, is transcribed from the Gentleman's Magazine vol. LXI [1791] p.852.]

THE BEGGAR'S PETITION

> Pity the sorrows of a poor old man,
> Whose trembling limbs have borne him to your door;
> Whose days are dwindled to the shortest span:-
> Oh, give relief, and Heav'n will bless your store!
>
> These tatter'd cloaths my poverty bespeak;
> These hoary locks proclaim my lengthen'd years;
> And many a furrow in my grief-worn cheek
> Has been the channel to a flood of tears!
>
> Yon house, erected on the rising ground,
> With tempting aspect drew me from my road;
> For Plenty there a residence has found,
> And Grandeur a magnificent abode.
>
> Hard is the fate of the infirm and poor!
> Here, as I crav'd a morsel of their bread,
> A pamper'd menial drove me from the door,
> To seek a shelter in a humbler shed.
>
> Oh, take me to your hospitable dome!

Keen blows the wind, and piercing is the cold!
Short is my passage to the friendly tomb;
For I am poor, and miserably old!

Should I reveal the sources of my grief,
If soft Humanity e'er touch'd your breast,
Your hands would not withhold the kind relief,
And tears of Pity would not be represt.

Heav'n sends misfortunes! why should we repine?
'Tis Heav'n has brought me to the state you see!
And your condition soon may be like mine,
The child of Sorrow, and of Misery!

A little farm was my paternal lot;
Then, like the lark, I sprightly hail'd the morn!
But, ah! Oppression forc'd me from my cot;
My cattle died, and blighted was my corn.

My daughter, once the comfort of my age,
Lur'd by a villain from her native home,
Is cast, abandon'd, on the world's wide stage,
And doom'd in scanty poverty to roam.

My tender wife, sweet soother of my cares,
Struck with sad anguish at the stern decree,
Fell, ling'ring fell, a victim to Despair,
And left the world to wretchedness and me!

Pity the sorrows of a poor old man,
Whose trembling limbs have borne him to your door;
Whose days are dwindled to the shortest span;
Oh, give relief, and Heav'n will bless your store!

1800. Sheriff. Hertfordshire. Justinian Casamajor of Potterells.

10 January 1800. As Mr. Hobdell, wheelwright, at Ridge Hill, in Hertfordshire, was hastily putting on his coat, in stretching out his arm he struck one of his children, of about two years old, who was standing on a chair at the breakfast table; and the poor infant, falling with the back of its head against the edge of a chair, received so dreadful a hurt as to occasion its death the next day, notwithstanding every possible assistance was afforded. The coroner's jury have brought in a verdict of Accidental Death.

4 March. Hertford. The assizes finished here this day, when W. Criswell and James Burgess received sentence of death for a burglary in the dwelling house of Nathaniel Camp. It appeared on the trial, that the prosecutor Camp, an old man, with his wife, resided in a cottage near half a mile from Stansted [Abbots?]; that it was generally understood about the country, that he had acquired money, which he kept in his house, which is supposed to have been the reason that induced the prisoners to select him to make their prey of; and accordingly, on the night of December 19, when he and his wife were in bed, they broke into the house, knocked him down with a large ashen stick, and cut him with a knife in the neck, and across the calves of his legs; they also cut his wife through her stays and shift to the skin, and in the neck, threatening, with the most horrid imprecations, to finish them by cutting their throats, if they did not discover where the money was; and, after searching the whole house without finding any money, took some spoons and other things, and set the old man in a chair telling him he might sit and bleed to death. They were ordered to be executed near the spot where the offence was committed, which was accordingly done, on Friday the 13th, amidst the greatest concourse of people ever assembled in the county, except at an election: the lane, being narrow, was entirely filled. The criminals behaved in the most daring and abandoned manner. Criswell, who was a native of Hoddesdon, was of gigantic and savage appearance, always armed with a bill, and ready for every desperate action, and it was found necessary to chain him by the arm in his cell after conviction. Burgess was born at Ware. The wife of the prosecutor had the fairest opportunity of knowing the persons of both by the clear light of the moon, which came into the room through two opposite windows, so that the trial was short.

Waters was executed on the Wednesday for robbing the Duke of Leeds' steward, on the highway near North Mimms.

May 1800. A large Library of 15,000 volumes has been lately discovered by Mr. Todd, Editor of Milton's Comus, at Ashridge, near Little Gaddesden, Hertfordshire, in which there is a Dido, much finer than Mr. S.'s, which fetched almost £20.

23 May 1800. General Manners, and two more gentlemen, in a postchaise and four, were stopped near Wade's Mill, on the road to Cambridge, by two highwaymen; one of whom, demanding the General's money with threats, was shot dead by him, and the other immediately rode off.

REVIEW OF THE HERTFORDSHIRE MILITIA, HATFIELD PARK

12 June 1800. This country affords no spectacle, perhaps, so splendid as a review of the domestic military force of a county. Were it confined to mere martial parade, much praise indeed would be due to the spirit of so many individuals sacrificing much private interest to so patriotic a purpose. But from that high and generous feeling which has always characterised the aristocracy of England, this species of military exhibition is in many instances combined with all the merit that ever attached to English hospitality also. Instead, therefore, of an entertainment to which each individual has contributed a share, the great expense is to be defrayed by one. Few are equal to such an undertaking, and consequently it is only from the first in rank and fortune in the county that it can be expected. On no one in Hertfordshire, therefore, could this part devolve with more propriety than on the Marquis of Salisbury; by no one could it be sustained with more munificence and elegance of manners; nor could any theatre be so favourable to its display as Hatfield Park. Nearly a month past has been exhausted in busy preparations; but this was the grand day of increasing activity for their completion. In this business above 100 of his Lordship's servants and labourers were employed, under the immediate inspection of the Marquis, who was indefatigable in his exertions to arrange the tents and waggons, so as to accommodate all the spectators to the best advantage. Among the innkeepers of the neighbourhood also, all was bustle and confusion. Their cellars and larders were stripped of their wines and provisions, and transferred to booths erected in the park, which were scattered among the distant clumps of trees, commanding a view of the tents and the whole scene of military display. The park, from the nature of the ground, is extremely well adapted to such a purpose. It rises with a gentle ascent in front of the house, and it was upon the lower part of it that the several corps were formed in line, while the various vehicles in which the company came were removed to the upper extremity, where they formed the exterior circle, overlooking all beneath. In making this arrangement, the Marquis was assisted by the Marchioness, who came at 2 o'clock; and, by their directions, tables and seats of oak planks were placed inside the vehicles, for the farther accommodation of the spectators, many of whom arrived in the evening. Securing a bed at the Salisbury Arms was the first consideration, and they could only be procured at a guinea a night. The stalls for horses were equally difficult of attainment; the Duke of York having engaged one; the Earls of Chesterfield, Harrington, Clarendon, and Spencer, the others. No accommodations could be had for even the volunteer cavalry, who came into the town that morning, and were obliged to put their horses in the cow-house and barn. 40 beds were made up at Hatfield House for the accommodation of visitors. As early as 4 o'clock yesterday, the company began to assemble in every kind of vehicle. At 6 the noble peal of bells sounded Malbrook in a very superior style, which aroused the drowsy visitors, by summoning them to prepare for the pleasurable scene. When the clock struck 7, the gates of Hatfield Park were thrown open to admit the carriages. The waggons were very gaily decorated with oak boughs, and the company in them consisted principally of ladies, dressed in virgin white. About half after 8 the whole line was formed by the carriages and waggons, extending near three miles from one extremity to the other, in the form of an horse-shoe; the open part in the front of Hatfield House. At 9 their Majesties, in a chariot with four horses, entered through the principal lodge at the southern extremity of the park, having been only one hour and three quarters in coming. Next followed one of the carriages, in which were the Princesses Elizabeth, Augusta, Mary, and Amelia. In the next, the Prince and Princess of Orange and the Duke of York. Punctually at a quarter after nine, the King came out of the south door, mounted; the Queen with the princesses followed in the open landau of Lady Salisbury; and next came in another landau, the Princess Mary, Princess of Orange, Countess of

Harcourt, Ladies Georgina and Emily Cecil. The Prince of Orange was in his own coach. These carriages kept to the left, until they arrived at the Queen's marquee, which was on a rising ground, commanding a view of the line. Its elegance was worthy of the noble Marquis. It was boarded with oak in the most finished style, and covered with a beautiful Brussels carpet, of an octagon pattern, planned to the floor; the lining cotton, of a straw colour, with a small sprig. Eight chairs were placed on each side for the accommodation of the royal and illustrious visitants. Projected panels of mahogany, with sash doors, commanded a full view of the east and western front. The adjoining tents were erected, one for the Cabinet ministers; the other for the Maids of Honour, the Marchioness, and her friends. An elegant breakfast was laid for their Majesties in a service of gold, which was prepared for them in the summer dining-room.

The Line was formed punctually by half past seven, and a serjeant from each corps was on the ground by 7 o'clock at latest. When his Majesty was seen approaching the Line, after mounting his horse at Hatfield House, a royal salute was fired of 21 guns. When the King took his station in front of the Line, one gun was fired, to present arms and salute; and a second, to shoulder. The King then passed along the front of the Line, and returned by the rear of the Infantry, and between the ranks of the Cavalry; during which time the drums and music played, but there was no salute. As soon as his Majesty was seen returning to his station in front of the Line, the ranks were closed by order of the Commanding Officers of the corps. On the third gun, the Infantry wheeled backward on their left by divisions; and the Cavalry wheeled, by threes, to the right. Fourth gun;- to march off at ordinary time—the moving at the same moment. At the last wheel before passing by, the Cavalry formed their divisions (as had been marked to them); and, at 150 paces from the King, the ranks opened, and arms carried. The officers saluted, and Colours were dropped on passing his Majesty, and the ranks were closed by each division 40 yards after it had so passed. The column then entered its former alignment by the left, and proceeded, with distances accurately kept, to its old ground; on which the Infantry halted by word of command from the Exercising Officer, which word was instantly repeated by the Commanding Officer of each corps. The words "Wheel into Line!"—"March!"—were then given in the same manner. The Cavalry trotted on when the Infantry halted, formed subdivisions, and passed the King afterwards in single file on a walk, formed its column of subdivisions again after passing, and, on a trot, took up its original alignment, which it entered near the right of Infantry. The eldest Officer of the Cavalry, at the proper moment, gave the words "Halt!"—"Wheel into Line!"—"March!"—the Infantry loaded while the Cavalry passed by. Fifth gun; fired a volley from right to left by corps, the firelocks pointed in the air. Sixth gun; a volley, in the same manner. Seventh gun; a volley, as before. Eighth gun; open ranks. Ninth gun; salute. Tenth guns; shoulder.

As soon as his Majesty returned to Hatfield House after the review, the Cavalry repaired to the riding-house, and there dismounted, and the Infantry ordered their arms. On the eleventh gun, the whole proceeded by corps to the dining-tables, which were marked for each; and there remained, at a little distance from their places, till a twelfth gun was fired as signal for them to sit down. The arms were regularly piled near the table. The thirteenth cannon was fired on drinking the King's health; and a fourteenth, for the Cavalry to mount, the Infantry to repair to their arms, and the whole to proceed to lines both sides of the road from the house to the lodges, previous to his Majesty's departure. The Cavalry, being best able to reach the most distant point in time, were posted nearest the lodges. Arms were presented, colours dropped, music played and officers saluted, as his Majesty passed between the ranks on this occasion.

We ought not to pass over in silence the admirable manner in which the various corps acquitted themselves in the field. With very few exceptions, indeed, we never heard better firing; the King, Prince of Wales, and Duke of York, expressed the most flattering approbation of the strict order and regularity of the different corps, and of their general appearance, conduct, and manoeuvring. The ground was kept by the 7th or Queen's Light Dragoons, commanded by Lord Paget, who was uncommonly active on the occasion. The Surrey Yeomanry and the Hampstead Association also assisted; and several others attended for that purpose. Besides whom, a great number of other Gentlemen Volunteers, horse and foot, were present. At a quarter after one their Majesties left the field, and returned to Hatfield House. In three quarters of an hour after, the Volunteers (officers 75, privates 1482) sat down to dinner. 80 hams; 80 rounds of beef; 100 joints of veal; 100 legs of lamb; 100 tongues, 100 meat pies, 25 edge-bones of beef; 100 joints of mutton; 25 rumps of beef, roasted; 25 briskets; 71 dishes of other roast beef; 100 gooseberry pies. Killed at the Salisbury Arms; 3 bullocks, 16 sheep, 25 lambs. The Volunteers occupied 24 tables. 38 covers were laid for the Cabinet ministers. 60 regular servants, and 60 extra, were employed on the occasion. At a quarter after two the Royal family assembled in King James's room, in Hatfield House, where they sat down to a most sumptuous dinner. At the head of the tables sat their Majesties; on the right of the King, the Duke of Gloucester, Prince of Orange, Prince of Wales, Duke of York, Duke of Cumberland, and Prince Ernest. The Queen's side; Princess of Orange, with Princesses Elizabeth, Augusta, Mary, and Amelia. At the lower end; Marquis and Marchioness of Salisbury, Countesses of Harrington and Chesterfield, Lady Georgina and Amelia Cecil.

The dinner was served up on gold and silver plate. The table frame was elegantly decorated with china figures of various devices, all of them bearing the initial of "G.R." and the Crown in enamel, adorned also with military trophies; the frame, thrown in sand, represented at the upper end two light-horsemen performing the sword exercise; the other end, a warrior, having a shield, on which was inscribed "Vivat Rex!". The centre pieces delineated with military emblems, and the colours of the Hertfordshire militia. At the four corners were placed Savoy cakes, on which were affixed the King's arms, the arms of the Marquis of Salisbury, the portrait of Admiral Nelson, and also his coat of arms and mottos; four pastry baskets had suspended on each side medallions of their Majesties, the Duke of York, and the four naval admirals, Howe, Duncan, Nelson, and St Vincent.

On a shield of the portrait of Lord Nelson; "O God, thy arm was with him; and not to us, but to thy arm alone ascribe we all".

The room, which was most superbly furnished, was decorated with pictures; on the right of the chimney-piece, a whole-length portrait of his Majesty, and the words, in gold letters on a wreath, "Preserved of GOD, beloved of his People!". On the left, was a whole-length portrait of the Queen, and in gold letters the words, "Favoured of Heaven, the glory of her sex!".

Portraits of the Marquis and Marchioness of Salisbury, King Charles I and Lord Ranelagh, also adorned this apartment.

The Cabinet ministers and General Officers of State were entertained, to the number of 30, in another room. When the Volunteers had dined, upon a signal gun being fired, the whole together drank his Majesty's health, and gave three cheers with an enthusiasm that cannot be described, and afterwards sung "God save the King!" in chorus. During dinner the bands of the several corps played on the lawn before their Majesty's window. At half past four, the Royal family set off in their carriages, when a royal salute was fired, and three cheers given. The music struck up, and soon after the nobility retired. Almost all the people of distinction in Hertfordshire and the adjoining counties were assembled on this occasion; and the concourse altogether, including the different corps, could not be estimated at less than 50,000 persons. The day being remarkably fine, contributed particularly to the gratification of this assemblage.

The mansion of the Cecils, which had never received a sovereign since James I resigned it by exchange to the present family, was honoured once more with a royal visit, without the fatiguing state of formal introduction of any of the nobility, clergy or gentry of the country, to the sovereign; to whom, it may be truly said, every person present was his own introducer, and more familiar and heartfelt expressions of satisfaction and joy were never witnessed.

His Majesty having reviewed the Yeomanry, Cavalry and Volunteer corps of Hertfordshire, at Hatfield, on the 13th instant the following letter, was, by his Majesty's command, written to the Marquis of Salisbury on the occasion.

Downing Street, June 13.

My Lord,

I am commanded by his Majesty to convey to your Lordship, and through you to the Militia and Volunteer Corps of Hertfordshire, the assurance of his Majesty's perfect satisfaction at the good order, regularity, and military appearance, they have this day exhibited in his Majesty's presence . . . (et seq.)

I am, &c.   H.DUNDAS

16 June 1800. Yesterday, a single highwayman, in a soldier's dress, robbed two gentleman, in a chaise, near Ware. The same morning he stopped and robbed Mr. Tattersall, between Barley and Hare Street; after which he had the folly to come forward to Foulmire [Fowlmere, in Cambridgeshire], where he put up his horse at a public house. An alarm being given, he mounted his horse, in the presence of several people, leaped over some pales, and took the road to Royston; but, being immediately pursued, after a chase of several miles, he was secured near Haydon, and, being carried before a magistrate for Hertfordshire, was committed to Hertford Gaol.

20 June 1800. This day was committed to Hertford gaol, Ann Mead, aged 15, for poisoning the infant child of her master, Mr. Proctor, of Royston. A powder was found in its stomach, which, from some experiments that were made, was declared to be arsenic. After many declarations of her innocence, on cross-examining her closely, it came out that the child had swallowed a powder; and she afterwards confessed that she had given it half a spoonful of arsenic, and had assigned, as a reason for the diabolical act, "that her mistress called her a slut, and she resolved to spite her."

15 July 1800. A dreadful fire broke out in the barns and out houses of Mr. Young, an eminent farmer, near Essendon, Hertfordshire. On the first alarm, the neighbouring gentlemen, and the inhabitants of the contiguous towns and villages, readily came to give all the assistance in their power: 5 engines, one from Lord Salisbury's, one from Hatfield, one from Mr. Whitbread's, one from Hertford, and one from Essendon, immediately repaired to the spot; but, notwithstanding they were extremely well served, and copiously supplied with water from the river which runs close to the farm, nothing could quench the fury of the destructive element, till the house and barns were entirely consumed to ashes. The horses and cows were, with great difficulty, saved; an immense quantity of corn, of hay, and of straw, was destroyed in a moment. The property, we hear, was insured to its full value. It is almost certain, on accurate examination of the circumstances, that the fire was not caused, but designed. Our readers will recollect a similar accident, to less extent, at the same farm, 5 years ago.

18 August 1800. As ————— Brown, Esq., of North Mimms, was returning home at 10, this evening, he discovered a fire just breaking out in the stable of his farm-house, by the church, occasioned by a boy, who was returning, with a team, from the harvest field, having his candle knocked out of his hand by the horses. Mr. Brown fortunately, by his personal exertions, saved the lives of two other boys who were asleep in the loft; but, the whole square of buildings, which had been just put into excellent repairs, and were insured only a few days before, together with 200 loads of hay, and all the wheat, just brought in, from 15 acres, oats, peases, and tares, and two stacks, consisting together of 8000 faggots, 2 horses, and 2 calves, fell a prey to the devouring flames; and it was with difficulty that the farm-house was saved, being built of brick, and defended by five engines. The blaze was seen all round the country, and was visible, in a degree, the following night; nor was it extinguished within the week.

November 1800. In a review of the book *Anecdotes of the Arts in England; or, Comparative Observations on Architecture, Sculptures, and Painting, chiefly illustrated by Specimens at Oxford.* By the Rev. James Dallaway, M.B., F.S.A., Earl Marshal's Secretary:

... Mr. Dallaway passes next to old portraits: "At Kingsweston is a series* of the Cliffords, Cromwells, and Southwells; at Wrest, of the Greys; at Gorhambury, of the Barons. ..."

*At Broxbourne, Hertfordshire, before the present possessor of the family seat sold it to Mr. Bosanquet, 1786, was a fine series of the Monsons, now removed to Burton, Lincolnshire. ...

BIRTHS

29 November 1740. Wife of Mr. Humphries of Berkhamsted in Hertfordshire, childless above 25 years, delivered of 2 boys and 2 girls.

January 1746. The wife of one Plumer, a labourer at Mill Wimley [Wymondley?], near Hitchin, Hertfordshire, delivered of four boys, three born alive.

17 July 1757. Lady of Edward Gardiner of Pishiobury, Hertfordshire, of a daughter.

May 1782. The lady of Rev. Mr. Jones, curate of Broxbourne and Hoddesdon, a son.

11 November 1789. Lady of Nathaniel Barnardiston, Esq., of Theobalds, Hertfordshire, a son, which died the same day.

22 February 1791. At Sandridge Lodge [Marshalswick], near St. Albans, the lady of Charles Bourchier, Esq., a son.

Charles Bourchier purchased Marshall's Wick in 1788, and changed the name of the house to Sandridge Lodge. His wife Anne was daughter of Thomas Foley, M.P., for the county. Charles Bourchier had been Governor of Madras. On his return from India he had rebuilt Colney House in Shenley. He was sheriff of Hertfordshire in 1788. [AJ]

9 July 1791. At Bishop's Stortford, Hertfordshire, the lady of E.G. Clarke, Esq., of the 1st. Battalion of Royals, a son.

8 October 1792. In Hill Street, Berkeley Square, the lady of William Baker, Esq., M.P. for Hertfordshire, a son.

27 October 1792. At Totteridge, the lady of John Fiott, a daughter.

10 June 1793. At Sandridge Lodge [Marshalswick] near St. Albans, the lady of Charles Bourchier, Esq., a son.

13 August 1793. At Hatfield, Hertfordshire, the Marchioness of Salisbury, a daughter.

24 August 1794. At Kelshall, Hertfordshire, the lady of the Rev. George Law, a son.

2 September 1794. At his villa in Hertfordshire, the lady of Thomas Tyrwhitt Jones, Esq., a son.

8 January 1795. At Northaw Place, Hertfordshire, in child-bed, the lady of A. Watt, Esq.

c January 1795. At Sandridge Lodge [Marshalswick], St. Albans, the lady of Charles Bourchier, Esq., a son.

c June 1795. Lately, at Hampton Court Palace, the lady of John Thomas Ellis, Esq., of Wyddiall Hall, Hertfordshire, a son.

c June 1796. Lately, at Hamels, Hertfordshire, the lady of John Mellish, Esq., a daughter.

March 1797. The lady of John Mellish, of Hamels, Hertfordshire, a son.

26 March 1797. At Epping House, Little Berkhamsted, Hertfordshire, the wife of William Breton, jun., a son.

31 July 1797. At Ayot St. Lawrence, Hertfordshire, wife of Charles Ashwell, a daughter.

28 August 1797. At Kelshall, Hertfordshire, the wife of Rev. George Law, a son.

19 January 1798. At Woolmers, Hertfordshire, Mrs. Whitbread, a daughter.

c September 1798. At Hadley, near Barnet, the wife of John Henderson, Esq., a daughter.

29 September 1799. At Kelshall, Hertfordshire, the wife of Rev. George Law, a son.

11 October 1799. At Cheshunt, Hertfordshire, the wife of Rev. W.A. Armstrong, a daughter.

25 April 1800. At Hadley, Middlesex, the wife of Alexander Dury, Esq., a daughter.

21 May 1800. At Cheshunt, Hertfordshire, the wife of ———— Vincent, Esq., a son.

14 July 1800. The wife of Drake Garrard of Lante [Lamer, Wheathampstead], Hertfordshire, a daughter.

The male line of the Garrard family of Lamer died out in 1767. The estate passed to a cousin, Charles Drake, then aged 12, who assumed the name Garrard. (The name Lante in this entry seems to be a mistake for Lamer). [AJ]

2 September 1800. At his seat in Hertfordshire, the wife of Charles Morgan, Esq., M.P., a son.

13 November 1800. In Baker Street, Portman Square, the wife of George Beeston Prescott, Esq., eldest son of Sir George William Prescott, Bart., of Theobalds Park, Hertfordshire, a son and heir.

5 December 1800. At Brickendonbury, Hertfordshire, the wife of William Dent, Esq., a son.

13 December 1800. At North Mimms Place, Hertfordshire, the wife of Henry Browne, Esq., a daughter.

15 December 1800. In Threadneedle Street, the wife of William Willoughby Prescott, Esq., second son of Sir George William Prescott, Bart., of Theobalds Park, Hertfordshire, a son.

20 December 1800. At St. John's Lodge [Welwyn], Hertfordshire, the wife of Lieut-General Cuyler, a daughter.

MARRIAGES

20 April 1731. The son of Mr. Graves of Baldock in Hertfordshire (a lad of 14 years of age) to Mrs. Luke, daughter to Sir Samuel Luke, a maiden lady aged 70.

The marriage (by licence) of John Grave aged 14 of Baldock and Catherine Luke, "granddaughter of Hudibras", aged 70, is recorded in the parish register of Clothall under the date 11 April 1731. The words "granddaughter of Hudibras", seem to have been inserted later, though in the same hand as the main entry. Catherine would appear to be the child baptised at Cople in Bedfordshire, 18 October 1660, daughter of Oliver and Elizabeth Luke. In the transcript of the Cople register in Bedfordshire Record Office there is a note that "The grandfather, Sir Samuel, was almost certainly the original of Samuel Butler's satire 'Hudibras'", who is portrayed as a pedantic Presbyterian. [JP].
The marital arrangements of the Grave/s family of Baldock seem to have been somewhat eccentric. By 1745 a later Mrs. Grave was installed at Quickswood as the mistress of James, 6th Earl of Salisbury. See obituary, 2 December 1789. [AJ]

29 January 1732. George Hill of Hertfordshire, Esq., to the eldest daughter of Tyringham Backwel, of Buckinghamshire, Esq.

June 1732. William Burnace of Moor Park, Hertfordshire, Esq., to Miss Mary Bendysh of Bedford Row.

August 1732. Thomas Window, Esq., of East Barnet, to Mrs. Main, widow, of St Albans, with a fortune of £4000.

August 1733. William Gape, whose brother was late representative for St. Albans, to the daughter of Thomas Putland, Esq., of Chelsea.

October 1733. William Robinson, of Wrexham, Denbighshire, Esq., to his first cousin, one of the daughters of the late Robinson Lytton, of Knebworth, Hertfordshire, Esq.

December 1733. George Knapp of Hertfordshire, Esq., to Miss Norris of Panton Square.

July 1734. Francis Hamilton of Wrexham, Denbighshire, Esq., to the daughter of James Middleton of Broxbourne, Hertfordshire, Esq.

November 1734. Henry Popple, Esq., Under-Treasurer of the Queen's Household, to the eldest daughter of the late Sir Joseph Edmund Moore, of Hertfordshire, Bart., with a fortune of £6,000.

8 May 1735. Sir James Marwood, of Bushy [Bush? Bushey?] Hall, Hertfordshire, Bart., to Miss Nancy Pierson of Stokesly, a £10,000 fortune.

December 1735. Thomas Gladman, of Barnet, Esq., to Miss Lane, with £8,000 and £200 per annum.

December 1735. George Shelley, Esq., of Broxbourne, Hertfordshire, to Miss Ladyeman, £7000.

December 1735. George Capel of Watford, to Miss Jane Russel of Harrow on the Hill, £8000.

14 February 1736. Dr. Ingram of Barnet, to Miss Mary Nicolls worth £10,000.

23 March 1736. George Ingram of Saffron Walden, Esq., to Miss Emerson of Hatfield.

5 April 1736. Jacob Jones of Hertford, Esq., to Miss Sarah Duncombe, with £15,000.

9 May 1736. William Langham Burton, Esq., to Miss Self of Hertford, with £5000.

21 May 1736. William King, Esq., of Ingatestone, Essex, to Miss Barns of Watford, with £12,000.

7 November 1736. Henry Toucher of Kimbolton, Huntingdonshire, Esq., to Mrs. Smallwood, relict of ————— Smallwood, Esq., of St. Albans.

11 November 1736. George Harwood of Worcester, Esq., to Miss Jones, only daughter of John Jones, Esq., of Rickmansworth, Hertfordshire.

4 December 1736. Philip Samson Esq., of Hertfordshire to Miss Wade, an heiress worth £14,000.

12 June 1737. George Harrison, of Balls [Park] in Hertfordshire, Esq., to Miss Field of Stanstead.

26 August 1737. Mr. Fred Bull to Miss Dickinson of Ware, £3000.

5 October 1737. Dr. Hughes, physician of Oxford, to Miss Finch of Watford, Hertfordshire, £15,000.

11 March 1738. Charles Caesar, jun., Esq., of Bayford, Hertfordshire, to Miss Grindall of Ware.

6 July 1738. Edmund Ball, Esq., a Paymaster of Exchequer-Bills, to widow Buckeridge of Ware, £30,000.

6 March 1739. ————— Cooley, Esq., of Hertfordshire, to the daughter and sole heiress of late Sir Fisher Trench of Low-Layton, Bart.

14 March 1739. Christopher Wyvil, Esq., Comptroller of Cash in the Excise Office, to Miss Asty of Northaw, with £12,000.

13 July 1739. Mr. Dimsdale, a Quaker surgeon, to a daughter of Nathaniel Brassey, Esq., member for Hertford.

Thomas Dimsdale commenced the practice of medicine at Hertford in about the year 1734. In 1739 he married Mary, the only child of Nathaniel Brassey, Esq., of Roxford in the parish of Hertingfordbury, an eminent banker in Lombard Street and representative for the Borough of Hertford in four successive parliaments. She died without issue in 1744. In the following year Thomas Dimsdale gave up his Hertford practice and joined the army of the Duke of Cumberland in the north of England. He returned home in 1746 and married Ann Iles, a relation of his first wife. For a time he retired from practice, but subsequently took the degree of M.D. at the University of Aberdeen in 1761 and was admitted to the College of Physicians of London. His important work in the field of innoculation, and two famous visits to the court of Catherine the Great, were to follow. Dimsdale's second marriage lasted thirty years and brought ten children. Ann died in 1779, and Thomas married as his third wife Elizabeth, daughter of his cousin William Dimsdale of Bishop's Stortford, who outlived him. (Sources: Clutterbuck, 2.33; A.G. Cross. An English Lady at the Court of Catherine the Great. *1989.) [AJ]*

10 September 1739. Thomas Ansell of Ickleford, Hertfordshire, to Miss Hackwell, £10,000.

29 December 1740. Mr. Thomas Toller of Hertford to Miss Mary Bisby, with £10,000.

21 April 1741. James Hinson of Hertford, Esq., to Miss Leake of Kensington with £25,000.

18 November 1741. Mr. Rogers of Bartholomew Close, to Miss Mary Honeywood, and Clark Willshaw, M.D. of Hempstead, Hertfordshire, to Miss Rebecca Honeywood, both sisters, of £12,000 each.

3 December 1741. William Gore, of Tring, Member for Hertfordshire, to a daughter of the late Sir Orlando Humphrys, with £20,000.

12 December 1741. Richard Mead, Esq., eldest son of Dr. Mead to Miss Gore, sister to Charles Gore, of Tring, Esq.

8 January 1742. Ephraim Miller of Hertingfordbury, Esq., to Lord Bettenden's sister.

6 May 1742. John Sabine of Tewin, Hertfordshire, Esq., son of the late General Sabine and Colonel in the Guards, to Miss Osbourn of Essex.

14 July 1743. Dr. Thomas Butt of Ware, Hertfordshire, to Miss Snashwell, of Hurstpierpoint, Sussex, with £5000.

22 July 1743. William Abney, of the Inner Temple, Esq., to Miss Wooton, only daughter of ———— Wooton, Esq., of Cannons [Shenley], Hertfordshire, with upwards of £40,000.

12 August 1743. ———— Brightman of St. Albans, Esq., to Miss Bodicoate with £20,000.

5 August 1743. Mr. Bellamy, of Kingston upon Thames, to Miss Anne Lomax, eldest daughter of the late Caleb Lomax, Esq., formerly a Representative for St. Albans, Hertfordshire.

23 September 1743. Mr. Whitbread of Cannon Street, to Miss Hinde, daughter of Peter Hinde of Hertfordshire, Esq., with £15,000.

15 December 1743. Crayle Crayle of Beechwood [Flamstead], Hertfordshire, to Miss Skreen of Ashtead, near Epsom, with £10,000.

18 March 1744. George Grimstone, Esq., son of Lord Viscount Grimstone, to Miss Clover, only daughter and heiress of the late Mr. Clover of Redbourn Mills, Hertfordshire, with £20,000.

Mary, the eldest daughter of Sir Harbottle Grimston, Bart., had married (c.1649) Sir Capel Luckyn of Messinghall, Essex. As a result of the failure of the Grimston male line their grandson William Luckyn (born 1683) was adopted as heir by his uncle Sir Samuel Grimston. When Sir Samuel died in 1700 William took the surname Grimston, and was created Viscount Grimston in 1719. He married Jane Cooke, and George (born 1714) was the fourth of their six sons. [AJ]

12 April 1744. John Robinson Lytton of Knebworth, Hertfordshire, Esq., to Miss Brereton of Gloucester Street, with £50,000.

30 August 1744. General Oglethorpe to Miss Sambrooke, a sister of the late Sir Jeremy Sambrooke, Bart. [But see following entry].

15 September 1744. General Oglethorpe, to the only daughter of the late Sir Nathan Wright, Bt., of Craneham Hall, Essex. (Erase this Gent, &c, 30 August 1744). [Note as printed in G.M.]

17 June 1745. Mr. Ogburn of the India House to Miss Pitcairn of Barking [sic], Hertfordshire.

23 December 1745. William Hale of Abbots Langley, Hertfordshire, Esq., to a sister of Sir Thomas Farnaby, Bart., of Kippington (?) Kent.

6 January 1746. Mr. Spencer, mercer in Aldermanbury, to Widow Slemaker of Cheshunt, Hertfordshire, with £4000.

18 June 1746. James Grimston, eldest son of Lord Viscount Grimston, to Miss Bucknall of Hertfordshire.

10 December 1746. Mr. Moses da Costa of Totteridge, Hertfordshire, to the eldest daughter of Mr. Alvaro Mendez, a Jew merchant of London, with £10,000.

12 June 1747. Sir Edward Smith, Bart., of Hill Hall, Essex, to Miss Salmon of St. Albans.

18 July 1747. Henry Wrench, Esq., of Hertfordshire, to Miss Jane Hartley, of Mile End, with £8,000.

3 November 1747. William Browning of Surrey, Esq., to Miss Shipton of Watford, Hertfordshire.

6 November 1747. Stephen Miller of Hertfordshire, Esq., to Miss Beckley of Shitlington, Bedfordshire.

11 December 1747. Henry Hyde of Hertfordshire, Esq., to Miss Colston of Hempstead in the same county.

14 June 1748. Ben Huguen of Watford, Hertfordshire, to Miss Rebecca Aldridge of Hoxton.

20 December 1748. Mr Richard Milward, attorney at Hatfield to widow Chappelow £10,000.

25 January 1749. William Woodley of Little Parndon, Essex, Esq., to Miss Newth of Hertfordshire.

16 September 1749. Thomas Plumer Boyd, of Ware Park, Hertfordshire, to Miss Hope, daughter of the late Andrew Hope, brewer at Norton Folgate, £30,000.

30 November 1749. Thomas Craven, Esq., was married to Miss Byron at Cheshunt.

24 February 1750. Fitzwilliams Barrington of Lilley, Hertfordshire, to Miss Hall of Norfolk Street, about £20,000.

April 1750. Henry Loon of Hertford, Esq., to the only daughter of the late Dennis Hooper of Tottenham.

4 May 1750. Gilbert Matthews of Redbourn, Esq., to Miss Mary Philipps of Watford, Hertfordshire.

4 June 1750. ———— Wellington of Hertford, Esq., to the relict of Charles Caesar, Esq., of ditto.

10 October 1750. Alex Edmonds of Hertford, Esq., to Miss Harris of Hitchin.

February 1751. Edward Bearcroft of Hertfordshire, Esq., to Miss Susannah Ambrose, £10,000.

19 March 1751. John Shaw of Cheshunt, Esq., to a daughter and coheiress of Thomas Huxley of Eaton Park, Bedfordshire, £25,000.

16 June 1751. Mr. James Farland, merchant in Cannon Street, to the only daughter of David Howell of Hempstead, Hertfordshire, Esq.

24 July 1751. Samuel Harcourt, Esq., possessed of a large estate in Hertfordshire, to the only daughter and heiress of late Sir Roger Gore, a beauty, with £300,000.

9 August 1751. George Hawkins, Esq., of Elstree, Middlesex [sic], to Miss Barker of Great Russell Street, with a very large fortune.

31 August 1751. Ralph Bernard of Hitchin, Hertfordshire, Esq., to Miss Castle of Bloomsbury.

4 October 1751. Mr William Owen, merchant, of Southwark, to a daughter of Daniel Skipton of Watford, Hertfordshire, Esq, £10,000.

30 November 1751. Thomas Lawrence of Cheshunt, Hertfordshire, Esq., to Miss Amy Charlton of Low Layton.

21 December 1751. Martin Madan, Esq., eldest son of Martin Madan, Esq., member for Hindon, to Miss Hale of Hertfordshire.

2 January 1752. James Comyn, Esq., to Miss Nanny [sic] Sharp of Hertfordshire.

17 June 1752. George Hatley of Hertfordshire, Esq., to the only daughter of late James Goodwin of Hatton Garden, Esq.

14 September 1752. Edward Lomax, Esq., of St. Albans to Miss Shallett of the Bankside, Southwark, with £40,000.

12 November 1752. Ambrose Eyre of Bishop's Stortford, Esq., to Miss Marra.

17 March 1753. Rev. Mr. Secker of Yardley [Ardeley], Hertfordshire, to Miss Bird, daughter of John Bird of Coventry, Esq.

3 April 1753. George Holmes of Hempstead, Hertfordshire, Esq., to Miss Saunders of Gloucester.

16 April 1753. William Dyson of Throcking, Hertfordshire, Esq., to Miss Lydia Smith of Chiswick.

2 February 1754. Mr. Garrard of Cheshunt to Miss Townshend of Oxford, £5000.

22 October 1754. Dr. Willshaw of Hempstead to Miss Steward of Cheshunt in Hertfordshire.

19 May 1755. Hon. Charles Yorke, Esq., second son to the Lord Chancellor, to [Catherine, daughter of Rev. William] Freeman of Hertfordshire.

20 November 1755. Rev. Dr. Jubb to Mrs. Mason of Porters [Shenley], Hertfordshire.

20 January 1756. Richard Harcourt of Pendley, Hertfordshire, Esq., to Miss Eames of Little Gaddesden. £5000.

23 February 1756. Richard Bard Harcourt of Pendley, Esq., to the only daughter of the late ———— Nesbit, Esq.

April 1756. Peter Brook of Chester, Esq., to Miss Langford of Theobalds, Hertfordshire.

November 1756. John Seane of the Grove near Tring in Hertfordshire, Esq., to Miss Grantham of High House in Essex.

February 1757. Richard Charleton, Esq., of Bloomsbury, to a daughter of the late John Radcliffe, Esq., of Hitchin, in Hertfordshire.

April 1757. Rev. Mr. Whitehurst of St Peter's College, Cambridge, to Miss Hitchin [sic] of Hitchin, Hertfordshire, with £15,000.

May 1757. James Thompson of Hertfordshire, Esq., to Miss Sally Clark.

June 1757. John Mason of Greenwich, Esq., to Miss Finch of Bushey, Hertfordshire.

July 1757. John Leman of Northaw, Hertfordshire, Esq., to Miss Worth.

July 1757. Rev. Mr. Barnard of Caxton, Cambridgeshire, Esq., to Miss Jones of Hoddesdon.

August 1757. John George of Hertford, Esq., to Miss Sally Bryan of that place.

September 1757. John Calvert of Albury, Hertfordshire, to a daughter of Sir Edward Hulse, Bart.

September 1757. Mr. Young, apothecary at Barnet, to Miss Cox of the same place, £2000.

September 1757. Mr. Lovis to Miss Glass of Hertford, £2000.

22 March 1758. Robert Chester of the Temple, Esq., to Miss Caesar of Hertfordshire.

27 April 1758. Row. Aynsworth of the Inner Temple, Esq., to Miss Legg of Hertford.

29 May 1758. Charles Lowman of Stevenage, Esq., to Miss Jackson of Hatfield.

29 June 1758. William Turton of Oxfordshire, Esq., to Miss Clarke of Hertford.

19 July 1758. William Ward of Birmingham, Esq., to Miss Selby of Hertford.

4 November 1758. Thomas Baynton of Jamaica, Esq., to Miss Porter of Cheshunt.

20 January 1759. Rev. Mr. Franklin, Vicar of Ware and Thundridge, Hertfordshire, to Miss Venables.

17 April 1759. Rev. Mr. Willis, Rector of St Christopher's, Threadneedle-street, to Miss Seller of Cheshunt, Hertfordshire.

7 May 1759. Thomas Western of Abington Hall, Cambridgeshire, to Miss Calvert, of Aubrey [Albury], Hertfordshire.

19 May 1759. Richard Nicholl of Aldenham, Hertfordshire, to Miss Hughes of Amersham.

12 September 1759. Joseph Treves of Mincing-lane, Esq., to Miss Rebecca da Costa of Totteridge.

3 October 1759. James Lee of Highgate, Esq., to Miss Bond of Barnet.

24 September 1760. Rev. Mr. Alexander, Vicar of Rickmansworth, to Miss Brown.

2 June 1761. Rev. Mr. Jefferys, Rector of Great Berkhamsted, Hertfordshire, to Miss Darrell.

18 June 1761. Mr. Charles Gardiner, of Lockleys in Hertfordshire, to Miss Halford.

17 September 1761. Rev. Mr. Smallridge, to Miss Capper of Bushey, Hertfordshire.

6 December 1761. Cornet Randal of the Royal Forresters, to Miss Russel of Northaw.

28 January 1762. Timothy Caswell, Esq., member for Hertford to Miss Rolt of Sacombe Park, Hertfordshire.

13 May, 1762. Sir William Beauchamp Proctor, Bart., Knight of the Bath, to Miss Johnson of Berkhamsted.

3 June 1762. Rev. Mr. Jenner to Miss Hazeland of Hertford.

November 1763. Thomas Shuttleford of Newark upon Trent, Esq., to Miss Seares of Barnet.

5 September 1764. ————— Moore of Hitchin, Hertfordshire, Esq., to Miss Webb of George Street, Hanover Square.

27 September 1764. Rev. Mr. Barford, orator of Cambridge University, to Miss Herver of Royston.

18 October 1764. John Manners, Esq., to Miss Peggy Manners of Moor Park.

22 January 1766. Mr. John Skedmore, a Quaker, to Miss Emmett of Rickmansworth, Hertfordshire. £10,000.

11 February 1766. John Searancke of Hatfield, Esq., to Miss Durnford of Little Berkhamsted.

25 March 1766. Charles Clarke of Adscombe Place, Surrey, to Miss Radcliff of Hitchin.

2 April 1766. Richard Bingham of Melcombe Regis, Esq., to Miss Sophia Halsey of Great Gaddesden.

5 June 1766. Mr. Uriah Bristow, of St. John's Square, Clerkenwell, to Miss Bristow of Hertfordshire.

17 July 1766. Rev. Mr. Collins, minister of Tring, Hertfordshire, to Miss Randolph of the same place.

29 June 1767. Hon. Colonel Pool to Miss Hyet of Hertfordshire.

15 July 1767. Thomas Baldwin, Esq., of Hertfordshire, to Miss Lesley of Bloomsbury.

22 July 1767. Colonel Blackwood to Miss Janssen of Cheshunt.

13 December 1767. Thomas Ellington, Esq., of St. Albans, to Miss Henrietta Anson of Southampton Row.

March 1768. John Radcliffe, Esq., member for St. Albans, to Lady Fr. Howard, sister to the Earl of Carlisle.

March 1768. Richard Warburton Lytton, Esq., of Knebworth to Miss Joddrell of Bedford Row.

6 September 1768. Rev. Mr. French to Miss Sally Liptrott of Totteridge.

18 September 1768. Rt. Hysham, Esq., to Miss Chipp of Paul's Walden, Hertfordshire.

23 September 1768. Kilham Haylon, Esq., of Ivinghoe, Buckinghamshire, to Miss Clara Duncombe of Stocks, Hertfordshire.

21 October 1768. Rev. Dr. Hollingworth of Northaw to Miss Clayton.

4 March 1769. Francis Morland, Esq., of Ongar, to Mrs. Hinde of Cheshunt.

15 June 1769. Rev. Mr. Whateley, to Miss Jane Plumer of Blakesware, Hertfordshire.

2 November 1769. Captain Richardson, of the Hertford Militia, to Miss Jackson of the Strand.

15 November 1769. Mr. Thomas Avery, to Miss Amelia Smith of St. Albans.

26 February 1770. Mr. Sheen of Theobalds Park, Hertfordshire, to Miss Hume, Pall Mall.

1 March 1770. John Ellington, Esq., St. Albans, to Miss Anson.

19 April 1770. Thomas Clutterbuck, jun., Esq., of Stanmore, to Miss Thurgood of Baldock, Hertfordshire.

24 June 1770. Isaac Scott, Esq., of South Mimms, to Miss Newton of Barnet.

3 July 1770. William Snell, Esq., Salisbury Hall, to Miss Eliz. Wilsonn [sic] of Lombard Street.

10 July 1771. John Ellington, Esq., of St. Albans, to Miss Harriot Anson, Golden Square.

1 October 1771. Thomas Byde, Esq., of Byde Place, Hertfordshire, to Miss Knight of Hackney.

4 October 1771. Samuel Hawkins, Esq., of Ware, to Miss Henderson of Hempstead.

October[?] 1771. Thomas Prescott, Esq., of Theobalds Park, to Miss Frederick, daughter of Sir Charles.

20 February 1772. John Wilkings, Esq., Hanover Square, to Miss Jackson, Hertford.

3 March 1772. William Aylmer, Esq., Cheshunt, Hertfordshire, to Miss Ellis of Enfield.

21 April 1772. Francis Blake, jun., Esq., only son of Francis Blake, Esq., of Twizel Castle, to Miss Douglas of Hoddesdon, Hertfordshire.
[Republished in the following month, but dated 25 April]

19 May 1772. Rev. Mr. Barron of Watford, to Miss Cruikshanks, of Piccadilly.

30 July 1772. Rev. Edward Heysham, LL.D., to Miss Anne Maria Smith of Watford.

25 August 1772. Lt.-Colonel Townsend, of the 34th Regiment, to Miss Ford of Northaw, Hertfordshire.

11 November 1772. Abraham Cromick, Esq., of Charing Cross, to Miss Smith of Barnet.

17 November 1772. William Tash, Esq., of Shenley Hill, Hertfordshire, to Miss Mary Jackson of Broomfield House, Southgate.

27 May 1773. Thomas Calvert, Esq., Albury, Hertfordshire, to Miss Calvert.

20 June 1773. Theo. Mayhew, Esq., captain in the guards, to Miss Foster of Theobalds, Hertfordshire.

17 August 1773. John Parker, Esq., of Tring, Hertfordshire, to Miss Williams of Kensington.

8 October 1773. Daniel Brook, Esq., to Miss Graham, both of Hatfield.

20 October 1773. William Pere Doddington, Esq., to Miss Brooksbank, of Ware.

2 December 1773. Lord Viscount Cranbourne, son of the Earl of Salisbury, to Lady Mary Hill, daughter of the Earl of Hillsborough.

14 December 1773. The Rev. Mr. Sandford, jun., of Georgeham,

Devonshire, to Miss Amy Pointz, youngest daughter of the late Newdigate Pointz, Esq., of Hexton, Hertfordshire.

20 April 1774. John Conesbee, of Lilley, in Hertfordshire, to Mrs. Whalby, relict of ———— Whalby, Esq., of Ormond street.

23 April 1774. George William Prescott, Esq., eldest son of George Prescott, Esq. [of Hertfordshire?] to Miss Long, eldest daughter of Beeston Long, Esq.

28 July 1774. The Rt. Hon. Lord Viscount Grimston, to Miss Walters, only daughter of Edward Walters, Esq., of Stalbridge, and member for Milborne Port, in Somersetshire.

6 October 1774. Thomas Estcourt, Esq., to the Hon. Miss Grimstone, sister to Lord Viscount Grimstone.

18 October 1774. The Rev. Mr. Brackley Kennett, morning preacher at Berkeley chapel, son of Alderman Kennett, to Miss Sarah Mahew, daughter of ———— Mahew, Esq., of Hertford.

22 December 1774. ———— Gestier, Esq., late a Governor in the East Indies, to Miss Law, of Brookbourne [Broxbourne?], in Hertfordshire.

3 January 1775. George Innis, Esq., of Theobalds Row, to Miss Jackson, daughter of ———— Jackson, Esq., of Higham Place, near Hoddesdon.

March 1775. ———— Angus, Esq., at Theobalds, Hertfordshire, to Miss Treadway, niece to Sir Andrew Lindsey, Bart.

17 June 1775. J.R. Hadsley, Esq., of Ware Priory, Hertfordshire, to Miss Goodwyn, of St. Paul's Churchyard.

Cussans records that Ware Priory became the property of Robert Hadsley, Esquire, of Great Munden, in 1685. His son, also Robert, died without issue, having bequeathed the property to Jeremiah Rayment, a distant relative, who assumed the name Hadsley as required by the testator. He died two years after his marriage, leaving one daughter, Sarah. [AJ]

August[?] 1775. Rev. Mr. Benjamin Round, of Maidstone, to Miss Sally Haynes, of Hertford.

7 October 1775. William Baker, Esq., of Hertfordshire, to Miss Sophia Conyers, third daughter to the late John Conyers, Knight of the Shire for Essex.

This was William Baker (1743—1824) of Bayfordbury, whose second wife, Sophia, was third daughter of John Conyers of Copped Hall near Waltham Abbey (but actually in the parish of Epping). Both are buried in the parish church at Bayford. [AJ]

3 November 1775. Rev. Jos. Jenkins, A.M., of Wrexham, in Denbighshire, to Miss Foster, of Market-street [Markyate], Hertfordshire.

26 March 1776. William Knight, Esq., of Lowton, in Essex, to Mrs. Chamberlain, of Hertford.

6 June 1776. John Rooper, Esq., of Berkhamsted castle, in Hertfordshire, to Miss Bonsoy, of Abbot's Ripton, in Huntingdonshire.

The Roper family held the lease of Berkhamsted Place from 1720 until 1807, when John Roper assigned his interest to the Earl of Bridgewater. [AJ]

7 August 1776. Sebastian Finch, Esq., of Hatfield, to Miss Templeman, of Cripplegate.

14 October 1776. Gregory Stonehouse, Esq., of Stevenage, Hertfordshire, to Miss Eleanor Hawkins of Old Fish Street.

3 April 1777. William Hale, Esq., jun., of Walden, Hertfordshire, to Hon. Miss Grimstone, sister to Lord Viscount Grimston.

July[?] 1777. William Calvert Benn, Esq., of Great Hormead, Hertfordshire, to Mrs. Sales, of Hampstead.

5 August 1777. Thomas Bishop, Esq., of Whetstone, in Middlesex, to Miss Archer, of Colne-brook-green, in Hertfordshire [Buckinghamshire?].

2 March 1778. John Bennet, Esq., of Rothamsted, Hertfordshire, to Miss Bigg, of Mackereye End.

22 January 1778. William Creasey, Esq., of Ware, to Miss Langford.

25 June 1778. Thomas Duncombe, Esq., of Duncombe Park, Yorkshire, to Miss Charlotte Hale of King's Walden, Hertfordshire.

29 June 1778. William Smart, Esq., of North Church Court, Hertfordshire, to Miss Hows of Friesden.

1 July 1778. David Taylor, Esq., of Queen Square, to Miss Weldon of Little Gaddesden, Hertfordshire.

15 July 1778. Richard Malone, Esq., of Baronstown, Ireland, to Miss Roper of Berkhamsted Place, Hertfordshire.

9 September 1778. John Young, Esq., of Hare Hatch, to Miss Meetkerke, of Julians in Hertfordshire.

5 May 1779. Rev. Mr. Smyth, rector of Greenstead, to Miss Bland, of Great Berkhamsted.

6 September 1779. Thomas Gore, Esq., of Ashlyns Hall [Berkhamsted], Hertfordshire, to Miss Thorpe of Salisbury.

9 September 1779. Henry Cowper, Esq., of Boswell Court, to Miss Cowper of Hertingfordbury Park.

1 December 1779. Hon. Thomas Dimsdale, baron of the Russian Empire, to Miss Dimsdale.

9 June 1780. At Marylebone church, Jeremy Milles, Esq., eldest son of the Rev. Dr. Milles, dean of Exeter, and president of the Society of Antiquaries, to Miss Gardiner, daughter and sole heiress of Edward Gardiner, Esq., late of Pishobury [Sawbridgeworth], Hertfordshire.

9 June 1780. Mr. Vincent, of Salisbury Court, Fleet Street, to Miss Phillimore, eldest daughter of John Phillimore, Esq., of New Broad Street, and Cheshunt.

20 July 1780. Mr. Joseph Barber, stationer, to Miss Lines, of Winchmore Hill, Hertfordshire [sic].

30 August 1780. Mr. J.B. Dickenson, of Ware, Hertfordshire, to Miss Dickenson, of St. Margaret's Hill.

23 December 1780. By special licence, at Bedwell Park, Hertfordshire, the Rt. Hon. Lord St. John of Bletsoe, to Miss Emma Whitbread, second daughter of Samuel Whitbread, Esq., M.P. for Bedford, with a fortune of £30,000.

31 May 1781. At Stevenage, Hertfordshire, William Mount, Esq., of St. Catherine's by the Tower, to Miss Berrie.

12 October 1781. Sir Frederick Reynolds, Knt., of Hatfield, Hertfordshire, to Miss M. Townshend of Hatton Street.

25 September 1781. Mr. George Berner of Enfield Mills to Miss Mansfield of St. Albans.

18 April 1782. Edward Dering, Esq., eldest son of Sir Edward Dering, Bart, to Miss Anne Hale, fourth daughter of William Hale, Esq., of King's Walden, Hertfordshire.

6 July 1782. Rev. John Bishop, B.D., rector of Cold Higham, Northamptonshire, to Mrs. Ellis, of Widdial Hall, Hertfordshire.

19 July 1782. John Fiott, Esq., to Miss Harriot Lee, 2nd daughter of the late William Lee, Esq., of Totteridge Park, and grand-daughter of the late L.C.J. Lee.

19 September 1782. Rev. Mr. Fawcett at Ware, dissenting minister at Walthamstow and Sunday lecturer at Old Jewry, to Miss French, daughter of Rev. Mr. French, of Ware.

14 October 1782. At Totteridge chapel, by the Rev. Mr. Lintrot, chaplain, Osmund Beauvoir, DD., late master of the free school at Canterbury, to Miss Sharpe, of South Bailey Lodge, Enfield Chase, aged 29, only daughter and heiress of the late Fane William Sharpe, Esq., member for Callington who died October 21, 1771.

18 October 1782. Samuel Vear, Esq., of Leicester Fields, to Miss Proctor, of Ware, Hertfordshire.

21 November 1782. Rev. Edward Conyers, M.A., vicar of Epping and Walthamstow, to Miss Turvin, youngest daughter and co-heiress of Jas. Turvin, Esq., of Tarlings in Gilston, Hertfordshire.

Edward Conyers was the brother of Sophia, for whose marriage to William Baker see 7 October 1775. [AJ]

30 January 1783. Hon. Mr. Grimston (brother to Lord Viscount Grimston), to Miss Sophia Hoare, co-heiress of the late Richard Hoare, Esq., of Borham, Essex.

26 February 1783. Mr. Moses Lindo, of Devonshire Square, to Miss da Costa, daughter of the late M. da Costa, Esq., of Totteridge, Hertfordshire.

11 March 1783. At Cheshunt, Thomas Blackmore, Esq., of Biggins, in Hunsdon, Hertfordshire, to Miss Anne Tatnall, youngest daughter of Mr. Tatnall of Theobalds.

28 March 1783. James Ibbetson, Esq., of Bushey, to Miss Agnes Thompson.

15 July 1783. J.K. Sandon, Esq., of Cheshunt, Hertfordshire to Miss Vincent.

8 September 1783. Dr. Cooke, to Miss Priest, of Waltham Cross.

30 October 1783. Rev. Mr. Poole, curate of Stanmore Parva alias Whitchurch, Middlesex, to Miss Millar, of Cheshunt.

9 December 1783. By the Archbishop of Canterbury, William Strode, Esq., of Northaw, Hertfordshire, to the widow of the late William Leman, Esq., of the same place.

The manor of Northaw was purchased by an earlier William Leman in 1632. It passed through three generations of Lemans, and thence successively to Richard Alie and John Granger, each of whom assumed the name Leman. John Granger Leman d. 1781, leaving the property to William Strode who married his widow. [AJ]

5 February 1784. By the Rev. Dr. Peckwell, at Cheshunt church, Hertfordshire, Miss Eliza Graham, of Botolph Lane, London, to Mr. William Marchant, surgeon, of Waltham Cross.

18 February 1784. Thos Halsey, Esq., of Great Gaddesden, M.P. for Hertfordshire, to Miss S. Crawley, of Cheshunt, youngest daughter of the late J. Crawley, Esq., of Stockwood, Bedfordshire.

14 April 1784. N. Kirkman, Esq., of Gaddesden, Hertfordshire, to Miss Bulkeley.

May[?] 1784. At St. Albans, George Bradshaw, Esq., of 56th regiment, to Miss Cotton, daughter of the late Dr. Cotton.

31 July 1784. At Hertford, Captain Thomas Spence, in the Antigua trade, to Miss Susanna Platt.

23 August 1784. At Cheshunt, Mr. Waller, calico printer, of Edmonton, to Miss Scott, daughter of Mr. Scott, carpenter, of Cheshunt.

2 September 1784. At Broxbourne, Hertfordshire, Mr. Almon, late bookseller in Piccadilly, to Mrs. Parker, widow of the late Mr. Parker, printer of the General Advertiser, who died 7 May.

11 October 1784. In the English church at Rotterdam, Charles Gore, Esq., of Tring House, Hertfordshire, to Miss Rochford.

14 October 1784. Alexander Cottin, Esq., of Cheverell's Green [Flamstead], Hertfordshire, to Mrs. Newe [sic] Barwick, of Charterhouse Square.

27 January 1785. Thomas Blachford, Esq., of Northaw, Hertfordshire, to Miss Moore.

2 March 1785. Rev. Baron French, of Ware, Hertfordshire, to Miss Dickinson.

29 March 1785. Rev. William Murgutroyd, of Ashwell, Hertfordshire, to Miss Rushworth.

27 April 1785. Mr. John Andree, surgeon, of Cary Street, to Miss Proctor, of Ware.

11 August 1785. At Ippollitts, near Hitchin, William Wiltshire, jun., Esq., of Hitchin, to Miss Martha Wortham, 2nd daughter of the late, and sister to the present Hale Wortham, Esq.

15 November 1785. At Weymouth, Thomas Watson, Esq., of Watford, to Miss Mary Smith.

8 December 1785. At Ashton [Aston?], Hertfordshire, Henry Dickenson, Esq., of the East India house, to Miss Anne Wood, of Frogmore.

10 January 1786. At Enfield, Rev. Mr. Shaw, schoolmaster on Fourtree Hill, to Miss Morris, eldest daughter of Mr. Morris, schoolmaster at Cheshunt.

2 March 1786. At St. Catharine, Creechurch Lane, Mr. Benjamin Fairfax, of the Bull Inn, Hoddesdon, to Miss Kirby, of the Ryehouse, Stanstead, Hertfordshire. [See also 19 October 1786].

19 March 1786. Mr. Sayer, of Gutter Lane, to Miss Mihill, of Ware.

8 April 1786. W. Boscawen, Esq., son of the late General Boscawen and nephew to the late Lord Falmouth, to Miss Charlotte Ibbetson, daughter of the late Archdeacon of St. Albans.

23 April 1786. N.W. Lewis, Esq., to Mrs. Young, of Bush Hall [Hatfield], Hertfordshire.

20 July 1786. Richard Corrie, Esq., of Hertford, to Mrs. Jenkins, relict of the Rev. Dr. Jenkins.

17 October 1786. Rev. R. Hughes, of Aldenham, Hants [Herts?] to Miss A. Reid.

19 October 1786. At Stanstead Abbots, Mr. John Kirkby, of Rye House, to Miss Maria Fairfax, of the Bull Inn, Hoddesdon. [See also 2 March 1786].

14 December 1786. Hale Young Wortham, Esq., of Aspenden, Hertfordshire, to Miss Proctor, daughter of Mr. Thomas Proctor, brewer.

Cussans records the following memorial tablet on the north wall of the chancel of Aspenden church:
"Hale Young Wortham, Esq., of this parish, many years Gentleman-Usher to his Majesty George III, and Lieut.Colonel of the Militia of this County, died 3rd March 1820, aged 73. Anne, his wife, daughter of Thomas Proctor of Bengeo Hall, Esq., died 2 June 1824, aged 62." [AJ]

25 January 1787. At Brington, Northamptonshire, Charles Bourchier, Esq., of Bramfield, Hertfordshire, to Miss Preedy.

10 May 1787. Dudley Johnson, Esq., to Miss A. Feast, of Cheshunt.

27 May 1787. At Porter's Lodge [Shenley], Hertfordshire, the Earl of Altamont to Louisa, youngest daughter of Lord Howe.

Lord Howe purchased the Porters Estate in 1772. [AJ]

12 July 1787. At Norwich, Mr. David Lindoe, of Ware, Hertfordshire, to Miss Sarah Smyth, daughter of Mr. James Smyth, attorney at law.

31 July 1787. At Porter's Lodge, Hertfordshire, Ashton Curzon, Esq., to the Hon. Miss Howe, daughter of Lord Viscount Howe.

31 August 1787. At the Quakers' Meeting house, Tottenham, Mr. William Squires, maltster, of Hertford, to Miss Elizabeth Hooper, daughter of Mr. Hooper, surgeon in Tooley Street. The speakers on this occasion were ———— West, of Hertford, and Special Vyse, of Northaw; and an excellent prayer was pronounced by Mrs. Bevington, of Gracechurch Street.

25 October 1787. Mr Charles Hollinsworth, butcher and grazier at Ware, Hertfordshire, to Mrs. Johnson, widow of the late Daniel Johnson, Esq., of Stratford Green.

31 October 1787. Mr. John Forster, of Royston, Hertfordshire, to Miss Cooper, of the same place.

17 November 1787. Mr. Thomas Clementson of Ware, Hertfordshire, to Mrs. Jones, widow, of Bruton Street.

29 November 1787. John Amherst, Esq., of Farleigh, Kent, to Miss Elizabeth Lomax, daughter of the late Caleb Lomax, Esq., of Chiswick Bury [Childwickbury, St. Albans], Hertfordshire.

15 December 1787. William Clarkson, Esq., of London Wall, to Miss Anne Goodwyn, of Baldock, Hertfordshire.

23 December 1787. Henry Hawkins, Esq., of Hitchin, Hertfordshire, to Miss Charlotte Wortham, of the same place.

7 February 1788. Mr. Wortham of Royston, Hertfordshire, grocer, to Miss Adams, of the same place.

9 May 1788. Mr. Slovin, of Newark upon Trent, to Miss Diana Sabine, daughter of the late John Sabine, Esq., of Tewin, Hertfordshire, and colonel of the Coldstream regiment.

24 May 1788. George Fothergill, Esq., of Park Street, to Miss Whetham, eldest daughter of Thomas Whetham, Esq., of Stagenhoe Park, Hertfordshire.

26 May 1788. At St. Martin in the Fields, Mr. George Weissenborn, of May's Buildings, man's mercer, to Miss Elizabeth Capreol, of Hitchin, Hertfordshire.

14 July 1788. Mr. G.A. Smith, of Abchurch Lane, to Miss French, of Ware.

21 August 1788. Mr. Langford, surgeon, of St. Albans, to Mrs. Allen, of Basinghall Street.

23 August 1788. At Margate, Mr. John Fordham, brewer, of Hertford, to Miss Cooper, of the same place.

2 September 1788. By special licence, at Clermont, the seat of the Rt. Hon. Earl Tyrconnel, Chas Grimstead, Esq., of Leatherhead, Surrey, to Miss Charlotte Walsh, younger daughter of Jn. Walsh of Redbourn.

14 September 1788. Thomas Edwards, Esq., captain in the East India service, to the Hon. Mary Grimston, relict of George Grimston, Esq., brother to Lord Viscount Grimston.

7 October 1788. At the Abbey church, St. Albans, Mr. Brasbridge, of Fleet Street, to Mrs. Greenhill.

4 November 1788. At Cheshunt, Rev. Mr. Taylor, of Ely Place, to Miss Porter, daughter of Benjamin Porter, Esq., of Theobalds Park, Hertfordshire.

7 December 1788. George Hankin, Esq., of Hertfordshire, to Mrs. Kennet, widow of the late Alderman Kennet.

16 December 1788. At Eton College, Rev. William Foster, vicar of Kew, and chaplain to the Prince of Wales, to Miss Pigott, only daughter of Grenado Pigott, Esq., of Ashton [Aston?], Hertfordshire.

22 December 1788. At Hatfield, Hertfordshire, William Church, Esq., of Woodside, to Miss Bellis, of the same place.

10 January 1789. Rev. Mr. Price, rector of Knebworth, Hertfordshire, to Miss Grove, of Leicester Fields.

24 January 1789. John Scott of Hadham Hall, Hertfordshire, to Miss Eliza Hudson, daughter of Thomas Hudson, Esq.

29 January 1789. Mr. Hancock, of Crutched Friars, to Miss Greenhill, daughter of Thomas Greenhill, Esq., of Watford, Hertfordshire.

1 February 1789. William Ward, Esq., of Morney Hill House, near Rickmansworth, Hertfordshire, to Miss Loder, of Goodman's Fields.

5 February 1789. Mr. Litler, oilman, Leadenhall Street, to Mrs. Parker, widow of the late Thomas Parker, Esq., of Yardley [Ardeley], Hertfordshire.

9 March 1789. At Baldock, Isaac Hindley, Esq., to Miss Mary Roe, daughter of the late Rev. Mr. Samuel Roe of Stotfold.

30 March 1789. William Wraxall, Esq., M.P. for Luggershall, to Miss Lascelles, eldest daughter of the late Peter Lascelles, Esq., of Knights, Hertfordshire [sic].

18 April 1789. At Newbold upon Avon, Warwickshire, Ambrose Proctor, Esq., of Bengeo Hall, Hertfordshire, to Miss Hume, eldest daughter of Alex Hume, Esq., of Wimpole Street.

24 April 1789. At Broxbourne, Hertfordshire, Mr. Robert Hilton, surgeon, of East Grinstead, Sussex, to Miss Charlotte Moore, only daughter of William Moore, Esq., of Hoddesdon, Hertfordshire.

8 May 1789. Mr. Dyson, of Botolph Lane, to Miss Ilbery, of Tunford [Turnford?] Hall, Hertfordshire, milliner at Enfield.

14 May 1789. William Hall, Esq., of Northaw, Hertfordshire, to Miss Cooke, of Aldersgate Street.

May[?] 1789. Mr. James Mawdsley, of Waltham Cross, to Miss Stubbs, of Margaret Street.

June 1789. Mr. Kemble, partner with Nathaniel and Smith, grocers, Cannon Street, to Miss Gill, niece to the late Mr. Cooke, of Cheshunt, Herts.

4 June 1789. Mr. E. Cooper, tea-dealer in the Borough, to Miss E. Palmer, of Bishop Stortford.

10 July 1789. By special licence, James Gordon, jun., Esq., of Moore Place, Rickmansworth, to Miss Whitbread, eldest daughter of Samuel Whitbread, Esq.

18 July 1789. At Kensington, Walter Hills, Esq., of Gray's Inn, to Miss Clarissa Hutchinson, 2nd daughter of late Norton Hutchinson, Esq., of Mardock House, Hertfordshire.

Norton Hutchinson who had purchased the manor of Mardock, Wareside, in 1767, was succeeded in 1781 by his eldest son, the Rev. Julius Hutchinson. Three years before Clarissa's marriage he sold it to Ambrose Proctor. [AJ]

September[?] 1789. Mr. Moor, master of the Four Swans Inn at Waltham Cross, to a niece of Mrs. White, who lately kept that inn.

1 September 1789. Rev. Mr. Price, vicar of High Wycombe, and chaplain to the Marquis of Lansdown, to Miss Seabrook, of Kensworth, Hertfordshire.

The parish of Kensworth was transferred from Hertfordshire to Bedfordshire in 1897. [AJ]

26 September 1789. Mr. Thomas Young, of Hertford, to Miss Rachel Gosling, youngest daughter of the late Mr. Robert Gosling of Fenchurch Street.

November 1789. Lately, Mr. Brown, coach-maker, of Bishop Stortford, aged 21, to Mrs. Hayton, of the Hoops Inn, Saffron Walden, aged 50.

5 November 1789. At the Protestant church at Latour, in the valley of Luzerne, near Turin, Frederick Lewis Baron de Fulitzsch, of Saxony, to Mrs. Letitia Houblon, of the Priory near Bishop Stortford, only daughter of the late Jacob Houblon, Esq., of Hallingbury.

16 December 1789. John Clarke, Esq., of Bunkers [Sandridgebury?], Hertfordshire, to Miss Cotton, daughter of late Dr. Cotton of St. Albans.

22 December 1789. At Broxbourne, Mr. W. J. Eade, of Wood Street, Cheapside, to Miss Robinson, of Hoddesdon, Hertfordshire.

March[?] 1790. Mr. Sanders, of Aldgate, to Miss Chandler, of Sawbridgeworth, Hertfordshire.

20 May 1790. William Pope, Esq., of the Exchequer Office, Temple, to Miss Willis, only daughter of the Rev. Sherlock Willis, late rector of Wormley, Hertfordshire.

10 June 1790. Mr. Green, tanner, of Buntingford, to Miss Vaughan, daughter of the late Mr. Vaughan, tanner, of Enfield.

29 June 1790. At St. Albans, Mr. Butcher, attorney, of Northampton, to Miss Judith Pemberton.

7 July 1790. Rev. Mr. Heinchen, of Ware, Herts, to Miss Yallowley, of London.

29 July 1790. Rev. Lynch Salusbury, of Offley, Hertfordshire, to Miss Offley, of Ormond Street, eldest daughter of the late William Offley, Esq.

27 August 1790. At Westmill, Hertfordshire, Henry Dampier, Esq., of the Middle Temple, to Miss Law, eldest daughter of the Rev. Dr. Law, archdeacon of Rochester.

11 September 1790. Mr. Thomas Bayles, of Russel Court, Covent Garden, to Miss Whalley, of Ridge, Hertfordshire.

28 September 1790. Mr. Edward Howell, of Vine Street, Piccadilly, to Miss Langford, of St. Albans.

28 October 1790. At Shenley, Hertfordshire, Charles Martin, Esq., of Duke Street, to Miss Osmond, of Shenley Hill.

October[?] 1790. Lately, Alex. Mair, Esq., of the Adelphi, to Miss Baronow, of Watford, Hertfordshire.

25 November 1790. John-Peter Boileau, Esq., of Hertfordshire, to Miss Pollen, daughter of the Rev. George Pollen, of Guildford, Surrey.

November[?] 1790. Lately, Thomas Chinnel Porter, Esq., son of Benjamin Porter, Esq., of Theobalds, Hertfordshire, to Miss Ker, of Fulham.

November[?] 1790. Lately, at South Warnborough, Hampshire, Robert Thornton Heysham, Esq., of Stagenhoe Park, Hertfordshire, to Miss Hawkins.

Robert Heysham of London purchased the manor and park of Stagenhoe in 1703. When he died in 1722 he was succeeded briefly by his son Robert, who died unmarried at the age of 22, after which the estate passed to a kinsman, Giles Thornton, on condition that he took the additional name of Heysham. Giles was succeeded by his son Robert Thornton Heysham (died 1781), and by a grandson of the same name who married Miss Hawkins. [AJ]

17 December 1790. At Amwell, near Ware, Hertfordshire, Rev. John Young, LL.B., younger son of Richard Young, Esq., of Orlingbury, Northamptonshire, and rector of Akeham, Buckinghamshire, to Miss Mary Wood, of Ware.

5 January 1791. By special licence, at St. George's chapel, Windsor, Henry Earl Fauconberg, to Miss Cheshyre, daughter of the late John Cheshyre, Esq., of Bennington, Hertfordshire.

11 January 1791. Rev. Charles Proby, eldest son of Commissioner Proby of Chatham, to Miss Cherry, the eldest daughter; and the Rev. Henry Sawbridge, to Mrs. Blachford, widow of the late Thomas Blachford, Esq., of Northaw, second daughter of George Cherry, Esq., one of the commissioners for victualling the navy.

26 March 1791. Thomas Nicholl, Esq., to Miss Blackwell, both of Watford, Hertfordshire.

6 April 1791. At Mary-la-Bonne, John Goodaker, jun., Esq., of Peatling Hall, Leicestershire, to Miss Knipe, eldest daughter of Rob. Knipe, Esq., late of Berkhamsted, Hertfordshire.

17 April 1791. At Essendon, Benjamin Cherry, Esq., eldest son of the late Alderman Cherry of Hertford, to Miss Frances Orme, sister of Rev. Robert Orme, rector of All Saints, Hertford, and of the united livings of Essendon and Bayford.

7 June 1791. Arnott Howard, Esq., of St. Julian's, Hertfordshire, to Miss Randall, only daughter of Rev. Mr. Randall, minister of New Brentford, Middlesex.

5 July 1791. At Ealing, Middlesex, William Seger, Esq., of Harrow, to Mrs. Hunt, relict of James Hunt, Esq., late of Union Hall [?], Hertfordshire.

12 July 1791. At Stanstead [Abbots], Hertfordshire, Captain Stephen George Church, of the Royal Navy, to Miss Maria Kempe, eldest daughter of John Tabor Kempe, Esq., of St. Margaret's Place, in same county.

19 July, 1791. Rev. Dr. Lewin, of Bushey, to Miss Elizabeth Capper, of the same place.

The manor of Bushey was purchased in 1719 by Richard Capper, Esq., and remained in the Capper family for four generations. His great-grandson Robert sold in 1814. It seems that the Lewin/Lewen family may have been tenants for part of this time. [AJ] [See also marriages dated 12 September 1791, 29 November 1791].

25 August 1791. At St. Stephens, Hertfordshire, Mr. James Nicholls, of Aldenham, Hertfordshire, to Miss Gascoyne, of Tower Hill.

30 August 1791. Mr. Bunny, jun., of Newbury, surgeon, to Miss Elizabeth Worsley, youngest daughter of the Rev. Mr. Worsley of Cheshunt.

12 September 1791. At St. Pancras, Captain Thomas Nixon, to Miss Isabella Capper, daughter of Richard Capper, Esq., of Bushey, Hertfordshire.

15 October 1791. Joseph Howgate, Esq., of Norwood House, Hertfordshire, to Miss Price, of Fleet Street.

17 October 1791. Rev. James Wiggett, to Miss Lyde, daughter of Samuel Lyde, Esq., of Ayot St. Lawrence, Hertfordshire, and niece to the late Sir Lionel Lyde, Bart.

31 October 1791. At Radwell, Hertfordshire, Mr. J.L. Siordet, jun., merchant, of Great Winchester Street, to Miss Maria Sampson, of Radwell.

29 November 1791. Richard Holbrook, Esq., surveyor to the Crown for the parish of St. James, to Miss Betsey Lewen, daughter of Francis Lewen, Esq., of Bushey Hall, Hertfordshire.

29 November 1791. John Tyrell, Esq., of Hatfield Place, near Chelmsford, Essex, to Miss Tyssen, only daughter of the late William Tyssen, Esq., of Cheshunt, Hertfordshire.

November[?] 1791. Edward Clarke, Esq., younger son of George Hyde Clarke, Esq., of Hyde, in Cheshire, to Miss Prevost, only daughter of the late General Prevost, of Greenhill Grove [East Barnet], Hertfordshire.

November[?] 1791. Lately, Mr. Vaughan, tanner, at Enfield, to Miss Beldam, of Royston.

24 December 1791. Rev. John Procter, of Woodhouse, Great Horksley, Essex, to Miss Simmons, of Hertfordshire.

16 January 1792. William Deathe to Miss Sarah Jones, both of Bishops Stortford.

1 March 1792. At Watford, Humphrey Bache, Esq., one of the sixty clerks in Chancery, to Miss Clutterbuck, grand-daughter to — Clutterbuck, Esq., of Watford.

17 August 1792. Christopher Hodgson, Esq., banker, of Malton, Yorkshire, to Miss Elizabeth Gilder, daughter of the late Rev. Jonathan Gilder, rector of Aspenden, Hertfordshire.

4 October 1792. Mr. Thomas Maynard, of Hatton Garden, to Miss Nourse, of Colney, Hertfordshire.

5 October 1792. At Hemel Hempstead, Hertfordshire, Rev. J. Hamilton, master of the academy there, to Miss Greatrake, of King's Langley, in same county.

6 October 1792. At Kensington, Jens Wolff, Esq., son of the Danish consul-general, to Miss Isabella Hutchinson, daughter of the late Norton Hutchinson, Esq., of Mardock House, Hertfordshire.

13 October 1792. At Derby, John Gisborne, Esq., to Miss Pole, daughter of the late Edward Sacheverell Pole, Esq., of Redbourn.

1 December 1792. John Bury, Esq., of Ware, to Miss Pryce, of Fleet Street.

14 May 1793. Rev. Edmund Harvey of Willian, Hertfordshire, to Miss Greave of York.

13 June 1793. James Penrose, Esq., of Hatfield, Hertfordshire, to Miss Henrietta Graham, 2nd daughter of Rev. R. Graham, of Aldenham Park, Hertfordshire.

The marriage took place at St. Leonard's Shoreditch, the bride being daughter of the Rev. Richard Robert Graham. James Penrose, the son of James Penrose senior, was assistant surgeon, H.E.I.C.S. He died in India in November 1799. [HG]

25 June 1793. Mr. Blayney, surgeon, to Miss Birch, both of Hemel Hempstead, Hertfordshire.

27 June 1793. At Great Gaddesden, Hertfordshire, the Rev. Mr. Perry, to Miss Halsey, youngest sister of the late Thomas Halsey, Esq., formerly M.P. for Hertfordshire.

1 July 1793. Mr. Bruce, of London, to Mrs. Good, of Tring, Hertfordshire.

16 July 1793. Mr. Robert Richard Mawley, of the Borough High Street, to Miss Jane Stevens, niece of John Wakefield, Esq., of Cheshunt, Hertfordshire.

18 July 1793. Benjamin Porter, Esq., of Gower Street, Bedford Square, to Mrs. Barne, widow of George Barne, Esq., of Theobalds, Hertfordshire.

August[?] 1793. Benjamin Henshaw, Esq., of Moor Hall, Essex, to Miss Clinton, of Sawbridgeworth, Hertfordshire.

7 September 1793. Paul Benfield, Esq., M.P. for Shaftesbury, to Miss Swinburne, of Hamsterley, Durham.

The jointure said to be settled on Mrs. Benfield, the lady of Paul Benfield, Esq., so well-known at Madras, is £3000 a year, besides £500 per annum for pin-money. Each of their children is to have £10,000; and his Hertfordshire estate, worth £4000 a year, is also settled on their eldest son. His house in Albemarle Street is also given to Mrs. Benfield after his death; and he has taken two of her sisters, to bring up under his immediate care and protection. Besides this, a few days before his marriage he presented his intended bride with a diamond ring from off his finger, of the value of 3000 guineas.

Paul Benfield had been an official of the East India Company who amassed a large fortune through his trade contacts and by moneylending. Doubt was thrown on the propriety of some of his transactions, and he was called home under a cloud in 1777, but subsequently restored to his position. He finally returned to England in 1793, in which year he married, and also purchased several Hertfordshire properties from the trustees of Sir Thomas Rumbold, including the manors of Aston and Watton Woodhall. Benfield was declared bankrupt in 1798, and his properties were sold by trustees in 1801. He died in Paris in 1810 in indigent circumstances. [AJ]

4 October 1793. Mr. Ewer, of Hill Farm, Hertfordshire, to Mrs. Beard, of Long Acre, London.

October[?] 1793. Mr. Davies, to Miss Penrose, of Hatfield.

21 December 1793. Francis Wheeler, Esq., of Little Gaddesden, Hertfordshire, to Miss Walford, daughter of Mr. Walford, surgeon, Red Lion Square.

21 December 1793. Rev. Thomas Rivers, rector of Marsfield, Sussex, to Miss Louisa Smith, daughter of Culling Smith, Esq., of Popes, near Hatfield.

1 January 1794. Rev. Thomas Barnard, M.A., of St. John's college, Cambridge, vicar of Amwell, Hertfordshire, to Miss Everilda Martin, 2nd daughter of Sir Mordaunt Martin of Burnham, Norfolk.

11 February 1794. At Enfield, Mr. Saunders, son of Mr. Saunders, apothecary, at Cheshunt, to Miss Ninny, daughter of Mr. Bartholomew Ninny of Enfield, entitled to a large fortune on her coming of age.

14 April 1794. At Buntingford, Mr. Nash, currier, of Enfield, to Miss Mackly, of Buntingford.

25 April 1794. At Edmonton, John Oakes Hardy, Esq., captain of his Majesty's ship Thisbe, to Miss Susan Woodcock, daughter of the late Dr. Woodcock, rector of Watford, Hertfordshire.

7 May 1794. Rev. Mr. Rippon, vicar of Hitchin, Hertfordshire, to Miss Roycroft, daughter of the late Samuel Roycroft, Esq., of Bray, Berkshire.

21 June 1794. Mr. Archibald Bell, son of Rev. Archibald Bell, master of the boarding school at Cheshunt, Hertfordshire, to Miss Maria Kitching, of the same place.

25 June 1794. At Little Canfield, Essex, Mr. John Green, of Ware, Hertfordshire, to Miss Mary-Anne Broadley, of Dover.

19 July 1794. At Great Berkhampsted, Mr. Prentice, surgeon, of St. Albans, to Miss Healey, daughter of Mr. Healey, surgeon, of the former place.

25 August 1794. At Hertingfordbury, Hon. William Brodrick, to Miss Preston.

30 August 1794. At Braughing, Hertfordshire, Rev. R. Hervey, jun., vicar of St. Laurence, in the Isle of Thanet, to Miss Anne Wade, of Braughing.

3 September 1794. At Beechwood [Flamstead], Henry Lascelles, Esq., 2nd son of Edward Lascelles, Esq., M.P. for Northallerton, to Miss Sebright, daughter of the late and sister of the present Sir John Sebright.

18 September 1794. At Oxford, Rev. Henry Richards, B.D., rector of Bushey, Hertfordshire, and late Fellow of Exeter College, to Miss Badcock of Oxford.

25 September 1794. John Herbert Toley, Esq., of Bridgeway, Pembrokeshire, to Miss Chambers, daughter of the late A. Chambers, Esq., of Totteridge, Hertfordshire.

27 September 1794. At the English minister's chapel at Venice, Louis Comte de Darfort, late ambassador from the Court of France, to Miss Seymour, daughter of Henry Seymour, Esq., of Pensanger [Panshanger], Hertfordshire.

6 October 1794. John Portal, Esq., to Miss Corrie, daughter of the late John Corrie, Esq., of Hoddesdon.

14 October 1794. At Beaconsfield, Buckinghamshire, Mr. Hall of Gracechurch Street, to Miss Stevenson, daughter of Joseph Stevenson, Esq., of White's [?], Hertfordshire.

16 October 1794. At North Mimms, Hertfordshire, Frederick Booth, Esq., to Miss Bowman, of Muffetts.

25 October 1794. At Wormley, Hertfordshire, Mr. Thomas Evitt, of Haydon Square, to Miss Elizabeth Welstead, second daughter of George Welstead, Esq., of the Custom House.

November[?] 1794. John Stratton, Esq., of Gays [i.e. the Gage, formerly Gazes Place, Little Berkhamsted], Hertfordshire, to Miss Charlotte Lucadon, daughter of John D. Lucadon, Esq., of Lombard Street, banker.

John Stratton purchased The Gage in 1780, and nine years later built in the grounds, apparently as an observatory, the 155 ft. tower ("Stratton's Folly") which is still one of the most prominent buildings in the village. [AJ]

2 November 1794. Thomas Jones, Esq., of Little Gaddesden, Hertfordshire, to Miss Blittenberg, of Kensington.

5 November 1794. John Dodd, Esq., of Red Heath House, Rickmansworth, Hertfordshire, to Miss Goulds, only daughter and heiress of the late Marval Goulds, Esq., of Beaumont Hall [Redbourn], in the same county.

3 December 1794. At Bishop's Stortford, Hertfordshire, the Rev. James Dalton, rector of Copgrove, and vicar of Catterick, Yorkshire, to Miss Gibson, daughter of the Rev. Edmund Gibson, vicar of Bishop's Stortford, and chancellor of the diocese of Bristol.

12 February 1795. At Whitchurch, Hampshire, Rev. Jn. Filmer, of Abbots Langley, Hertfordshire, to Miss Portal, daughter of Jos. Portal, Esq., of Freefolk [sic].

7 April 1795. Rev. N. May, of Hemel Hempstead, to Miss Isabella Oliphant, tenth daughter of the late Mr. James Oliphant of Cockspur Street.

9 June 1795. Thomas Frederick, Esq., eldest son of General Frederick, to Miss Glasse, eldest daughter of the Rev. Mr. Glasse, of Percombe [sic], Hertfordshire.

16 June 1795. Mr. John Crisp, of Hertford, draper, to Miss Worsley, daughter of Mr. John Worsley, late of Hertford, now of Hackney.

18 June 1795. At Essendon, Hertfordshire, Captain Grey, of the Royal Navy, third son of Sir Charles Grey, K.B., to Miss Whitbread, daughter of Samuel Whitbread, Esq., of Bedwell Park, Bedfordshire.

24 June 1795. At Hartingfordbury, Mr. Smith of Thavies Inn, Holborn, to Miss Smith, of Cole Green, Hertfordshire.

25 July 1795. Mr. Roebuck, of Laytonstone, Essex, to Mrs. Hase, of Berkhamsted, Hertfordshire.

August[?] 1795. Mr. William Henry Gibson, of Lombard Street, public notary, to Miss Felicia Harriet Smith, of Watford, Hertfordshire.

October 1795. At Arcot, in the East Indies, Cotton Bowerbank Dent, Esq., of Madras, senior member of the Board of Trade at that presidency, to Miss Harriet Neale, daughter of the late Rev. William Neale, rector of Essendon and Bayford, Hertfordshire.

13 October 1795. At Clothall, Hertfordshire, Mr. John Ironmonger, silk merchant, to Anne Phillips, of St. Botolph, Bishopsgate.

7 December 1795. At Northampton, Mr. Crispin, surgeon, of Royston, Hertfordshire, to Miss Clark, daughter of the late Alderman Clark of Northampton.

December[?] 1795. Lately, at Witham, William Gaskell, Esq., of the Hertfordshire Militia, to Miss Elizabeth Kynaston, second daughter of Thomas Kynaston, Esq., of the Grove, Essex.

21 January 1796. Rev. John Jeffreys, M.A., rector of Barnes, Surrey, son of Dr. Jeffrey, canon-residentiary of St. Paul's, to Miss Charlotte Byron, daughter of Richard Byron, Esq., of Hertford.

10 March 1796. George Garrett, Esq., of Portsmouth, to Miss Peirce, of Watford, Hertfordshire, daughter of the late Captain Richard Peirce, of Kingston, Surrey.

31 March 1796. Rev. John Collins, of Betterton, Berkshire, vicar of Cheshunt, Hertfordshire, to Miss Smith, daughter of James Smith, Esq., of College House, Chiswick, Middlesex.

2 May 1796. Rev. William Armstrong, eldest son of Edmund Armstrong, Esq., of Forty Hall, Enfield, to Miss A.M. Charlotte Hassell, one of the daughters and co-heiresses of the late Richard Hassell, Esq., of Barnet, with a fortune of £10,000.

4 May 1796. Richard Hey, Esq., fellow of Magdalene college, Cambridge, to Miss Martha Browne, 2nd daughter of the late Thomas Browne, Esq., of Camfield Place, near Hatfield, Hertfordshire.

10 May 1796. George Granville Marshall, Esq., of Charing, Kent, to Miss Hutchinson, eldest daughter of the late Norton Hutchinson, Esq., of Woodhall Park, Hertfordshire.

According to Cussans the manor of Woodhall had been in the possession of Thomas Hutchinson, brother of Norton Hutchinson. When Thomas died in 1774 it passed to his nephew, the Rev. Julius Hutchinson, son of Norton, who eventually sold it to the Marquess of Salisbury in 1792. [AJ]

24 May 1796. At Chelmsford, Essex, George Porter, Esq., of Stanstead Bury, Hertfordshire, to Miss Tindal, eldest daughter of Robert Tindal, Esq., of Chelmsford.

28 May 1796. Mr. Edward Brome, of Watford, Hertfordshire, to Miss Foard, of Petworth, Sussex.

22 July 1796. At St. George's, Hanover Square, the Rev. Wollaston Pym, of Radwell, Hertfordshire, to Miss Mary Cartwright, second daughter of the late Thomas Cartwright, Esq., of Aynho, Northamptonshire.

16 August 1796. Colonel Stephen Poyntz, of the 1st Regiment of Life Guards, to Mrs. Whitfield, widow of John Whitfield, Esq., of Watford, Hertfordshire.

17 September 1796. At Elstree, John Woodcock, Esq., to Miss Mary Ann Graham, third daughter of R.R. Graham, of Aldenham Park, Hertfordshire.

4 February 1797. At Tring, Hertfordshire, John Rolfe, aged 83, to Miss Turner of Ewell, Surrey.

24 April 1797. Lord Dunsany of Ireland to Miss Smith, sister of Drummond Smith of [Tring] Hertfordshire.

May[?] 1797. At Fornham, Suffolk, Hammond Alpe, Esq., of Hardingham, Norfolk, to Miss Hassel, eldest daughter and coheiress of the late Richard Hassel, Esq., of Barnet.

21 June 1797. At St. George's, Hanover Square, Thomas Howard to Miss Sedgwick, both of Rickmansworth, Hertfordshire.

6 July 1797. At Rickmansworth, Lord Holland to Lady Vassal, only daughter of the late Richard Vassal.

11 August 1797. At Cheshunt, Rd. Bally, attorney, to Miss Feather of Red Lion Passage, Holborn

23 August 1797. At Bushey, Hertfordshire, John Smythe, jun., of Uttoxeter, Staffordshire, to Miss Pickering of Bushey.

27 August 1797. At Hadham, Hertfordshire, Thomas Andrews of Basinghall Street to Miss Vigne.

30 August 1797. At Hitchin, Hertfordshire, Rev. Thomas Carter, M.A., to Miss Anne Collison.

August[?] 1797. Lately, John Wilson of Watling Street, to Miss Howard, daughter of Simon Howard of Rickmansworth.

4 September 1797. At Cheshunt, Hertfordshire, Ellerington Laing, Lieutenant 57th. Regiment, to Miss Roberts, daughter of John Roberts, of Cheshunt, and sister to Captain Roberts of the same regiment.

5 December 1797. Joseph Hight of Bovingdon Hay [Hay Farm, Bovingdon?], Hertfordshire, to Miss Collet of Hemel Hempstead.

26 December 1797. E. Haywood of Tooley Street to Miss Mary Crawley of Welwyn, Hertfordshire.

1 January 1798. Rev. George Bell, of Kimpton, Hertfordshire, to Miss Denbiggin, of Northampton.

11 January 1798. At Cardiff, Glamorganshire, Robert Clutterbuck, Esq., of Watford, Hertfordshire, to Miss Capper, eldest daughter of Colonel James Capper of Cathays, near Cardiff.

6 March 1798. At Wormley, Hertfordshire, Mr. Charles Wellstead, deputy collector of the customs in the coast business inwards and outwards, to Miss Porter, of Enfield, sister of — Porter, Esq., of Stanstead Abbots.

6 March 1798. Mr. John Telford, of London (son of Mr. Telford of York), to Miss Salusbury, daughter of the Rev. Thelwall Salusbury, rector of Graveley, Hertfordshire.

March[?] 1798. Lately at Wheathampstead, Hertfordshire, Rev. George Bell, M.A., vicar of Bloxham, Oxfordshire, to Miss Sarah Dowbiggin, daughter of the late Dr. Dowbiggin, subdean of Lincoln.

12 April 1798. Rev. John Keet, of Hatfield, Hertfordshire, to Miss Crawley, daughter of the late John Crawley, Esq., of Stockwood, Bedfordshire.

21 May 1798. At Stapleford, Hertfordshire (by the Rev. Thomas Maurice), Thomas Blore, Esq., of Benwick Hall, in that parish, to Mrs. Gell (Dorothy), relict of Philip Gell, Esq., of Hopton, Derbyshire, and youngest daughter and coheir of William Milnes, Esq., of Aldercar Park, Derbyshire.

22 May 1798. Colonel Buller, of the Norfolk militia, to Miss E.W. Lytton, of Knebworth, Hertfordshire.

18 June 1798. At Saffron Walden, Essex, Rev. Mr. Newton, rector of Tewin, Hertfordshire, to Miss Douglas, only daughter of the late J.C.S. Douglas, Esq., of Jamaica.

26 June 1798. John Booth, Esq., distiller, of Red Lion Street, Clerkenwell, to Miss Elizabeth Williamson, 2nd daughter of John Williamson, of Baldock, Hertfordshire.

16 July 1798. At Dresden, Michael Brown, Esq., of the Saxon horse-guards, to Miss Augusta Prescott, of Theobalds, Hertfordshire.

25 July 1798. At Totteridge, Hertfordshire, Richard Bowzer, Esq., of St. John's, Southwark, to Mrs. Denison, of Bedford Row.

4 August 1798. At Islington, Mr. William Vanning, of Copthall Court, Throgmorton Street, to Miss Rogers, of East Barnet, Hertfordshire.

7 August 1798. Rev. Richard Vivian, rector of Bushey, Hertfordshire, to Miss Emmett, daughter of John Emmett, Esq., of St. Albans.

8 August 1798. At Bushey, Hertfordshire, the Rev. Samuel Pickering, rector of Bishop's Cleave, Gloucestershire, to Miss Ramas, of Merry Hill farm, Bushey.

27 September 1798. Mr. Charles Baker, of Isleworth, to Miss Clark, late of Hartingfordbury, Hertfordshire.

9 November 1798. Mr. Cornelius Pateman Herbert, brewer, at Setchbridge, Norfolk, to Miss Anne Fitzjohn, daughter of Mr. George Fitzjohn, an eminent maltster, at Baldock, Hertfordshire.

The Fitzjohn family had a network of connections with malting, brewing and banking interests in Baldock and Hertford. Martha, the widow of John Fitzjohn, brewer of Baldock, married John Pryor, brewer, who subsequently bought the Fitzjohns' brewery in Baldock. George continued malting, and another daughter married John Williamson, maltster and mealman, who in 1807 joined with Samuel Wells, brewer of Biggleswade, to establish the Baldock Bank. [AJ]

20 November 1798. At St. Saviour's, Southwark, the Rev. Samuel Burder, of St. Albans, to Miss Newsom, daughter of Mr. Newsom of Highgate.

22 November 1798. At Stevenage, Hertfordshire, R. Whitington, Esq., to Miss Catharine Amelia Hinde, daughter of the late Robert Hinde, Esq., of Preston, near Hitchin.

27 November 1798. At Cambridge, the Rev. William Wade, B.D., rector of Lilly, Hertfordshire, vicar of Corley, Warwickshire, and fellow and junior bursar of St. John's college, to Miss Margaret Serocold, daughter of the late Rev. Walter Serocold, vicar of Cherry Hinton.

12 December 1798. Captain J. Edwards, of the Royal Navy, to Miss S. Doo, of Chipping [Buckland], Hertfordshire.

19 December 1798. Rev. Thomas James, of Brecon, to Miss Young, daughter of the late Thomas Young, Esq., of Bush Hall [Hatfield], Hertfordshire.

22 December 1798. Captain James Crook, of the East and West Lothian Light Dragoons, to Miss Fayrer, daughter of late Rd. Fayrer, Esq., of Sacombe Green, Hertfordshire.

7 February 1799. John Castleton Miller, Esq., of Queens college, Cambridge, to Miss Pagett, eldest daughter of the late Rev. William Pagett, of Totteridge, Hertfordshire.

11 June 1799. At Mary-le-Bonne William Willoughby Prescott, second son of Sir George Prescott, Bart., of Theobalds Park, to Miss Blackmore, sister of T. Blackmore of Briggins [Hunsdon], Hertfordshire.

19 August 1799. At Cheshunt, Hertfordshire, George Beeston Prescott, eldest son of Sir George William Prescott, Bart., of Theobalds Park, to Miss Mills, daughter of the late Sir Thomas Mills.

22 October 1799. James Torkington of Stukeley, Hunts, to Miss Bourchier, daughter of Charles Bourchier of Sandridge Lodge [Marshalswick, St. Albans], Hertfordshire.

21 November 1799. At Hertingfordbury, William Baron, late of the University of Cambridge, to Miss Mary-Anne Hickman, of Hertford.

5 January 1800. Rev. Wiltshire John Emmett, only son of John Emmett of St. Albans, to Miss Smith of Watford.

23 January 1800. William Wilson, Esq., of Wellingborough, Northamptonshire, to Miss Harriet *Augusta* Hinde, youngest daughter of the late Robert Hinde, Esq., of Preston Castle, Hertfordshire.

June[?] *1800.* At Lambeth, Joseph Biddle, Esq., of Cuper's Bridge, to Miss Mary Anne Smith, of Kingsbury, St. Albans. Also, Stephen Smith, Esq., of Kingsbury, to Miss E. Biddle.

5 August 1800. At Great Gaddesden, James Pickford, Esq., of Market-street [Markyate], to Miss Grant.

12 August 1800. Mr. Holmes, exciseman, Bishop's Stortford, to Miss Sarah Hobkirk, of the George Inn, Enfield.

August 1800. At Hitchin, Mr. John Bedford, printer and bookseller, to Miss Margerson.

5 September 1800. At Aldenham, Hertfordshire, Captain Henry Graham, of the 1st Dragoon Guards, to Miss Clutterbuck, of Stanmore, second sister of Robert P.[sic], Esq., of Cardiff, Glamorganshire.

September[?] *1800.* Lately, at Berkhamsted, Mr. Jones, to Miss Fall, daughter of the late Colonel Fall, governor of Jersey.

2 October 1800. James Howard, Esq., of West Fields, St. Albans, Hertfordshire, to Miss Mary Louisa Ekins, daughter of the late Rev. Randolph Ekins, rector of Pebmarsh, Essex.

11 October 1800. W.G. Times, attorney, to Mrs. Sworder, both of Much Hadham, Herts.

18 October 1800. John Wood, Esq., of Austin Friars, to Miss Frances Heysham, daughter of the Rev. Edmund Heysham, rector of Little Munden, Hertfordshire.

6 November 1800. At Hertford, John Brickwood, Esq., of Croydon, Surrey, to Miss Bowyer, daughter of the late Calvert Bowyer, Esq., of Coles.

The Bowyers were established at Coles in Westmill by 1674, until the death of Calvert Bowyer shortly before 1800. Other Bowyers continued elsewhere in the village for a few more years. In the early days they seem to have been Quakers. [AJ]

5 December 1800. At Colney Hatch, Hertfordshire [sic], Thomas Sheppard, Esq., of Basinghall Street, to Miss Sarah Down, daughter of Richard Down, Esq., banker, Bartholomew Lane, London.

13 December 1800. Mr. Thomas Pitt Stead, of London Bridge, to Miss Anne Skey, of Welling [Welwyn], Hertfordshire.

BANKRUPTCIES

February 1733. John MARSHAL of St. Albans, stage coachman.

March 1734. Benjamin MITCHELL of St. Albans, Hertfordshire, brewer.

July 1734. Compton MORRES of St. Albans, linen draper.

March 1735. John BRANTON of Ashwell, Hertfordshire, butcher.

May 1735. John SIBLEY of Hunsdon, Hertfordshire, mercer.

June 1735. Jeremiah GODFREY of Ashwell, Hertfordshire, mealman.

July 1735. Robert FRENCH, sen., of St. Albans, vintner.

August 1737. Wentworth George PITT of St. Stephens, Hertfordshire, chapman.

February 1742. Lucy STRUDWICK of Watford, Hertfordshire, draper.

September 1743. John STOUGHTON of St. Albans, grocer.

December 1743. Richard MILLBANK late of Cheshunt, Hertfordshire, mealman.

April 1744. Thomas DEAR of Royston, linen draper.

March 1745. John GALBRAITH of St. Albans, Hertfordshire, apothecary.

April 1745. Thomas KIDDALL of Weston, Hertfordshire, mealman.

July 1745. Barnardiston NELSON of Redbourn, Hertfordshire, inn-keeper.

October 1745. George GOLDSMITH of Windridge [St. Michaels], Hertfordshire, maltster.

November 1745. William BARTON of Cheshunt, Hertfordshire, victualler.

November 1745. John ASHTON of Stanstead [Abbots], Hertfordshire, mealman.

February 1746. Henry HICKS of Munden, Hertfordshire, grocer.

February 1746. Jeremiah GODFREY of Ashwell, Hertfordshire, linen draper.

April 1746. Thomas AYRES of Buckland, Hertfordshire, shopkeeper.

April 1746. Thomas ROBERTS of St. Albans, Hertfordshire, linen draper.

April 1747. James NORMAN of Redbourn, Hertfordshire, carrier.

November 1748. George SLEATH of East Barnet, Hertfordshire, maltster.

January 1749. William COOKE of St. Albans, cheesemonger.

March 1749. Humphrey THURSTANS of Ware, Hertfordshire, ironmonger.

June 1749. Robert HARROW of Cheshunt, Hertfordshire, dealer.

October 1751. John GRAVENOR of South Mimms, Middlesex, chapman.

December 1751. Justinian MORSE of Barnet, Hertfordshire, coach maker.

October 1752. Thomas BRENTNALL of Hertford, victualler.

November 1753. Anthony FREEMAN of St. Albans, dealer and chapman.

January 1754. John SAUNDERS of Hertford, grocer.

September 1754. William SHEPHERD of Hemel Hempstead, grocer.

February 1755. Joseph FOWDEN of Wormley, Hertford, cyder merchant.

September 1755. Archibald FINNEY of St. Albans, innholder.

January 1756. John CLOPPELL of Tring, Hertfordshire, chapman.

January 1756. Silvanus PERROT of Hemel Hempstead, chapman.

March 1756. Samuel COWELL of Hunsdon, Hertfordshire, tanner.

June 1757. Thomas ADCOCK of South Mimms, Middlesex, innkeeper.

June 1757. John BEECH of Great Gaddesden, tanner.

August 1757. James SMITH of Widford, Hertfordshire, mealman.

October 1757. Tempest LOCKWOOD of Sawbridgeworth, innholder.

October 1758. Lancelot SANDERSON of Market Street [Markyate], innholder.

May 1759. James WYER of Cheshunt, innholder.

July 1759. John SMITH of Hertford, draper.

November 1760. Robert SPENCER, of Barkway in Hertfordshire, chapman.

January 1761. John BOND of Rickmansworth, surgeon.

March 1762. David WHEATLEY of Barnet, dealer in coals.

September 1765. William GILL of South Mimms, inn-holder.

November 1765. Benjamin BAYRON of Barley, Hertfordshire, linen draper.

December 1765. John HOUGH of St. Albans Street [London?], wine merchant.

June 1766. Thomas CLAYDEN of Tring, Hertfordshire, victualler.

November 1766. Thomas REYNOLDS of Bishops Stortford, shopkeeper.

October 1767. Thomas BECKINGTON of Cheshunt in Hertfordshire, surgeon and apothecary.

November 1767. William HOWARD, jun., of Hatfield, Hertfordshire, innholder.

January 1768. Abraham NORTH, jun., of Ware, maltster.

February 1768. James DUEWICK, of Hertingfordbury, linen draper.

April 1768. H. WANKFORD, Rickmansworth, Hertfordshire, dealer.

May 1768. Henry BOWKER, of Hertford, vintner and innholder.

July 1768. Henry RIDER, of Hertford, shopkeeper.

October 1768. Robert WILLIAMSON, of Hatfield-street, pasteboard-maker.

December 1768. William SMITH, of Watford, Hertfordshire, corn chandler.

January 1769. Hannah APPLEBY, Sawbridgeworth, Hertfordshire, grocer.

October 1769. Zachary HOUSE, Hertfordshire, papermaker.

January 1770. Matthew IREMONGER, Hertfordshire, shopkeeper.

May 1770. Arthur UPTON, Hertford, linen draper.

September 1770. Ralph TURNER, Hitchin, Hertfordshire, pot seller.

January 1771. G. OXFORD, Much Hadham, Hertfordshire, haberdasher.

August 1771. Benjamin KING, of Northaw, Hertfordshire, dealer.

January 1772. Edmund LONG of Widford, Hertfordshire, mealman.

March 1772. Richard PEECHY, Aldenham, Hertfordshire, butcher.

April 1772. W. WARNER of Barnet, peruke maker and brick maker [sic].

April 1772. John CLARKE, of Much Hadham, Hertfordshire, dealer in cattle.

November 1772. George HAWKINS, of Redbourn in Hertfordshire, mercer and draper.

April 1773. Peter SPRECKLESON, of Chipping Barnet, Hertfordshire, coach and coach-harness maker.

August 1773. Edward PARKER, Little Hadham, Hertfordshire, bays [baize?] maker.

November 1773. J. HILL, of Codicote, Hertfordshire, innholder.

February 1774. John HOLLAND, Barkway, Hertfordshire, innholder.

April 1774. Samuel BARTLETT, of Barnet, wheelwright.

July 1744. John HUMPHRYS, Tring, Hertfordshire, wheelwright.

November 1774. John CONNER, Chipping Barnet, Hertfordshire.
[NB. No trade given]

July 1775. Edward HILL, Hatfield, Hertfordshire, victualler.

December 1775. James MACKLIN, Buntingford, Hertfordshire, apothecary.

January 1776. John READ, South Mimms, Middlesex, dealer and chapman.

April 1776. Robert SMITH, St. Albans, linen draper.

November 1776. James LATTIMER, St. Albans, Hertfordshire, linen draper.

November 1776. John ARNOLD, Barnet, innholder.

November 1776. William KENDAL, Baldock, Hertfordshire, innholder.

February 1777. Elizabeth SMITH and John RALPH, Bishop Stortford, in Hertfordshire, shopkeepers.

February 1777. John HAMMOND, of Hertford, maltster.

April 1778. Thomas GLADMAN, Studham, Hertfordshire [Bedfordshire], dealer.

June 1778. John KEIRBY, late of Layston, Hertfordshire, fellmonger.

June 1778. Thomas BRUGIS, Hatfield, Hertfordshire, innholder.

February 1779. Elisha FIELD, Watford, Hertfordshire, dealer.

March 1779. John BIGGS of Scotch Bridge Mill, Rickmansworth, Hertfordshire, papermaker.

July 1779. Francis BROWN, Hitchin, Hertfordshire, shopkeeper.

August 1779. John BYRCHMORE of St. Albans, Hertfordshire, distiller and brewer.

September 1779. Thomas JOHNSON, Gustard Wood, Hertfordshire, woolstapler.

November 1779. William TURPIN, Harpenden, Hertfordshire, butcher.

September 1780. John SUTTON, of Hitchin, Hertfordshire, brazier.

January 1781. Dorothy WOODCOCK, Puckeridge, Hertfordshire, linen draper.

June 1781. John LUCAS, Hitchin, Hertfordshire, shopkeeper.

February 1782. David JONES, St. Albans, Hertfordshire, innholder.

August 1782. John GODDARD, Watford, Hertfordshire, shopkeeper.

March 1783. William THOMPSON, of Hertford, grocer.

May 1783. Henry RIDER, Wadesmill, Hertfordshire, linen draper.

May 1783. Richard BROWN, Hemel Hempstead, Hertfordshire, wool spinner.

February 1784. Henry COOK, jun., Waltham Cross, Essex, patent sponge maker.

April 1784. Moses HARRIS, Brown-End [BOURNE END?], Hertfordshire, paper maker.

May 1784. Francis BANKS, sen., and Francis BANKS, jun., St. Albans, millers.

July 1784. Robert WALTERS, Watford, Hertfordshire, victualler.

April 1785. Andrew POUPARD, Ware, Hertfordshire, slopseller.

January 1786. George SAVAGE, Hatfield, Hertfordshire, innkeeper.

January 1786. Moses BEST, Rickmansworth, Hertfordshire, shopkeeper.

June 1786. Richard NICOLL, Ware, Hertfordshire, malt factor.

June 1786. J.C. CLARKE, Barnet, innholder.

February 1789. Jeremiah DOUTON, Barntet [Barnet?], baker.

May 1789. Richard HEMMING, Ware, shopkeeper.

DEATHS

15 February 1731. HAMILTON. The second son of the Rt. Hon. the Lord Paisley, about this time, at Mr Plummer's seat in Hertfordshire.

The eldest son of James, 6th Earl of Abercorn, was known by his courtesy title of Lord Paisley until he succeeded his father as the 7th Earl in 1734. On 3 April 1711, at Widford, he married Anne, eldest daughter of Colonel John Plumer of Blakesware, which is where this sad death of their second son took place on a visit to her family.

Paisley's grand-daughter Jane, 6th daughter of his third son, became in 1761 the second wife of William Plumer (1736–1822) of Gilston Park, MP for Hertfordshire 1768–1807, nephew of Anne above. Her second husband was Commander Richard John Lewin, RN, but her third marriage on 16 July 1828, to Robert Plumer Ward of Gilston Park (1765–1846) retained the Hamilton-Plumer link begun in 1711 and ended only by her death on 26 March 26 1831. For a full account of Ward see DNB. He took the Plumer surname on marriage. [PW]

15 March 1731. GALE. Robert Gale, Esq., at Barret [Barnet?], son of Benjamin Gale of Abbots Langley in Hertfordshire.

Robert Gale presumably died at Barnet. See Cussans III (Cashio) p.101 for monumental inscriptions of several members of the Gale family of Abbots Langley but not one for Robert. [PW]

18 March 1731. GULSTON. Richard Gulston, Esq., at Wydial Hall in Hertfordshire.

Richard Gulston (1669–1731), eldest son of James and his wife Mary, daughter of John Rowley of Barkway. He was MP for Hertford, 1701–1705, 1710–1715 (when unseated). Descended from John Gulston of Leicestershire, Prothonotary of the Common Pleas, who purchased Wyddial in 1628. See Cussans I (Edwinstree) p.121 for a pedigree. Cussans extracted all Gulston entries in the Gentleman's Magazine from 1737 to 1806 on p.120. [PW]

26 March 1731. WILMOT. The Rev. Mr. Wilmot, going to Stapleforth [Stapleford] in Hertfordshire, his horse fell with him and killed him on the spot.

The Rev. Thomas Wilmot was rector of Stapleford, 1724–31. He was buried at Stapleford on 30 March. His brother, George Vernon, was presented to succeed him but died on 28 August, 1731, and was buried 31 August, the day when he should have been instituted, according to Cussans II (Hertford) p.31. [PW]

May 1731. JOCELYN. The Lady of Sir Strange Josselin, Bart., at Hide in Hertfordshire.

Lady Jocelyn was the wife of Sir Strange Jocelyn, 2nd baronet of Hyde Hall, Sawbridgeworth. She was buried at Sawbridgeworth on 24 May. She was Mary, dau. of Tristram Conyers, Copped Hall, Epping, Essex. See Cussans I (Braughing) pp.80–90 for an account of the family. Sir Strange, who died in 1734 and was also buried at Sawbridgeworth, was succeeded in the baronetcy in order by his two sons. [PW]

21 May 1731. NORTON. The Rev. Dr. William Norton, preacher of Grays Inn, vicar of Deptford in Kent, and rector of Walkern in Hertfordshire.

Dr William Norton, rector of Walkern 1722–23, was educated at Eton and Kings College Cambridge of which he was elected a Fellow in 1709. His doctorate was a Cambridge one in Divinity awarded in 1728. From 1729 he was preacher at Grays Inn. In 1728 he also became vicar of St. Nicholas Deptford and in 1730 vicar of St. Pauls Deptford, all of which jointly with Walkern he held at his death. [PW]

27 November 1731. HANSCOMBE. James Hanscombe, of Pirton Grange, in Hertfordshire.

James Hanscombe of Pirton Grange was the very epitome of the English country landowner as the monumental inscription to him on the floor of the nave in Pirton church amply testifies. Cussans II (Hitchin) p.20 prints it in full. [PW]

11 January 1732. FINCH. Mr Isaac Finch of Watford in Hertfordshire, aged 104. He followed the trade of a leatherseller 80 years, and died worth £15,000.

6 February 1732. BYDE. Thomas Byde, Esq., Lord of the Manors of Ware and Hertford.

23 March 1732. PHEASANT. Mr. Pheasant, at Northaw in Hertfordshire, Turkey merchant.

25 March 1732. GOODWIN. The Rev. Mr. William Goodwin, vicar of Pirton, in Hertfordshire.

12 April 1732. FLOYER. Relict of Sir Peter Floyer, at Cheshunt in Hertfordshire.

14 April 1732. RUSSEL. John Russel, Esq., at Theobalds in Hertfordshire.

1 July 1732. SHEPHERD. Nathaniel Shepherd, Esq., at Abbots Langley, Hertfordshire, in the Commission of Peace, one of the projectors of the late Sir Richard Steele's Fish-pool Scheme.

Sir Richard Steele (essayist, dramatist and politician) had obtained authority under letters patent for a project ('the Fishpool') which involved bringing live salmon from Ireland in a well-boat. The scheme was eventually unsuccessful [PW]

15 July 1732. STONE. Mr Stone, Mayor of St. Albans, the first who died in that office for 150 years.

18 November 1732. LYTTON. William Robinson Lyttleton [Lytton], Esq., of Knebworth, Hertfordshire, beloved by rich and poor.

11 December 1732. GAPE. Thomas Gape, Esq., Member of Parliament for St. Albans.

2 March 1733. BLOOM. Thomas Bloom, Esq., at Hoddesdon, Hertfordshire.

4 March 1733. GLOVER. John Glover, Esq., at Cheshunt, Hertfordshire.

8 March 1733. THORNBURY. John Thornbury, Esq., at Cheshunt in Hertfordshire, formerly a merchant.

10 March 1733. CARR. Mr William Carr, mayor and post-master of St. Albans. [See Main Sequence February 1733]

19 March 1733. RAYMOND. Sir Robert Raymond, Kt., Lord Raymond of Abbots Langley, Hertfordshire. In 1710 he was appointed Solicitor General to Queen Anne, elected Member for Lymington in Hants, and so continued during that reign, but in 1714 his patent was revoked. In 1720 he was appointed Attorney General to his late Majesty [George I]; and in 1723–24 was made a Serjeant at Law, and the next day appointed one of the Justices of the King's Bench, in the room of Lord Chief Justice Pratt; in 1730 he was elected a Governor of the Charterhouse, in the room of Lord Trevor; and in January 1730–1, created a Peer of Great Britain. He married a daughter of the late Sir Edward Northey, Attorney General to Queen Anne, by whom he has left one son aged 16.

21 March 1733. TALMAN. Mrs. Talman, relict of an ingenious virtuoso of that name, at Hinxford [Hinxworth], Hertfordshire.

John Talman (d. 1726) was an amateur artist and antiquary, best know for his drawings of antiquities. He was elected first director of The Society of Antiquaries in January 1717/18. [DNB]

25 April 1733. BLUNDEL. Mr. Blundel, of Hoddesdon, in Hertfordshire, formerly wine merchant.

25 May 1733. COMBS. John Combs, Esq., at Hertford, formerly Turkey merchant worth £20,000.

4 August 1733. KILLEGREW. Mrs. Jane Killegrew, at St. Albans, daughter of the late Admiral of that name.

17 August 1733. BARD. The relict of Sir Bard, Kt., near Watford, Hertfordshire.

30 August 1733. LEWIS. John Lewis, at Berkhamsted, Hertfordshire, Esq., formerly Commander of a Man of War.

7 September 1733. WALLINGFORD. John Wallingford, Esq., at Cheshunt, Hertfordshire, wine-merchant.

15 December 1733. CAPEL. The relict of the late Sir William Capel at her house at St. Albans.

31 January 1734. MILLECHAMP. The Rev. Mr. Millechamp, at Broadwater, Hertfordshire.

11 March 1734. OSBORNE. Bridget, Duchess Dowager of Leeds; she was the Lady of Peregrine [Osborne], Duke of Leeds, and sole daughter and heir of Sir Thomas Hyde, of North Mimms in Hertfordshire, Bart.

In 1658 Sir Thomas Hyde, lord of the manor of Aldbury, purchased also the manor of North Mimms. Two years later, at the age of 66, he married (for the first time). His wife was Mary, née Whitchurch, whose two sisters had married respectively William Emerton, the bailiff of Sir Thomas's Aldbury estate, and his brother Richard who had been made bailiff of the newly acquired estate at North Mimms. Bridget, the only child of Thomas and Mary, was born two years later at North Mimms. Within three years her father had died and her mother very soon remarried—to Sir Robert Vyner, a generous creditor and banker to Charles II, who urgently needed to improve his finances. An arranged marriage for his step-daughter Bridget—a wealthy heiress in her own right—offered considerable benefits. A union between Bridget and Peregrine, son of Thomas Osborne (Earl of Danby, Lord High Treasurer of England, and soon to become the first Duke of Leeds) was being discussed when it was discovered in 1674 that this extremely wealthy young girl (she was then only twelve years old) had been inveigled into a form of marriage with her cousin, the son of William Emerton. This notorious 'clandestine marriage', the annulment of which was not achieved until April 1683, became the scandal of the 1670s and 80s, especially when Bridget bigamously married Peregrine at Marylebone on 22 April 1682, and bore him a son in March 1683. By that time both her parents were dead, and she had inherited both the Aldbury and North Mimms estates.

The apparent love match between Bridget and Peregrine ended in tears, and they separated at some time before 1715. In that year history tried to repeat itself when their daughter, also Bridget, also entered into a clandestine marriage, with Rev. William Williams, the chaplain to her brother's family at Kiveton Hall in Yorkshire. This time however, after some violent scenes with her mother and determined efforts by the family to have the marriage annulled, there was a short-lived happy ending: in 1716 the court declared the marriage valid, and influence secured for Williams a prebend at Chichester Cathedral. But he died less than four years after their marriage. Bridget, the dowager Duchess, died 8 March 1733/34, and was buried at Aldbury. (Sources: Jean Davis. The case of the pretended marriage. Aldbury, 1976; Lawrence Stone. Uncertain unions: marriage in England 1660–1753. OUP, 1992). [AJ]

1 April 1734. HUSSEY. Edward Hussey, Esq., nephew of Sir Charles Hussey, Bart., at St. Albans.

7 May 1734. GAPE. John Gape, Esq., representative for St. Albans in several Parliaments.

24 May 1734 PHILIPS. George Philips, Esq., at Barnet.

26 July 1734. SELBEY. John Selbey, Esq., at Cheshunt, Hertfordshire.

19 August 1734. LEBAND. Joseph Leband, Esq., at Watford, Hertfordshire.

3 September 1734. JOCELYN. Sir Strange Jocelyn, of Hertfordshire, Bart.

17 December 1734. JOCELYN. Mrs. Katherine, daughter of Sir Strange Jocelyn of Hertfordshire, Bart.

18 December 1734. CLENCH. Mr. Clench of Barnet, aged 70 who diverted the town many years, with imitating the Drunken Man, Pack of Hounds etc.

8 June 1735. HUGHES. George Mileman Hughes, Esq., at St. Albans. He changed his name from Mileman to Hughes for an estate of £754 per annum.

22 November 1735. PARNS. Sir Peter Parns, Kt., of Watford, Hertfordshire.

1 December 1735. SWINFORD. Philip Swinford, Esq., at Barnet.

24 January 1736. HILL. Philip Hill, Esq., at Moor Park, Hertfordshire.

11 April 1736. SEABRIGHT. Sir Thomas Saunders Seabright, Bart., Knight of the Shire for Hertford. £4000 per annum descends to his [son?] aged 13.

23 May 1736. LADYMAN. Christopher Ladyman, Esq., of Rickmansworth, Hertfordshire.

26 May 1736. SUNLEY. George Sunley, Esq., just come of age to £4000 per annum, at St. Albans.

28 July 1736. HUGHES. Captain Hughes, at Herford [Hertford, Hereford ?], aged 70, and worth £20,000. He had served 48 years; at the Battle of Schellenberg was shot through the cheek; at Namur through the wrist, and wounded in the head.

30 August 1736. CLARK. Dr. Clark, a physician, at Hertford.

20 September 1736. MONTGOMERY. Jos. Montgomery, Esq., at Barnet.

18 November 1736. KIRBY. William Kirby, Esq., at Rickmansworth.

12 December 1736. PEARSON. John Pearson, Esq., at St. Albans.

14 January 1737. BUCKNELL. The Lady of William Bucknell, at Oxhey, Hertfordshire.

This was Mary, wife of William Bucknell, Esq., of Oxhey. Their daughter Mary married 19 June 1746 James Grimston, 2nd Viscount Grimston. [AJ]

8 March 1737. JENKINSON. Jos. Jenkinson, Esq., at Ware, Hertfordshire.

5 April 1737. STANLEY. George Stanley, Esq., at Hertford.

c. June 1737. CECIL. The Right Rev. Father in God, Dr. Charles Cecil, Lord Bishop of Bangor, who held in Commendam the rich living of Hatfield, Hertfordshire.

Charles Cecil, grandson of third Earl of Salisbury, Rector of Hatfield 1719–1737, bishop of Bristol 1733–1734, bishop of Bangor 1734–1737. The drawing-room of the former rectory— now Howe Dell School, Hatfield—has a fine plaster ceiling, decorated with medallions of the arms of the Cecil family, for which the bishop was no doubt responsible. [RHW]

19 July 1737. ANDREWS. John Andrews, Esq., at Rickmansworth.

1 August 1737. GORE. Hon. Lady Mary Gore, at Tring, Hertfordshire.

20 August 1737. CORNFORTH. Gabriel Cornforth, Esq., at Rickmansworth.

3 September 1737. PITT. John Pitt, Esq., at Rickmansworth.

8 July 1738. FREEMAN. ————— Freeman, Esq., of a great estate at Cheshunt, Hertfordshire.

13 September 1738. STUBBS. Dr. Stubbs, Archdeacon of St. Albans, and chaplain of Greenwich Hospital.

13 January 1739. HALSEY. Henshaw Halsey, Esq., of Gaddesden, Hertfordshire.

4 April 1739. STYLES. Benjamin Haskyns Styles, Esq., of Moor Park, Hertfordshire; member in last Parliament for Calne.

Benjamin Styles purchased Moor Park in 1720. It was he who cased the house with stone, and added the portico on the south front and two wings. Styles died at Moor Park and was buried in the chapel there. [AJ]

4 November 1740. STARKS. Philip Starks, Esq., Chancellor at Law, at Ware in Hertfordshire.

2 April 1741. CAESAR. Charles Caesar, Esq., Member for Hertfordshire.

1 November 1741. JOCELYN. Sir John Jocelyn, Bart., at his seat of Hyde Hall [Sawbridgeworth], Hertfordshire, who was succeeded by his brother Sir Conyers. He desired by his will to be buried in the avenue before his house, and that one of his largest oxen should be given to the poor on the occasion.

25 November 1741. CHACE. Richard Chace of Hertfordshire, Esq. His real estate of £2000 per annum goes to his only son, and his personal estate of £100,000 to be divided among his three daughters.

23 February 1742. CARLETON. Thomas Carleton, of Broxbourn, Hertfordshire, Esq., who was to have gone out with the Turkey fleet, as consul to the Company at Smyrna.

7 May 1742. FALLE. Mr. Philip Falle, rector of Shenley, Hertfordshire, and a prebendary of Durham. He was author of *An Account of the Island of Jersey* of which he was a native, and left his fine library for the use of that island.

13 May 1742. WHEATLEY. Charles Wheatley, M.A., vicar of both Pelhams in Hertfordshire. He published some sermons and an exposition of the liturgy.

Cussans (Edwinstree, p.151) shows Wheatley b. 6 February 1685/6, d. 13 May 1742, buried in the church at Furneux Pelham. [PW]

13 June 1742. FREEMAN. Ralph Freeman of Aspeden Hall, Hertfordshire, aged 76. 33 years Member for that county.

15 June 1742. GAPE. Thomas Gape, Esq., formerly Member for St. Albans.

11 November 1742. COPPIN. John Coppin of Market-Cell [Markyate], Hertfordshire, Esq., greatly regretted. He has left a son and a daughter to whom he bequeathed his estate.

8 January 1743. CAPEL. William Capel, Earl of Essex, Viscount Malden and Baron Capel of Hadham, a Lord of the Bedchamber, Captain of the Yeomen of the Guard, Lord Lieutenant and Cust. Rot. of Hertfordshire, P.C., and F.R.S. He is succeeded by his eldest son, a minor.

29 January 1743. ASHBY. Thomas Ashby, Esq., representative for St. Albans.

30 May 1743. SHORT. Samuel Short of Hertfordshire, Esq.

7 December 1743. BULL. George Bull, near Watford, Hertfordshire, Esq.

23 January 1744. FLOYER. Thomas Floyer of Brent Pelham, Hertfordshire, Esq.

Cussans (Edwinstree) p.137 gives the pedigree of the Floyer or Flyer family. Thomas was born in 1695. [PW]

21 February 1744. SAMBROOKE. Lady Sambrooke, mother of Sir Jeremy Sambrooke of Gibbons [Gobions], Hertfordshire, Bart.

Lady Sambrooke was the widow of an earlier Sir Jeremy, who died in 1705. He had been deputy chairman of the East India Company. [PK]

5 April 1744. TOLLER. Thomas Toller of Hertford, Esq.

17 April 1744. SALE. George Sale of Watford, Hertfordshire, Esq.

22 August 1744. WYNN. William Wynn, Esq., of a large Estate in Hertfordshire.

23 March 1745. HEASLINGFIELD. Henry Heaslingfield of Hertfordshire, Esq.

6 August 1745. MONTGOMERY. William Montgomery Esq., of Hertfordshire.

2 September 1745. DRAPER. George Draper, Esq., at Lilley, Hertfordshire, brother to Lady Barrington of Hitchin.

29 September 1745. JEKYLL. Relict of Sir Jo. Jekyll at Bell Bar, Hertfordshire.

2 March 1746. PLUMER. Walter Plumer, Esq., formerly Member twice for Aldborough also twice for Apulby [Appleby]. Leaving no issue, his large estate goes to his two brothers, William Plumer of Blakesware, Hertfordshire, Esq., and Richard Plumer, Esq., one of the lords of trade.

21 March 1746. HIND. Peter Hind of Cheshunt, Hertfordshire.

1 July 1746. DUNCOMB. ———— Duncomb, Esq., Hertfordshire.

24 March 1747. SAVAGE. John Savage, D.D., Rector of Clothall, Hertfordshire, and lecturer of St. George, Hanover Square; called the Aristippus of the age.

John Savage (Westminster School and Emmanuel College, Cambridge) was tutor to the 5th Earl of Salisbury, with whom he travelled for many years on the continent. He was rector successively of Bygrave (1701–8) and Clothall (1708–47), to which he was presented by his former pupil the Earl of Salisbury whose manor of Quickswood lay within the parish. He was president of the Royston Club (see Main Sequence, October 1780 and October 1783), and earned the tag 'the Aristippus of the age' — after the pupil of Socrates credited with the doctrine of Hedonism, that pleasure or happiness is the chief good and chief end of man. The antiquary William Cole (1714–1782) recorded that Savage died as a result of falling down the steps of the scaffolding which had been erected at Westminster Hall for the trial of Lord Lovat, concluded several days before. [AJ]

For a further biographical note by the Editor, G.M., see Main Sequence October 1783.

10 December 1747. TOPHAM. Henry Topham Esq., at St. Albans.

28 December 1747. EVANS. George Evans of Fanham Hall, near Ware, Hertfordshire, Esq.

February 1748. ASHFORDBY. John Ashfordby Esq., at Cheshunt, Hertfordshire.

4 April 1748. ASTON. Lord Aston, a Roman Catholic, at his seat at Tickills, Hertfordshire.

6 April 1748. HALSEY. Charles Halsey, Esq., near Hempstead, Hertfordshire.

The rectory of Great Gaddesden, having been granted in 1544/45 by Henry VIII to William Hawsè or Halsey, descended in that family and was in due course inherited by Charles Halsey in 1739, he being the sixth son of Thomas and eldest surviving brother of Henshaw Halsey who previously held the estate. Charles was county Sheriff in 1746. [AJ]

15 May 1748. METCALFE. Sloper Metcalfe, Esq., in Hertfordshire.

23 September 1748. WITTEWRONGE. James Wittewronge, Esq., of Rothamsted, Hertfordshire.

26 September 1748. HARMAN. William Harman of Cole Green, Hertfordshire, Esq.

22 October 1748. BISSE. James Bisse, Esq., M.D., at Codicotebury, nr. Welwyn, Hertfordshire, aged 80.

Dr. James Bisse was born in 1766 in West Ham, son of Edward Bisse, a draper who had made his money in the City of London, and had moved out of town to live the life of a gentleman. James attended Merchant Taylors School and Wadham College, Oxford, where he obtained the degrees of B.A., M.A., M.B., and, in 1701, M.D. By December, 1701, Bisse was paying poor rates on the "wood and Lordship" in Codicote, and in 1703 he married 25-year-old Anne Poyner, sole surviving child of the late George Poyner, lord of the Manor of Codicote. They occupied the manor house Codicote Bury. Bisse appropriated the former Sissevernes Chapel in the nearby parish church, and upset fellow parishioners in 1706 by erecting a screen around it, in so doing encroaching upon another private pew. In 1730/1 he and Edward Gilbert of St. Paul's Waldenbury donated the current tower clock to Codicote church. However, by 1735 Bisse was in trouble for neglecting the fabric of his chapel. Therefore the following year he reconstructed the building, erecting two Latin inscriptions detailing the work carried out, and enlarged its vault, filling it with the remains of his ancestors. He himself was buried there in 1748. Bisse's two sons and four daughters were born in Codicote, and the second and sole surviving son, George Poyner Bisse, inherited the manor and Bury, which he sold in 1771. (Main source: E.H.A.S. Transactions, 1910–11). [NM]

23 November 1748. MORRIS. Nicholas Morris of Hitchin, Hertfordshire, Esq.

6 July 1749. LEMAN. Richard Leman, Esq., at Northaw, Hertfordshire.

23 August 1749. ROBERTS. Thomas Roberts, Esq., at Barnet.

23 August 1749. MIMMS. ———— Mimms of South Mimms, Hertfordshire, Esq.

24 April 1750. THOROWGOOD. Ralph Thorowgood, Esq., at Ware, Hertfordshire.

6 June 1750. BENNET. James Bennet, Esq., at Cheshunt.

14 June 1751. MOORE. Francis Moore, Esq., possessed of a large estate near Hertford, of a mortified toe.

14 July 1751. WIGLEY. Nicholas Wigley, Esq., near Ware, Hertfordshire.

10 September 1751. WILLIS. George Willis, Esq., of Hertfordshire.

7 October 1751. COLTSWORTH. Charles Coltsworth, Esq., at Bath, of a large estate near Cheshunt, Hertfordshire.

15 October 1751. MARTIN. Ambrose Martin, Esq., at Cheshunt.

25 November 1751. BURR. Edward Burr of Bishops Stortford, Hertfordshire, aged 69, who had employed himself 48 years in no other business than as a journeyman tailor, at £10 a year wages and board, and died possessed of an estate of £48 a year and above £1140 in cash.

7 January 1752. BUCKNELL. Robert Bucknell, Esq., of Cheshunt, Hertfordshire.

22 January 1752. SNELL. Anthony Snell, Esq., of Hertfordshire.

3 June 1752. BETSWORTH. Mrs. Jane Betsworth at Bovington, Hertfordshire, aged 40. Falling down stairs, a pair of pointed scissors she carried about her stuck in her groin, of which she died in a few hours, worth £8000. She left £2000 to charitable uses.

9 June 1752. HAYNES. Dr. Samuel Haynes, Canon of Windsor, and possessed of the livings of Hatfield and Clothall, Hertfordshire, the former above £800 per annum.

Formerly tutor of the Earl of Salisbury, he was rector of Hatfield 1737–52 and of Clothall 1747–52. Published a volume of the State Papers (1542–1570) preserved at Hatfield House. [HG]

21 October 1752. ELWYS/ELWES. Thomas Elwys of Throcking, Hertfordshire, Esq., possessed of £4000 per annum, which, after the decease of his widow, descends to his only son, Thomas, of Isleworth, Middlesex.

23 October 1752. TIPPING. Rev. Mr. Thomas Tipping, Rector of Yardley [Ardeley], Hertfordshire.

29 November 1752. HAYDEN. Philip Hayden of Hertfordshire, Esq.

16 January 1753. DA COSTA. Joseph da Costa of Totteridge, Hertfordshire, Esq.

20 July 1753. FELTON. Arnold Felton, of Cheshunt, Esq.

24 September 1753. ALIE. Mrs. Alie of Northaw, Hertfordshire. She has left £500 to the Foundling Hospital.

The manor of Northaw was purchased by William Leman in 1632. It remained in the Leman family until 1745 when it passed to a cousin, Richard Alie or Aley, who took the surname Leman. Richard's heir was his unmarried sister Lucy, who was buried at Northaw 8 October 1753, aged 63. [AJ]

24 September 1753. LUCAS. Rev. Mr. Lucas, minister of Benington, Hertfordshire.

18 November, 1753. LANCE. John Lance of Hadley, near Barnet, Esq., of grief for the loss of his wife, who died three weeks before.

3 December 1753. FORRESTER. Pulter Forrester of Baldock, Hertfordshire, Esq.

The Pulter (later Forester) family owned the estates of Delamere (Gt. Wymondley) and Broadfield (adjoining Cottered). Pulter Forester (1690–1753) served as sheriff of Hertfordshire in 1717. He had received a considerable marriage portion from his wife Agnes (Harvey) in 1713, but his fortunes subsequently declined and Delamere and some other properties were sold in the year before his death. [AJ]

11 April 1754. STRACEY. John Stracey of St. Albans, Esq.

29 August 1754. COLE. Rev. Mr. Cole, Archdeacon of St. Albans.

4 October 1754. SAMBROOKE. Sir Jeremy Sambrooke of Gubbins [North Mimms] in Hertfordshire, Bart.

26 October 1754. CLARKE. Sir Thomas Clarke, Bart., who many years represented the borough of Hertford.

4 April 1755. HALE. Paggen Hale, Esq., member for Hertfordshire. His large estate, for want of issue, devolves to his relations.

19 April 1755. RIDER. Rev. Dr. Henry Rider, Rector of Hertford.

15 June 1755. CALVERT. Felix Calvert of Furneux Pelham, Hertfordshire, Esq.

12 December 1755. FOX. George Fox of Northam [? Northaw], Hertfordshire, Esq.

25 January 1756. EWER. Anthony Ewer of Bushey Hall, Hertfordshire, Esq.

7 June 1756. WINSLOW. Rev. Mr. Winslow of Puckeridge, Hertfordshire.

10 July 1756. COWPER. Rev. Dr. Cowper, Rector of Great Berkhamsted, Hertfordshire.

21 August 1756. ST. JOHN. Sir Fr. St. John, at Little Ayot, Hertfordshire.

21 August 1756. DIPPLE. Rev. R. Dipple, Rector of Stapleford, Hertfordshire.

21 August 1756. LEVETT. Edward Levett of Hertfordshire, Esq.

19 September 1756. RAYMOND. Lord Robert Raymond, Baron of Abbot's Langley in Hertfordshire.

6 March 1757. KEATE. Rev. Sir William Keate, Bart., aged 72, at Digswell near Welwyn, Hertfordshire.

23 April 1757. HORE. Charles Hore, Esq., at Hadley, near Barnet.

5 January 1758. MEETKERKE. Rev. Mr. Meetkerke, Rector of Ickleford and Vicar of Rickmansworth, Hertfordshire.

Robert Meetkerke (1714–1758) was born at Julians (Rushden), the youngest brother of Adolphus Meetkerke V; descended from Sir Adolphus Meetkerke, formerly President of the Flemish Council, who had fled to England after an abortive revolution in 1587, the year before the Armada. [AJ]

23 January 1758. HASSEL. Rev. Mr. Hassel, Rector of St. Laurence Egot [Ayot St. Lawrence], near Welwyn, Hertfordshire.

January 1758. COCKBURN. Captain Cockburn, at Barnet, aged 94. He lost a leg at the battle of Blenheim.

17 May 1758. LANGFORD. James Langford of Theobalds, Hertfordshire.

1 July 1758. DICKENS. James Dickens of Hertfordshire, Esq.

14 October 1758. ITHEL. Benedict Ithel of Hitchin, Hertfordshire.

4 December 1758. WEBSTER. Dr. Webster, Vicar of Ware and Thundrich [Thundridge].

8 December 1758. INGRAM. James Ingram, Esq., at Barnet.

5 February 1759. LOVE. Jacob Love, Esq., at Barnet.

26 February 1759. WILKINSON. Rev. Mr. Wilkinson, Rector of Wallington, Hertfordshire, and headmaster of the free school in Birmingham.

September 1759. REYNOLDS. Thomas Reynolds, L.B., Fonesbury [sic], Hertfordshire.

3 December 1759. HARRISON. George Harrison, Esq., of Hertfordshire, aged 80.

4 December 1759. HARRISON. George Harrison, Esq., member for Hertford.

Duplicate entry as in G.M. [AJ]

25 March 1760. REYNOLDS. Rd. Reynolds, Esq., at Hoddesdon, Hants [sic].

27 March 1760. RAMSAY. Rev. Mr. Ramsay, Vicar of Abbot's Langley, Hertfordshire.

12 May 1760. JOHNSON. Henry Johnson, Esq., at Great Berkhamsted, Hertfordshire.

11 December 1760. RADCLIFFE. Lieut. Radcliffe, of the Hertfordshire Regiment, at Winchester.

22 December 1760. HIRST. Rev. Dr. Hirst, Rector of Benwell [Northumberland] and Sacombe, Hertfordshire.

1 January 1761. CHARLTON. Richard Charlton, Esq., at Hitchin.

5 January 1761. ROLT. Miss Rolt of Sacombe Park, Hertfordshire.

28 September 1761. BLOUNT. Relict of Sir Harry Pope Blount, Bart., at Hatfield.

25 October 1761. SEBRIGHT. Sir Thomas Saunders Sebright of Beechwood, Hertfordshire, Bart.

1 December 1761. GARRARD. Sir Samuel Garrard, Bart., at Lamer [Wheathampstead], Hertfordshire.

Sir Samuel died unmarried at the age of 69, the eldest in a generation in which all three sons died without issue, and the estate passed to Drake cousins who assumed the additional name Garrard. [AJ]

3 December 1761. PLUMER. Wife of William Plumer, Esq., of Hertford.

11 January 1762. RYDER. Relict of Rev. Dr. Ryder, of Hertford.

19 January 1762. REYNOLDS. R. Reynolds, Esq., recorder of Hertford.

26 January 1762. SMITH. Rev. Mr. Smith, at Baldock, Hertfordshire.

5 February 1762. TURVIN. John Turvin, Esq., at Gilston, Hertfordshire.

17 February 1762. CROMWELL. Rob. Cromwell, Esq., at Cheshunt,

Hertfordshire, great great grandson of the Protector. [See Main Sequence, June 1777].

10 April 1762. LEGG. John Legg, of Hertford, Esq.

14 April 1762. SPILLER. Henry Reynell Spiller of Hertfordshire, Esq.

14 May 1762. NEWDICK. Joseph Newdick, Esq., at Cheshunt.

June 1762. SPEDDING. Rev. Mr. Spedding, of Watford, Hertfordshire.

2 August 1762. COWPER. Relict of Dr. Cowper, Rector of Berkhamsted.

12 September 1762. TWELLO. Wife of Edward Twello, Esq., at Royston.

16 September 1762. HURME. John Hurme, Esq., at Flamstead, Hertfordshire.

26 October 1762. NEWTON. Alderman Newton, of Leicester, aged 79; he died worth £14,000 the greater part of which he has left to educate poor children. At Leicester 35; at Ashby de la Zouch 25; at Earl Shilton 20; at Northampton, St. Neot's, Hertford, Huntingdon, Bedford, and Buckingham, 25 each.

In Hertford, Gabriel Newton's benefaction enabled the development of the Green Coat School, which probably existed already in a more modest form. All the pupils were boys, though the trustees later assisted a charity school for girls. The original school built in 1812 just north of All Saints' Church, still exists but is used for other purposes. [AJ]

29 October 1762. RAY. H. Ray, Esq., at Bovingdon, Hertfordshire.

17 March 1763. KEET. Rev. Mr. Keet, Rector of Hatfield, Hertfordshire.

John Keet was presented to the rectory of Hatfield by the Earl of Salisbury in 1752. Seven years earlier the Earl had caused a sensation by his marriage to Keet's sister, his steward's niece, and daughter of a barber in Canterbury. [HG]

29 April 1763. BALK. Ben Balk, near Buntingford, Hertfordshire, Esq.

6 May 1763. REDMAN. Dr. Redman at Berkhamsted, Hertfordshire.

12 May 1763. PARNELL. Rev. Mr. Parnell of Kelshall, Hertfordshire.

5 June 1763. WITHONGER. Thomas Withonger, Esq., near Redbourn, Hertfordshire.

18 June 1763. PROUDFOOT. Edmund Proudfoot, Esq., at Totteridge; he died worth £100,000.

21 June 1763. HAZELAND. Dr. Hazeland, master of the free grammar-school at Hertford, and lecturer of Whitechapel.

2 August 1763. GROVER. John Grover at Flaunden, Hertfordshire, Esq.

30 December 1763. NASH. William Nash, Esq., at Hoddesdon, Hertfordshire.

8 February 1764. GROVER. Israel Grover of Hertfordshire, Esq.

28 April 1764. SMITH. Mrs. Smith at Hemel Hempstead, aged 100.

11 June 1764. BOUCHER. Lieut.-Colonel Boucher at Berkhamsted.

3 August 1764. OSBORNE. The duchess of Leeds, suddenly, while she was at dinner at her seat [North Mimms] in Hertfordshire.

The duke, as lord of the manor of North Mimms, and duchess resided at North Mimms Park, (obit. 11 March 1734). Mary, duchess of Leeds, was the second and youngest daughter and co-heir of Francis (Godolphin), 2nd Earl of Godolphin by Henrietta suo jure duchess of Marlborough, first daughter and co-heir of John Churchill 1st duke of Marlborough. Mary married Thomas (Osborne), 4th Duke of Leeds on the 26th June 1740 at St. Martins-in-the-Field. She died 3rd August 1764, aged 41, and was buried on the 12th at Harthill, co. York. Will proved 1764. [BW]

18 August 1764. RICHARDS. Jn. Richards, Esq., of Bovingdon, Hertfordshire.

23 August 1764. CHESTER. Edward Chester, Esq., Albury, Hertfordshire.

13 September 1764. DEAWN. Thomas Deawn, Esq., near Watford.

24 September 1764. GEERS. Rev. Mr. Geers, Rector of Astley, Worcestershire and Vicar of Hatfield, Hertfordshire.

9 October 1764. WALLBANK. E. Wallbank of Hitchin, Hertfordshire, Esq.

17 October 1764. BOND. Arthur Bond of Hertfordshire, Esq.

31 October 1764. SMITH. T. Smith at Whitwell, Hertford, aged 99.

3 January 1765. HARWOOD. Joseph Harwood, Esq., near St. Albans.

28 January 1765. SMITHIES. William Smithies of Hertfordshire, Esq.

13 March 1765. GRIMSTEAD. Viscountess Dowager Grimstead in Hertfordshire.

5 April 1765. YOUNG. The celebrated and ingenious Dr. Young, Rector of Welwyn in Hertfordshire, author of Night Thoughts, The Brothers, a tragedy, performed at one of the theatres in March 1753; the benefits arising from the performance he gave to the Society for Propagating the Gospel, (See Vol.xxiii p.135,146) and many other ingenious works; his first piece, called the Last Day, was published in 1704. He married a lady nearly related to the Earl of Litchfield, by whom he had only one son, to whom his late Royal Highness the Prince of Wales stood godfather. He was buried with the utmost privacy, under the altar-piece of his parish church, by the side of Lady Betty, his late wife; and though he was both the founder and endower of a charity-school in this parish, neither the master nor the children attended his funeral. His pall was supported by the rectors or vicars of the neighbouring parishes. The mourners were his son, his nephew, another near relation, his housekeeper, most of the bearers, and the whole town of Welwyn. All his manuscripts he ordered to be burnt; an irreparable loss, say some, to posterity, as he was the intimate acquaintance of Addison, one of the writers of the Spectator, and excepting Dr. Pearce, the present Bishop of Rochester, the last surviving genius of that incomparable group of authors.

    The altar-piece in the church of Welwyn is the most curious in this or any other kingdom, being adorned with an elegant piece of needle-work, wrought by the Lady Betty Young, wife to the late Dr. Young. In the middle is inscribed, in capital letters, the following sentence: 'I AM THE BREAD OF LIFE.' On the north side of the chancel is the following inscription, supposed to be by the order of the late Dr. Young: "VIRGINIBUS, Increase in stature and in wisdom:" and on the south side, "PUERISQUE, and in favour with God and Man." Dr. Young has, in his will, left all his possessions to his son, after his legacies are paid.

18 May 1765. BAGSTER. Mill [sic] Bagster, Esq., at Ashton [Aston], Hertfordshire.

24 May 1765. BERNEY. Lady Berney at Hoddesdon, Hertfordshire.

30 November 1765. MARTIN. Rev. Mr. Martin, Rector of Hunsdon, Hertfordshire; he lately changed his name for an estate of £600 per annum.

15 January 1766. STAMP. Peter Stamp of Hertfordshire, Esq.

6 April 1766. HULLET. J. Hullet, Esq., of Rickmansworth, Hertfordshire.

15 July 1766. SHEPHERD. T. Shepherd, Esq., at Benjey Hall [Bengeo], Hertfordshire.

28 September 1766. AUBER. Peter Auber, Esq., at Cheshunt.

15 January 1767. CHEEKE. Robert Cheeke, Esq., at Cheshunt.

23 May 1767. REDSHAW. William Redshaw, Esq., of Cat's Hill [Stanstead Abbots?], Hertfordshire.

12 July 1767. POOR JOE ALL ALONE, a remarkable character, aged 105. He was well known in the royal army in the time of the last rebellion, and employed as a spy in the rebel army, in which he used to sell gingerbread and whisky. He died at Ware, and though he never had any settled habitation, is said to have died worth £3000 which he has left to charitable uses.

There is no other record of the death of "poor Joe all alone" and his burial is not recorded in the registers of either Ware or Great Amwell, although both registers record the burial of many other strangers or soldiers during the 17–18th centuries. [DP]

17 July 1767. CASWELL. Lady of Timothy Caswell, member for Hertford.

22 August 1767. RACKET. Major Racket, near Hertford.

12 December 1767. PLUMER. William Plumer, Esq., member for Hertfordshire.

14 December 1767. HEYSHAM. Giles Thornton Heysham, Esq., of Hertfordshire.

8 January 1768. DUNCOMBE. Mrs. Duncombe, relict of John Duncombe, Esq., at Stocks [Aldbury] in Hertfordshire.

15 February 1768. GORE. Charles Gore, Esq., of Tring, in Hertfordshire, member for Tiverton.

April 1768. HICKS. Sir Robert Hicks, Bart., of Hemel Hempstead, Hertfordshire.

April 1768. GORDON. Ja. Gordon, Esq., of Moor Place [Rickmansworth], Hertfordshire.

April 1768. THOROWGOOD. Henry Thorowgood, Clerk of the Peace at Hertford.

28 June 1768. HAYGARTH. Rev. Mr. Haygarth, curate of Much Hadham 40 years.

1 July 1768. THOMPSON. Colonel Thompson, at his seat near St. Albans.

November 1768. JOHNSTON. Lieut.-Colonel William Johnston of the invalids, at Aldenham, Hertfordshire, aged 127.

2 January 1769. OSWALD. James Oswald, Esq., at Knebworth, Hertfordshire.

May 1769. BRUDENELL. William Brudenell, Esq., of Hertfordshire.

25 July 1769. HAUGHTON. Frederick Haughton, Esq., at Welwyn, Hertfordshire.

22 September 1769. BETHELL. William Bethell, Esq., of Welwyn, Hertfordshire.

1 October 1769. ELLIS. Thomas Ellis, Esq., Hertford.

2 October 1769. MUSGRAVE. William Musgrave, Esq., of Langley, Hertfordshire.

11 October 1769. SWAIDE. Thomas Swaide, D.D., Hertfordshire.

15 February 1770. HOUBLIN. Jacob Houblin Esq., of Hertfordshire.

6 March 1770. LONG. Philip Long, Esq., of Hatfield, Hertfordshire.

7 March 1770. WEBSTER. Whistler Webster, Hertfordshire.

16 March 1770. HASSEL. Richard Hassel, Esq., Barnet.

16 April 1770. SANDYS. As Lord Sandys was returning to town from his son's seat in Hertfordshire, he was overturned in his post-chaise coming down Highgate hill. At first it was thought, he was not much hurt, but afterwards it appeared, he received a contusion in his head that cost him his life.

18 May 1770. ELLIS. Samuel Ellis, Esq., Barnet.

14 July 1770. WALTHAM. Joseph Waltham, Esq., at Hertford.

18 August 1770. WHITEHEAD. Rev. Mr. Whitehead, dissenting minister of Box Lane, near Hempstead, Hertfordshire.

Rev. Thomas Whitehead was educated for the dissenting ministry at Kendal (he married the daughter of his tutor, Dr. Caleb Rotherham) and Daventry Academies. He was seemingly minister of the dissenting chapel at Box Lane (built about 1697) Boxmoor, at the time of his death, having been appointed in the 1750s, although some sources do not mention him as being connected with this chapel. (See Surman Index at Dr. Williams's Library). [AR]

29 August 1770. SPARHAUKE. Lawndey Sparhauke, Esq., Chesfield, Hertfordshire.

In 1703 the manor of Graveley and Chesfield was conveyed to Edward Lawndey of Baldock, attorney-at-law. His daughter married the Rev. Samuel Sparhauke, and had three children — Edward, William and Katherine. At Edward Lawndey's death in 1714 the property passed to his grandson, the Capt. Edward Sparhauke, who died without issue in 1741. The manor was then inherited successively by Lawndey and Edward Sparhauke, infant sons of his brother William, who also died without issue, when it passed to the sons of Katherine and Richard Perkins. [AJ]

15 September 1770. WHITE. John White, Esq., Berkhamsted, Hertfordshire.

23 September 1770. BEAN. Calv. Bean, Esq., Buntingford, Hertfordshire.

23 October 1770. SHEPPARD. Nathaniel Sheppard, Esq., at Watford.

3 November 1770. BEALE. John Beale, Esq., merchant, Hertford.

11 January 1771. GILDART. Richard Gildart, Esq., Totteridge, Hertfordshire.

8 March 1771. BURRELL. Rev. Alexander Burrell, rector of Adstock, Buckinghamshire, cum Puttenham, Hertfordshire.

25 July 1771. RICHARDSON. William Westbrooke Richardson, Esq., at Mount Pleasant, near Barnet.

11 September 1771. STOCKDALE. Adrian Stockdale, Esq., at Cheshunt in Hertfordshire.

15 September 1771. HILTON. Mrs. Hilton, wife of ———— Hilton, Esq., at Cheshunt.

29 September 1771. HUTCHINSON. Rev. Julius Hutchinson, at Hartfield [Hatfield?] in Hertfordshire.

3 November 1771. OSMAN. Joseph Osman, Esq., at Flamsteadbury, Hertfordshire.

9 November 1771. SEWELL. ———— Sewell, Esq., at Hadley, Hertfordshire.

November 1771. BOGDANI. William Bogdani, Esq., at Hitchin, Hertfordshire, F.R.S. etc.

"An eminent arithmetician" (Hine, Hitchin, 1. 62), son of James Bogdani, Hungarian painter of still life, who had settled at Hitchin and sought a lease of Hitchin manor which his son was eventually granted. By 1757, when he was appointed a trustee of the Hitchin, Shefford and Bedford Turnpike Trust, he was referred to as Bogdani of Charlton. [AJ]

22 January 1772. MATTHISON. Richard Matthison, Esq., at Barnet.

26 February 1772. DUNCOMBE. Miss Martha Duncombe, sister of Arnold Duncombe, Esq., of Stocks [Aldbury], Hertfordshire.

17 May 1772. SHAW. John Shaw, Esq., at Cheshunt.

May[?] 1772. PERRAM. ———— Perram, Esq., at his seat in Hertfordshire.

29 May 1772. INGRAM. Paul Ingram, Esq., Watford, Hertfordshire.

18 June 1772. NORTH. Rev. Mr. North, vicar of Codicote, Hertfordshire.

29 June 1772. FREEMAN. Rev. Ralph Freeman, D.D., Hamels, Hertfordshire.

17 August 1772. ANDREWS. James Andrews, Esq., Royston.

10 October 1772. HUME. Sir Abraham Hume, Bart., Wormleybury, Herts.

January 1773. SAMBORNE. Mrs. Mary Samborne, of Herford [Hertford?]. She has left £100 to the poor of Hatfield; £100 to twenty poor housekeepers of St. Andrew's, Holborn; £500 to St Luke's Hospital; and £500 more after the deaths of George Becher and Lucy Mayne.

February 1773. JOHNSON. Rev. Mr. Johnson, Vicar of Hemel Hempstead, and Prebend of Lincoln.

13 May 1773. ROSEN. Mr. Rosen, of Redbourn, Hertfordshire. He has left to each of his tenants half a year's rent; £10 a year to the poor of Redbourn; and the remainder of his fortune to his poor relations.

June 1773. MILLS. Mrs. Mills, at St. Albans. About 5 years ago she obtained a prize of £10,000 in the English lottery and another of nearly the same value in that at Utrecht.

16 July 1773. BUCKRIDGE. Henry Buckridge, Esq., at Cheshunt, Hertfordshire.

11 August 1773. SMITHSON. At his seat near Butt's-mills [sic], Hertfordshire, John Smithson, Esq.

19 August 1773. HARCOURT. John Harcourt, Esq., at St. Albans, possessed of a large estate in South Carolina.

8 September 1773. CHOLWELL. The Rev. Nicholas Cholwell, archdeacon of Huntingdon, and rector of Stevenage, Hertfordshire.

30 October 1773. SALISBURY. At his seat in Hertfordshire, Sir Thomas Salisbury, LL.D., judge of the High Court of Admiralty, Chancellor of St. Asaph, and Commissary of the Dean and Chapter of St. Paul's.

c. November 1773. GRIMSTON. At his seat [Gorhambury] in Hertfordshire, of the gout, James Grimston, Viscount Grimston, Baron of Dunboyne, and Bart. His Lordship was born 9 October, 1711, succeeded his father, William, the late and first Viscount, 15 October 1756, and married Mary, daughter of William Bucknall, of Oxhey, Esq., (which Lady was born 28 April, 1717) by whom he has issue, 1. The Hon. James Bucknall, born 9 May, 1747; 2. Jane, born 18 September, 1748; 3. William, born 23 June, 1750; 4. Harbottle, born 14 April, 1752; 5. Mary, born 28 May, 1753; 6. Susannah-Askell, born 28 September 1754; 7. Francis-Cook, born 27 March, 1757; and 8. Joanna, born 10 September, 1759.

2 January 1774. INGRAM. The Rev. ———— Ingram, D.D., vicar of Harfordbury [Hertingfordbury], Hertfordshire.

February[?] 1774. MUNNS. At St. Albans, Mrs Rachael Munns, aged 107.

February[?] 1774. FRAMPTON. At Hoddesdon, in Hertfordshire, Peter Frampton, Esq., aged 107. He has a son now living, 84 years old.

14 March 1774. DUNCOMBE. Arnold Duncombe, Esq., of Stocks [Aldbury], Hertfordshire.

c. March 1774. CHANCELLOR. At Hertingfordbury, in Hertfordshire, ———— Chancellor, Esq.

1 April 1774. ADDERLY. At Bishops Stortford, Hertfordshire, Thomas Adderly, Esq., a Justice of the Peace.

4 April 1774. KENTISH. At St. Albans, Hertfordshire, Thomas Kentish, Esq., aged 76.

A prominent nonconformist; baptised 13 December 1697 at St. Peter's, St. Albans, only son of Robert Kentish of Nast Hyde. Married Martha, sister of Alderman Matthew Iremonger of St. Albans. Identified by Clutterbuck as sheriff of Hertfordshire in 1723. Buried at St. Stephen's, St. Albans. [HG]

29 August 1774. DOUGLAS. At North End, near Barnet, Mrs. Douglas, aunt of John St. Leger Douglas, Esq., member for Hindon, in Wiltshire.

6 February 1775. THURGOOD. Mr. Thurgood, at Baldock, in Hertfordshire, one of the most considerable brewers in the kingdom.

This was Robert Thurgood, the son of John. Between them, they owned Baldock brewery from 1730 till 1775. The brewery and malting premises were in Baldock High Street. In 1770 Robert's daughter Sarah married Thomas Clutterbuck, brewer of Watford and Stanmore. Clutterbuck eventually sold Baldock brewery in 1799 to John Izzard Pryor. [AJ]

26 April 1775. GRIMSTONE. The Hon. Henry Grimstone, of a paralytic stroke.

c. July 1775. NAPIER. Dr. Napier, physician, at Cheshunt, Hertfordshire.

16 September 1775. THOMPSON. George Thompson, Esq., St. Albans.

7 October 1775. EDWIN. Humphrey Edwin, Esq., St. Albans.

c. 14 October 1775. RAWLINS. Sir Benjamin Rawlins, Knt., Hertfordshire.

12 November 1775. GRESHAM. John Gresham, Esq., Hoddesdon, Hertfordshire.

14 December 1775. HILL. Charles Hill, Esq., Barnet.

25 March 1776. SOUTHERNWOOD. Rev. Mr. Southernwood, rector of Walkern, in Hertfordshire.

30 March 1776. WOODFIELD. William Woodfield, Esq., at Barnet.

c. September 1776. DOBYNS. Joseph Dobyns, a shepherd, at Rickmansworth, Hertfordshire, aged 102.

15 December 1776. NOYS. Thomas Herbert Noys, Esq., of Berkhamsted.

1 February 1777. BODIMEAD. William Bodimead, Esq., of Bushey.

11 February 1777. JENKINS. Sa. Jenkins, Esq., on Barnet common.

8 March 1777. LE STRANGE. Walter Le Strange, Esq., Hatfield.

8 May 1777. COTTON. Thomas Cotton, Esq., at Northaw, Herts.

12 June 1777. NELSON. Timothy Nelson, Esq., near Barnet.

15 July 1777. SMITH. Thomas Smith, Esq., at King's Langley, near Watford.

18 August 1777. STIRLING. John Stirling, D.D., vicar of Great Gaddesden, Hertfordshire.

5 December 1777. DUNCOMBE. At Berkhamsted, Hertfordshire, Mrs. Elizabeth Duncombe, a maiden lady, sister to the late Arnold Duncombe, Esq., of Stocks.

10 December 1777. NICHOLLS. ———— Nicholls, Esq., of Hadley, near Barnet.

18 March 1778. LISTER. Rev. William Lister, a dissenting minister, many years preacher to a congregation at Ware.

William Lister (1715–1778) was born in Yorkshire and educated for the dissenting ministry at Northampton Academy from 1734. Following a short ministry at Banbury he became assistant to Rev. Daniel Neal at Jewin Street Chapel in London 1739–43. He married Neal's youngest daughter (see death of Mrs. Lister 6 January 1783) and was minister at the Independent Chapel, Ware 1743–1778. "Distinguished by piety, prudence and good temper, he kept a good congregation to the last. After his death the people divided, and both interests were reduced to a very low state." (see Surman Index, Dr. Williams's Library; Urwick, Herts. p.719). [AR]

August 1778. WALTHOE. John Walthoe, Esq., at St. Albans.

17 September 1778. SPRIGG. Nathan Sprigg, Esq., at Barnet.

18 November 1778. MARSDALE. William Marsdale, Esq., at Hatfield in Hertfordshire.

30 January 1779. GARDINER. Edward Gardiner, Esq., of Pishobury, Hertfordshire.

14 March 1779. FEWTRELL. John Fewtrell, Esq., of Cheshunt, Hertfordshire.

15 May 1779. SEARANCKE. John Searancke, Esq.

Baptised at Hatfield 30 January 1719/20, son of John Searancke, brewer. He was high sheriff of Hertfordshire 1777. The family had been brewing in Hatfield since the 16th century, and acquired considerable property. With his death the male line of the family came to an end, although the business was continued by his sisters and nephew, F.C. Searancke (formerly Niccoll), till sold by the latter in 1815. The Hatfield Brewery (then Pryor Reid & Co.) finally closed in 1920. [HG]

30 December 1779. BICKERTON. Near Hertford, Constantine Bickerton, Esq., aged 72.

February 1780. KIRBY. At Hertford, Mr. Kirby, aged 104.

11 March 1780. DUNSTER. At Hampstead, Mrs. Dunster, wife of H. Dunster, Esq., of Hertford.

16 March 1780. BARNES. At his seat at Theobalds, George Barnes, Esq.

18 March 1780. HALE. In Grosvenor Place, the lady of W. Hale, Esq., of King's Walden, Hertfordshire.

20 March 1780. ASH. Samuel Ash, Esq., of Buntingford.

c. May 1780. WHITEHEAD. At Great Berkhamsted, the Rev. George Whitehead, fellow of Queen's College, Oxford.

c. May 1780. DEACON. At Bath, Thomas Deacon, Esq., of Watford.

14 June 1780. MONTAGU. Near Hempstead, Hertfordshire, Sir J. Montague, Knt., aged 91.

18 July 1780. MIDDLETON. Near Hatfield, Sir Andrew Middleton, Bart.

The entry also appears in the 'London Magazine', but in a contemporary newspaper cutting in Upcott's 'Collections for Hertfordshire' (Hine Colln: Herts C.R.O.) the entry reads: "At his Seat near Hatfield in Hertfordshire, Sir Andrew Middleton, Knt. aged 79". But who was he? He was not buried at Hatfield, and there seems to be no record of the existence of a knight or baronet of these names. [HG]

16 August 1780. CLAY. W. Clay, Esq., of Coles [Westmill], Hertfordshire, aged 87.

c. September 1780. FIELD. At Boxford [Boxmoor?], Hertfordshire, Thomas Field, a labouring man, aged 102. His father was 104, his uncle 93, his brother 95, and scarce any of the family have died under ninety.

4 September 1780. FIELDING. At Brompton, near Knightsbridge, Sir John Fielding, Knt., one of his Majesty's Justices of the Peace for the counties of Middlesex, Essex, Hertfordshire, Kent, Surrey, and the city and liberty of Westminster.

17 September 1780. HAVERFIELD. Near Hemel Hempstead, Hertfordshire, Theophilus Haverfield, Esq., aged 74, formerly high sheriff for that county.

2 October 1780. BAKER. At Hertingfordbury, Richard Baker, Esq., second son of the late Sir William Baker and brother to William Baker, Esq., member for Hertford. He was sheriff of the county last year.

30 October 1780. THORPE. Near Stevenage, Mr. J. Thorpe, aged 109.

c. October 1780. SPRY. At Braughing, Hertfordshire, the Rev. Dr. Spry, prebend of Durham, and vicar of Potterne, Wiltshire.

c. October 1780. REYNOLDS. At Ware, Mrs. Reynolds, relict of Mr. Reynolds, many years master of a flourishing academy there.

There is no record of Mr. Reynolds's "flourishing academy". It was probably a Nonconformist boarding establishment for boys, since the Free Grammar School in the churchyard catered for Anglican boys. It was possibly situated in Thunder Hall, where William Taylor was running a similar academy in 1823 (Pigot). [DP]

2 November 1780. GARDINER. At Lockleys [Welwyn], Hertfordshire, Charles Gardiner, Esq.

Charles Gardiner obtained Lockleys by marriage to Elizabeth, second daughter of Edward Searle. She died in 1780. Lockleys was inherited by Charles, his son by his second wife Mary Holford. [TR]

17 December 1780. MANNING. Near Stevenage, Hertfordshire, Jos. Manning, Esq.

25 December 1780. SEARLE. At Enfield Mr. SEARLE, formerly an oilman in Cannon Street and brother to Mrs. Reynolds of Ware, beforementioned.

27 December 1780. LAMOTT. At Barnet, John Lamott, Esq., formerly a wine merchant.

c. January 1781. BOTELER. Edward Boteler, rector of Watton, Hertfordshire.

c. January 1781. ORME. At Hertford, Hon. Mrs. Orme, wife to Robert Orme, Esq., M.P., daughter of the late Viscount Townshend.

Mrs. Orme's father was Charles Townshend, 3rd Viscount (1700–64) and her mother Etheldreda or Audrey Harrison, of Balls Park. She was the sister of George, 4th Viscount and 1st Marquis Townshend, and Charles (1725–67), Chancellor of the Exchequer in Chatham's last Ministry, who was the author of the American Import Duties Act of 1767 which did so much to inflame discontent in the American colonies. [AG]

2 January 1781. WATSON. Near Hemel Hempstead, Hertfordshire, Sir Abraham Watson, Knt., aged 99.

2 January 1781. FOSTER. At Cheshunt, Hertfordshire, in an advanced age, J. Foster, Esq., formerly a seedsman in the Strand.

22 January 1781. BOWES. At Paul's Walden, Hertfordshire, Mrs. M. Bowes, mother of the present Lady Strathmore. By the decease of Mrs. Bowes, her jointure, which is £1600 per annum devolves to Andrew Robinson Bowes, Esq., one of the members in the present parliament for Newcastle upon Tyne.

February 1781. JEAVES. At Hoddesdon, Mr. Jeaves, formerly an eminent linen draper in London.

30 March 1781. RICHARDSON. At Great Berkhamsted, R. Richardson, Esq.

15 April 1781. VINCENT. At Northaw, Hertfordshire, Mrs. Vincent, aged 74, widow of the late Robert Vincent, Esq.

10 May 1781. WRIGHT. Mrs. Mary Wright, a widow lady late of Cheshunt, Hertfordshire, aged 96.

2 June 1781. LANE. At Barnet, George Lane, gardener, aged 102.

12 August 1781. IBBETSON. Dr. James Ibbetson, archdeacon of St. Albans, author of several polemical tracts.

25 August 1781. THACKERAY. Rev. Mr. Thackeray, rector of Walkern, Hertfordshire.

7 September 1781. WARWICK. Mr. Benjamin Warwick, farmer of Kit's End, near Barnet.

Kit's End, Kitts End or Kicks End, was a hamlet in Kitts End Road, which runs from the Great North Road at Hadley Highstone to South Mimms. The hamlet, which had a large number of inns, disappeared after Kitts End Road, the main road between Barnet and St. Albans (the Holyhead Road) was by-passed about 1827 by Telford's New Road, thus depriving Kitts End of its coaching trade. [GJ]

27 September 1781. RICHARDSON. In Dean Street, Soho, aged 50, the Rev. Robert Richardson, DD, F.R. and A., SS, prebendary of Lincoln, rector of St. Anne's Westminster, and of Wallington, Hertfordshire, and chaplain in ordinary to his Majesty. The rectory of St. Anne's is in the gift of the Bishop of London; the value of it is about £530 a year, resulting from a very good glebe land and a parish rate of £100 a year in aid to the Easter offerings and surplice fees. The glebe land alone is above £200 of the money. Dr. Richardson was the only son of the late Dr. William Richardson, master of Emmanuel College, Cambridge, and was some years chaplain to Sir Josef Yorke at the Hague.

c. October 1781. PLUMER. At Culver Lodge, near Hadham, Hertfordshire, Miss A. Plumer, sister to William Plumer, Esq., M.P.

9 November 1781. JENKS. Thomas Jenks, Esq., father of the Rev. David Jenks, rector of Northchurch and Gaddesden, Hertfordshire.

29 November 1781. SKEY. At Hedgrove [Aldenham], Hertfordshire, aged 82, John Skey, Esq., upwards of 50 years in the commission of the peace for that county, and one of the commissioners of the lieutenancy for London.

c. November 1781. HENDLEY At St. Albans, Jos. Hendley, Esq. By his desire he was buried in his wedding clothes, and wearing his gold watch, knee and shoe buckles. His hat was placed in the coffin, and his sword laid by his side.

3 January 1782. WILKINSON. At Baldock, Hertfordshire, Isaac Wilkinson, Esq.

6 January 1782. TOWNLEY. Near Barnet, aged 76, Thomas George Townley, Esq., formerly Governor of Fort St. George in the East Indies.

8 January 1782. REYNOLDS. At Hertford, aged 90, Mrs. Reynolds, relict of Richard Reynolds, Esq., formerly recorder of that town.

26 February 1782. HALSEY. In Jermyn Street, St. James's, Mrs. Halsey, mother of Thomas Halsey, Esq., M.P. for Hertfordshire.

3 April 1782. SMITH. At Hadley, near Barnet, Mrs. Smith, wife of Culling Smith, Esq., and sister to the Rev. Mr. Burrows, rector of St. Clement Danes.

11 May 1782. MARLOWE. At Redbourn, Hertfordshire, Abraham Marlowe, Esq. He was principally concerned in projecting the plan for the herring fishery.

28 May 1782. CALVERT. At Albury, Hertfordshire, Peter Calvert, Esq.

1 June 1782. NICCOLL. At St. Albans, Fra. Carter Niccoll, Esq., an alderman of that corporation, and in the commission of the peace for Hertfordshire.

Francis Carter Niccoll, born c. 1723, son of William Niccoll of St. Albans, brewer, by his wife Dorothy, daughter and heir of Francis Carter, alderman of St. Albans. Inherited his father's brewery, and was mayor 1750–1 and 1763–4. Married Ann (died 1793), sister and co-heir of John Searancke of Hatfield, brewer. Memorial in St. Albans Abbey. (See also 19 March 1793 & 9 March 1797). [HG]

15 June 1782. MOORE. At Hitchin, Hertfordshire, aged 72, Mr. Edward Moore.

June 1782. MANN. At Theobalds, Captain Mann of a deep consumption in the prime of life.

June 1782. KEYS. At Ware, Mr. Keys, formerly a farmer at Enfield Highway, where his house was broke open a few years ago by a gang of villains, whom he shot at, and who dangerously wounded his servant.

1 August 1782. JONES. At Ware, in Hertfordshire, aged 77, Mr. Ephraim Jones, one of the people called Quakers.

21 September 1782. BATLEY. At Hadley, near Barnet, John Batley, Esq.

16 November 1782. FRENCH. Rev. John French, many years head of the academy at Ware.

c. December 1782. BLACKDEN. The lady of Benjamin Blackden, Esq., of Tring, Hertfordshire.

c. December 1782. BENN. William Benn, Esq., of Hare Street, Hertfordshire, son of the late Calvert Benn, Esq., and nephew to the late Alderman.

4 December 1782. HAMILTON. At Hadham, the lady of Dr. Hamilton, rector of that parish, and of St. Martin's in the Fields, Westminster. She was youngest daughter of the late Dr. Terrick, bishop of London, and sister to the present Lady Harrowby.

6 January 1783. LISTER. At Ware, Mrs. Lister, relict of the late Rev. William Lister, many years pastor of a dissenting congregation there.

Mrs. Mary Lister was the youngest of the three children of Rev. Daniel Neal (1678–1743), and Elizabeth (m.1708, d.1748) who was sister of Rev. Dr. Nathaniel Lardner (1684–1768). The Listers are mentioned in the DNB entries for both Neal and Lardner. They had at least one son, Daniel (of Hackney, Middlesex). [AR]

3 February 1783. FEILDE. Paule Feilde, Esq., of Stansted Bury, Hertfordshire, late M.P. for the borough of Hertford, and one of the judges of the sheriff's court, London.

c. February 1783. PHAIP. At Watford, aged 72, Richard Phaip, Esq., many years in the commission of the peace for Hertfordshire.

c. February 1783. PRITCHARD. Near St. Albans, aged 103, Mrs. Mary Pritchard, a widow lady.

c. February 1783. COOKE. At Wormley, Mrs. Cooke, relict of the late Mr. Cooke, of Broad Street, merchant. She has left £10,000 in different legacies amongst poor families, and her servants, and £1000 to the Asylum for female orphans.

1 March 1783. LOWE. In Aldersgate, Mr. Thomas Lowe, singer at Sadlers Wells [etc.]. He took the Wells at Otter's Pool near Watford, about 12 years ago, and made other unsuccessful efforts to procure a comfortable livelihood. . ... Notwithstanding he was between twenty and thirty years in the receipt of an income little less than £1000 a year, yet he constantly dissipated the whole of it, and became, in the decline of his life, an object of charity as well as pity.

27 March 1783. BOWYER. At Coles, Hertfordshire, Calvert Bowyer, Esq., aged 63 years.

17 April 1783. PHILLIPSON. Christopher Phillipson of Hoddesdon, Hertfordshire.

21 April 1783. WILLIS. Rev. Sherlock Willis, rector of Wormley, Hertfordshire, and of St. Christopher's in London, prebendary of St. Paul's, and of Sarum, and nearly related to bishop Sherlock.

12 July 1783. HOUBLON. At his brother's house at Hallingbury, aged 48, John Houblon, Esq., captain in the Hertfordshire militia. [see 14 October 1783].

c. August 1783. WORSLEY. At Apsley, aged 105, Mrs. M. Worsley.

3 August 1783. HASSELL. Mrs. Hassell, wife of Richard Hassell, Esq., one of his Majesty's justices of the peace, at Barnet, Hertfordshire. . ... Her death was in consequence of being thrown out of a chaise some months before.

5 August 1783. TWYFORD. At Cheshunt, Hertfordshire, Mr. Twyford, aged 74, who many years kept the Queen's Head tavern in Paternoster Row, but, having acquired a competency, had retired.

21 September 1783. GREEN. At Hertford, Mr. Green, master of the nursery school in that town, belonging to Christ's Hospital, London.

1 October 1783. LAW. Hon. Mrs. Law, 3rd daughter of the late Lord Falkland, and lady of the Rev. Dr. Law, archdeacon of Rochester, and rector of Westmill, Hertfordshire.

14 October 1783. HOUBLON. Jacob Houblon, Esq., of Great Hallingbury, Essex, major of the Hertfordshire militia. [see 12 July 1783].

October 1783. WESTFIELD. At Cheshunt, Mrs. Westfield, a maiden lady, the bulk of whose fortune, after many charities and legacies to servants, goes to her niece, the lady of Mr. Pott, surgeon.

November 1783. WESTON. At Walthamstow, Mr. Weston, many years an eminent wine cooper, and one of the people called Quakers. He was buried at Hertford the 19th instant.

November 1783. CLEBBON/CLIBBON. In Hertford gaol, whither he had been removed from Chelmsford to take his trial at the next assizes, ———— Clebbon, whose father was shot in attempting to rob a farmer and his boy in Benfield [Bramfield] parish, near Hertford, last year.

Addition: The notorious Clebbon, mentioned as dead, is yet living. He was at the point of death, which gave rise to this report.

The Clebbons or Clibbons, of Babbs Green, Wareside, were a family of footpads, operating in the vicinity of Hertford and Ware. On 28 December, 1782, they had waylaid the son of Benjamin Whittenbury of Queen Hoo Hall, Tewin, but he managed to escape and raise the alarm. His father and other members of the family, accompanied by a servant George North armed with a fowling piece, went in search of the Clibbons whom they encountered in Canon's Wood, on the road between Bramfield and Bull's Green. A fight ensued during which Clibbon senior was shot dead, his son Joseph was captured and another son escaped. Clibbon's body was carried to Bull's Green where it lay overnight in a barn at the Horns Inn. John Carrington recorded: "A coroner came on the Monday following. Also Jury met, and they found he met his death as he deserved and they buried him by the road side where he was dead." The place of burial is still marked by a squared timber post over 6 feet high, inscribed "Clibbons Post, Dec. 28 1782." The original post was renewed in the 1930s by the East Herts. Archaeological Society.

Joseph Clibbon, to whom the above entry refers, was subsequently hanged on gallows on the Stanstead Road at Hertford. [AJ]

11 November 1783. MALLISON. At Hoddesdon, aged 91, William Mallison, Esq.

10 December 1783. JONES. At Hoddesdon, Hertfordshire, in his 70th year, Rev. Dr. Jones.

12 December 1783. SCOTT. At Amwell, Hertfordshire, John Scott, Esq., one of the people called Quakers, author of a pleasing poem, intituled, "Amwell" published 1776, 4to, and of other poetical works printed 1782, 8vo; also of a most useful *Digest of Laws respecting Highways, 1778,* 8vo. To this subject he had particularly turned his thoughts; and in this book not only the law respecting highways and turnpikes is to be found, but a number of judicious and well-founded remarks on the construction and preservation of roads. The loss of this most active and public-spirited man will be more easily felt than expressed in his neighbourhood, and in the wide circle of his acquaintance.

21 December 1783. RADCLIFFE. John Radcliffe, of Hitchin Priory, Hertfordshire, Esq., member in the two last, and the present parliament, for St. Albans. He married, in April 1768, Lady Frances Howard, daughter to the late, and sister to the present, Earl of Carlisle, by whom he had no issue. He was the lineal descendant, and last male heir, of Ralph Radcliffe, Gentleman (descended from Richard Radcliffe, of Radcliffe Tower, county of Lancaster, temp. Edward III), who died temp. Henry VIII having purchased the priory of White Carmelites at Hitchin of the first grantees after the dissolution, whose heir and representative was Ralph Radcliffe, of Hitchin Priory, Esq., and also of Devonshire Street, London, Turkey merchant, who, dying unmarried, was succeeded in the estate by his two brothers, Edward and Arthur Radcliffe, Esqrs., both also Turkey merchants, in Devonshire Street, neither of whom having any male issue, the estate and their fortunes devolved to John Radcliffe, Esq., above-mentioned, son of their younger brother, Mr. John Radcliffe, Turkey merchant.

8 January 1784. MEETKERKE. At Bath, aged 80, Adolphus Meetkerke, of Julians, near Buntingford, Hertfordshire, Esq. A very respectable and worthy character, universally esteemed by all his acquaintance. He was descended from Sir Adolphus Meetkerke, president of Flanders, who came over to England circa temp. Elizabeth, died here, and was buried in the church of St. Botolph Aldersgate (see Stow's Survey of London). His father married the eldest daughter and coheiress of the family of Stone of Julians, by whom he became possessed of a part of the estate, and purchased the rest. He has left one son, of his own name (to whom he some years since gave possession of the family estate, and retired to Bath), and four daughters. He was an old member of the Royston Club.

24 January 1784. PENROSE. Mrs. Penrose, wife of Mr. Penrose, surgeon, at Hatfield, Hertfordshire.

Buried at North Mimms. She was Elizabeth, daughter of James Bellis, of Pall Mall and Hatfield Woodside, silversmith and toyman. (See also April 1788, 1 November 1788 & November 1793). [HG]

24 January 1784. HOWARD. At Barnet, John Howard, Esq.

3 February 1784. LAWRENCE. At Cheshunt, Hertfordshire, Mrs. Prudence Lawrence, sister to the late Mrs. Cooke of the same place.

17 February 1784. COPPIN. Rev. Mr. Coppin of Markyate-Cell [Markyate]. Hertfordshire.

18 February 1784. JONES. At Offley, Hertfordshire, in his 53rd year, Rev. Jervas Jones, M.A., rector of Holwell, Bedfordshire, vicar of Offley, and minister of the donative of King's Walden, Hertfordshire.

22 February 1784. CAESAR. Mrs. Caesar, eldest sister to the late General Caesar. Mrs. Caesar was daughter of the Right Hon. Charles Adelmar Caesar, of Bennington Place, Hertfordshire, Esq., treasurer of the navy temp. Ann. The lineal descendant of Adelmar, Count of Genoa, and admiral of France, A.D. 806, from whom descended Sir Julius Adelmar Caesar, master of the rolls, &c. temp. Jac. I (grandson of a daughter of the Duke de Cesarini, from whom he had the name of Caesar), which office was held by his son Sir Charles Adelmar Caesar in the following reign. Mr. Caesar had also two sons and another daughter: the eldest son was of his own names, and was member for Hertfordshire, as several of his ancestors had been. He was remarkable for having a hand like a lobster's claw, on which he usually wore a glove. He married, and left issue two daughters, of whom one was married, 1. to the late Sir Charles Cottrell Dormer, master of the ceremonies, by whom she had Sir Clement Cottrell Dormer, and, 2. to the Hon. Lieut General George Lane Parker, brother to the Earl of Macclesfield; and the other is married to Robert Chester, Esq., receiver of the tenths, who have several children. Mr. Caesar's youngest son was the late Major General Julius Caesar, who died unmarried about 20 years ago: his eldest sister died at Hertford 22nd February last, aet. 83: her sister, Mrs. Elizabeth Caesar, is still living, about 80 years of age. These two ladies lived together, their income was formerly small, but afterwards very happily increased by a small pension, which their brother the General procured for them, and by legacies from several of their acquaintance, they being very much and generally respected by the ancient gentry of the county of Hertford.

15 March 1784. FRANCKLIN. In Great Queen Street, Rev. Thomas Francklin, D.D., chaplain in ordinary to his Majesty. This learned and ingenious author was the son of Richard Francklin well known as the printer of an anti-ministerial paper called "The Craftsman.". . . In December 1758, he was instituted vicar of Ware and Thundridge, which, with the lectureship of St. Paul, Covent Garden, and a chapel in Queen Street, were all the preferments he held till he obtained the rectory of Brasted in Kent. . .

26 March 1784. WEBSTER. At Redheath [Watford], Hertfordshire, aged 77, Mr. Thomas Webster, father of Edward Webster, Esq., in the commission of the peace for Middlesex.

28 March 1784. WILLIS. At Drayton, Middlesex, the relict of the late Rev. Sherlock Willis, rector of Wormley and St. Christopher in London, who died April 21, 1783.

9 April 1784. POPE. At Northaw, Hertfordshire, aged 75, J. Pope, Esq.

c. May 1784. KITCHEN. At St Albans, Thomas Kitchen, Esq., hydrographer to his Majesty.

c. 7 May 1784. PRITCHARD. Lately, near St. Albans, aged 103, Mrs. Jane Pritchard.

5 June 1784. DECAUX. At Broxbourne, Hertfordshire, Mr. David Decaux.

9 June 1784. DIMSDALE. At Hertford, Dr. Dimsdale of Bloomsbury Square, son of the Hon. Baron Dimsdale.

c. June 1784. GWILT. At her house at Cheshunt, the relict of Mr. Gwilt, and sister of the late Mr. Shaw, of Cheshunt House.

c. June 1784. COLLETON. At Baldock, Hertfordshire, Charles Colleton, Esq.

3 July 1784. ROBERTS. At Hadley, in her 63rd year, after languishing a considerable time with a paralytic stroke, Mrs. Roberts, wife of Peter Roberts, Esq., city remembrancer and comptroller of the Bridge House lands, and sister to Charles and Thomas Boddam, Esqrs., of Enfield, and to R.H. Boddam, Esq., governor of Bombay.

18 July 1784. LIPTROTT. At Totteridge, Rev. Bexworth Liptrott, minister of that place.

7 August 1784. COOKE. At Cheshunt, Hertfordshire, Mrs. Cooke, wife of R. Cooke, Esq., merchant in Crutched Friars.

c. September 1784. PYM. William Pym, Esq., of Little Wymondley, Hertfordshire, a lineal descendant from the celebrated Patriot.

William Pym was the son of John Pym, lawyer, of Little Wymondley. John is first recorded in that parish in 1724 when he was presented to the manor court for enclosing eight acres of the common field. He seems to have retained the land, on which he subsequently built a substantial house—now known as Wymondley House. John died at Wymondley 26 June 1770. The property remained in the family's possession until 1799. In spite of a contrary assertion by Reginald Hine (History of Hitchin) *no evidence has been found to connect this family with John Pym (1584–1643) 'the Patriot', who was one of the Five Members of Parliament impeached in January 1642. [NF]*

27 October 1784. HINDE. At Calcutta, of a violent flux, Captain Hinde, son of Robert Hinde, Esq., of Preston Castle, near Hitchin.

10 November 1784. YOUNG. Thomas Young, Esq., of Bush Hall [Hatfield], Hertfordshire.

9 December 1784. DORRIEN. In his 71st year, at Great Berkhamsted, Hertfordshire, John Dorrien, Esq.

c. January 1785. LAW. At Broxbourne, aged 77, after a tedious and painful illness, the lady of Stephen Law, Esq., formerly governor of Bombay, and one of the directors of the East India Company.

22 February 1785. PETER THE WILD BOY. At Broadway farm, near Great Berkhamsted, Hertfordshire, the person distinguished by the appellation of Peter the Wild Boy, who was picked up in a wood in Germany in the latter end of the reign of George I while the king was hunting, and by that monarch sent over to England, where he has remained ever since; and of whom Lord Monboddo has lately given a particular history, which see in our last, p.113; and also a singular anecdote of him in our vol. XXI, p.522. A half-length figure of him was for many years exhibited at Mrs. Salmon's, in Fleet Street.

1 March 1785. HALL. At the house of Richard Gough, Esq., Enfield, in her 49th year, regretted by all who had the pleasure of her acquaintance, Mrs. Elizabeth Hall, sister to Mrs. Gough and third daughter of the late Thomas Hall, Esq., of Goldings, Hertfordshire.

Elizabeth Hall, who, despite the 'Mrs', was presumably unmarried, was buried, like her father and others of the family, in the Hall family vault beneath the chancel of St. Leonard's Church, Bengeo, 'Goldings' at Waterford being then in that parish. The Hall monument in the chancel actually gives the date of her death as 15 March 1785. Thomas Hall himself died in 1748. He seems to have been responsible for the damage to the Norman chancel arch in St. Leonard's caused by the installation of a large family pew where the three-decker pulpit had formerly stood. Richard Gough, the Enfield antiquary, is today perhaps best known for his edition of Camden's Britannia. *[AG]*

c. April 1785. RAMSAY. Rev. Mr. Ramsay, rector of Bushey, Hertfordshire.

23 April 1785. SCOTT. Mr. Scott, many years an eminent carpenter at Cheshunt, hanged himself.

8 May 1785. WRIGHT. At Oakley, otherwise Ugley, near Quendon, Essex, Paul Wright, D.D., F.S.A., vicar of that place, and rector of Snoreham, in the same county. . ... He was also for some time curate and lecturer of All Saints, Hertford. In 1773 he published proposals for printing by subscription, in one volume 4to price one guinea, Sir H. Chauncy's *History of St. Albans and its Archdeaconry*, continued to the present Time, with the Antiquities of Verulam; including, among other MS. Collections, those of Mr. Webster, many years surgeon there, whose Drawings of various Antiquities in that Neighbourhood were to be engraved. In May, 1775, the work was promised to be put to press as soon as the editor should meet with sufficient encouragement; and a specimen of it was exhibited in our last volume, p.745. [See Main

Sequence, October 1784.]. In 1781 his name appeared to the "Complete British Family Bible", in 80 folio numbers; a literary manoeuvre on which the old adage, de mortuis, &c., forbids us to enlarge.

In June 1740 Paul Wright married (at Bengeo) Mary Bridgeman, daughter of Charles Bridgeman, twice mayor of Hertford. His antiquarian interests developed in the 1760s, when he first announced his intention to publish an 'accurate edition' of Chauncy's History of Hertfordshire (see August 1780), and he became a Fellow of the Society of Antiquaries in 1770. The Cambridge antiquarian William Cole withheld his support from both these proposals, having found Wright "to be a most odd and extravagantly ridiculous person, and by no means qualified to undertake such a work". The edition of Chauncy did not materialize. [AJ]

27 August 1785. WHIPHAM. At St. Albans, Mr. Whipham, sen., formerly a silversmith in Fleet Street.

c. September 1785. HALL. Mr. Hall, attorney, at Hertford.

October 1785. STONE. At Harding [Harpenden], near St. Albans, aged 106, Margaret Stone.

10 November 1785. TRISTRAM. At Hitchin, aged upwards of 70, Mr. Tristram, attorney at law.

12 November 1785. CHERY. Benjamin Chery, Esq., alderman of Hertford, an eminent butcher and dealer in cattle. He was talking to his bailiff at his farm at Jenningsbury, near Hertford, and, sending him to turn some persons out of an adjoining field, immediately threw himself into a moat. The bailiff returned in a quarter of an hour, but every method used to recover life was ineffectual. He has left a fortune of £30,000 acquired with a fair character. The only cause assigned for this rash action is, that he had bought up a larger quantity of barley for malt than he could immediately pay for, though the profit on it would have amounted to a considerable sum.

29 November 1785. DICKENSON. Richard Dickenson, of Ware.

4 December 1785. TATNALL. At Theobalds, in Cheshunt, of a paralytic stroke, aged 75, Mr. Tatnall, an eminent upholder in Queen Street, Cheapside.

6 December 1785. HUGHES. In Bishopsgate Street, aged 73, Mr. Hugh Hughes, druggist. He was buried in a splendid manner at Broxbourne, December 14, having a country residence at Hoddesdon, in that parish. He was sheriff of Hertfordshire in 177-.

Captain Hughes bought the Grange, Hoddesdon, in 1777. He also held the site of St. Paul's Church, Hoddesdon, which he sold in 1822. [TD]

14 December 1785. BOURCHIER. At Bramfield, Hertfordshire, the Rev. Edward Bourchier, M.A., rector of that parish, and of All Saints Hertford.

3 January 1786. MILLES. At Pishobury [Sawbridgeworth], Hertfordshire, the infant son and heir of Jeremiah Milles, Esq.

3 January 1786. BOND. At St. Albans, on his way to London, the Rev. James Bond, D.D., formerly chaplain to the late Bishop of London.

24 January 1786. POOL. At her house at Wormley, Mrs. Pool, only daughter and heiress of the late Mr. Millar, merchant, second wife of the Rev. Mr. Pool, minister of Little Stanmore, alias Whitchurch, near Edgware, and vicar of Hernehill, Kent, and to whom her very handsome fortune devolves.

26 January 1786. PALMER. At Hatfield, Hertfordshire, Mr. John Palmer, late wheeler to the Earl of Bristol. Being 100 years of age on Michaelmas day last, his birthday was celebrated at his Lordship's expense.

'Earl of Bristol' obviously an error for Earl of Salisbury. [HG]
[See Main Sequence, 29 September 1785].

c. January 1786. BLACKFORD. at Northaw, Hertfordshire, Mr. Blackford, goldsmith and refiner, nephew of the late Mr. Alderman Blackford.

10 February 1786. HUNTER. Mrs. Hunter, wife of John Hunter, Esq., of Gobions, Hertfordshire, M.P. for Leominster. She was daughter of Governor Hornby of Bombay.

Ann Hunter, a benefactor of the poor, is commemorated by a tablet in St. Mary's Church, North Mimms. John Hunter was deputy chairman of the East India Company and high sheriff of Hertfordshire in 1780–1. [PK]

3 March 1786. KECK. At his seat at Theobalds, aged 75, Anthony Keck, Esq., senior serjeant at law. He was buried at Cheshunt, to which parish he had been a great benefactor by his constant and extensive charity. He has left surviving two sons: the eldest a clergyman, the other a merchant in Holland. His eldest son (who sat in several parliaments) and his only daughter, died before him.

25 March 1786. WILLIS. Mr. Willis, master of the Rose and Crown at Edmonton, in consequence of a fall from his horse, which he wantonly attempted to ride into a public-house at Cheshunt 2 or 3 days before, but received a violent contusion on his skull from the lintel of the door.

c. March 1786. WORSLEY. In advanced age, at her son's school at Hertford, Mrs. Worsley, relict of the late Mr. Worsley, schoolmaster of that town, mother to the Rev. Mr. Worsley, pastor of the congregation of Protestant Dissenters at Cheshunt, and sister to the late Rev. Dr. Obadiah Hughes.

1 May 1786. BACHE. Mr. John Bache, of Fortunes, near Watford, Hertfordshire.

5 May 1786. PREVOST. At his house at East Barnet, at an advanced age, Major General Augustine Prevost, colonel of the 60th regiment of foot. His spirited defence of Savannah against Count d'Estaign and the American General Lincoln, in September 1779 (see our volume XLIX, p.633), whom he obliged to raise the siege, will render him respected by his country, as his private conduct endeared him to all his neighbours and acquaintance.

15 May 1786. ATTLAY. At Cheshunt House, of the gout in his stomach,

Stephen Attlay, Esq., of Yorkshire, where he was buried. His only daughter married Huxley Sandon, Esq., of whom see volume LIV, p.955.

July 1786. NORRIS. At Hitchenden [Hitchin?], Hertfordshire, John Norris.

3 September 1786. MONTAGU. At Hatfield, Hertfordshire, Mrs. Montagu, wife of Captain Montagu and daughter of Mr. L'Epine, of Great George Street.

6 September 1786. COOPER. At Turnford, Hertfordshire, the lady of Robert Harris Cooper, Esq., Portugal merchant.

29 September 1786. HINDE. At Preston Castle, near Hitchin, Robert Hinde, Esq., late captain of the royal regiment of light horse, whose "Discipline" he published in 1778, 8vo. He retired on half pay, having at that time a wife and 12 children alive, the eldest in the army.

10 October 1786. BRASSEY. At Hertford, of a paralytic stroke, Mrs. Brassey, relict of the late, and mother of the present, Nathaniel Brassey, Esq., banker, in Lombard Street.

21 October 1786. WITTENBOOM. At Watford, Mrs. Wittenboom.

c. November 1786. VILLIERS. At Watford, Hertfordshire, aged 78, the Right Hon. Thomas Villiers, Earl of Clarendon, Lord Hyde, Joint Postmaster General, and a Lord of Trade and Plantations. [Here follows a long biography irrelevant to Hertfordshire].

c. November 1786. SCOT. At Ware, of a cancer, Mrs. Scot.

21 December 1786. BOGDANI. At Hitchin, Hertfordshire, in her 39th year, universally lamented, Mrs. Bogdani, wife of William Maurice Bogdani, Esq.

c. December 1786. BUTTS. At Northaw, Hertfordshire, Mrs. Butts, formerly of Fleet Street.

23 December 1786. HALL. In Hatton Street Richard Hall, Esq., an East India Director, formerly an East India captain, son of Mr. Hall of Hertford, and brother to Mr. Hall, late attorney in that town; brother also to Mr. Hall of the city pavement office.

3 March 1787. BARTLET. At Hertford, aged near 70, of a confirmed dropsy, Mr. Benjamin Bartlet, F.R.S., one of the people called Quakers, formerly an eminent apothecary at Bradford, Yorkshire, in which he succeeded his father, who had for his apprentice the afterwards celebrated Dr. Fothergill. . . .

26 April 1787. NICHOLL. At St. Albans, Samuel Nicholl, Esq., late Accountant General to the East India Company.

7 May 1787. EARLE. At Moor House, near Rickmansworth, Hertfordshire, Timothy Earle, Esq., one of the gentlemen of his Majesty's Privy Chamber.

1 June 1787. SEARANCKE. At Hatfield, Hertfordshire, Mrs.

Searancke, widow of John Searancke, Esq., and owner of the site of Croyland Abbey, which she has left to Mr. Durnford, attorney at Winchester.

Mary, daughter of the Rev. Thomas Durnford, curate of Rockbourne, Hants., and vicar of Whitsbury, Wilts., married 1766 at Little Berkhamsted John Searancke of Hatfield, a prosperous brewer, who died without issue in 1779 (see above). Memorial to both in Hatfield church. Mr. Durnford was Mary's brother George. [HG]

1 July 1787. ANSTRUTHER. At Cheshunt, Miss Anstruther, lately arrived from the West Indies.

5 July 1787. HANCOCK. At Hertford, Nathaniel Hancock, Esq., formerly commander of the Norfolk East India-man.

20 July 1787. FRANCIS. At Start Hill, near Bishops Stortford, in his 101st year, Mr. William Francis, who was baptized September 16, 1686, and retained his faculties till within a few days of his death.

3 September 1787. DOMVILE. At St. Albans, Mr. John Domvile.

16 September 1787. HERBERT. Mr. Nathaniel Herbert, master of the White Hart inn at Baldock, Hertfordshire, and formerly master of a company of comedians.

19 September 1787. KENTISH. At St. Albans, Robert Kentish, Esq.

Born c.1738, second son of Thomas Kentish of St. Albans (see above, 4 April 1774). Died unmarried, buried at St. Stephen's. [HG]

20 September 1787. WALKER. Rev. John Walker, vicar of Sawbridgeworth, Hertfordshire, of Takely, Essex, and chaplain to the 7th regiment of foot.

5 October 1787. PEMBERTON. At St. Albans, Miss Anne Pemberton.

14 October 1787. FITCH. Mrs. Fitch, wife of Mr. Fitch, maltster at St. Albans.

3 November 1787. KING. At his house in Edward Street, after a few hours illness, being taken ill only the evening before, and dying in the morning, aged 55, the Rev. John Glen King, D.D., rector of Wormley, preacher at Spring Garden Chapel, F.R. and S.S.S.

13 November 1787. DOVE. At Stevenage, Hertfordshire, Mr. Simon Dove, attorney.

19 November 1787. BUSH. At Hatfield, Hertfordshire, Mr. James Bush. His death was occasioned by the kick of an ass on Saturday evening the 3rd instant.

No entry of burial in Hatfield registers, but may have been father of James Bush who held gamekeeper's certificate for Lord Salisbury's manors of Hatfield and Bedwell Lowthes 1784–89. [HG]

6 December 1787. MANNING. At his house near Stevenage, Hertfordshire, aged 106, Joseph Manning, Esq. He served as a volunteer in the royal army against the rebels, and has ever since lived a retired life in the house where he died.

7 December 1787. PITT. At Hertford, Mrs. Mary Pitt, youngest sister of the late Earl of Chatham.

21 December 1787. BLACKMORE. At Cheshunt, Hertfordshire, Mr. William Blackmore, jun., late of Henrietta Street, Covent Garden.

25 December 1787. LESON. ———— Leson, a young miller. About ten o'clock in the morning, as he was walking in the middle of the road with two friends, his hat flapped over his eyes against the falling snow, meeting a post-chaise, belonging to Mr. Picard of Broxbourne, going to fetch some company to dinner from Edmonton, the pole struck him on the chest, of which he languished till next morning, at four o'clock, and then died. He was to have been married, on New Year's Day, to a daughter of Mr. Mansfield, a wealthy farmer of Cheshunt, and to have been placed in Broxbourne Mill, as agent for Mr. Brookland, miller, of Cheshunt. He desired 50 guineas, which he had saved, and his watch, to be given to his intended bride. What is remarkable in this catastrophe is, that the very same chaise occasioned the death of the late Sir Barnard Turner, in 1784, being then the property of Mr. Saunders, apothecary at Cheshunt, who sold it to Mr. Picard, and it is since said to have been broken in pieces, to counteract its evil destiny in future. There was, however, this difference in the catastrophes, that Sir Barnard lost his life by riding against the chaise in consequence of conviviality; while Mr. Leson, perfectly sober, had not the good fortune to hear the calls of the driver, warning him of his danger in a road rendered trackless by a sudden and violent fall of snow.

25 December 1787. TYSSEN. Of the dropsy in his chest, William Tyssen, Esq., of Cheshunt, Hertfordshire, nephew to the late ———— Tyssen, Esq., lord of the manor of Hackney. He has left a widow and only daughter to deplore his loss.

13 January 1788. FREEMAN. Jn. Cope Freeman, Esq., of Abbot's Langley, Hertfordshire.

4 February 1788. KECK. At Theobalds, Hertfordshire, after six months confinement of the dropsy in her chest, Mrs. Keck, relict of Anthony Keck, Esq., late senior serjeant at law.

5 February 1788. HARRIS. Aged 68, of an abscess in his liver, at his house in Great St. Helen's, William Harris, Esq., treasurer of the East India Company; which place he had held in the highest respect 50 years. He was, in every sense of the word, a worthy man. Dying a widower without issue, his fortune, which is considerable, will be divided among his nephews and nieces. He was buried at Ware.

13 February 1788. NICHOLS. At his son's house, near Hempstead, Hertfordshire, aged 79, Mr. Thomas Nichols, who kept a mercer's shop near Carnaby Market more than 40 years, but had lately retired from business. He was found dead in his bed in the morning, after having been apparently cheerful and well the preceding day.

14 February 1788. MORRIS. At Cheshunt, aged 58, Mr. Morris, many years master of an academy there.

23 February 1788. STAINES. At Hertford, Mr. Staines, formerly a hosier in London, but had retired many years.

c. February 1788. CHASE. Sir Richard Chase, Knt., of Much Hadham, Hertfordshire. His fortune, which is very considerable, devolves between his two nephews, Francis and Richard Stanley, sons of Francis Stanley, rector of Hadham, and grandsons of Dr. William Stanley, dean of St. Paul's; the former of these is vicar of North Weald, Essex, and rector of Eastwick, Hertfordshire; the latter a barrister of the Inner Temple, and recorder of Hertford.

March 1788. BELLIS. At Woodside, near Hatfield, Hertfordshire, the widow of the late William Hartley, Esq., late principal secretary to his Excellency the Hon. Mr. Villiers, lately Lord Hyde and Earl of Clarendon, on his embassy to Saxony and Poland, and also wife of Mr. Bellis, late a jeweller in Pall Mall; mother of the late Mrs. Penrose, wife of Mr. Penrose, surgeon at Hatfield, and of Captain Bellis, of Bombay.

Elizabeth Hartley married James Bellis 2 April 1746, at St. James's, Clerkenwell, and was buried 11 March 1788 at North Mimms. (see also 1 November 1788). [HG]

March 1788. GRAVE/GREAVES. At Clothall, Hertfordshire, the Rev. Thomas Cecil Greaves, rector of that parish, and of the rich rectory of Hatfield, to which last he was presented by the Earl of Salisbury, 1772, and to the former in 1780. He is succeeded at Hatfield by the Rev. Mr. Keate, vicar of Cheshunt, and rector of Little Berkhamsted.

Two brothers are confused here, both of them illegitimate sons of the sixth Earl of Salisbury. The Rev. William Cecil Grave, rector of Hatfield from 1772, died 8 March 1788, aged 40. He has a memorial in the church at Clothall, where he is buried. The Rev. Thomas Cecil Grave, (1757–1816) was rector of Clothall from 1780 until his death. [RHW]

16 March 1788. CLARE. At Hempstead, Hertfordshire, aged 114, Mrs. Anne Clare, relict of Colonel Clare, who served under the Duke of Marlborough, and was killed at the battle of Blenheim.

22 March 1788. CLUTTERBUCK. At Watford, Mrs. Clutterbuck, wife of Thomas Clutterbuck, Jun., Esq.

29 March 1788. GRIFFIN. At Cheshunt, Hertfordshire, Rev. Thomas Griffin, M.A., senior fellow of St. John's College, Oxford, curate of Cheshunt, one of the surrogates of the London diocese, and one of the preachers at Whitehall.

31 March 1788. REED. At Weston, Hertfordshire, Rev. Jos. Reed, near 57 years vicar of that parish. His immediate predecessor in the living held it 64 years; so that it had been in possession of two successive incumbents above 120 years.

12 April 1788. SHAW. In Great Russell Street, Bloomsbury Square, Mrs. Shaw, relict of John Shaw, Esq., of Cheshunt House, Hertfordshire, and sister to Mrs. Huxley, of Edmonton. The estate is entailed on the relicts of the respective lords, and on females in the direct line. By Mrs. Shaw's death, an estate in Edmonton devolves to Mr. Willis, son of the late Rev. Mr. Willis, vicar of Wormley, who married her niece, Miss Sandon; and the rest of her fortune to the Sandons.

17 April 1788. BOYS. At his apartments in the Inner Temple, aged 74, Rev. John Boys, vicar of Redbourn, Hertfordshire, to which he was presented by the late Lord Grimston, 1746.

26 April 1788. DALMEIDA. At Watford, Joseph Dalmeida, Esq.

c. May 1788. TROLLOPE. In the prime of her life, Mrs. Penelope Trollope, wife of the Rev. William Trollope, rector of Cottered, and vicar of Rushden, Hertfordshire, younger son of the late Sir Thomas Trollope of Casewick, Lincolnshire, Bart., and uncle to his successor, Sir Thomas William Trollope, the present baronet. She was the second daughter of the late Adolphus Meetkerke, Esq., of Julians, Hertfordshire; and has left a son, now at Winchester College, and three daughters, Penelope, Diana, and Isabella.

5 June 1788. LEWIN. At Cheshunt, advanced in years, Mrs. Lewin, relict of ———— Lewin, Esq., and mother to the Lady of Colonel Craig, of the same place.

15 June 1788. COOKE. At Cheshunt, after a very long and painful illness, Richard Cooke, Esq., late a linen-draper in Houndsditch brother of William Cooke, Esq., of Woodford, who died June 21, 1787, and father of the first lady of Nathaniel Barnardiston, Esq.

19 June 1788. SEARANCKE. At Hatfield, Hertfordshire, Mrs. S. Searancke.

Sarah, daughter of John Searancke, brewer, baptised at Hatfield 27 August 1727. Youngest sister and co-heir of John Searancke who died 1779. [HG]

2 July 1788. BROWNE. At Marlers [Marlowes?], near Hemel Hempstead, Hertfordshire, aged 88, Mrs. Browne, widow of the late Dr. Thomas Browne, of Arlesey, Bedfordshire.

5 July 1788. HARDING. At Tring, Hertfordshire, John Harding, Esq., only son of the late Mr. Harding of Edmonton and London, wine merchant. He married Miss Jackson, of Southgate, by whom he has left a son and a daughter.

2 August 1788. COTTON. At St. Albans, Dr. Cotton, many years physician there, and author of "Visions in Verse, for the Instruction of younger Minds". He was distinguished for his great care, humanity, and attention to those unhappy objects to whose cure he had devoted his principal study; and is succeeded by Dr. Peller, who assisted him in his practice.

7 August 1788. CHURCH. John Church, Esq., of Wood-side [Hatfield], Hertfordshire, a partner in the house of Messrs. Child and Co., bankers, Temple Bar. Dying a bachelor, he has left his fortune, which was very considerable, to his numerous relations: his house, which he built, and an estate of £1000 a year, to his brother and his children.

Baptized at Hatfield 28 February 1724/25, son of Thomas Church, described as a "labourer", and tenant of a cottage and a few acres at Hatfield Woodside. He made his way to London, became a clerk, then a partner in Child's Bank, and amassed a fortune, enabling him to purchase the Woodside estate at Hatfield, and rebuild the old mansion there. He was buried in Hatfield church (memorial tablet there). (See also Hatfield and its People, part 11b, pp.74–76). [HG]

11 August 1788. RUSS. At Barnet, aged 107, Thomas Russ, Esq., formerly a merchant of London.

23 August 1788. CLARKE. At Hertford, in her 86th year, Mrs. Clarke, relict of Dr. Clarke, formerly physician in that town. She was the daughter of the Rev. Charles Proby, D.D., rector of Tewin, Hertfordshire, and had resided the whole her life in the county. To a most engaging and beautiful external deportment (the remains of which she carried to her grave) she added the graces of a well-informed and observant mind... Except the infirmities of old age, she enjoyed a good share of health till within a few weeks of her death. She has left one son, Edward Clarke, Esq., of Lisbon; and one daughter, married to William Turton, Esq., of Soundes, Oxfordshire (who died in 1779), by whom she had three sons, all of whom are now living. Mrs. Clarke, was nearly allied to several of the nobility: to the late Dowager Lady Townshend, Lord Viscount Dudley and Ward, Earl Carysfort, &c...

c. August 1788. NEWMAN. At Watford, Hertfordshire, aged 87, Mrs. Mary Newman, widow.

20 September 1788. SHULDHAM. At St. Margaret's Place, Hertfordshire, very greatly and deservedly lamented by her family and friends, Catherine-Maria Shuldham, wife of Arthur Lemuel Shuldham, Esq., and daughter of the late Sir William Anderson, Bart. Her remains were interred on the 27th at Lea, near Gainsborough, Lincolnshire.

c. September 1788. WYNNE. Lately, at St. Albans, Mrs. Wynne, widow of Captain John Wynne, late of the navy.

9 October 1788. HALSEY. At his seat at Gaddesden Place, Hertfordshire, Thomas Halsey, Esq., formerly M.P. for that county in four parliaments. He married, March 18, Miss S. Crawley, of Stockwood, Bedfordshire.

November 1788. SAPSARD. At Sawbridgeworth, aged 82, Mrs. Sapsard, widow.

November 1788. WHITE. Mr. White, son of Mrs. White, of the Four Swans Inn at Waltham Cross.

1 November 1788. BELLIS. At his house at Hatfield Woodside, of an asthmatic complaint, Mr. Bellis, formerly a jeweller and toyman in Pall Mall. His wife died in April last.

James Bellis. He was father-in-law of William (Beck) Church of Hatfield Woodside and of James Penrose, surgeon, of Hatfield. Buried at North Mimms, 7 November 1788, aged 68. (See also April 1788 and 23 November 1789). [HG]

17 November 1788. EASTGATE. At St. Albans, aged 70, Mr. Thomas Eastgate, formerly hosier in Great Russell Street, Covent Garden.

20 November 1788. MARTIN. Samuel Martin, Esq., of Marshalswick, Hertfordshire, a gentleman well known in the political world, particularly from his having fought a duel, about 25 years ago, with Mr. Wilkes. Mr. Martin had the reversion of the ushership of the Exchequer, at present in the possession of the Hon. Horace Walpole, worth about £4000 per annum. By his death, after Mr. Walpole dies, the office goes to the Crown.

24 November 1788. MITCHIE. At his house at Muffits, North Mimms, after a lingering illness, John Mitchie, Esq., deputy chairman of the East India Company.

28 November 1788. GOODMAN. Aged 98, Mrs. Goodman. She kept a school at Abbots Langley, Hertfordshire, till within three days of her death.

7 December 1788. MOAKES. Near Barnet, aged 107 years and 6 months, George-Frederick Moakes, Esq., commander of an East Indiaman in 1719.

14 December 1788. NEWMAN. After a lingering illness, Mr. Joseph Newman, wool stapler, of Hempstead, Hertfordshire.

29 December 1788. BELFIELD. At Berkhamsted, the Rev. Henry Belfield, M.A., Fellow of Exeter College, Oxford.

14 January 1789. PARNELL. At Hadham, Mrs. Parnell, relict of Hugh Parnell, Esq.,

18 January 1789. BLACKMORE. Of an apoplexy, aged 47, ———— Blackmore, Esq., of Briggins in Eastwick [Hunsdon], Hertfordshire. He married to his third wife the daughter of ———— Tatnall, Esq., of Cheshunt, who survives him.

27 March 1789. FISHER. At Ware, suddenly, just as he had dismounted at his son-in-law's door, Mr. Fisher, clerk in the Three per Cent Office at the Bank, formerly master of a livery stable in Moorfields.

28 March 1789. WATSON. At Sion House, near Bishop Stortford, Mrs. Watson, wife of Mr. Alex. Watson, formerly of Billiter Square.

4 April 1789. BARTON. Mr. John Barton, of Hertford.

9 April 1789. DICKINSON. At Islington, Mrs. Dickinson, relict of R. Dickinson, Esq., of Ware, Hertfordshire.

13 April 1789. CHOLMLEY. At Theobalds, Hertfordshire, Mrs. Sarah Cholmley.

30 April 1789. JOHNSON. At Richmond, William Johnson, Esq., of Clayhill, Enfield, son of the late vicar of Hemel Hempstead, Hertfordshire.

4 May 1789. WILSON. At Chorley Wood, Hertfordshire, George Winfield Wilson, Esq.

11 May 1789. KIRBY. At Hertford, advanced in years, Mr. Kirby, an eminent bricklayer, and one of the aldermen of that corporation.

27 May 1789. WRAXALL. At Cheshunt, Hertfordshire, after two days illness, Mrs. Wraxall.

8 June 1789. SEARANCKE. At Hatfield, Hertfordshire, Mrs. Elizabeth Searancke, a maiden lady of considerable property.

Baptized at Hatfield 23 October 1718, daughter of John Searancke, brewer. She was one of the three sisters and co-heirs of John Searancke who died 1779. [HG]

26 June 1789. SMITH. At his seat at East Barnet, Hugh Smith, M.D., of Hatton Street. He raised himself into celebrity by his medicine chests, and by several publications on Respiration, and had the reputation of performing great cures in asthmatic complaints. He married the eldest daughter of the late Archibald M'Clean, merchant, by a second marriage; and, on the death of her mother's sister, inherited an ample estate at East Barnet.

Dr. Smith was author of Philosophical Inquiries into the Laws of Animal Life *and* Letters to Married Women, *a treatise on child rearing and childhood diseases which ran to a number of editions. His residence was Trevor Park, sold for housing development in 1934; only the lodge remains in Church Hill Road, East Barnet. [GJ]*

1 July 1789. BEAUVOIR. At his lodgings on the North Parade, Bath, Rev. Osmund Beauvoir, D.D., formerly master of the free school at Canterbury. He was of St. John's College, Cambridge, where he proceeded B.A. 1742; M.A. 1746. He had a doctor's degree from the archbishop of Canterbury; and was elected F.A.S. 1784. By his first wife he had two daughters, both married. He took to his second wife Miss Sharpe, only daughter and heiress of Fane William Sharpe, Esq., of East Barnet, late M.P. for Callington, October 14, 1782.

11 July 1789. CHAMBERLEYNE. At Hoddesdon, Hertfordshire, Mrs. Chamberleyne, widow of the late Richard Chamberleyne, Esq., of Rise, in Hatfield Broadoak parish, Essex, and mother of Stanes and Richard Chamberleyne, Esqrs. She was the daughter and heir of Thomas Smith, Esq., of West Kennet, Wiltshire, and heir of Rob. Plumer, Esq., late of Hoddesdon, Hertfordshire, and married Mr. Chamberleyne in 1745.

3 August 1789. CATHCART. At Tewin Water, Hertfordshire, in her 98th year, Rt. Hon. Elizabeth Lady-dowager Cathcart. She was one of the four daughters of ——— Malyn, Esq., of Southwark, and of Battersea in Surrey. She was four times married, but never had any issue: first, to James Fleet, Esq., of the city of London, lord of the manor of Tewin, (believed to be son and heir to Sir John Fleet, lord mayor of London 1693, and to have died April 30, 1733); secondly, to Captain Sabine, younger brother to General Joseph Sabine of Quino Hall, in Tewin aforesaid; thirdly, in 1739, to the Rt. Hon. Charles, eighth Lord Cathcart, of the kingdom of Scotland, commander in chief of the forces in the West Indies, who died at Dominica, December 20, 1740; and, fourthly, May 18, 1745, to Hugh Macguire, late an officer in the service of the Queen of Hungary, for whom she bought a lieutenant-colonel's commission in the British service, and whom she also survived, but was not encouraged, by his treatment of her, to verify her resolution, which she inscribed as a poesy on her wedding ring, "If I survive, I will have five."

Her avowed motives for these multifarious engagements were, the first to please her parents, the second for money, the third for title, and the fourth because "the devil owed her a grudge, and would punish her for all her sins." In the last she met with her match. The Hibernian fortune-hunter wanted only her money. Soon after she married him, she found that she had made a grievous mistake, for that he was desperately in love, not with the widow, but with the "widow's jointured land"; and apprehending that he designed to carry her off, and to get the absolute power of all her property, she endeavoured to prepare for the worst, by having some of her jewels plaited in her hair, and others quilted in her petticoat, and constantly wearing them. The Colonel's mistress insinuated herself into his wife's confidence so well, that she learnt where her will was; and Macguire getting sight of it, insisted on her altering it in his favour, threatening to shoot her.

Her apprehensions proved to be not without foundation; for one morning, when she and her caro sposo were out to take an airing from Tewin in the coach, she proposed to return, but he desired to go a little further. The coachman drove on; she remonstrated, "they should not be back by dinner time." At length the Colonel told her, that "she might make herself easy, for they should not dine that day at Tewin; they were in the high road to Chester, and to Chester they should go." Her efforts and expostulations were vain.

Upon her disappearing, her friends found out what had happened, and whither she was gone. They sent an attorney in pursuit of her, with a writ of habeas corpus, or ne exeat regno, who overtook her at an inn at Chester. The Colonel was not deficient in expedients. The attorney found him, and demanded a sight of my lady, but he did not know her person. The Colonel told him, that he should see her immediately, and he would find that she was going with him to Ireland with her own free consent. The Colonel persuaded a woman, whom he had properly tutored, to personate her. The attorney asked the supposed captive if she was going with Colonel Macguire to Ireland of her own free will? "Perfectly so." Astonished at such an answer, he begged her pardon, made her a low bow, and set out again for London.

The Colonel thought that possibly Mr. Attorney might recover his senses, find how he had been deceived, and yet stop his progress; and, in order to make all safe, sent two or three fellows after him, with directions to plunder him of all he had, and particularly his papers. They faithfully executed their commission; and when the Colonel had the writ in his possession, he knew that he was safe. He then took my lady over to Ireland, and kept her there, in a solitary place in the country, till his death, which, to her great satisfaction, happened in or about 1764. While she was in this state of confinement, she sent, by a crazy woman whom she could depend on, her jewels to a Mrs. Johnson, to be taken care of. After some time, Mrs. Johnson's husband failed, and she returned all the jewels safe to the owner, and in reward for her fidelity, my lady bought her son a commission.

When the Colonel died, his widow returned in triumph to Tewin, which he had let to Mr. Joseph Steele; but her ladyship, at her return, turned him out, and on his resisting her ejectment, she brought a suit against him at the assizes, which she attended in person, and cast him.

She danced at Welwyn assembly, with the spirit of a young woman, when she was past 80. On July 18, 1783, the reversion of her manors of Tewin and Wimley, in Hertfordshire, together with other property, particularly Bear Quay in London, was advertised to be sold in chancery; and we believe that in Hertfordshire was purchased by Earl Cowper. An annuity of her life was purchased by the same nobleman, at a time when it was said her life was less valuable because she had just left off dancing.

Her brother married, and left two daughters, Mrs. Frances and Mrs. Valentina Malyn, now of Berners Street. One of her sisters was Mrs. Jesses, late of Mortlake in Surrey; and another was Susannah, married to George Paul, LL.D., his Majesty's advocate-general, &c. who died March 1, 1755, as she also did April 8, 1757. What her ladyship had to leave she has left among her domestics. Her body was dressed in linen, and laid in a leaden coffin: the outside coffin was covered with velvet, trimmed with gold, on which was a gold plate, whereon were engraven the names of her husbands, her age, &c. She was carried in a hearse and six, followed by two coaches and six, and a prodigious concourse of people, to the church of Tewin, where she was buried in a vault near her first husband. Hat-bands and gloves were given in general to all who chose to attend, and a sumptuous entertainment was provided for them.

26 August 1789. GLEGG. At Baldock, James Glegg, Esq.

28 August 1789. JEPHSON. Mrs. Judith Jephson, wife of Richard Jephson, Esq., many years serjeant at arms to the Lord Chancellor, and serjeant at mace to the House of Lords. Her death was attended with the following singular circumstances: Mr. Jephson being in his 78th year, was become exceedingly feeble; and his wife, who was about ten years younger, was particularly careful of him. They took lodgings at Sydenham, for the sake of the old lady's drinking the waters at Sydenham Wells. Going down stairs, with Mr. Jephson and having hold of his coat, she was seized with a paralytic stroke on the staircase, and fell to the bottom, dragging Mr. Jephson with her. She fell with so much violence that she never spoke afterwards. It was with difficulty Mr. Jephson could be persuaded that he had not caused his wife's fall, and consequent death, and survived her only till the 2nd. of September instant. They were buried on the 9th. in one grave at Cheshunt, Hertfordshire, where they had lived.

29 August 1789. JONES. Mrs. Margaret Jones, relict of Rev. Richard Jones, late of Hoddesdon, Herts.

15 September 1789. WRIGHT. Aged 85, Mrs. Wright, mistress of the boarding school at Cheshunt, sister of the late Mr. James Johnson, who died July 19, aged 75.

29 September 1789. SMITH. Henry Smith, Esq., of Newhouse, St. Albans.

2 October 1789. PORTEUS. At St. Albans, Mrs. Judith Porteus, relict of Rev. Mr. Porteus, rector of Hatley Port, alias Cockayne Hatley, Bedford. It pleased the Almighty to bless her with an unusual share of health, and even a perfect enjoyment of all her faculties to the great age of 87. She was a pattern to the old of cheerfulness and contentment, and most instructive to the young by her advice as well as example. Her husband was brother to the present respectable Bishop of London.

October 1789. COTHERY. After a lingering illness, at Hadley, Mrs. Cothery, wife of Mr. Cothery, formerly master of the Green Man livery stables, Coleman Street.

23 November 1789. CHURCH. At Woodside, Hatfield, ———— Church, Esq., who married, in January last, the only surviving daughter of Mr. Bellis, of Pall Mall.

William Church (formerly William Beck), the nephew of John Church who died August 1788 (above). Changed his name on inheriting his uncle's estate. Baptized at Essendon 11 June 1746, married at Hatfield 22 November 1788 Sarah Bellis; buried at Hatfield (memorial in the parish church). (See also 1 November 1788). [HG]

2 December 1789. GRAVE. At Baldock, after a lingering illness, Mrs. Grave, the well-known favourite of the late Lord Salisbury, and mother of the late rector of Hatfield and Clothall.

Mrs. Mary Grave, mistress of the sixth Earl of Salisbury ("the Wicked Earl"). His relationship with her pre-dated his marriage in 1745. Within a few years he separated from his Countess and lived as a recluse with Mrs. Grave for the remaining 30 years of his life at Quickswood, in the parish of Clothall. "He lives upstairs . . .. surrounded with old trunks and boxes and scattered books. Well or ill he never quits this chamber, never sees or converses with any but his old Dame, as he calls her, and his physician, who occasionally visits him. The servants are old and rusty like the dwelling." (Letter from C. Price, 1771, Hatfield House archives). Mrs. Grave received over £50,000, besides jewellery, silver and furniture removed from Hatfield. They had seven children, to whom the Earl bequeathed £43,000. The will was unsuccessfully contested by the seventh Earl of Salisbury, who demolished Quickswood. [RHW]

13 December 1789. WARLEY. Found suffocated in a ditch between Hertford and Ware, Mr. Peter Warley, an elderly gentleman, and well-respected lawyer.

26 December 1789. MILBOURNE. At Watford, Hertfordshire, Mrs. Milbourne, relict of Gordon Milbourne, Esq.

7 January 1790. TROWER. At Newhouse, St. Albans, the infant son of James Trower, Esq.

10 January 1790. COCKAYNE. At Ilford [Ickleford?], near Hitchin, Hertfordshire, Mrs. Cockayne, wife of Thomas Cockayne, Esq.

13 January 1790. GORDON. At Hinxworth, Hertfordshire, in his 13th. year, after a long and painful illness, Master Brydges O'Bryen Gordon, the only child of Sir Adam and Lady Gordon.

24 January 1790. BACKHOUSE. In his 74th. year, Mr. Robert Backhouse, of Collier's End, Hertfordshire.

c. February 1790. EAMES. At Little Gaddesden, Hertfordshire, Mrs. Elizabeth Eames.

13 March 1790. LYTTON. At her seat at Knebworth, Hertfordshire, after a lingering illness, Mrs. Lytton, relict of John Robinson Lytton, Esq.

26 March 1790. IBBETSON. At Bushey, Hertfordshire, after a long illness, James Ibbetson, Esq., barrister at law, eldest son of the late Dr. Ibbetson, archdeacon of St. Albans.

c. April 1790. WADE. Lately, at Braughing, Hertfordshire, Rev. William Wade, of Jesus College, Cambridge.

16 April 1790. PARIS. At Hertingfordbury, Mrs. Paris, wife of Mr. John Paris of Gough Square, Fleet Street.

17 April 1790. HASKINS. At Essendon, Hertfordshire, Mrs. Haskins.

21 April 1790. PRESCOT/PRESCOTT. At his house in Cavendish Square, aged 78, George Prescot, Esq., an eminent Italian merchant and banker of the city of London, immensely rich. He was seized with the gout in his stomach on the 17th, in the evening, after his return from his seat at Theobalds, but was so well recovered as to be supposed out of danger, when, sitting in his chair, he expired without a groan. . ... Mr. Prescot married for his first wife a beautiful young lady, without fortune, who died in child-bed at Albury, near Theobalds. He married to his second, who survives him, a daughter of Abraham Elton, merchant, of Bristol, and sister to Isaac Elton, banker, of that city, who died March 29. By her he had two sons, Thomas and George-William, and a daughter, Mary, who died 1775, aged 20. His elder brother, Thomas, of Newport, co. Salop, Esq., died November 5, 1768, and left his fortune, amounting to at least £100,000 acquired by ship-building at Liverpool, to his brother's eldest son, who also succeeds to the paternal one in Hertfordshire. . ... In the year 1770, he purchased, for £75,000 exclusive of timber, of the Duke of Portland, the manor of Theobalds, formerly a royal palace by exchange with the Cecil family, and granted by William III to the first Duke of Portland, containing 3000 acres, within a brick wall reduced almost to the foundation. On the site of the palace, Mr. Lewis the builder contracted to erect several handsome houses, occupied by genteel families; and on a rising ground to the southward, Mr. Prescot built himself a handsome mansion. In 1782, he purchased, for £1750 of Lord Monson, the manor of Cheshunt; so that almost the whole parish was his property, and considerably improved by his good management. He was buried, on the 26th, in a vault provided by himself, on the south side of Cheshunt church-yard.

George Prescott, Esq., was the son of a wealthy lead merchant from Chester. As a young man he travelled in Italy where he learned banking. He returned to England about the year 1760 and, being supported and sponsored politically by Henry Fox became Member of Parliament for Stockbridge in 1761. He purchased the Theobald estates in Cheshunt in 1763. A survey of the estates in that year records "the former Palace of Theobalds now in a ruinous condition". He chose a site about three-quarters of a mile south-west of the palace to build the mansion now known as Theobalds Park, as his country seat. In 1782 he purchased the Manor of Cheshunt, and became very much the local squire. This property remained with the family until 1955. In 1620 the estates of Theobalds had been enlarged by King James I and enclosed within a wall some nine and three-quarters miles long. From the death of Charles I until the purchase of the property by Prescott the wall seems to have served as a quarry for local people. Very few fragments now survive, although the line of the wall, which has remained the estate boundary, can be clearly seen on modern Ordnance maps. [JE]

29 April 1790. DUNNE. Mrs. Dunne, relict of Mr. John Dunne, shopkeeper at Hatfield, Hertfordshire. She went to her chamber as usual, in order to go to bed, the preceding night, but was discovered the next morning lifeless, kneeling by her bedside, and not undressed.

May 1790. HALLOWS. At her lodgings in Hertford, aged upwards of 80, Mrs. Hallows, many years housekeeper to the late celebrated Dr. Young, author of the '*Night Thoughts*', etc.

[See also Main Sequence, June and July, 1790].

May 1790. BOGDANI. At Hitchin, Hertfordshire, William Bogdani, Esq., late fellow of King's College, Cambridge.

6 June 1790. BERNARD. At Sawbridgeworth, aged 83, Mrs. Bernard.

17 June 1790. ORME. At Mr. Bourchier's house, in Queen Street, Mayfair, Robert Orme, Esq., of Hertford.

3 July 1790. WINTER. Much lamented, aged 77, Mrs. Leader Winter, relict of Joshua Winter, Esq., of Bishop Stortford, Hertfordshire.

4 July 1790. BOURCHIER. At her house in St. Albans [probably Sandridge Lodge], Mrs. Bourchier, relict of the Rev. Edward Bourchier, formerly rector of All Saints, Hertford.

23 July 1790. YOUNG. At his mother's at Enfield, of a deep decline, Mr. Young, butcher, at Hoddesdon.

c. July 1790. HEYMAN. Lately, at the house of Jn. Hale, Esq., at Hertford, aged 70, Sir Peter Heyman, Bart., of Somerfield, Kent. He was formerly in the navy; and at the age of 17 married Miss Kempe, daughter and sole heiress of ———— Kempe, Esq., of Plymouth, by whom he had three children, who, as well as his lady, are long since dead; and he leaving no issue, the title devolves to the Rev. Henry Pixe Heyman, M.A., of Canterbury, fellow of Emmanuel College, Cambridge, grandson of his father's second brother.

3 August 1790. KENTISH. At Leicester, Tho. Kentish, Esq., of St. Albans.

Born c. 1735, eldest son of Thomas Kentish of St. Albans (see above 4 April 1774). Died unmarried, buried at St. Stephen's, St. Albans. [HG]

15 August 1790. CAESAR. At Hertford, in an advanced age, Mrs. Elizabeth Caesar, last surviving sister of the late General Caesar of the Coldstream regiment of guards.

24 August 1790. HEPWORTH. At Hertford, Mr. William Hepworth, late of the Red Lion livery stables in Gray's Inn lane.

24 August 1790. SENIOR. At Uffington, Berkshire, Mrs. Senior, relict of Nassau-Thomas Senior, Esq., late of Bath, and formerly of Hoddesdon, Herts.

c. August 1790. DANCER. At Ely, Mr. Charles Dancer, formerly an eminent surgeon and apothecary at Barnet.

c. August 1790. CHIPPINDALE. At Welwyn, Hertfordshire, aged 75, Mr. W. Chippindale.

3 September 1790. CLARENDON. At Stoney Stratford, the Countess of Clarendon. Her ladyship was going to Dunham Massey, in Cheshire, accompanied by the Earl of Clarendon and Lady Charlotte Villiers, on a visit to the Earl of Stamford. She was suddenly taken ill on the morning of the 1st instant and carried to a gentleman's house in Stoney Stratford. Lord Villiers was immediately sent for, but did not arrive until after her ladyship's decease. Her remains were interred in the family vault at Grove, near Watford, Hertfordshire on the 11th.

9 September 1790. NORTH. At Ware, aged 29, Mrs. North, wife of Mr. North, of the New Road, Mary-la-Bonne.

12 September 1790. DAUTIVILLE. In the abbey of Holyrood House, Miss Anne Dautiville, daughter of the late Andrew Dautiville, Esq., of Broxbourne, Hertfordshire.

14 September 1790. CHESTER. At Jenningsbury, Hertford, aged 64, Robert Chester, Esq., of Curzon Street.

15 September 1790. CUTLER. Dr. Cutler, of Hertford, one of the aldermen of that borough. On his return from visiting a patient, he suddenly dropped down dead at his own door.

c. September 1790. NEALE. At Hemel Hempstead, Hertfordshire, the Rev. Mr. Neale.

The Rev. James Neal, aged 50 years, buried at Hemel Hempstead 22 September 1790. [HG]

13 October 1790. LATEWARD. At Much Hadham, Hertfordshire, Mrs. Lateward, wife of John Lateward, Esq., of Portman Square. She was the daughter of Mr. Wildman, salesman, in Red Lion Street, Clerkenwell, and relict of ——— Green, Esq., of Huntingdonshire, and married August 26, 1782, to John Schreiber, Esq., who, on the death of his maternal grandfather, assumed the name, and inherited the estate, of Lateward.

16 October 1790. JEFFERSON. At King's Langley, Hertfordshire, the Rev. John Jefferson, curate and lecturer of St. Anne, Soho, vicar of King's Langley, and chaplain to the Earl of Hardwicke.

c. October 1790. EMMOTT. In St. James's Street, in her 81st year, Mrs. Emmott, widow of the late Richard Emmott, Esq., of Emmott Hall, co. Lancaster, and mother of ——— Emmott, Esq., of Golding, near Hertford, and of Mrs. Ross, wife of ——— Ross, Esq., army agent.

11 November 1790. ELTON. At Gaddesden Hall, Hertfordshire, Thomas Elton, Esq.

15 November 1790. DENNE. At Watford, Mrs. Denne, widow of John Denne, Esq., formerly partner with the late Sir Benjamin Trueman, brewer; and mother to the banker in the Strand.

20 November 1790. BOULTON. At Clissen [?], after a long illness, George Boulton, Esq., of South Mimms, Hertfordshire, formerly largely concerned in stage-coaches at the Gold Cross, Charing Cross.

George Boulton appears as the occupier of the Black Horse P.H. South Mimms, though according to the Licensed Victuallers' lists not its licensee from 1780 to 1790, when it was owned by Mrs. Elizabeth Hughes. The Black Horse P.H., Blackhorse Lane, was on the main Holyhead Road, an important coaching road. At the same time he was tenant of the Deeves Hall lands, the bulk of which were in the parish of Ridge, but some small fields along Bentley Heath Lane, South Mimms were included in the estate, once the property of Sir Edward Turner. (Land Tax South Mimms and Ridge; Licensed Victuallers' List South Mimms). [BW]

13 December 1790. MARCHANT. At Waltham Cross, Mr. William Marchant, surgeon to his Majesty's powder-mills at Waltham Abbey.

4 January 1791. ORME. At Hertford, Miss Audrey Orme, eldest daughter of the late Robert Orme, Esq., and sister of the Rev. Robert Orme, rector of All Saints, in that town.

7 February 1791. MOUNSLOW. At East Barnet, in his 82nd year, Mr. Edward Mounslow, who had been 54 years clerk of that parish.

16 February 1791. HANWORTH/HAINWORTH. At Graveley, Hertfordshire, Mr. John Hainworth, silk manufacturer of the Old Jewry.

A note in issue of G.M. for March 1791 records that Mr. Hanworth, having died suddenly at Graveley on the 6th [February?] had been buried in Bassishaw church, in the city of London. "His family were remarkable for sudden deaths." [AJ]

4 April 1791. SPRANGER. At West Farm, Barnet, aged 19, Mr. Richard Spranger, second son of John Spranger, Esq., master in chancery.

April 1791. BELL. At his house at Hertford, in his 75th year, Mr. Jonathan Bell, one of the people called Quakers, formerly an eminent shopkeeper in Tottenham, but retired many years, and elder brother to Mr. Daniel Bell, coal merchant, at Stamford Hill. Mr. Bell's integrity, communicative and friendly disposition, will make him remembered with esteem by all who knew him.

3 June 1791. HATT. Mrs. Hatt, wife of Mr. Richard Hatt, of Wormley, Hertfordshire.

10 June 1791. STREET. At Abbot's Langley, Hertfordshire, aged 75, Mrs. Street, relict of Mr. George Street, of Bucklersbury.

20 June 1791. JOCELYN. At Stortford, aged 94, Mrs. Sarah Jocelyn, daughter of the late Sir Strange Jocelyn, Bart., and sister of the late Sir Conyers Jocelyn, Bart., of Hide Hall, Hertfordshire.

25 June 1791. LYDE. After a very short illness, Sir Lionel Lyde, Bart., of Bedford Square, and of Ayot St. Lawrence, Hertfordshire, where our readers will recollect he rebuilt the parish church, from a design of Mr. Revett; of the consecration of which, see our volume XLIX, p.374; LIX, p.972. He was created a baronet of Great Britain in 1772, and had been an eminent tobacco merchant. His large property, both in Hertfordshire and London, was, by the express direction of his will, sold by public auction immediately after his decease.

5 July 1791. BOWMAN. Suddenly at Hoddesdon, Hertfordshire, George Bowman, son of William Bowman, banker in Lombard Street.

15 July 1791. COLLETT. At Hemel Hempstead, Hertfordshire, aged 73, Mrs. Collett.

28 July 1791. GIBSON. At Gilston, Hertfordshire, Rev. William Gibson, rector of St. Magnus, London Bridge, of Gilston, and of Wickham Bishop's, Essex, 1779.

15 August 1791. WHALLEY. At Ridge, Hertfordshire, in her 73rd. year, Mrs. Elizabeth Whalley, relict of Rev. Robert Whalley, vicar of that place.

31 August 1791. BARWICK. At South Mimms, John Barwick, Esq.

John Barwick purchased Clare Hall, South Mimms, from the son of Temple West c.1779, though he was already in occupation before this date. He enlarged the estate with the purchase of a 16¼ acre field called Westmead, and it is possible that the park was created during his ownership. [BW]

29 September 1791. MOORE. At Hoddesdon, Hertfordshire, in her 55th year, Mrs. Martha Moore, wife of William Moore, Esq.

30 September 1791. MANN. John Mann, of the Crown, Barnet.

20 October 1791. BEAUCLERK. At the Hoo, near Welwyn, Hertfordshire, the Rt. Hon. Lady Georgiana Beauclerk, daughter of the Duke of St. Albans.

8 November 1791. KIRKMAN. In an advanced age, at Little Gaddesden, Hertfordshire, Mrs. Kirkman, relict of Joseph Kirkman, Esq.

9 November 1791. BATHURST. Suddenly, in a fit, at his seat at Lydney, in Monmouthshire, Thomas Bathurst, Esq., eldest of the thirty-six children of the late Hon. Benjamin Bathurst, the brother of the late Allen first Earl Bathurst. He married, 1745, Anne, daughter and heir of William Fazakerley, of Totteridge, Esq., but leaving no legitimate issue, his estate, worth between 2 and £3000 a year, is said to descend to ———— Bragg, Esq., of the Temple, whose father married his eldest sister Anne. His personal property will be divided between two young ladies, his natural daughters. He was of a very hospitable and cheerful disposition, and sustained the character of an English country gentleman with great credit. The widow of his father, who had two wives, is the daughter of the late Rev. Dr. Lawrence Broderick, of Mixbury, in Oxfordshire, brother of Alan first Viscount Middleton of the kingdom of Ireland.

10 November 1791. RUMBOLD. At his house in Queen Anne Street West[minster], of an inflammation in his liver, to which, as an East India disorder, he had been frequently subject, Sir Thomas Rumbold, Bart., so created in 1779, when governor of Madras. Who his first wife was we have not learned. He married to his second, when M.P. for Shoreham, May 21, 1772, Miss Law, daughter of the late Bishop of Carlisle, by whom he had several children. His eldest daughter married Mr. Hale, son of the late General Hale, March 3, 1775. His eldest son, William, a captain in the guards, dying in his passage from France, in January 1786, he is succeeded by his second son by his first lady. Another son, Thomas Henry, is a student at Trinity College, Cambridge. His property, at the time of the Restraining Bill, was said to be £2000 a year in real estates, and £150,000 personal. He purchased the reversion of the fine estate of the ancient family of Butler, at

Watton, in Hertfordshire, which Philip, grandson of the late John Butler, Esq., had sold to the late Lord Clive, and his lordship made over to the late Henry Verelst, Esq., governor of Bengal. Sir Thomas took down what remained of the old mansion, and built another on the western extremity of the park, which was executed during his second government of Madras, and now boasts a greater profusion of hot walls and forcing fruit-houses than perhaps any garden in the kingdom. The whole fortune he has left behind him will not exceed £80,000 which he has thus bequeathed; after directing that his seat in Hertfordshire and other estates should be sold, he wills £1000 per annum to Lady Rumbold, during her life; the interest of £10,000 to his son succeeding to the title; and £300 per annum to the rest of his children; but having left no residuary legatee, the present baronet will probably obtain further possessions.

By Sir Thomas Rumbold's will, which is a tedious and formal repetition of provisos and conditions, he has ordered his Hertfordshire estates, except the church living of Watton, and the house, to be sold; and leaves £2000 per annum to his lady during her life, issuing from £40,000 to be raised by the sale of the estates, which is to be placed in the funds, with remainder to his children. Fify pounds a-year is bequeathed to his sister, Mrs. Ives, of Kendall, in Westmoreland; and £300 per annum to his eldest son, George Berriman Rumbold, during life, with many reservations as to its allotment afterwards. The executors are Evan Law, of Grafton Street, Esq., Mr. E. Law, the counsel, and the Rev. William Sheepshanks, of Leeds, in Yorkshire, who is appointed with a view of retaining the living of Watton for one of the sons of Sir Thomas Rumbold. An hundred pounds is also bequeathed to each of the executors, and some legacies to servants. This will, it is said, has given discontent to many persons, and, among others, to his daughter, Mrs. Hale Rigby. This lady's fortune, at her marriage was to have been £20,000; but Sir Thomas had, by consent, hitherto paid only the interest. He has now, by will allotted her only £15,000 of the £20,000.

23 November 1791. HICKS. At his seat at Hoddesdon, Hertfordshire, Sir John Baptist Hicks, Bart., of Beverston, Gloucestershire. He is succeeded in title by Howe Hicks, Esq., of Whitcombe Park, Gloucestershire.

23 November 1791. MANNING. At his house at Totteridge, Hertfordshire, of a paralytic stroke, William Manning, Esq., a West India merchant, and one of the directors of the Royal Exchange Assurance office.

November 1791. HASSELL. At Barnet, Richard Hassell, Esq., of Trinity College, Cambridge, where he proceeded B.A. 1756, M.A. 1759, and one of his Majesty's justices of the peace for the county of Middlesex. His lady died April 3, 1783, in consequence of being thrown out of a single-horse chaise; and by her he has left two daughters. His brother Robert, of Lincoln's Inn, commissioner of bankrupts, died April 3, 1783.

27 December 1791. MONRO. At Hadley, near Barnet, in his 77th year, Dr. John Monro, physician to the united hospitals of Bridewell and Bethlem. His son, Dr. Thomas Monro, was appointed, in 1782, assistant physician to Bethlem hospital, by the unanimous consent of a full general court; and most probably will be elected successor to his father at the next court, which is summoned for Thursday the 2nd. of January.

2 January 1792. DAVENPORT. At Cheshunt, Hertfordshire, of a schirrous liver, William Davenport, eldest son of late Rev. John Davenport, formerly vicar of St. Nicholas, Leicester. He was bred a printer, under the patronage of Mr. Johnson, who put him apprentice to the late William Strahan. About 15 months ago he stood candidate for and obtained the legacy of £30 p.a. bequeathed by the late Mr. Bowyer in trust, to Members, Warden of Court of Assistants of the Stationers Company to be by them paid to the compositor best skilled in the Greek language.

22 February 1792. ROOKE. At Willian, Hertfordshire, Rev. John Rooke, M.A., many years rector of that place, and in the commission of the peace for Hertfordshire.

2 April 1792. HINDE. At Hunsdon House, Hertfordshire, Venables Hinde, Esq., late a lieutenant and captain in the 2nd troop of horse grenadier guard, younger son of Captain Rob. Hinde, who died in 1786.

13 April 1792. BAUGH. At Sion Hill, near East Barnet, where he was on a visit to General Morrison, Lt.-General Launcelot Baugh, Colonel of the 6th regiment of foot.

c. May 1792. VANDER MEULEN. Lately, at St. Albans, Miss Vander Meulen, daughter of Joss Vander Meulen, merchant of London.

The Vander Meulen family vault was discovered in the abbey beneath the St. Albans Shrine during excavation, in 1991. [RA]

c. May 1792. PEARCE. Lately, at Hoddesdon, Hertfordshire, in his 75th year, Bert Pearce.

6 June 1792. PLANTIN. At Bushey, Hertfordshire, of a violent fever, Benjamin Plantin.

8 June 1792. SPRY. At Yardley, of a consumption, aged 57, Rev. Matthew Spry, prebend of Salisbury, vicar of Yardley, and of Sandon, Hertfordshire, M.A., Oxon.

12 June 1792. BARCLAY. In her 49th year, universally lamented, Mrs. Rachel Barclay, wife of Mr. David Barclay, of Youngsbury [Standon], Hertfordshire. On the 19th, her remains were interred in the burial ground of the Society of the Quakers at Winchmore Hill. She was peculiarly engaging in her manners, quick in perception, sound in judgement, anxious to know her duties, and firm in fulfilling them; and was so possessed with the milk of human kindness, that the woes of a numerous neighbourhood were daily softened by her lenient hand. She was a most zealous friend to the widow, and a fostering parent to the rising generation.

15 June 1792. EKINS. At Berkhamsted, in her 90th year, Mrs. Ekins, mother of the late Dean of Carlisle, and of the present Dean of Salisbury.

July 1792. DE LAET. The late Charles De Laet, Esq., of Pottrells, in Hertfordshire, has left the whole of his landed estate to his neighbour, Mr. Casamajor. An immense sum of ready money was found in his house, of which £7000 is left to Colonel Sibthorpe. Many of his other friends, and all his servants, have also legacies. His estates in distant counties are to be sold, to buy land for Mr. Casamajor in Hertfordshire.

1 July 1792. SEARE. At his house at Grove, near Tring, Hertfordshire, after a lingering illness, Jn. Seare, Esq.

26 July 1792. BRAMHALL. At Ware, after a long illness, Mr. Bramhall, wholesale haberdasher in Aldersgate Street.

17 September 1792. PRESCOTT. At her house in Cavendish Square, Mrs. Prescott, relict of George Prescott, Esq., of Theobald's Park, Hertfordshire; and on the 22nd her remains were deposited in the family vault at Cheshunt.

24 September 1792. BARRINGTON. At his house in Great James Street, Bedford Row, in his 85th year, having been afflicted with the palsy the last ten years of his life, Sir Fitzwilliam Barrington, Bart., of Swaynston, in the Isle of Wight. By his death, a very fine estate at Hatfield Broadoak, Essex, with other considerable property, descends to his son, now Sir John Barrington, Bart., M.P. for Newton, Hampshire. His only daughter married the Rev. William Brown, of Camfield Place, Hatfield, May 18, 1791.

29 September 1792. SAVAGE. At Bishop Stortford, Hertfordshire, in her 74th year, Mrs. Elizabeth Savage, widow of the Rev. Thomas Savage, formerly rector of Darley, Derbyshire.

c. September 1792. PROCTOR. After a lingering illness, the wife of Mr. Proctor, brewer, at Ware.

7 October 1792. WINDUS. At Ware, Hertfordshire, Mr. Windus, an eminent attorney, and many years under-sheriff of that county.

10 October 1792. MASON. At Cheshunt, Mr. Mason, gardener and seedsman, formerly servant and partner with Mr. Foster, afterwards with the late Mr. Minier, whose sons carry on the business in the Strand.

c. October 1792. CROMWELL. At Hampstead, Mrs. Elizabeth Cromwell, eldest daughter and last surviving child of Mr. Richard Cromwell, grandson of Henry, Lord Lieutenant of Ireland. Her sisters, Anne, died in 1777, and Letitia in 1789. She has left the bulk of her fortune to Mr. Oliver Cromwell, attorney, clerk of the Million bank, &c; £500 to the children of Mr. —————Field, of Newington, late an apothecary, of Newgate Street, London, who married her cousin, her uncle Thomas's daughter; and a handsome legacy to Mrs. Moreland, relict of Richard Hinde, Esq., whose mother was her maternal aunt, and who, with her brother, jointly possessed Cheshunt Park, the moiety of which, on his death, devolved to them, subject to his widow's jointure.

23 November 1792. BALLENDEN. At Westmill, Hertfordshire, aged 91,

Mary Lady Ballenden, widow of John, second Baron Ballenden of Ireland, and grandmother to the present Lord Ballenden.

c. December 1792, and Supplement. BARFORD. Lately, at Kimpton, Hertfordshire, in an advanced age, Rev. Dr. Barford, rector of that place, fellow of Eton college, prebendary of Canterbury. He printed 1. "In Pindari primum Pythium Dissertatio habita Cantabrigiæ in Scholis publicis, 7 kalend Julias, A.D. 1750, 1751," 4to; 2. "A Latin Oration at the Funeral of Dr. George, Provost of King's 1756," 4to. He proceeded B.A. 1742, M.A. 1746, S.T.P. 1771.

Dr. W. Barford was elected public orator of the University of Cambridge in 1763, on the cession of Mr. Skinner; and married, September 27, 1764, Miss Hewer, of Royston. In December following he was presented to the rectory of Pilton, Northamptonshire; chosen fellow of Eton, 1784; presented to the rectory of Allhallows, Lombard Street, with the vicarage of Kimpton, March, 1778.

10 December 1792. WILLIAMS. At Sarratt Green, Hertfordshire, Sir David Williams, Bart. His title (which was conferred on his ancestor by Charles I 1644) and estates devolve to his son, Mr. David Williams, of Aston Clinton, Buckinghamshire.

David Williams of Goldingtons, son of the Rev. Gilbert Williams, vicar of Sarratt, had purchased the manor of Sarratt from Arnold Duncombe in 1752. His father Gilbert claimed succession to the baronetcy when the fourth baronet died without issue, but his relationship was remote and the claim was not officially recognized. Nevertheless the title was assumed successively by his son and grandson. The statement in G.M. about (Sir) David's disposal of the estate is at variance with that in Cussans and (substantially) the Victoria County History, where the property is said to have passed via trustees for his wife Rebecca, to his grandson John. After two further sales the property was acquired in 1814 by Sophia, relict of his son—also Sir David Williams of Goldingtons. [AJ]

10 December 1792. KENTISH. At her home in St. Peter's Street, St. Albans, Mrs. Martha Kentish.

Born c.1738, eldest daughter of Thomas Kentish of St. Albans (see above, 4 April 1774). Died unmarried, buried at St. Stephen's. [HG]

23 December 1792. CLUTTERBUCK. At a very advanced age, Thomas Clutterbuck, Esq., of Watford, Hertfordshire.

17 January 1793. SCHREIBER. At her father's house at Tewin, aged 19, Miss Anne Louisa Schreiber, youngest daughter of O. Schreiber, in consequence of the injuries received by her clothes taking fire as she was putting up some paintings over the chimney of her apartment on the 3rd instant and on 24th she was deposited in the family vault at Enfield.

17 January 1793. SHEPPARD. At Offley, Hertfordshire, aged 80, Thomas Sheppard, Esq.

20 January 1793. CARR. At Hertford, Mrs. Carr, wife of Dr. Carr, the very masterly translator of Russian.

2 February 1793. WILLIAMS. At Pointer's Grove, Totteridge, Hertfordshire, Mrs. Williams, relict of Edward Williams, formerly of the Inner Temple, barrister.

7 March 1793. BAYLEY. At Tring, Hertfordshire, in his 59th year, after a lingering decline, Mr. William Bayley, late an eminent surgeon there. His reputation was very high in the various branches of that most useful art; and it must be regarded to his praise, his humanity and tenderness were not inferior to his distinguished professional abilities. He was universally loved in the neighbourhood and died most sincerely lamented.

19 March 1793. NICOLL. Mrs. Nicoll, relict of Francis Carter N. Esq., of St. Albans. She left the world infinitely regretted, not only by the large circle of acquaintance, but (which is still a more speaking evidence of departed merit) by the poor and indigent, whose wants her benevolence pitied, and her charity abundantly relieved.
Baptized at Hatfield 1 October 1724, she was Ann, daughter of John Searancke, brewer, and sister and co-heir of John Searancke who died 1779. Her husband died in 1782 (see above), and she was buried with him at St. Albans Abbey. [HG]

22 March 1793. CURRY. Aged 63, by his horse suddenly falling down in Cheshunt Street, Hertfordshire, Mr. Curry of Hoddesdon. He was taken up sensible, but survived the accident only 2 hours, and was buried at Bramfield, near Hertford, with his wife.

16 April 1793. WRIGHT. At Cheshunt, Hertfordshire, in his 69th year, R. Wright, druggist of London.

21 April 1793. ROSS. Andrew Ross, in his 65th year, of Knight's Hill, Hertfordshire.

4 May 1793. CALVERT. At his brother's house at Portland Place, in his 68th year, Nicholas Calvert of Hunsdon House, Hertfordshire, formerly M.P. for Tewkesbury.

23 May 1793. WORSLEY. At Hertford, suddenly, Mrs. Worsley, wife of John Worsley, schoolmaster in that town.

20 June 1793. DUNDAS. At Moneyhill House [Rickmansworth], Hertfordshire, Captain James Dundas, of the Earl Fitzwilliam East Indiaman.

26 June 1793. NASH. Of a deep decline, in the prime of life, Miss Nash, only daughter of Mr. George Nash of Tring, Hertfordshire.

c. June 1793. LAMBORNE. At Buckland, Hertfordshire, aged 95, Mrs. Lamborne, formerly of Cambridge, and mother of Mr. P.C. Lamborne, late portrait painter there.

7 July 1793. GORDON. Near Hertford, the lady of the Rev. Sir Adam Gordon, Bart., rector of Hinxworth; whose loss will be long regretted, particularly by her poor neighbours, for her amiable manners and great goodness of heart.

29 July 1793. GREATRAKE. At an advanced age, much and justly regretted by all who knew her, Mrs. Greatrake, wife of Mr. Greatrake of Apsley Mill, Hertfordshire.

4 August 1793. GINGER. At his seat at Hemel Hempstead, William Ginger, Esq., attorney, much respected in his profession.

18 August 1793. WORTHAM. In London, whither he came two days before, for medical assistance, Hale Wortham, Esq., attorney, of Royston.

24 August 1793. ROBINSON. Of a decline, at St. Albans, aged 66, Thomas Robinson, who had been 40 years waiter at the White Hart inn in that town, and, by his attention and acquaintance with the antiquities of the place, rendered himself useful to all the guests. He left two daughters, one of whom succeeded, in a small shop, her mother, who died about 6 years ago.

25 August 1793. JENKS. Rev. David Jenks, M.A., rector of Northchurch and Little Gaddesden, Hertfordshire.

c. August 1793. IBBETSON. At her house at Bushey, Hertfordshire, Mrs. Ibbetson, relict of the archdeacon of St. Albans.

29 August 1793. DOMVILLE. At Bath, whither she went for the recovery of her health, Mrs. Domville, wife of William Domville, of St. Albans, Hertfordshire.

14 September 1793. HALE. At Chelsea, in his 78th year, William Hale, Esq., of King's Walden, Hertfordshire.

c. November 1793. PEMBROKE. Lately, at Reading, Berkshire, in his 80th year, George Pembroke, in the commission of the peace for Hertford and formerly Receiver-general of the land and window tax for that county.

1 November 1793. BLACKWELL. Suddenly, at Watford, Hertfordshire, Mrs. Blackwell, relict of Mr. Charles Blackwell of the Strand.

9 November 1793. SEDGWICKE. At his house at Cheshunt, Nathaniel Sedgwicke, Esq., of the Inner Temple.

14 November 1793. KENTISH. At Bath, Mrs. Kentish, wife of John Kentish, Esq., of St. Albans.

Born c.1742, she was Hannah, daughter and heir of Keaser Vanderplank, and married 1766 John Kentish (third son of Thomas Kentish, above, 3 April 1774) who was mayor of St. Albans 1787 and 1794, and died 1814. Both buried at St. Albans Abbey. [HG]

20 November 1793. WEBSTER. Thomas Webster, Esq., of Organ Hall [Aldenham], near Shenley, Hertfordshire.

The English Place-name Society (Hertfordshire) records the name Orgonehalle as early as 1272, but 'the precise reason for the name is lost beyond recovery.' [AJ]

26 November 1793. WEST. At his house in Harley Street, Cavendish Square, John Balchen West, Esq., receiver-general for the county of Hertford, and second son of the late Admiral West.

1 December 1793. CHITTY. at Great Berkhamsted, Rev. George Henry Chitty, late rector of Upper Winchendon, near Aylesbury, together with the second portion of Waddesdon, both in the gift of the Duke of Marlborough.

14 December 1793. SMITH. Mrs. Elizabeth Smith, wife of William Smith, Esq., of Nascott, near Watford, Hertfordshire.

26 December 1793. WILD. Found drowned in a ditch, near the Bell, at

Bushey, Hertfordshire, Mr. John Wild, of the Axe and Gate, Downing Street; the oldest publican in Westminster, and, perhaps, the tallest, as he was six feet three inches high. He had been a yeoman of the guards, and kept the Axe and Gate upwards of forty years. His circumstances were affluent; but he could never be prevailed on to make a will, in the weak, though not uncommon, persuasion, that the distance between making his will, and his mortal dissolution must be small.

Mr. Wild was buried at Bushey January 1; and the company returning were attacked by a highwayman, who fired into a chaise fortunately without doing mischief; and, being immediately pursued by the postillion on one of the horses, was taken on the Edgware road near Kilburn, but not before he had twice fired at his pursuers; after which he was knocked down, and carried before Mr. Addington at Bow Street, where it appeared he was the son of a gentleman of independent property in Ireland, of the name of Hawkins.

10 January 1794. CAMPBELL. At his seat at Hemel Hempstead, in his 87th. year, the Right Hon. Hugh Hume Campbell, Earl of Marchmont, Viscount Blassonbury, Lord Polwarth, Red Braes, and Greenlaw, in the county of Berwick, and a baronet. . . . [et seq]

c. January 1794. HARE. Lately, at Hatfield, Hertfordshire, much lamented, the Rev. Samuel Hare, rector of Beachampton, and vicar of Wolverton, near Stony Stratford, Buckinghamshire. The former living, which he had held almost 42 years, is in the patronage of the Marquis of Salisbury. The latter, of the Trustees of the late Dr. Radcliffe, of Oxford.

c. January 1794. SMITH. At Hertford, aged 67, Mr. John Smith.

29 January 1794. HIDE. At Stanstead [Abbots], near Ware, Hertfordshire, Mr. Jn. Hide, late malt meter [sic] of that place. He had acquired a large fortune with a fair character.

23 February 1794. SEABRIGHT. At his house in Curzon Street, Mayfair, Sir John Seabright, Bart., of Beachwood, Hertfordshire, a general in the army, and colonel of the 18th regiment of foot. He was the younger son of Sir Thomas Saunders Seabright, Bart., and succeeded his brother, the late baronet, in 1765. He once represented the city of Bath in parliament; and married, in June 1766, Sarah daughter of Edward Knight, Esq., of Wolverley, Worcestershire, by whom he has left one son.

23 February 1794. BYDE. In Wigmore Street, Cavendish Square, in her 73rd. year, Mrs. Byde, relict of Thomas Plumer Byde, Esq., of Ware Park, Hertfordshire.

26 February 1794. HAWKES. In his 39th year, Mr. William Hawkes, of Bishop's Stortford, brewer and banker. He was possessed of fine abilities, which he much improved and enlarged by reading. Of an amiable disposition, exemplary in every rank and relation of life; and particularly eminent for his liberality to the poor, as well as for promoting every scheme and work of a benevolent kind.

William Hawkes was the son of Thomas Hawkes and Elizabeth née Woodham. From about 1787, William Woodham, William Hawkes and Thomas Bird, important Bishop's Stortford maltsters, brewers and barge-owners, were carrying out 'quasi-banking activities' in the town, following the increase in trade following the opening of the Stort Navigation in 1769. By 1794, they were known as Woodham, Hawkes and Bird, bankers, but apparently had closed by 1799, when Mortlock & Co. opened an office in North Street, Bishop's Stortford. Hawkes Brewery, Northgate End, Bishop's Stortford was built in 1780. Under the owner-ship of the Hawkes family with various partners, it expanded until 1898, when it was acquired by Benskins. Brewing at the site ceased in 1916, but it was used as a depot until 1987. The buildings have now been demolished and the site is about to be developed. [WW]

c. February 1794. NEWBERY. Suddenly, Rev. Samson Newbery, B.D., rector of Bushey, Hertfordshire, and late fellow of Exeter College, Oxford.

c. February 1794. CALVERT. Mrs. Calvert, relict of Peter Calvert, Esq., late of Hadham, Hertfordshire.

c. March 1794. DELAMAR. Lately, at Cheshunt, in the house where Richard Cromwell ended his days, 1712, Mr. Isaac Delamar, many years an eminent silk weaver in Spitalfields, but had retired from busi-ness. He was brother to the late Mr. John Delamar of Cheshunt, and was interred in the family vault in Bunhill burial ground, aged about 70.

18 April 1794. KENT. At St. Albans, aged about 70, Mrs. Martha Kent.

19 May 1794. ST. JOHN. At her house, St. John Lodge, near Welwyn, Hertfordshire, Mrs. Frances St. John, eldest daughter and one of the co-heiresses of the late Sir Francis St. John, Bart., of Long Thorpe, Northamptonshire.

14 June 1794. WILLIAMS. In Theobalds Park, Enfield, aged 95, Mr. Williams, farmer.

21 June 1794. PLACKETT. At Totteridge, Hertfordshire, in his 68th. year, John Plackett, Esq., of Monks House, Northumberland.

25 June 1794. FIOTT. At Totteridge, much regretted by all her acquain-tance, and a real loss to her relations and friends, the lady of Jn. Fiott, Esq.

25 June 1794. GORING. In Theobalds Park, Mrs. Goring, aged 82, of which she had been 12 years totally blind, wife of Mr. Goring, farmer; and on 11th July, she was buried in Cheshunt churchyard in a brick grave 9 feet 6in. deep.

28 June 1794. MATHER. Suddenly, at his house at Hoddesdon, Hertfordshire, in his 45th year, William Mather, Esq.

19 July 1794. KITCHINER. Suddenly, while at breakfast, having been slightly indisposed some days, in his 64th year, William Kitchiner, Esq., of Beaufort Buildings, Strand. Mr. Kitchiner came to London from Hertfordshire early in his life, having little more to introduce him than a good constitution and a countenance which engaged regard. He found, what many good citizens have done before him, that merit would be his best friend, and that "virtue is its own reward". He began as porter at a coal wharf, and in that business he succeeded. By a steady industry he realized a very large fortune, not less than £2000 a-year. Being in the commission of the peace for Westminster, he occasionally filled the judi-

cial chair at Bow Street with credit to the bench and to himself. He sometimes went down to the watering-places for a season, but kept no country
house. He resigned business, a few years ago, in favour of two young men
who were his clerks. His only daughter, by his first wife, who was dead,
was sent to a boarding school, where was also a young lady nearly related
to a noble marquis and to the late Rev. William Cecil Grave, rector of
Bishops Hatfield, Hertfordshire. An acquaintance thus commenced, was
kept up, and in due time these young friends were more nearly allied. Mr.
Kitchiner found this gentlewoman deserving, and married her. By this
lady, who survives him, he has left an only son, now 16, and a promising
youth, on whom, it is said, he has settled £30,000. About three years ago
he unfortunately lost an eye by a dangerous boyish custom, too frequent
at school, of throwing a paper arrow, armed with a pin, at each other. By
an advantageous contract with the Earl of Salisbury, he has a clear £500
a-year from a coal wharf on that nobleman's estate. Mr. Kitchiner was
buried, on the 26th, in the vault of his parish church, St. Clement Danes.

22 July 1794. COOKE. At her house on Turner's Hill, Cheshunt,
advanced in age, Mrs. Cooke.

31 August 1794. SMALL. At Ware, in Hertfordshire, aged 84, Alexander
Small, Esq., F.A.S., formerly an eminent surgeon in London.

2 September 1794. COTTIN. Alexander Cottin, Esq., of Cheverells
[Flamstead], Hertfordshire, in the commission of the peace for that
county.

12 September 1794. PIERSON. At Hitchin, in a deep decline, aged 22,
Mr. J. Pierson, eldest son of Mr. J.M. Pierson, banker there.

*Joseph Margetts Pierson, a maltster, brewer and grocer, was one of the four founding part-
ners of the Hitchin Hertfordshire Bank in 1789. It had been intended that son John should
enter the business, but after he died, the only surviving son, J.M. Pierson junior took over
on his father's retirement in 1805. [JP]*

30 September 1794. GROVE. At the Rev. Mr. Price's, at Knebworth,
Hertfordshire, aged 85, Mrs. Grove, late of Leicester Square.

5 October 1794. DASENT. At Northaw, Hertfordshire, Mr. George
Dasent, son of the Hon. John Dasent, deceased, late chief justice of the
island of Nevis.

11 October 1794. STEELE. At Cheshunt, Hertfordshire, after a long and
painful illness, the lady of Samuel Steele, Esq.

7 November 1794. WHITE. Miss Rebecca White, eldest daughter of Mr.
Peter White of Broxbourne, Hertfordshire.

10 November 1794. PAXTON. At Watford Place, Hertfordshire, Mrs.
Paxton, the lady of Archibald Paxton, Esq., and daughter of William
Gill, Esq., alderman of London.

12 November 1794. HAMMOND. At Enfield, in her 25th year, after having been a fortnight delivered of a daughter, her first child, Mrs.
Hammond, wife of Mr. Thomas Hammond, apothecary there, and
daughter of Mr. Complin, formerly an eminent apothecary in Prescot

Street, Goodman's Fields; and, on the 18th, her remains were deposited in the family vault in St. Andrew's church at Hertford.

20 December 1794. PYNER. Suddenly, at the house of William Newdicke, Esq., of Cheshunt, Hertfordshire, the affectionate and much lamented wife of Francis Pyner, Esq., of Brook House, Cheshunt; and formerly an auctioneer in London.

25 December 1794. CRABB. At Royston, in Cambridgeshire, the Rev. Habakkuk Crabb, who (to adopt his own modest language) "conducted the devotions" of an independent congregation of Christians.

[Here follows a very long obituary. No further reference to Hertfordshire people or places.]

26 December 1794. STRUTT. Aged 70, Joseph Strutt, Esq., of Rickmansworth, Hertfordshire, brother to Jed Strutt, Esq., of New Mills, Derbyshire.

8 January 1795. WATT. At Northaw Place, Hertfordshire, in child-bed, the lady of A. Watt.

2 February 1795. PYNSENT. At Cheshunt House, Mr. William Pynsent, many years steward to John Shaw, Esq., lord of that manor.

8 February 1795. PARSONS. At Shantock Farm, near St. Albans, Hertfordshire, after a lingering illness, Mrs. Parsons, wife of Mr. John Parsons, farmer, and daughter of the late Mr. Fulham, archdeacon of Landaff.

19 February 1795. ADAMS. At Enfield, aged about 50, of an asthmatic complaint, Mrs. Adams, relict of Mr. Adams of the Court of Chancery. Mrs. Adams, who died at Enfield, February 19, was relict of the late Mr. Patient Adams, one of the silazers of the Court of Common Pleas.

Mr. Patience-Thomas Adams (not Mr. Patient Adams as there printed) held the office of silazer, exigenter, and clerk of the outlawries, in the Court of King's Bench, now filled by a son of Lord Kenyon. Mr. Adams was of Hatton Street, London, and of Bushey Grove, Hertfordshire, and died within these two or three years.

February 1795. STOCKWELL. After a long and lingering illness of a high scorbutic complaint, amounting almost to a leprosy, the Rev. Thomas Stockwell, rector of Wotton and vicar of Broxbourne, Hertfordshire; the former, to which he was presented in 1781, in the gift of the lord of the manor, and, we believe, reserved for a son of the late lord, on the sale of the estate, a turn having been purchased by Mr. Stockwell of the Butler family, in which Mr. Stockwell succeeded Mr. Rothwell, after 1728; the latter in the gift of the Bishop of London. Mr. Stockwell was of Oriel or Corpus Christi college, Oxford.

27 February 1795. MONK. At her house at Edmonton, of a paralytic stroke, aged 64, Mrs. Monk, mother of Mr. Monk of Bury Green, Cheshunt, and of eight daughters.

1 March 1795. GORE. After a long and lingering illness, at her house in

Albemarle Street, Mrs. Susan Gore, youngest daughter of the late John Gore, Esq., of Bush Hill, and sister to the two Mrs. Mellishes, who died last year. Her remains were interred, in the family vault at Tring, March 10.

17 March 1795. HERBERT. At his house at Cheshunt, in his 77th year, of a dropsical complaint, the learned and industrious Mr. William Herbert. The various labours of this good man's life demand the public acknowledgement. His career commenced in the service of the East India Company, as purser's clerk to three of their ships. [A long and detailed obituary follows].

3 April 1795. CROSHOLD. At Norwich, of a dropsical complaint, Mrs. Sarah Croshold, sister of Mrs. Herbert, wife of the late Mr. W. Herbert who died last month, at Cheshunt.

April 1795. HINDE. At Preston Castle, near Hitchin, of a decline, Charles Venables Hinde, Esq., third son of the late Captain Peter Hinde. [But see June 1795, below].

18 April 1795. BROWNING. At Watford, Hertfordshire, aged 82, Mrs. Browning.

14 May 1795. CARTER. At the house of his son, in Upper Gower Street, Thomas Richard Carter, Esq., of Bayford, Hertfordshire.

c. June 1795. HINDE. At Hunsdon House, Hertfordshire, Charles Venables Hinde, Esq., son of Colonel Hinde late of the 2nd troop guards. [But see April 1795, above].

22 August 1795. GOODALL. At Barnet, aged 70, John Goodall, Esq., of the South Sea House.

9 September 1795. BARRON. Mr. Charles Barron, wine merchant, of Ware, Hertfordshire.

13 September 1795. DENT. At Cheshunt, Hertfordshire, aged 90, Mrs. Dent, one of the oldest inhabitants of that town.

c. September 1795. BARWICK. At Clare Hall, Hertfordshire, Mrs. Barwick, relict of John Barwick, Esq.

c. November 1795. BOWLBY. At Jenningsbury, Hertfordshire, Thomas Bowlby, Esq., Commissary-General of the Musters.

6 December 1795. GRIFFITHS. At Hitchin, Hertfordshire, aged 59, the Rev. Jn. Griffiths, upwards of 20 years minister of the Independent congregation of Protestant Dissenters at that place.

John Griffiths was born in 1736, and was minister at Stockwill Chapel, Hinckley 1767–1772, then at Hitchin 1772–1795. He was educated for the dissenting ministry at Abergavenny Academy. (See also Hine, History of Hitchin, v.2, 118–124). [AR]

10 December 1795. GARROW. At Barnet, William Garrow, M.D., brother of the Rev. Mr. Garrow, master of the academy at Hadley, near Barnet, and uncle to the celebrated Serjeant. Many hundred persons, of all ranks, in that extensive and populous neighbourhood, will long regret the loss of a physician whose private and professional worth they have many years known and experienced. His loss to the poor will not easily be repaired. Two letters from Dr. Garrow, written so long ago as the year 1752, relative to the controversy between the late Dr. Hunter and the two Professors Monro, of Edinburgh, are inserted in the Medical Commentaries published by Dr. Hunter.

16 December 1795. BARED. Aged 69, at his seat at Beechen Grove, Watford, William Bared, Esq.

26 December 1795. FIRMIN. At Turnford, Hertfordshire, Mrs. Firmin, wife of Mr. Firmin of the Strand.

January 1796. JACKSON. Rev. Samuel Jackson, M.A., of Merton college, rector of Little Gaddesden, Hertfordshire.

20 February 1796. STRATTON. Thomas Stratton, Esq., of the Grove, Hackney. He has left a son, resident at Essington [Essendon?], Hertfordshire; and a daughter, married to the Rev. Mr. Fuller, formerly minister of the Presbyterian congregation at Enfield.

21 February 1796. SAUNDERS. In Theobalds Park, aged 24, after the birth of her second child at 7 months end, the wife of Mr. Saunders, farmer, and only daughter of Mr. Ninny, of Enfield.

10 March 1796. AMSINCK. At Little Gaddesden, Hertfordshire, Mrs. Amsinck, respected while living, and now lamented by all who knew her.

20 March 1796. AYRE. At Cheshunt, Hertfordshire, in his 56th year, the Rev. A. Ayre, rector of Leverington, in the Isle of Ely, and Outwell, Norfolk; to both which he was presented by the bishop of Ely, 1774. He was chaplain to Dr. Law, bishop of Carlisle; B.A. 1760; M.A. 1772; and married a sister of the Rev. Mr. Underwood, rector of East Barnet.

13 April 1796. NORTON. Far advanced in years, at her house at Little Gaddesden, Hertfordshire, Mrs. Anne Norton, youngest daughter and co-heiress of the late Gervas Norton, Esq., of Kettlethorp, Yorkshire.

13 April 1796. LITTLEHALES. At Berkhamsted, on her way home, Miss Sophia Littlehales, youngest daughter of the Rev. Dr. Littlehales, of Bicester, Oxfordshire.

1 May 1796. WOODCOCK. May 1. At Enfield, of spasms in the stomach, just after her return from visiting Mrs. Hardy, one of her daughters, whose only child was lately dead under inoculation, Mrs. Woodcock, relict of the late Dr. W. rector of Watford, who died June 6, 1792. She was (the) only daughter of Thomas Whitfield, Esq., of Watford Place, Hertfordshire, formerly in the profession of the law, and had a handsome fortune. She had also the manor of the Wick in Hackney parish, bought by her father-in-law. Her remains were interred on the 8th in the church of West Haddon, Northamptonshire, where her husband had an estate and was buried.

29 May 1796. VANDER MEULEN. At St. Albans, Hertfordshire, Mrs. Vander Meulen, wife of Joseph Vander Meulen, Esq., of Tokenhouse Yard, merchant.

11 June 1796. WHITBREAD. At Bedwell Park, Hertfordshire, in his 76th year, Samuel Whitbread, Esq., whose abilities, integrity, benevolence, and public spirit, will transmit his character with respect to the latest posterity. His father was a yeoman of Bedfordshire, who lived at the Barns, at Cardington in that county, on an estate of about £200 per annum, which devolved to his eldest son, who much improved it by building, and spent much of his time at it after he purchased Bedwell Park. He is said to have died worth a million at least; the bulk of which he has bequeathed to his son. He was half-brother to Ive Whitbread, Esq., hardwareman, of Cannon Street, and sheriff of London with Mr. Beckford, in 1755. By his first wife, Harriet, daughter of Haytor, an eminent attorney, of London, whom he married in 1757, and who died in 1764, he has left issue a son, Samuel, gentleman-commoner of Christ Church, Oxford, and representative of the town of Bedford in several parliaments after his father gave it up, and two daughters; the eldest married, 1789, to James Gordon, junior, Esq., of More Park, Hertfordshire; the younger, Emma, to Henry Beauchamp Lord St. John of Bletso, 1780. Mr. Whitbread married to his second wife, 1769, Lady Mary, youngest daughter of the late Earl, and sister to the present Marquis, Cornwallis, who died in 1770, in childbed of an only daughter, married, in June 1795, to Captain George Grey, late of the Boyne man of war, of 98 guns (see vol. LXV p.433), third son of Sir Charles Grey, KB, and nephew of Sir Harry Grey, Bart., whose sister was married in 1788 (see vol. LVIII p.82), to the present Mr. Whitbread and by whom he has several children.

His extensive establishments in the brewery were long unrivalled, and perhaps, to a certain point, remain so still, and excited the envy even of a poet, who spares not royalty, though, in this instance of his satire, he has perpetuated a compliment to the sovereign and the man of malt by coupling them together. (Of the royal visit see our vol. LVII P.633). Mr. Whitbread's liberal charity will be witnessed by every parish where he had property, and in the distribution of his private benevolence, which is said to have exceeded £3000 per annum; for no proper application met with a repulse; and to his honour let it here be recorded, that, several years before his death, he settled on St. Luke's Hospital of Lunatics, a perpetual rent-charge of one hundred guineas, payable out of his extensive premises in Chiswell Street. As a senator, he maintained his independence and integrity, his walk through life being uniform and unostentatious. His speech on the inequality of the land tax, in which he mentioned his estates in the counties of Lincoln and Leicester, may be seen in vol. XLVIII p.197; on a corn bill in relief of a great scarcity, 1788, LVIII, 110; on the loan of that year, ibid, 736; on the evasion of the receipt tax, LIV, 474, 619.

20 June 1796. VEARY. At St. Albans, aged 56, Martha Veary, 26 years a true and faithful servant to the venerable clerk of the abbey church.

4 July 1796. SCUDAMORE. At his seat at Kentchurch, Herefordshire, in his 68th year. John Scudamore, Esq., a few weeks before elected, for the sixth time, to represent the city of Hereford in parliament, by the unanimous voice of the citizens. His death was occasioned by a cold caught, after hunting in his park, by the too sudden check of perspiration; every effort of the ablest of the faculty to preserve so valuable a life was ineffectual. In his public character, as an useful and disinterested member of parliament, and an active magistrate, he was deservedly respected; as the pleasant and amiable friend and accomplished gentleman, he will be long sincerely lamented. Mr. Scudamore married, August 26, 1756, Miss Wescomb, only daughter of Nicholas Wescomb, Esq., of Langford, Essex, of Lincolnshire, and of Cheverill's Green [Flamstead], Hertfordshire, with a fortune of £3000; whom he has left a widow, with two sons, the eldest a lieutenant-colonel in the Essex fencibles, and a deserving candidate for the honour so repeatedly bestowed on his father; and one daughter, married to James Hereford, Esq., of Saffron Court, near Hereford. Mrs. Scudamore was interred in Kentchurch, the burial place of his ancestors for many generations, the Scudamores being one of the oldest families in Herefordshire.

26 July 1796. FIELD. At Stoke Newington, in his 78th year, Mr. John Field, many years an eminent apothecary in Newgate Street. Of a man so greatly esteemed by an extensive circle of relations and friends, we presume a short biographical sketch will not be unacceptable. He was descended from an ancient family of that name, who had been long settled in the northwest parts of Hertfordshire. His grandfather (the common ancestor of a numerous family, now residing chiefly in London) was Thomas Field, of Cockernhoe [Offley], a gentleman farmer, who lived upon, and farmed, his own lands. [Here follows a long biography which has no more mentions of Hertfordshire families and places].

25 August 1796. BUCKNALL. At Gorhambury, Hertfordshire, in his 79th year, John Askell Bucknall, Esq., of Oxhey, in the same county, uncle to the present Viscount Grimston, whose father, James, 2nd Viscount, married Mary, daughter of J.R. Bucknall, Esq., and has by her James Bucknall Grimston, 3rd and present Viscount, to whom Mr. Bucknall has left his fortune, amounting to £150,000. James Bucknall, Esq., M.P. for St. Albans is a distant relation.

31 August 1796. HOLMES. In Portman Place, Mr. Edward Holmes, many years an eminent paper-maker at Two Waters, Hemel Hempstead, Hertfordshire.

4 September 1796. HAWKINS. At Gaddesden, near Hemel Hempstead, Hertfordshire, Mrs. Hawkins. She was 2nd wife of Charles Hawkins, Esq., 2nd son of Sir Caesar Hawkins, surgeon, late of London, but retired from practice a few years ago to Gaddesden.

27 September 1796. DOO. In his 70th year, Mr. John Doo, of Chipping [Buckland], in Hertfordshire.

7 October 1796. COLLINS. Aged 102, at Little Berkhamsted, Hertfordshire, Jane Collins, a poor industrious widow, who, a very few days before her death, walked more than four miles, carrying a basket of vegetables under her arm.

5 November 1796. DAINTRY. After a short illness, at Royston,

Cambridgeshire, to the inexpressible loss of his family, Mr. Daintry, postmaster of that place, treasurer for the county, and land steward to the Earl of Hardwicke.

The Daintry family continued postmasters in Royston until 1866. The estate of the Earl of Hardwicke was Wimpole Hall, about five miles north of Royston. [AJ]

13 November 1796. WHITE. Miss Elizabeth White, daughter of Peter White, Esq., of Broxbourne, Hertfordshire.

c. December 1796. INGLIS. At Portsmouth, on his way to Lisbon, for the recovery of his health, Robert Inglis, surgeon, at Stratford by Bow, brother to Hugh Inglis, Esq., deputy chairman of the East India Company. He was buried in the family vault at Cheshunt, Sunday, November 15.

9 January 1797. BOSCAWEN. At Haydon, in Essex, the Hon Mrs. Jane Boscawen, relict of the late Hon. and Rev. Dr. Nicholas Boscawen, prebendary of Westminster, who was brother to the deceased admiral of that name, and to the late Lord Falmouth. She was daughter of ———— Woodward, and relict of ———— Hatton, of Stratford-upon-Avon, Warwickshire, Esqrs., and had by Dr. Boscawen two sons; Hugh, born 1755, died the next year, and Nicholas, born 1756.

11 January 1797. CLARKE. Mrs. Clarke, wife of John Clarke, Esq., of Sandridgebury, Hertfordshire, and daughter of the late Dr. Cotton, of St. Albans.

On a plaque in the chancel of St. Leonard's church, Sandridge: "Sacred to the memory of a beloved and most affectionate father John Clarke of Sandridgebury, Esq., who for many years was a zealous and active magistrate for this County. He departed this life the 27th. August AD 1820, ætat 63. Also of Elizabeth his wife, youngest daughter of Nathaniel Cotton, of St. Albans M.D., who departed this life the 10th January AD 1797, ætat 43, and of Phoebe Susannah, their infant daughter who departed this life the 22nd February AD 1793 aged 9 months. Their bodies are interred beneath this marble which was erected by their only surviving daughter." [RA]

March 1797. BOSCAWEN. Mrs. Boscawen died at Sawbridgeworth, Hertfordshire.

4 March 1797. WILDER. In the Fleet prison, in his 40th year, of a mortification in his arm, Mr. Peter Wilder, late of St. James's Street. He was brought up a cook, and married a daughter of Mr. Connor, who kept the Mitre at Barnet, by whom he had Major Francis Wilder of the 106th regiment. This young gentleman was educated at Eton, where he was entered in the name of Lockhart, and, no expense being spared, he had the tuition of the best masters.

9 March 1797. NICCOLL. At Mrs. Chawner's, in Hart Street, Bloomsbury, aged about 40, of an inflammation on her lungs, Miss Niccoll, of St. Albans, who conducted a great brewery in that town, and was sister to Mr. Searancke, brewer, at Hatfield, and to Mrs. Rideout, wife of the Rev. Mr. Rideout, of Court Lodge. She came to town for a few days, in her way to Brighthelmstone [Brighton]; was of a respectable family in the County of Hertford; and, by her life and manners, every way worthy of them. Her greatest pleasure was to support the Christian character, not by reservedness and austerity, but by acts of religion and

charity, good humour and affability; thereby rendering herself agreeable to all, and useful to many. She will therefore, for a long time, be
missed by the rich as well as the poor.

*She was Elizabeth, daughter of Francis Carter Niccoll by his wife Ann, sister and coheir of
John Searancke of Hatfield, brewer. Baptized 28 February 1754 at St. Albans Abbey, and
buried there. Her sister Sarah married (1) Samuel Niccoll of Court Lodge, Mountfield,
Sussex, and (2) the Rev. Richard Rideout, rector of Westmeston, Sussex. Their brother,
Francis Carter Niccoll changed his name to Searancke in 1781 in compliance with his
uncle John Searancke's will, and eventually inherited both the Searancke brewery of
Hatfield and the Niccoll brewery of St. Albans. (See also 15 May 1779, 1 June 1782, etc).
[HG]*

31 March 1797. DOO. Mr. John Doo, of Buckland, Hertfordshire, son of
the late Mr. John Doo of Chipping.

2 April 1797. NEWCOME. At his sister's at Hadley, near Barnet,
Middlesex, aged upwards of 70, of an inflammation on his lungs, occasioned by a neglected cold, the Rev. Peter Newcome, rector of Shenley,
Hertfordshire, which was purchased by his mother about 1742, just
before the death of Philip Falle, the historian of Jersey, and was held
two years by another Peter Newcome, and seven more by Dr. Lewis,
curate of Hackney, for Mr. Newcome, who held a living for some other
person, which was filled before Shenley, to which he was instituted, on
his own petition, in 1751; and, in 1786, to the rectory of Pitsey, in
Essex, on the presentation of Sir Gilbert Heathcote, Bart. He was likewise possessed of a prebend in the church of Llandaff, and of a sinecure
in the diocese of St. Asaph; to both of which he was collated by his
uncle, Bishop Newcome,. He was educated at Hackney school, under his
relation, Dr. Newcome; whence he removed to Queen's college,
Cambridge, where he took the degree of B.LL. in 1750. Some years
since, he preached Lady Moyer's lectures, which were so much
approved, that he had once intended to have made them public. He
printed, 1787, "Maccabeis," a Latin poem, 4to; and, in 1793, published,
in two volumes, 4to, the "History of the Abbey of St. Albans," which has
been well received. His general and useful knowledge rendered him a
valuable member of the community; and his abilities, activity, and
impartiality as a magistrate, will make him long remembered in
Hertfordshire. He made the rectory of Shenley worth near £400 per
annum, and his predecessor improved it by building a very good parsonage house and offices; and Mr. Newcome has left his living to his
nephew.

11 April 1797. SAUNDERSON. Suddenly, while at Hitchin market, Mr.
Lawrence Saunderson, of Radwell Grange, Hertfordshire, an opulent
farmer.

22 April 1797. MILLES. At his house in Harley Street, in his 47th year,
after a very severe and tedious illness, Jeremiah Milles, Esq., of
Pishobury, Hertfordshire, F.A.S., eldest son of the late Dean of Exeter,
by Edith his wife, third daughter of the most Rev. John Potter, late
archbishop of Canterbury. He married in June 1780 Rose, sole daughter
and heiress of Edward Gardiner, Esq., of Pishobury aforesaid; by whom
he has left issue four daughters.

Jeremiah Milles, Esq., was Lord of the Manor of Pishobury. His wife, Rose, only child of Edward Gardiner of Pishobury, died 21 May 1835 age 78. They are commemorated on a wall tablet in Great St. Mary's Church, Sawbridgeworth. [WW]

23 April 1797. GRANT. At Potterells [North Mimms], Hertfordshire, aged 85, Mrs. Grant, relict of Duncan Grant, Esq., late of Antigua.

c. April 1797. COUNTESS OF MARCHMONT. Lately, at her house near Hemel Hempstead, Hertfordshire, Elizabeth Countess of Marchmont. She was the daughter of Mr. Crompton, an eminent silk mercer of London, and second wife of Hume Campbell, Earl of Marchmont, by whom, 1747, she had one son, Lord Polwarth, who married Annabel, eldest of the two daughters of the late Marchioness Grey, and was created Baron Hume in England, but died without issue 1781. She survived her husband, who made so distinguished a figure in the opposition to Sir Robert Walpole, little more than three years, he dying January 10, 1794. The retirement in which they had been for many years will prevent their being missed by the very honourable circle in which they formerly lived; but the loss of both will be most severely felt by those who were relieved by their benevolence, and lamented by the few who shared their society. The late Lord Marchmont had the MSS. of Pope bequeathed to his care, but they were never published. Now that her ladyship is dead also, it is to be hoped that the world will yet be favoured with the papers, as Lord Marchmont had too much taste to destroy them, however unwilling he might be to undergo the trouble of revision and publication.

24 May 1797. FYSH. Mr. B. Fysh, draper, of Watford.

June 1797. SPARHAUKE. At Hinxworth, Hertfordshire, the Rev. John Sparhauke, rector of that place, and vicar of Great Hormead, both in that county, and formerly fellow of St. John's college, Cambridge.

16 September 1797. NEWPORT. At Topsham, Devon, Mrs. Mary Newport, wife of William Newport of St. John's, of Pelham Hall, Hertfordshire.

23 September 1797. IRESON. At Northchurch, Hertfordshire, Miss Ireson, only daughter of the late George Ireson of Hoddesdon.

c. September 1797. SEDGEWICKE. Lately, at Cheshunt, Hertfordshire, Mrs. Penelope Sedgewicke, relict of Nathaniel Sedgewicke.

c. September 1797. HILL. Lately, at St. Albans, Thomas Hill of the White Hart inn there.

14 October 1797. COWPER. in her 71st year, Mrs. Cowper, relict of Major General William Cowper, of Hertingfordbury Park, Hertfordshire.

18 October 1797. BOSANQUET. At Bristol, of a decline, Mrs. Bosanquet, wife of Jacob Bosanquet, of Broxbourne, Hertfordshire, and relict of ————— Grady, Esq., sister of Sir George Armitage, Bart. She was married to Mr. Bosanquet in 1790 and has left him five children.

30 October 1797. HENSHAW. At Barking, Essex, Mrs. Henshaw, relict of the late Mr. Henshaw, of Cheshunt, where her remains were interred November 6.

c. October 1797. MORELL. Lately, at Scarborough, Rev. Thomas Morell, D.D., rector of Buckland, Hertfordshire.

Dr. Thomas Morell was rector of Buckland from 1737 until his death in 1784. Cussans reports that he was buried at Chiswick (where his wife's family resided). He was a man of considerable literary accomplishments, and had been librettist for Handel's Oratories. (If the above entry really does refer to him, the word 'lately' has been rather overstretched). [AJ]

16 January 1798. GREENHILL. At his house at Watford, Hertfordshire, Thomas Greenhill, Esq.

17 January 1798. PENROSE. At his son's house at Hatfield, Dr. Francis Penrose, of Stonehouse, Plymouth.

January 18, 1798. STOWE. At Cheshunt, after lying-in, Mrs. Stowe, wife of Mr. Stowe of that place.

21 January 1798. WILLIAMS. At Clifton Court, after a few hours illness, Sir David Williams, Bart., of Goldingtons [Sarratt], in Hertfordshire.

11 March 1798. HAMMOND. Francis Hammond, Esq., of Potter's Bar, Hertfordshire.

22 March 1798. HERIOT. At Berkhamsted, Hertfordshire, in his 80th year, John Hartwell Heriot, eldest son of John Heriot, Esq., Catherine Street, Strand.

4 April 1798. PARSONS. At Rickmansworth, in his 75th year, John Parsons, Esq., only son of the late Humphry Parsons, Esq., of Reigate, twice lord mayor of London, and brother to the lady of the late Sir John Cotton, of Madingley, Bart. He married Domitilla, sister of Barberini the dancer, who died about two years ago.

9 April 1798. MELLISH. At the Magpie at Hounslow, John Mellish, Esq., of Albemarle Street, St. James's, Westminster and Hamels [Braughing], Hertfordshire, eldest son of the late William Mellish, Esq., of Blythe, by his second wife. The case of this gentleman, whilst peculiarly distressing to his family, is a reproach on the police of this kingdom. He was returning, the Tuesday evening before, from following the royal hounds, with his friend, Mr. Joseph Bosanquet and Mr. ———— Poole, in chaise and four, to town, when they were stopped, on Hounslow Heath, by three highwaymen, who, after robbing them, without resistance, of their money and gold watches, fired wantonly into the chaise as they went off; the ball, supposed to be fired by the third villain, after the robbery was committed, penetrated Mr. Mellish's forehead, just below his hat, and was believed to have found its way down towards the back of his neck, so that it would have been impossible for the united skill of Messieurs Rush, Blizard, and Cline, to extract it. In this situation it was supposed to have remained, without any visible effect on Mr. Mellish's health; who immediately executed his will, and was, till Sunday, perfectly composed. A delirium and violent fever then came on, in which he continued till five in the morning, when he died. His head was opened by the surgeons, but no ball could be found; whence it is conjectured to have dropped out shortly after he was wounded. The brain had received a very violent contusion. Mr. Mellish married, February 17, 1795, Miss Charlotte Pinfold, who died April 8, 1797, with her infant daughter, leaving him an only daughter, born 1796. The murderers afterwards stopped Mr. Frogley, the surgeon, who was sent for; and not only robbed him, but obliged him to turn back from his errand, which they made him tell, so that he was forced to return in a hired carriage.

14 April 1798. RIVETT. At Moresfield, Sussex, Mrs. Rivett, wife of the Rev. Thomas Rivett, rector of that place, and youngest daughter of Culling Smith, Esq., of Popes, Hertfordshire.

28 April 1798. WADE. At Standon, Hertfordshire, Mrs. Margaret Wade, widow of the Rev. William Wade, late of Braughing, in that county.

15 May 1798. CROOK. In Lambs Conduit Street, Mrs. Crook, wife of John Crook, Esq., late of Bushey Grove, Hertfordshire.

8 June 1798. CARTER. At Exmouth, Miss Harriet Carter, daughter of the late Thomas Richard Carter, Esq., of Bayford, Hertfordshire.

9 June 1798. FOWLER. In his 59th year, at his rectory house, of an extraordinary complaint in his stomach, the Rev. Barnard Fowler, B.LL., rector of Wormley, Hertfordshire, to which he was presented by Sir Abraham Hume, in 1788, on the death of Dr. Glen King. He married Miss Skinner, aunt to Miss Egerton, by whom he has left a son, in the East Indies, and three amiable daughters. He held also the rectory of Southminster, Essex, to which he was presented by the governors of the Charterhouse, 1769. He was of Magdalen college, Cambridge, where he took the degree of B.LL. 1769.

11 June 1798. JENNINGS. At her house at Bull's Cross, Enfield, aged 60, of a deep decline, Mrs. Elizabeth Jennings, sister of Mr. Joseph Jennings, deputy warehouse-keeper for the East India Company at Botolph wharf. The grandfather of Mrs. Jennings (who came from St. Albans to Abbots Langley, Hertfordshire) was a first cousin of the late Sarah Duchess of Marlborough's father, whose name was Jennings. [This entry is as amended in G.M. July 1798].

16 June 1798. GRAY. At Hartsbourne Manor Place [Bushey], Hertfordshire, Edward Gray, Esq., of Edward Street, Portman Square, in the commission of the peace for Middlesex.

18 June 1798. BRETON. At his house on Epping Green, Little Berkhamsted, Hertfordshire, in his 55th year, Michael Harvey Breton, Esq., eldest son of the late Eliab [sic] Breton, Esq., of Forty Hill, Enfield. He was admitted a fellow-commoner of Trinity college, Cambridge; and married Miss Martin, by whom he has left a son, and daughter married to her first cousin, a counsellor.

19 June 1798. DOMVILLE. At St. Albans, after a very severe illness, Mrs. Elizabeth Domville.

20 June 1798. LLOYD. At Hertford, Mrs. Lloyd, wife of the Rev. T. Lloyd.

2 July 1798. SMITH. After a lingering illness, at Popes, Hertfordshire, Miss Smith, the only remaining daughter of Culling Smith, Esq., of that place.

28 July 1798. BYRON. At his house at Hertford, Rd. Byron, Esq.

July 1798. BOWRA. The wife of Mr. Bowra, master of the school belonging to Christ's hospital in Hertford.

Rev. William Bowra was the first Grammar Master (as opposed to 'Writing Master') *appointed to Christ's Hospital, Hertford, holding the post from 1783 until his death in 1801. A former pupil, W.P. Scargill, in* Recollections of a Blue Coat Boy *(1829), described him as 'one of the most kind and gentle beings that ever lived; and I feel he rather spoiled us by his too great leniency and neglect.' [AG]*

12 September 1798. KENT. At St. Albans, aged 80, John Kent, plumber and glazier, but better known to the lovers of antiquity as the venerable and intelligent Clerk of the Abbey, which place he filled near fifty-two years, being appointed October 26, 1746, by the Rev. John Cole, archdeacon and rector of St. Albans, who died September 1, 1754 (see volume XXIV p.435). That truly pious Divine, that this favourite of his should not be displaced by his successors, procured him, in July, 1754, a licence under the episcopal seal of Dr. Sherlock, then bishop of London, through which he maintained his place in the church. This year his father died. In July, 1767, his wife died, aged 45; and his mother, aged 84. The latter end of this year, he became, and continued, a very active member of an independent party, termed Blue; and, from his spirit and fortitude during the contest, was called Honest John. This character he maintained to the last, for he was truly an honest man. This spirited election in 1768 terminated in favour of John Radcliffe, Esq., who continued an independent M.P. for this borough until his death 1783 (see volume LIII p.1066). In December, 1794, he lost his eldest son John, aged 48; and, in October, 1795, this was followed by the death of his second son Walter, aged 47. By these strokes he felt heavily the hand of Providence almost to his last, but murmured not.

The Antiquary and the curious Traveller have lost the guide through that sacred pile the Abbey church; the beauties of which he familiarly pointed out, with an accuracy that at once described his wonderful mind and memory. With the late reverend and learned antiquary, Dr. Browne Willis, he was intimate, and also with the Rev. Paul Wright. The celebrated and ingenious Mr. Gough has noticed his intelligence in the second volume of his "Sepulchral Monuments of Great Britain". The late Rev. Peter Newcomb expressed his thanks for the variety of information he had received when compiling his "History of the Abbey," accompanied with a copy of that instructive and laborious work. His veneration for the sacred particles deposited there often created disputes; the monks could not have taken more care of the shrine of St. Alban that he did of the remains of good Duke Humphrey; for he would not suffer, if he knew it, a thread of his cloak to have been purloined; and, 40 years ago (as he told some gentlemen who visited the Abbey in August, 1798), he caused the wooden stall to be made which inclosed the Duke's remains. The following circumstance, known to the writer of this, was related by Mr. Kent. Some years ago, Kent suspected a gentleman, now deceased (who never passed the town without taking a view of the church), of having taken a piece of bone from this hallowed tomb; and frequently mentioned his suspicion whenever the gentleman came again, which usually passed with a smile. But their last interview was, "Kent, I am come for the last time to look at your Abbey". When in the vestry together, the person said, "I am come on purpose to deposit this piece of bone into that sacred place from which it was taken; for, I could not depart easy with it in my possession". At another time he received, from an unknown hand, a piece of bone in a parcel, desiring him to take care and put it into Humphrey's tomb.

He had not less veneration for the building itself; and perhaps there is not its equal in the kingdom, wherein the beauties of ancient architecture are so magnificently displayed. This ancient edifice was his constant care, and engrossed his attention so much, that it would have given him great concern to have seen any part thereof despoiled by the crude architect of the present day. It must be added, that he was not alarmed for the safety of the church, like the architect who wrote an account of the storm in volume LXVII, p.928 [see Main Sequence, Sept.-Oct. 1797]; for, when looking into the magazine (of which he was a constant reader), he smiled at the idea. With that gentleman Mr. Kent was well acquainted; and it may be lamented that he will lose some information he may want in the completion of his laborious and architectural designs of that much-admired place.

As a convivial and social companion, Mr. Kent's company was courted. The Society of College Youths, of which he was a member, he annually entertained with his favourite ditty called The Old Courtier; which also was annually called for at the mayor of St.Albans feast, by the nobility and gentry, and received with a thunder of applause. In his official station as parish clerk, it may not be presumption to say that in psalmody he was excelled by no one, and equalled by few, particularly in the old Hundredth Psalm. He had a voice strong and melodious, and was himself a compleat master of church music; always pleased to hear the congregation join. It has been often remarked, when country choristers came from a neighbouring parish to perform in the Abbey, with instruments termed by him a box of whistles, with which the congregation could not join, he, on those occasions, gave out the Psalm or Anthem in this way: "Sing YE to the praise and glory of God". He was rarely absent from his desk; and, though of late he laboured under much weakness, and was frequently confined during the week, "he was always in the Spirit on the Lord's Day".

So wonderfully was he assisted in the church, that, notwithstanding, in the month of June, 1793, he had a first stroke of the palsy, which he called a body blow, and much distorted his mouth, and occasioned him to stammer in conversation, in worship it could not be discerned. His last essay was on a public occasion, Monday, September 10, that of the consecration of a pair of colours presented to that spirited corps, the St. Albans Volunteers, by the Honourable Miss Grimstone, when he sang the Twentieth Psalm before one of the most respectable and largest congregations that ever assembled within those sacred walls (once the pride of mitred abbots). He performed with all the strength and vivacity of youth. To adopt the language of the present popular and respectable rector, in his funeral sermon, "To have heard him on that day, Nature seemed to have re-assumed her throne, and, as if she knew it was to be his last effort, was determined it should be his best".

It was so. He was interred in the abbey September 19, in a spot marked by himself. His funeral was respectfully attended; and his death is universally felt amidst the neighbourhood, and particularly by his relict, one son, a daughter, and eight grandchildren. Death, which was always familiar to him, eased him this last year, by taking his only sister, aged 83; and her husband, aged 85. In this he had his prayer granted, "That they both might depart before him". May those who are left behind him tread in his pious steps! T.C.

In this memorial of a lay officer of St. Albans Abbey, John Kent, 1718–1798, four aspects are of special interest: the gothic revival, the functioning of the abbey in the eighteenth century, the corporate life of the town in that period and the Kent family genealogy. The achievements of the great antiquaries like Browne Willis, 1682–1760, Richard Gough, 1735–1809 and the Rev. Peter Newcome of Shenley are well known, but here we see them gathering their material, in earnest concourse with a local historian. Kent's intimate knowledge of the abbey, acquired over a lifetime, had made him an unrivalled specialist on this particular building. Against this must be placed his complacency over the structural safety of the decaying fabric. From 1550 to 1845, the archdeaconry of St. Albans lay in the Diocese of London. Interesting glimpses emerge of eighteenth century parish life, the role of the parish clerk in the conduct of worship, the provision of church music in voice and instrument, burials still common within the building and a Romantic pre-occupation with the macabre.There are glimpses of civil life, in the conduct of elections, the precarious life expectancy, and social strata and the festivities enjoyed. Of the Kent family itself, genealogical details over five generations: indeed, two of Kent's descendants achieved later roles in local government: John Walter Kent, plumber, served three terms as Town Councillor in the 1840s, while Thomas Weedon Kent, brewer of Holywell Hill, served variously as Councillor and Alderman between 1862 and 1880 and was elected Mayor in 1880. [ER]

18 September 1798. BRASSEY. At the Green Man on Blackheath, on his way from Ramsgate, aged 46, Nathaniel Brassey, Esq., banker, of Lombard Street; and, on the 25th, his remains were interred at Hertingfordbury with his father, who was also a banker, and represented the town of Hertford, and died in 1765. Mr. Brassey married the eldest daughter of Aston Lee, Esq., banker, by whom he had several children.

20 September 1798. GARROW. At Totteridge, Hertfordshire, Mrs. Garrow, wife of Edward Garrow, Esq. She was taken suddenly with a pain in her head at the card-table on the 17th, and never recovered.

20 September 1798. SANDERS. At Shenfield Place, Essex, Mrs. Sanders, wife of Mr. Thomas Sanders, surgeon and apothecary of Cheshunt, Hertfordshire.

24 September 1798. BOUVERIE. At her seat at Teston, in Kent, in her 72nd year, Mrs. Elizabeth Bouverie, eminent for the moderation with which she enjoyed, and for the beneficent use she made of a large fortune.

Mrs. Bouverie, who died September 22, became possessed of Teston by the will of Sir Philip Boteler, Bart., who married as his first wife her aunt, Anne, daughter of Sir Edward Desbouverie, and died, without issue, 1772. He bequeathed one moiety of all his estates, both real and personal, without any specific allotments, to this lady, then of Chart

Sutton, and the other to Elizabeth dowager Viscountess Folkstone, and her son, William Bouverie, Earl of Radnor, since deceased. They, by private agreement, made a partition of these estates, in which Teston manor and advowson, and the house heretofore called Barham Place, were, with the advowson of Nettlested, the tithes of West Barming, the manors of Tusham and Ewell, with other premises, were allotted to Mrs. Bouverie, who enjoyed Teston house, with the park, gardens, and lands thereto belonging; all which she had been for some years improving, with such elegance of taste, that this seat is become one of the greatest ornaments of that part of the country. (See Hasted's Kent, II 292.) Christopher Desbouverie, Knt., of Chart Sutton, 7th son of Sir Edward Desbouverie, Knt., of Cheshunt, Hertfordshire, married Elizabeth daughter of Ralph Freeman, Esq., of Beechworth, Surrey, and was father of Mrs. Bouverie, who, on the death of her two brothers and her sister, wife of John Harvey, Esq., of Beechworth, became possessed of that estate also.

c. September 1798. BULKELEY. At Hatfield, Hertfordshire, Lady Frances Bulkeley, wife of the Rev. Samuel Bulkeley and eldest daughter of the late Earl of Peterborough, born in 1736.

c. September 1798. RADCLIFFE. At Hitchin Priory, Hertfordshire, of a lingering illness, Sir Charles Farnaby Radcliffe, Bart., of Kepington, in Sevenoaks parish, Kent, M.P. for Hythe. He married, 1762, Penelope daughter of Ralph, and niece of John, Radcliffe, Esqrs., of Hitchin; and, on the death of the latter, December 21, 1783 (see volume LIII, p.1066), succeeded to his estate, and assumed his name. Dying without issue, the Radcliffe estate devolves to Mr. Clark, son of another sister of the late Mr. John Radcliffe.

c. October 1798. WILSHERE. Advanced in years, after having been long confined by illness, William Wilshere, sen., Esq., of Hitchin, Hertfordshire, attorney at law.

In 1523 the Wilshere family obtained a lease from Holywell Priory, Shoreditch, of The Frythe in Welwyn. Wilsheres remained in occupation there until the present century. During the nineteenth century the family took a prominent part in public affairs, but the William Wilshere who died in 1798 was an intensely private person, notable mainly for the fact that between 1754 and 1775 he fathered fifteen children. He lived appropriately in a house in Hitchin called The Hermitage, in which a later resident, William Seebohm, discovered a secret chamber bearing the date 1789. It was fitted with shelves, and a tube for communication with the outside world. Reginald Hine (Hitchin Worthies, p.328) concluded that Wilshere, like many rich men of his day, expected the French Revolution to spread to England, and was preparing for the worst. [AJ]

9 October 1798. ROPER. At the Rev. Dr. Hay's, canon of Christ Church, Oxford, in her 81st year, Lady Henrietta Roper, widow of the late Robert Roper, Esq., of Muffetts [North Mimms], Hertfordshire, and one of the daughters of George, 7th Earl of Kinnoul.

Robert Roper was Doctor of Law. His marriage settlement of 1771, of which the archbishop of York was a trustee, provided £110 per annum for Lady Henrietta. [PK and WK]

c. October 1798. CUNDELL. At Wormley, Hertfordshire, aged 70, Mr. Cundell, an eminent maltster and contractor, and churchwarden of that parish.

19 November 1798. CLAPHAM. At Cheshunt, of an inflammation in his bowels, aged about 60, Mr. Clapham, a respectable farmer, and many years one of the churchwardens, of that parish, who has left a widow and eleven children to lament him.

20 November 1798. JEFFERYS. At Richmond, Surrey, in his 81st year, the Rev. John Jefferys, D.D., many years canon-residentiary of St. Paul's, and rector of Great Berkhamsted, Hertfordshire.

27 November 1798. COLE. At Hackney, Mrs. Cole; and, on December 5, her remains were interred in Cheshunt church-yard.

12 December 1798. PAGETT. At Totteridge, Hertfordshire, aged 71, the Rev. William Pagett, rector of North Wingfield, Derbyshire.

25 December 1798. CLARKE. At Buntingford, Hertfordshire, Mr. Thomas Clarke, many years a respectable merchant at Cambridge.

31 December 1798. WINDUS. At Ware, in her 84th year, Mrs. Windus, relict of William Windus, Esq., of Hertford.

December 1798. STREET. At Barkway, Hertfordshire, aged 72, the Rev. John Street, vicar there, being patron in his own right, by purchase of the Jennings family. He was of Merton college, Oxford; M.A. 1772.

12 January 1799. MEETKERKE. At her son's house at Julian's, Hertfordshire, aged 72, Mrs. Mary Meetkerke, widow of Adolphus Meetkerke of that place.

13 January 1799. BRACE. At Rickmansworth, Hertfordshire, aged 80, Harris Thurloe Brace, Esq., formerly of the 1st Regiment of dragoon guards.

1 February 1799. ROUS. Suddenly, at Moor Park, Hertfordshire, Thomas Bates Rous, Esq.

Thomas Bates Rous purchased the Moor Park estate in 1785. It was Rous who demolished the two wings which had been connected by colonnades to the main house. he died without issue and the property passed to his widow. [AJ]

6 February 1799. CRAWLEY. At Great Gaddesden Place, Hertfordshire, Mrs. Crawley, relict of the late John Crawley, Esq., of Stockwood, Bedfordshire, in his [sic] 91st year.

7 February 1799. SPOONER. In Northumberland Street, Mrs. Spooner, relict of the late Rev. Joseph Spooner, rector of St. Albans, Hertfordshire.

9 February 1799. COLLINSON. After a lingering illness, John Collison, Esq., of Hitchin.

10 February 1799. READ. Aged 78, at Little Berkhamsted, Hertfordshire, Mrs. Read, relict of the late Samuel Read, Esq., of Balancebury [sic], in that county.

11 February 1799. FITZJOHN. At Baldock, Hertfordshire, aged 52, Mr. George Fitzjohn, maltster, of that town.

12 February 1799. COWPER. At his seat at Cole Green, Hertfordshire, in consequence of the bursting of a blood vessel on the lungs, on the 17th ultimo and in his 23rd year, George Augustus Clavering Cowper, Earl Cowper, Viscount Fordwich, Baron Cowper of Wingham, a baronet, and also a prince of the Holy Roman Empire. The disorder which produced this much-lamented event was an abscess on the lungs, which baffled all the medical skill of Sir Walter Farquhar and Dr. Turton. He had the misfortune, in the spring of last year, to fall from his horse; and to his refusal to be bled at the time, the physicians who attended him attribute his premature death. His Lordship was never perfectly well after this accident, though it was only lately that he was obliged to confine himself to his house. His indisposition commenced with a severe cold, which he caught while doing duty with the Hertfordshire regiment of militia, in which he was a captain. He was born at Florence in 1766; succeeded his father 1789; and is succeeded by his brother, Peter Leopold Lewis Francis, born May 6, 1788. His Lordship was possessed of a fortune of £20,000 a year; and was entirely free from those indiscreet propensities which too often mark the character of our modern men of fashion. His disposition, manners, and intellectual endowments, promised that he would be an ornament to his rank and station. In short, his character cannot have higher praise bestowed on it than in reporting the opinion recently given of it by the worthy Chief Justice of the Court of King's Bench, who said of his Lordship, that he did not know a more promising young man among the peerage. What then must his friends feel for the loss of a promising youth, who, from his acquirements and virtues, bade fair to become a distinguished ornament of society! (For an account of the rejoicings at his seat on coming of age, see volume LXVII, pp. 706, 727).

5 March 1799. LEE. Mrs. Philadelphia Lee, relict of William Lee, Esq., of Totteridge, Hertfordshire, son of the chief justice, and mother of William Lee Antonie, Esq., and the late Mrs. Pyot.

19 March 1799. STRANGE. At Ridge, near Barnet, Middlesex, after a long and painful illness, aged 67, John Strange, Esq., of Portland Place, LL.D., F.R. and A.SS. 1766, and of the academies of Bologna, Florence, and Montpelier; and the Academia Leopoldina Curiosorum Naturæ; only son of Sir John Strange, master of the rolls. He was educated at Clare hall, Cambridge, where he proceeded M.A. 1755; was British resident at Venice, 1773. . ..

c. March 1799. ROOKE. At Hertford, the wife of Mr. Rooke, attorney, of that town.

22 April 1799. ADAMS. At Mr. Griffin's, in the Strand, aged 16, Mr. Joseph Adams, youngest son of Mrs. Joseph Adams, of Ware, Hertfordshire, and brother to Mr. Adams, goldsmith in the Strand.

May 1799. PAGET. At Totteridge, Hertfordshire, the Rev. Mr. Paget, chaplain to the late Lord Rodney, and his private secretary during the greater part of his active services on board the fleet in the West Indies and at St. Eustatia; from the emoluments of which employments, the share of prize money, and the appointment of distributing it to the ships' companies under the Admiralty's direct command, he made a competent fortune, and secured the favour of his patron to his death. Though very much deformed, he was remarkably active, both in body and mind, and particularly distinguished himself for laborious equestrian exercises. His extraordinary testamentary disposition would not have been noticed here, had not one of his friends communicated it to a similar Miscellany of last month. His not surviving the lady with whom he had passed 20 years in happy union, laid him under a necessity of discovering that she was his wife without the ceremony. He has left a son and two charming daughters, in the happiness and education of whom he was unceasingly employed.

20 May 1799. FRANCKLYN. Gilbert Francklyn, Esq., of Aspeden Hall, near Buntingford, Hertfordshire.

29 May 1799. BROTHERTON. At Elstree, where she had resided for the recovery of her health, aged 41, Mrs. Tho. Brotherton, of Margaret Street, Cavendish Square.

2 June 1799. SPURGEON. At his father's house in Welwyn, Hertfordshire, Daniel Spurgeon, junior, Esq.

3 June 1799. BROOKLAND. At Cheshunt, advanced in years, of a paralytic stroke, Mr. Brookland, a respectable corn chandler and baker, but had for some years retired from business.

3 June 1799. COGAN. At Cheshunt, aged 8, the eldest son of Rev. Mr. Cogan, schoolmaster.

4 June 1799. BYRON. At Hertford, Richard Isles Byron, Esq.

12 June 1799. STRINGER. At Barnet, Rev. Mr. Stringer, formerly rector of St. Paul's, Philadephia.

19 June 1799. GAPE. Aged 83, Thomas Gape, Esq., of the parish of St. Michael's, St. Albans, of which town he may be truly said to have been one of the most ancient and respectable inhabitants. He was eldest son and heir of William Gape, Esq., who was sheriff of Hertfordshire, 1738, and died June 12, 1741, aged 51, the descendant and representative of a numerous family, several of whom have been in the commission of the peace, mayors, and members of parliament, for the town of St. Albans, since Henry Gape who was mayor 1554 (being the second year that the town was empowered by charter to elect a mayor), and buried in St. Michael's church in 1558. He had long been grievously afflicted with the stone, the pains of which he bore with so much patience and magnanimity, that his friends seemed to feel more for him than he did for himself. The illness which ended his life came on with a shivering fit about a week before his death; but his faculties continued, and he at length calmly breathed his last in the bosom of his family. He married, in August, 1743, the Hon. Jane Grimston, eldest surviving daughter of William, the first Lord Viscount Grimston of the kingdom of Ireland, who died July 15, 1763, aged 44, leaving issue four sons and one daughter: 1. William, who died August 7, 1790, aged 46; 2. Thomas, an officer in the army, who died in Ireland; 3. Joseph, who died May 9, 1775, aged 25; 4. Rev. James Carpenter Gape some time of Trinity college, Cambridge, B.A. 1777, M.A. 1780, chaplain in ordinary to his Majesty, vicar of St. Michael's in St Albans, and of the adjoining parish of Redbourne, who succeeds to the family estates. He married a daughter of Mr. Fothergill, some time partner with the celebrated Mr. Boulton, of Soho, near Birmingham, by whom he has seven children. The daughter is married to Mr. Brideoake, late of London, merchant, by whom she has a son and daughter. The family, having at one time resided in the abbey parish, caused a spacious and excellent vault to be erected in the consistory court behind the high altar in the abbey church (the formation of which, in the year 1703, is said to have been the accidental cause of the discovery of the stairs leading to the famous vault of Humphrey, Duke of Gloucester), in which the body of Mr. Gape was deposited, with those of his father and mother, his wife, two of his sons and many others of his relations.

20 June 1799. COOMBE. At Brompton, in her 9th year, Miss Sophia Coombe, daughter of the Rev. Dr. Coombe, of Hertfordshire.

9 July 1799. WELSTEAD. At Wormley West End, Hertfordshire, Mrs. Elizabeth Welstead, widow of George Welstead, late of the Custom House, London.

13 July 1799. LIND. At Rev. Mr. G. Cogan's at Cheshunt, Mrs. Lind, relict of Mr. Lind, formerly packer to the East India Company, and daughter of the late Admiral Gascoyne. She left a son, a clerk in the bank, and 2 daughters.

13 July 1799. WILLIS. At Ridge, near Barnet, Hertfordshire, in his 78th year, Rev. John Willis, BD, vicar of that parish; formerly (before 1779) kept a school and published a translation "The Actions of the Apostles" 1789.

21 July 1799. HOOPER. At Cheshunt, Hertfordshire, advanced in years, John Hooper, a respectable surgeon and apothecary of that place.

6 August 1799. KING. At her house near Bromley, of a paralytic stroke, near 70 years old, Mrs. King, second wife and relict of the late Dr. Glen King, rector of Wormley, who died 2 November 1787, and daughter of John Hyde.

26 August 1799. NEAVE. At Watford, after many years of a severe illness sustained with Christian resignation, Miss Sarah Neave, one of the daughters of the late Edward Neave, merchant of London and sister to the lady of Cornelius Denne.

28 September 1799. CALVERT. At Great Berkhamsted, where he was curate, Rev. Francis Calvert, youngest son of Peter Calvert, of Theobalds, Hertfordshire.

c. September 1799. GILBEE. Lately, at St. Albans, Hertfordshire, J. Clarabut Gilbee, late of Arletty Place, Moorfields.

1 October 1799. OSBORN. At St. Albans, aged 61, two days after the expiration of his 3rd mayoralty, John Osborn. He was buried at Harpenden; and is succeeded as mayor by Thomas Baker, M.D.

4 October 1799. BODDAM. At Bull's Moor Place, Enfield, of a paralytic stroke, aged 74, Thomas Boddam, brother of Rawson Hart Boddam, late governor of Bombay. He married 1788 one of the daughters of Mr. Palmer, solicitor to the Post Office, by whom he has left one daughter. His remains were interred with his family in Wormley church, Hertfordshire.

10 October 1799. BASKERFIELD. At Redbourn, Hertfordshire, in his 81st year, Mr. Thomas Baskerfield. He had long been much indisposed by the infirmities of age, yet bore his decay with the utmost patience and resignation. . ... He had, for upwards of half a century, kept an oil-shop in Holborn. . ...

8 November 1799. DUESBURY. At Bishops Stortford, Mrs. Elizabeth Duesbury, widow of the late Robert Duesbury, of Scarborough.

18 November 1799. DESCHAMPS. At St. Albans, aged about 42, Mrs. Deschamps, wife of Mr. Deschamps, merchant in Bucklersbury, and one of the daughters of the late Mr. Alderman Gill.

25 December 1799. FIFIELD. In St. Alban's-street, Mrs. Fifield.

27 December 1799. SIMKINS. At Gorhambury, seat of Lord Grimston, James Simkins.

c. December 1799. ROSE. Lately, at St. Albans, Richard Rose, formerly of Chard, Somerset.

c. December 1799. TROTT. At Stevenage, Hertfordshire, aged 70, John Trott.

c. December 1799. VENABLES. At Stevenage, Hertfordshire, William Venables, aged 97.

January 1800. FARMAN. Aged upwards of 90, Mr. Farman, mealman and maltster, of Ware, Hertfordshire. He rode to London weekly till within a year of his death, which was hastened by an accidental fall down stairs in his own house.

4 January 1800. SAUNDERS. In Sloane Street, Knightsbridge, Edward Saunders, Esq., of Little Court [Layston], Hertfordshire, late a member of Government at Madras.

10 January 1800. FEILDE. At Stanstead Abbots, Hertfordshire, the wife of the Rev. Thomas Feilde, vicar of that parish.

28 January 1800. HUSSEY. At St. Albans, aged 63, William Hussey, formerly an apothecary in St. James' Street, but had retired from business some years.

19 February 1800. BARKER. In consequence of the unfortunate accident she met with by the fire catching her apparel on the 15th, Mrs. Barker, of Chesterfield Street, Mayfair. She was relict of Edward Barker, Esq., formerly consul at Tripoli; by whom she had two sons; Edward, of West Taring, Sussex, Esq.; and Francis, vicar of St.

Stephen's, near St. Albans, and of Northchurch, Hertfordshire; and a daughter, married to General Lake. She was daughter of Mr. Crompton, mercer, of London; and her sister married the late Earl of Marchmont, whose son, Alexander Lord Polworth, married Annabella, daughter of Philip Earl of Hardwick, now, on the death of her mother, Lady Lucas.

2 March 1800. BERNERS. In Queen Anne Street East, Mrs. Berners; and, on the 7th, she was interred in the family vault at Much Hadham, Hertfordshire.

3 March 1800. WHITHAM. At Brackwood, Hertfordshire [sic], Miss Whitham, youngest daughter of Thomas Whitham, Esq., and sister to Colonel Whitham, of the 1st guards.

6 March 1800. LUCAS. Mr. Lucas, apothecary at St. Albans.

6 March 1800. WORSLEY. At Cheshunt, Hertfordshire, the Rev. Samuel Worsley, pastor of the congregation of Protestant Dissenters in that town; to which charge he succeeded, 1763, on the death of the Rev. John Mason, who had held it 17 years. He was son of that good Greek scholar, Mr. John Worsley (who kept a school at Hertford, translator of the New Testament, edited by his son), by a sister of Dr. Obadiah Hughes, pastor of a dissenting congregation at Westminster. He published a sermon on the fast in the American war, 1777; and has left a widow, a son, and two daughters. He was interred in Cheshunt churchyard on the 13th; and his funeral sermon was preached on the 16th by the Rev. Mr. Gellibrand, pastor of the dissenting congregation at Edmonton.

8 March 1800 AYNSWORTH. At her house in Russel Street, Bloomsbury, aged 78, Mrs. Frances Aynsworth, relict of Rowland Aynsworth, Esq., bencher of the Inner Temple, who died December 12, 1791, and daughter of the late John Legge, Esq., of Hertford.

8 March 1800. WOOD. In Southwark, near St. George's church, Mr. Wood, many years a farrier of eminence at Cheshunt, famous for shoeing horses agreeable to nature and according to art. His father followed the same profession before him.

15 March 1800. CHAPMAN. In Charles Street, Berkeley Square, Dame Sarah Chapman, second wife (and relict) of Sir John Chapman, Bart. She has left her manor of Cockenach, in Barkway, which she inherited from the Chesters, and her house in Charles Street, with her plate and jewels, to Lady Mills, wife of Sir Francis Mills, of Chesterfield, an intimate friend, but not related; £7000 to relations of her son, Sir John Chapman; £3000 to a natural child of a near relation; £1000 to her own maid, who lived with her 24 years; and £100 to her coachman who lived with her 22 years. She was buried at Barkway.

A memorial in Barkway church carries the following inscription:

Near this place lie interred the remains of Dame Sarah Chapman, widow of Sir John Chapman, Bart. of Cokenach in this county. She deceased the XV day of March MDCCC aged LXV years. This lady was endued with many virtues and good qualities. She was an affectionate wife, a sincere friend and a much loved acquaintance.

Sir Francis and Lady Willes of Hampstead, Middlesex, and now of Cokenach, erected this monument to her memory as a small tribute of their gratitude.

Cussans describes this as "a large and unsightly monument of black and white marble, reaching from the floor to the cornice," and adds that "previous to her marriage Lady Chapman was housekeeper to Sir John." [TD]

17 March 1800. HAWKINS. At Bath, aged 83, Lady Hawkins, relict of Sir Caesar Hawkins of Kelstone, Bart., so created 1778, who died in 1786, shortly after the death of his eldest son, who was father of Sir John, the present baronet. She was the mother of many children, of whom Charles Hawkins, Esq., formerly of Pall Mall, surgeon, now of Hemel Hempstead, Hertfordshire, is probably the only survivor. . ..

31 March 1800. BENSON. At Hertford, after a lingering illness, aged 45, Miss Sarah Benson, 2nd daughter of the late Mr. Benson, brewer.

c. March 1800. LEWIN. At Broxbourne, Hertfordshire, Mr. Lewin.

12 April 1800. SCHREIBER. At his seat at Tewin, Hertfordshire, aged 80, John Charles Schreiber, many years an eminent fur merchant on Labour-in-Vain Hill.

Charles Schreiber and his son William lived at Tewin House. After his father's death William sold the house to Earl Cowper, who pulled it down. [AJ]

25 April 1800. COWPER. At East Dereham, Norfolk, William Cowper, Esq., of the Inner Temple, author of a poem intituled "The Task", and many other beautiful productions. This truly amiable and very interesting character was born at Great Berkhamsted, Hertfordshire, November 15, 1731. His father, the rector of that parish, was John Cowper, D.D., nephew to the Lord High Chancellor Cowper; and his mother was Anne, daughter of Roger Donne, gentleman, late of Ludham Hall, Norfolk. . . ..

Mr. Cowper was born at Berkhamsted in 1722, and educated at Westminster school; and, as the place of clerk of the House of Lords was reserved for him, he was sent to the Temple instead of the University, but never applied himself to the drudgery of the law or public business. He spent much of his time in retirement, at the house of his relation, Earl Cowper, at Cole Green, Hertfordshire, or at Huntingdon, with the Rev. Mr. Unwin; and after his death, he retired with his widow to Olney, Buckinghamshire, where was then minister Mr. Newton, who inserted in "The Olney Collection" some poems marked with his initial. At Huntingdon he formed a close friendship with Dr. Cotton, of St. Albans; and he was also intimate with Lord Thurlow. By intermarriage he was related to the author of "Thelyphthora", and to the present Bishop of Peterborough. He died of a lingering illness; and his funeral sermon was preached by Mr. Newton, at St. Mary Woolnoth church, May 11.

c. May 1800. WAKEFIELD. At Cheshunt, Hertfordshire, Mrs. Wakefield, wife of John Wakefield, Esq.

c. May 1800. SERGEANT. At Enfield, Mr. Robert Sergeant, of St. Albans, one of the people called Quakers.

5 May 1800. BEST. Suddenly, after eating a hearty dinner, Mr. Best, carpenter, and mayor of Hertford.

It sounds a very eighteenth century way to go! Carrington in his diary reports the funeral of John Best: ". . . . Saw Mr. Best, the Mayor of Hartford, buried at St. Andrews Church, Hartford, a Herss and pair 3 Mourning Coaches in pair, he was a Master Carpenter at Hartford, he was about 40 years of age, a good kind of Man and Died in the 8th Month of his Mayoralty all most Suddingly". Mayors of Hertford at this period were elected at Michaelmas. [AG]

21 May 1800. TAYLOR. Of a deep decline, Mrs. Taylor, wife of the Rev. Mr. Taylor, pastor of a Presbyterian congregation in Carter Lane, London, and daughter of the late Benjamin Porter of Theobalds, Hertfordshire. She was married 4 November, 1788, and has left several children.

Mary Porter married Thos. Taylor at Cheshunt parish church on 4 November 1788. Rev. Thomas Tayler, usually spelt with an 'e', (1735–1831) was educated for the dissenting ministry at Northampton and Daventry Academies, and probably met his wife while chaplain to the Abney family, circa 1760 who had connections with Theobalds. He was minister at Carter Lane Chapel, London, 1776–1811. (See Surman Index, Dr. Williams's Library). [AR]

c. June 1800. NICHOLL. Lately, at Watford, J.A. Nicholl, lieutenant of the Royal Navy, lately returned, on board the Bellerophon, from the Mediterranean.

18 July 1800. BEAUCLERK. At Paul's Walden, Hertfordshire, the lady of Aubrey Beauclerk, Earl of Burford (son to the Duke of St. Albans); to whom she was married in 1788 (LVIII p.658). She was daughter of the late —————— Moses, Esq., and niece to Sir Henry Etherington, of Hull.

26 July 1800. WHEELDON. At Wheathampstead, aged 65, the Rev. John Wheeldon, M.A., rector of that parish, with the adjoining chapelry of Harpenden, al. Harden, and prebendary of Lincoln. He married a niece of the late Dr. Green, Bishop of Lincoln, by whom he had a daughter, and son, married to the daughter of Mr. Pickford, an eminent waggon-master at Market Street [Markyate]. His living is deemed worth at least £800 per annum, and is in the gift of the Bishop of Lincoln. He was of St. John's college, Cambridge; B.A. 1759: M.A. 1762; and published a Latin Poetical Epistle to Mr. Pennant on his Tours; and "A new Delineation of Job's ancient Abode, by a Gentleman now contemplative in Arabia Petræa; transmitted from Alexandria to John Wheeldon, M.A. To which are added, a few Observations on the Book of Job, by the Editor, 1799."

30 July 1800. HASKINS. At Essendon, Hertfordshire, John Haskins, Esq.

c. July 1800. DEBELL. Lately, at his house in Green Park buildings, Bath, Peyto Debell, Esq., formerly of King's Langley, Hertfordshire.

c. July 1800. WAGSTAFFE. Rev. Thomas Wagstaffe, rector of Barley, Hertfordshire, in the gift of the Bishop of Ely, to which he was presented 1779. He married the sister of the Rev. B. Underwood, rector of Chipping and East Barnet, and of St. Mary Abchurch, London. He was of Christ's college, Cambridge; B.A. 1762, M.A. 1765.

5 August 1800. ANDREWS. At the vicarage of Ashwell, Hertfordshire, Miss Catharine Andrews.

18 August 1800. FORMAN. At Welwyn, Hertfordshire, aged 32, Mrs. Martha Forman, wife of Richard Forman, Esq., of Chatham.

c. August 1800. ENGLAND. At Northaw, of the injury he received from two footpads, labouring men in the neighbourhood, who had waylaid him, knowing he had been receiving the Duke's rents, Mr. England, steward to the Duke of Leeds. One of them has since been executed at Hertford, and the other transported for life.

14 September 1800. MARSHAM. Rev. Thomas Marsham, of Hatfield, Hertfordshire, many years rector of Alwalton, Huntingdonshire, in the gift of the Dean and Chapter of Peterborough. He was of King's college, Cambridge; B.A. 1755, M.A. 1758.

22 September 1800. CAPEL. At Russel Farm [Watford], Hertfordshire, Lady Diana Capel, eldest surviving daughter of William Earl of Essex, and aunt to the present Earl.

26 September 1800. KINGSMAN. At Langley Bury, Hertfordshire, after a long illness, which she bore with the greatest resignation, Miss Kingsman, eldest daughter of W.L. Kingsman, Esq. She possessed very superior accomplishments, particularly extraordinary talents in music and painting, a cultivated understanding, amiable disposition, and unassuming manners, added to the most exemplary piety.

10 October 1800. BLAND. At his house in Hertfordshire, Jos. Bland, Esq., of Mincing Lane, London, merchant.

13 October 1800. PINNOCK. At St. Ibb's, the Rev. Thomas Pinnock, vicar of St. Hippolits cum Wimley, Hertfordshire, and of Marsworth, Buckinghamshire, and formerly of Trinity college, Cambridge; B.A. 1767; M.A. 1770. The livings are in the gift of that college.

22 October 1800. BUXTON. At Great Hadham, Hertfordshire, the Rev. George Buxton, of Ham, Staffordshire, fellow of Worcester college, Oxford, and late curate of Great Hadham.

27 October 1800. AUBER. At Cheshunt, Hertfordshire, Mrs. Jane Auber, widow of the late Rev. John Auber, rector of Blaisden, Gloucestershire.

29 October 1800. SMITH. At St. Albans, aged 73, Mr. Ralph Smith, an opulent farmer, whose ancestors, for a generation or two, and himself, had been long tenants to the noble family of Grimston, of their manor-farm of Kingsbury, adjoining to that town. His mother was sister of Ralph Thrale, Esq., formerly M.P. for the borough of Southwark; and he was related also to the family of Halsy, of whom Anne (daughter of Edmund Halsy, Esq.) lady Viscountess Cobham, who died in 1760, is said to have been his aunt, and left considerable legacies to him and his family.

c. October 1800. ARCHER. At Hertford, Mrs. Archer, wife of Mr. Archer, butcher, and once mayor of that town, and sister to Mrs. Nash, of Enfield.

5 November 1800. NOYES. At Great Berkhamsted, aged 92, Mrs. Anne Noyes.

14 November 1800. HORTON. At Hadley, John Shadwell Horton, Esq., a director of the South Sea Company.

c. November 1800. WITHALL. At his house at Waltham Cross, Hertfordshire, Mr. Caleb Withall, sen.

1 December 1800. LUDLOW. At Wormley, aged 33, of an inflammation in his bowels, Mr. Ludlow, coal merchant.

8 December 1800. REYNOLDS. Shot himself through the head, by the side of the high road in the village of Harpenden, Mr. Reynolds, one of the sons of the predecessor of the late rector of Wheathampstead, to which Harpenden is a chapelry. Mental derangement is said to have been the cause of this unfortunate accident.

INDEX TO NAMES OF PERSONS AND PLACES

Out-of-county names have usually been excluded, and names of parishes have also been omitted when indexing the supplementary lists of births, marriages, bankruptcies and deaths. Only specific locations within parishes have been indexed from these lists.

Compound parish names in the main sequence have been indexed under the second element – e.g. Hadham, Little, not Little Hadham.